# THE MEDIEVAL HOUSES OF KENT:

## *An Historical Analysis*

ROYAL
COMMISSION
ON THE HISTORICAL
MONUMENTS
OF ENGLAND

# THE MEDIEVAL HOUSES OF KENT:
## *An Historical Analysis*

Sarah Pearson

ROYAL COMMISSION ON THE HISTORICAL MONUMENTS OF ENGLAND
LONDON: HMSO

Published by the Royal Commission on the Historical Monuments of England,
National Monuments Record Centre, Kemble Drive, Swindon SN2 2GZ.

© RCHME Crown copyright 1994

First published 1994

ISBN 011 300047 2

*British Library Cataloguing in Publication Data*
A CIP catalogue record for this book is available from the British Library

HMSO publications are available from:

**HMSO Publications Centre**
(mail, fax and telephone orders only)
PO Box 276, London, SW8 5DT
Telephone orders 071-873 9090
General enquiries 071-873 0011
(queuing system in operation for both numbers)
Fax orders 071-873 8200

**HMSO Bookshops**
49 High Holborn, London, WC1V 6HB
(counter service only)
071-873 0011  Fax 071-873 8200
258 Broad Street, Birmingham, B1 2HE
021-643 3740  Fax 021-643 6510
Southey House, 33 Wine Street, Bristol, BS1 2BQ
0272 264306  Fax 0272 294515
9-21 Princess Street, Manchester, M60 8AS
061-834 7201  Fax 061-833 0634
16 Arthur Street, Belfast, BT1 4GD
0232 238451  Fax 0232 235401
71 Lothian Road, Edinburgh, EH3 9AZ
031-228 4181  Fax 031-229 2734

**HMSO's Accredited Agents**
(see Yellow Pages)

*and through good booksellers*

Designed by Chuck Goodwin, 27 Artesian Road, London W2 5DA.

Printed by Staples Printers Rochester Limited

# Contents

# Commissioners

# Chairman's Foreword

Kent has long been celebrated for the richness of its timber-framed houses, but although these buildings form such a characteristic and well-loved feature of the county's rural landscape, their place in the overall development of timber-framed building has been little understood. At the same time, it was widely thought that Kent might contain more medieval dwellings than any other county in England and the sheer wealth of the surviving material had deterred the Royal Commission from undertaking a complete inventory. However, with the shift in the Commission's field-survey policy in the late 1970s, which involved a move away from the compilation of comprehensive county inventories towards the study of particular classes of building, a survey of the medieval houses of Kent became a viable project. In undertaking this work, the Commission decided to adopt a strategy of systematic, but selective sampling, aiming to produce a synthesis illustrative of the regional and chronological development of medieval housing in the county. It is hoped that the results presented here will lead to a greater understanding of Kent's rich legacy of medieval dwellings, set within a wider architectural, historical and geographical framework.

The survey took place between 1986 and 1992. During this time some 450 houses, built between the late 13th and the mid 16th centuries, were analysed and recorded, and an archive of drawings, photographs and written reports was compiled. This volume is one of three to have resulted from the project. It examines the evolution of medieval houses, the differences in their form, numbers, dates and distribution across the county, and considers the historical reasons for the resulting patterns. Its companion volume, *The House Within: Interpreting Medieval Houses in Kent*, is an illustrated handbook designed to promote the understanding of the layout, structure and detail of Kentish medieval buildings among owners, restorers and the general public. Both books are supported by *A Gazetteer of Medieval Houses in Kent*, which contains accounts of all the recorded buildings and reproduces a selection of the most important archive drawings.

The Commissioners wish to thank Sarah Pearson and her colleagues for their work on this project. Commissioners also wish to thank the large number of people both within and outside the Royal Commission whose help made it possible, particularly the staff of the Nottingham University Tree-Ring Dating Laboratory. Above all, the Commission is grateful to the owners and occupiers of the medieval houses that form the basis of the study for allowing access to their homes; without their generous co-operation this work would not have been possible, and we hope that they, along with all who read this book, will agree that the effort was worthwhile.

PARK OF MONMOUTH

# Acknowledgements

Many people contributed to the Commission's study of medieval houses in Kent, not least the members of the team who undertook the fieldwork and documentary research: Allan T Adams (who also drew all the illustrations), Dr Paul S Barnwell, Dr Martin Cherry and Dr Bridgett Jones. Peter Williams took the photographs and Jan Cornell typed numerous texts as well as supplying the administrative support necessary to keep the project on course.

J T Smith was in charge of the Royal Commission's architectural programme when this project began. His support and encouragement in the early years were vital, and it was his idea that we should carry out the dendrochronological work which has proved all-important to the final results. Dr John Bold, as his successor, also provided encouragement and constructive criticism. A number of Commissioners and members of staff gave their advice and commented on the text: in particular, we would like to thank Robyn Burgess, Bridget Cherry, Professor K Downes, Professor Peter Fowler, Nigel Fradgley, Tom Hassall, Professor G I Meirion-Jones, Anne Riches and Dr Robin Thornes. Outside the Commission I would also like to express my gratitude to Professor Peter Kidson, Eric Mercer, Jayne Semple and Dr Joan Thirsk, for both reading the text of this book at draft stage and for contributing their thoughts in the course of several stimulating discussions.

The conclusions of this book rest heavily on the use made of dendrochronology to date selected buildings. The Commission is grateful to Robert Howard, Dr Robert Laxton, Dr Cliff Litton and Dr Gavin Simpson of the Nottingham University Tree-Ring Dating Laboratory for undertaking this work on its behalf.

Many other people provided information, advice and encouragement during the course of our work, and the project would have been the poorer without their assistance. Among them were Jill Allibone, Jane Andrews, Dorothy and Robert Beck, Brian Brent, Andrew Butcher, Beryl Coatts, Richenda Codling, Dr Joanna Cox, Alan Dell, Professor Alan Everitt, Dr P W Fleming, Kenneth Gravett, Peter Gray, Joan Harding, Richard Harris, Margaret Lawrence, Maureen Lovering, Kinn McIntosh, the late Miss M Mansell, Barbara and David Martin, Miss A M Oakley, E W Parkin, Heather Pullen, Judith Roberts, Mary Scott, Tony Singleton, Margaret Sparks, Tim Tatton-Brown, John Thorp, Jane Wade and Patricia Winzar. In addition, we were given frequent and willing help by staff in the planning departments of Kent County Council and several of the Districts, and by the staff of the Centre for Kentish Studies, in both Maidstone and Canterbury.

The majority of houses visited in the course of this study are in private ownership, and the book would not have been possible without the generous co-operation of their owners and occupiers. We are immensely grateful for the interest and hospitality that we received throughout the county. We hope that many of our erstwhile hosts will find something to interest them in the books which we have produced.

Finally, a particular debt of gratitude is due to the late Stuart Rigold. This project was not formally announced until after his death, but his presence has pervaded the work at all stages. His all-too-brief publications on Kentish buildings offer new insights each time they are read, and the fact that he has not been here to debate controversial points has been our loss.

Sarah Pearson

# Illustration Credits

All illustrations are copyright of the Royal Commission on the Historical Monuments of England, with the exception of Figure 12 which is reproduced by kind permission of the British Architectural Library, RIBA, London and of Figures 104a and 122 which are reproduced by courtesy of the Country Life Picture Library. The maps are based on the 1974 Ordnance Survey Administrative map with the permission of the Controller of Her Majesty's Stationery Office © Crown copyright.

# Editorial Notes

The three books resulting from the RCHME project on medieval rural houses in Kent consist of *The House Within: Interpreting Medieval Houses in Kent* (abbreviated to *The House Within*), *A Gazetteer of Medieval Houses in Kent*, and this book which provides an historical analysis of the medieval houses. Most houses have been given a single date in the main text. Where this is preceded by *circa* (*c*), it indicates the mid date of a date range of varying length (as discussed in Chapter 6, p67 and Appendix 1). Where the date is followed by an asterisk (*), it indicates that the timbers have been tree-ring dated. The tree-ring dating was carried out by the Nottingham University Tree-Ring Dating Laboratory (NUTRDL). Techniques and results are discussed in Appendix 1.

The archive which results from this survey is held in the National Monuments Record at the Royal Commission on the Historical Monuments of England, National Monuments Record Centre, Kemble Drive, Swindon SN2 2GZ. Copies of the reports and drawings, and a selection of the photographs, are also held in the Centre for Kentish Studies, Kent County Council, County Hall, Maidstone ME14 1XQ. At the end of the illustration captions, the NMR negative numbers of the individual photographs are given (for example, BB89/9819).

# Abbreviations

| | | | |
|---|---|---|---|
| *AC* | *Archaeologia Cantiana* | KAS | Kent Archaeological Society |
| BL | British Library | NMR | National Monuments Record |
| *Cat Anct Deeds* | *Descriptive Catalogue of Ancient Deeds in the Public Record Office* 6 vols 1810–34 | NUTRDL | Nottingham University Tree-Ring Dating Laboratory |
| CKS | Centre for Kentish Studies (formerly known as the Kent Archive Office and the Kent Record Office) | PRO | Public Record Office |
| | | *The House Within* | *The House Within: Interpreting Medieval Houses in Kent* |
| DoE | Department of the Environment | *VA* | *Vernacular Architecture* |
| Hasted | Hasted, E 1797–1901. *The History and Topographical Survey of the County of Kent*, vols I–XII (2nd ed, reprinted 1972, with introduction by A M Everitt) | VAG | Vernacular Architecture Group |
| | | *VCH* | *Victoria County History* |

# Drawing Conventions

All the drawings in this book have been simplified, with post-medieval details largely omitted. For the original survey drawings see the companion book, *A Gazetteer of Medieval Houses in Kent* and the files in the NMR.

# Plans

Scale 1:300. Two dashed lines are used for beams; one dashed line for joists. The position of the open truss is marked by a dash/dot/dash line. Single lines indicate reconstructed walls. Surviving external doorways are shown by solid arrows; sites of former external doorways are indicated by open arrows.

# Sections

Scale 1:150. Dashed lines indicate features which have been removed. Diagonal hatching is used for sections through solid walls.

# Introduction

The present book is one of three arising out of the RCHME's recent work on medieval houses in Kent. It was never intended to cover all aspects of domestic architecture in the county, but to explore issues relating to the chronological development of building during the later Middle Ages, and the interaction between surviving examples and the social and economic circumstances of the people for whom they were built. In recent years a number of studies have been published which have attempted to put buildings into their historical context. Some of these have been national, others are confined to regions, but by and large they have tended to concentrate on periods from the 16th century onwards when documentation relating to individual households is more readily available.

This is not to say that the study of medieval building has been neglected. Since it has been an ambition of many students of domestic architecture to seek out the earliest surviving examples in their area, medieval houses have received considerable attention at national, regional and local levels. At a national level the seminal works on high-status houses, written in the 1950s or earlier, are generally recognised to be in need of revision, and there are signs that this is now occurring.[1] The development of smaller houses has been discussed in several excellent general works,[2] and at a regional level one or two important books or articles have recently appeared, or are likely to do so before this book is published.[3] Over many years, construction and carpentry have received special attention,[4] and numerous individual buildings have been described and analysed in national and local journals. Meanwhile, on the historical side, books have been written on standards of living among both nobles and peasants which have sought to draw upon the surviving material remains pertaining to the people of the time.[5] Yet, despite this, the study of medieval domestic buildings and the study of medieval history have remained curiously aloof from one another.

The reasons almost certainly lie in the complexity of the issues and the disparate approaches of the relevant disciplines. It is extremely difficult to handle unfamiliar evidence in a constructive way, and this difficulty besets both social and economic historians and architectural historians alike. The problem can be demonstrated by reference to the appropriate volumes of *The Agrarian History of England and Wales* which all have considerable sections

1

devoted to archaeology and architecture.[6] The treatment of buildings stands quite apart from the general questions of agricultural and economic development with which the rest of the books are concerned, and one doubts whether their potential significance has been perceived by social and economic historians. It is partly for this reason, no doubt, that few regional studies of the peasantry include chapters on buildings, and even when they do the evidence is largely documentary or hardly integrated into the rest of the volume.[7]

Among the matters which urgently need addressing are three which are of particular relevance: the status of houses and the extent to which the form of buildings, or even their mere survival, reflects status; the question of what might have preceded the houses that exist today; and the degree of certainty with which buildings can be dated. No doubt there are others, but until we have got some way towards resolving these, the study of medieval houses and the study of social and economic history will simply continue to follow parallel paths that never meet.

The distinctions between peasant houses and those built for people of higher status are not always as obvious as might be imagined. It is not difficult to identify the buildings which lie at the top of the social spectrum, but below that there is a subtle gradation, broken by no clear-cut dividing lines and extending downwards to the smallest and poorest houses remaining today. Since recent studies indicate that historians find the terms gentry, yeoman and peasant difficult to classify,[8] it is hardly surprising that architectural historians find it hard to distinguish the houses pertaining to these classes, particularly as we have little idea what proportion of peasant dwellings are represented among surviving buildings. This problem is not new. In Kent, which had an unusually free social structure, it was certainly recognised in the 17th century by Celia Fiennes who, when visiting the county, identified 'a sort of yeomanly gentry' to which she was clearly unaccustomed. In modern times it has been claimed that while the gentry had leaped a social gulf, there was little difference between yeomen and husbandmen.[9] This does not mean that contemporaries could not distinguish a man's rank, but that they had to know how to read the signs aright. Elsewhere in England, and in relation to a later period, it has been argued that architecture was used both to define status and to boost social aspirations.[10] In Kent, and in the Middle Ages, this is less obvious. For such reasons, gentry houses have not been treated separately throughout this book, but questions of status are considered, in particular in Chapters 1, 5 and 11. As a result, gentry houses are frequently discussed alongside other buildings. But the uncertainty in identifying members of that class or their dwellings suggests that it would be foolish to impose arbitrary distinctions. Instead, as an interim measure awaiting further research, houses have been classified according to type, size and number, and considerable work has gone into considering how common the various categories were, and into estimating what proportion of the population the surviving houses may have served. This is not a complete answer to the problems posed by status, but it is perhaps a step in the right direction.

The second problem relates to why buildings only start surviving from a given moment in time, for whom they were built and what came before them. Despite the considerable and increasing volume of archaeological activity, the links between standing and demolished structures and the question of continuity or change are only now being addressed by architectural historians.[11] Yet until we have a firmer grasp of this, it is almost impossible to put our surviving buildings into perspective. At present we simply do not know whether the earliest small buildings we see are the first potentially durable peasant houses to have been built, preceded by flimsy, short-lived structures, or whether their predecessors were equally sturdy but have been demolished because they lacked some other ingredient essential to survival. This book has come up with no firm answers, but through the analysis of surviving buildings, particularly those of fragmentary nature, it seeks to arrive at a better understanding of what may have occurred.

The third theme concerns chronology. It is impossible to set buildings into a wider historical context unless they can be accurately dated. Until this is done we cannot assess what the architectural response to a particular historical circumstance may have been. High-status houses can often be dated by documents, or assigned to reasonably specific periods on stylistic grounds. But this is seldom possible for smaller buildings, particularly those of medieval date. Various details, such as joints and mouldings, have been carefully analysed with a view to establishing their date range and the circumstances in which they were used,[12] and the question whether such details provide evidence for precise dating has been fiercely debated. The problem is that although there is a broad measure of agreement on the general typological sequence, there remain divergent views concerning the precise chronology. There was considerable practical wisdom in Mercer's conclusion that when dating by traditional means 'one must be content with broad statements ..... satisfied with a general distinction between "early" and "late" in the [medieval] period';[13] but the consequence of caution has been to make it extremely difficult to use evidence from medieval building studies in other historical fields.

Fortunately this survey was begun at exactly the moment when the prospect of scientific dating for at least some timber buildings was becoming a real possibility by means of dendrochronology, that is, the dating of timbers through the measurement and analysis of tree rings. A joint project was set up with Nottingham University Tree-Ring Dating Laboratory (NUTRDL), and timber samples for dating were taken from seventy-four buildings or phases of building. The method and the results are discussed in detail in Appendix 1. That this technique is an indispensable instrument by means of which a major breakthrough in house dating could be achieved became increasingly apparent as work in Kent progressed, and the results have informed the conclusions throughout this book.

It is with these three issues in mind that this book has been written. Though it cannot claim to have solved all the problems they pose, for each is a vast and complex subject which will keep archaeologists, historians and architectural historians busy for years to come, it will have achieved its purpose if it sets in motion the process of bringing the separate disciplines together, and forcing them to take notice of one another. The aim is neither architectural history in the narrow sense, nor social history as this is commonly understood, but an integrated study of houses as reflections of the people who built and lived in them.

It has long been recognised that Kent has an unusually high number of medieval houses surviving. Every general account of medieval domestic building in England has drawn attention to both the quantity and quality of timber-framed houses in the south east, often singling out Kent for special mention.[14] Much valuable work on this rich heritage has already taken place. The few – all-too-brief – articles published by the late Stuart Rigold in the 1960s and 1970s form an indispensable starting point for any student of Kentish architecture; Kenneth Gravett has accumulated an impressive array of knowledge on the subject; and a number of excellent studies of individual buildings or groups of buildings have been written by others, notably E W Parkin, The Canterbury Archaeological Trust and Jane Wade and her students.[15] But, while the wealth of Kentish medieval building was obvious, it was only appreciated in a general way. The numbers of medieval houses still surviving could only be surmised, their date range was unclear, and the density of distribution, both generally and at different dates, was unknown.

The modern county covers 1,440 square miles and contains 319 civil parishes or administrative units.[16] It was impossible, without conducting a parish-by-parish survey, to cover such a large area thoroughly in the search for medieval houses. Some method of reducing the task to manageable proportions had to be found. The simplest solution, to concentrate on a smaller area, was rejected, for, despite its size and diversity, Kent has evolved as a historical entity. Its customs and conditions of tenure were distinct from those of neighbouring counties, and although differences may be discernible between its regions, both in historical and architectural terms, the relationships between its parts were too important for one to be studied in isolation from the rest. A method of sampling was called for which took account of the whole county.

The first decision taken was to concentrate on rural buildings. Although there is no doubt that the development of Kentish towns in the later Middle Ages was critical for the history of the county as a whole, it is unlikely that much would have been achieved by including town houses in this study. Urban buildings are often a separate species from rural ones. Built-up areas have always imposed restrictions on size and layout of property, and specialised functions have led to the development of types which are not found in the countryside. In Kent this is apparent from the work that has already been done by others in Canterbury and Sandwich;[17] to have included the buildings of these towns would have meant introducing many additional architectural issues. Moreover, the full range of medieval buildings which occurs in towns is still imperfectly understood, and the fragmentary nature of much of the evidence means that knowledge of urban architecture is probably still best advanced through the study of urban building *per se*, or through the detailed study of individual towns. Not until more work of this nature has been done will one be in a position to consider the extent to which medieval urban building can be set in a regional context. It was therefore decided to exclude towns from this project.

But what constitutes a town in Kent? Kent is a county of scattered dwellings with a number of small nucleated settlements. These were not agricultural village communities of the kind found in large parts of the Midlands, but trading centres with markets, in other words, small towns.[18] In some cases, as in Chilham, Elham, Smarden or Wrotham, medieval nucleation consisted of a cluster of dwellings in the vicinity of the church; in others, such as Brasted and Charing, medieval houses lie adjacent to each other forming a complete street. Although there is some surviving evidence for purpose-built shops, and in some instances it is likely that the layout restricted the size of buildings, true urban forms were not necessary, and were seldom found in these small settlements. To exclude them seemed artificial, and they were therefore included in the survey. However, it is as well to be aware that houses studied in these locations may not always have been identical to those studied in isolation. Where such market towns grew to sizeable urban centres in the 16th century or later, they were avoided.[19] The time-consuming task of disentangling the medieval from the post-medieval, and estimating the significance of the reduced medieval remains, is better tackled in more detailed local studies, as has been done for Tenterden,[20] or in broader studies devoted to the specialised topic of urban recording.

All thematic studies have grey areas around the edge where one theme shades into the next. The central subject of this project was the timber-framed houses of the 14th and 15th centuries. But it was soon clear that they could not be divorced from earlier high-status houses, whether built of timber or of stone, and these accordingly became part of the study. But to have included castles, palaces and communal ranges of ecclesiastical institutions would have made the task unmanageable.[21] They have therefore not been looked at in detail, although they have been referred to where appropriate.

In order to look at the whole of the county, the possibility of surveying in randomly chosen grid squares or transects was considered.[22] This was rejected because it would not have allowed full advantage to be taken of the wealth of known historical circumstances. The geographical and historical background of Kent indicates a county structure of some complexity. Topography, settlement and agriculture varied widely. In addition, social and economic developments were dissimilar in different regions. All of that had to be taken into account when selecting areas for study. It was impossible to survey by manor since manors were seldom discrete, and the detailed work required to reconstruct their boundaries could not be undertaken. So, by a process of elimination, the decision was made to sample by parish. The parishes are not ecclesiastical or historical ones, but the modern civil parishes or administrative units. However, with some notable exceptions, their boundaries are not too dissimilar.[23] The parish, even allowing for this reservation, has historical significance, and it was considered that the relationship between buildings and the historical background from which they emerged would become more readily apparent this way than through any technique of random selection. The approach has, for example, enabled the incidence of surviving medieval houses to be correlated with information about wealth and population, which was collected and documented by parish or hundred. Parish-based sampling also made it possible to explore whether changing topography or different historical circumstances influenced the form and development of surviving medieval buildings within a restricted area. As will be discussed in Chapter 12 this produced some interesting results.

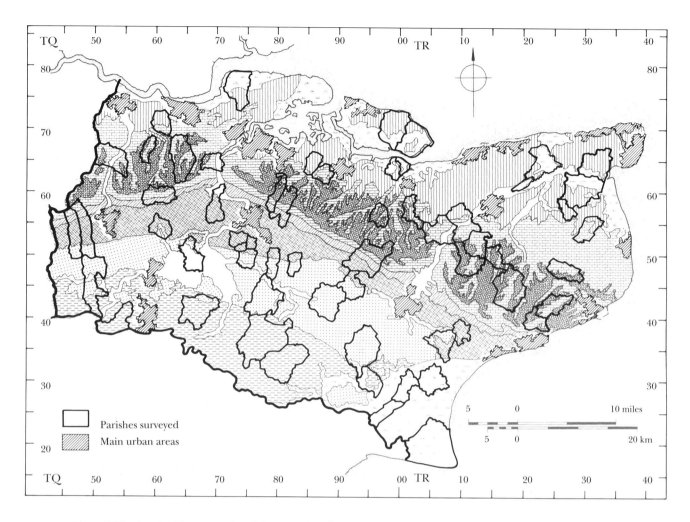

*Figure 1 The sixty parishes surveyed and the areas of modern development shown in relation to the geographical regions.*

In the event, 60 of the 319 civil parishes or administrative areas which make up the modern (post-1974) county were surveyed (Figure 1). They constitute 19 per cent of parishes, and 24 per cent of the county's total area.[24] They were not selected at random but were deliberately chosen to include as many geographical and historical variables as possible. Areas of modern development were avoided since very few rural medieval buildings survive in such circumstances. In addition to the information gathered from these particular parishes, other medieval houses were recorded on purely architectural grounds: that is, rare or important types of house were surveyed whatever their location.

Many medieval houses lie hidden within later structures (Figure 2), and since it was not possible to conduct an internal inspection of every property in each of the surveyed parishes, it is inevitable that some medieval buildings will have been missed.[25] In addition some houses, likely to be medieval, could not be visited. Thus the coverage is almost certainly not exhaustive. However, given the remarkable differences which emerge, both between individual parishes, and more importantly, between one part of the county and another, there is good reason to believe that the regional distributions revealed by the survey have genuine historical validity.[26]

By the end of the project some 380 houses had been surveyed from the sixty chosen parishes. In addition, another seventy buildings from other parts of the county were investigated; these include a high proportion of the mid 14th-century and earlier survivors which are too important to be left out, and too few in number to produce a representative sample from within the chosen areas. This total of 450 buildings, together with about fifty more

*Figure 2 Disguised houses: a) Chilton Manor, Sittingbourne, an early aisled hall (BB86/3345); b) Old Well Cottage, East Peckham, a 15th-century aisled house (BB89/4801).*

a

b

7

known from the work of other investigators, has provided the stock of material evidence for inferences concerning the nature and development of medieval houses in the county. As will become apparent, the number of examples actually cited varies according to the purposes for which they are required. These matters will be discussed in more detail where appropriate.

The general themes outlined above, relating to earliest survival, status and chronological development, are particularly applicable to the study of medieval building in Kent. Various questions arise concerning the extent and kind of accommodation found in houses of the 13th and early 14th centuries. Although all such surviving houses are of higher than peasant status, they were none the less built for people of differing wealth and social position, whose households and residential requirements varied enormously. The range they cover needs to be borne in mind, and since the total number of buildings is not large, generalisations can only be made with caution. It soon became apparent that early high-status houses do not occur in all parts of the county; there appears to be a pattern to their distribution, whether built of stone or timber, and this fact requires exploration and explanation.

At some point in the 14th century the houses built for those below the level of the gentry start to survive for the first time. That they exist by the end of the century is certain, but the moment of their first appearance is less clear. Distinguishing the largest and finest peasant dwellings from those of the lesser gentry is no easy task. Documentary evidence is unlikely to clarify the situation, for the owners of many potentially relevant houses will probably remain untraceable. In principle a combined study of documents and buildings might help to define the houses of each class, but unfortunately in this study the resources were not available to undertake the necessary documentary research. However, once houses of a particular type and date start occurring in considerable numbers it is likely that they represent the homes of wealthy peasants or yeomen – that is to say, of the top layer of landowners who were not of gentry status. Extensive parish surveys, combined with the more precise dating which dendrochronology allowed, made it possible to distinguish those parts of the county where this development took place in the late 14th century from those where the earliest surviving peasant dwellings are likely to be much later in date.

Distinguishing gentry from peasant dwellings remains an important issue throughout the later Middle Ages, not least because there is an apparent decrease in the actual number of gentry houses built between the mid 14th and late 15th century, at the very same time as there is a significant increase in the number of surviving peasant houses. Whether this is the reflection of a changing society, or whether it can be accounted for some other way, needs to be considered.

To look at these matters it was first necessary to identify the various kinds of building which were erected, in order to establish whether there were patterns to their use, either in terms of date, size or distribution. Most of the timber structures dating before the late 14th century were of aisled or 'quasi-aisled' form.[27] Aisled construction continued to be used during the 15th century, but from the late 14th century new types of house started to appear. Attention has previously tended to focus on the well-known Wealden house, whose design has been seen as the ultimate expression of medieval timber-framed architecture. It was generally agreed that the Wealden first occurred in the years around 1400, although its heyday was probably later, spanning an eighty or hundred year period, ranging from *c* 1430 to *c* 1530. Indeed Wealdens, like crucks in other parts of England, have captured the imagination and led to numerous specialised studies.[28] Already by 1970 some 350 examples had been identified in Kent and, since so many were obviously disguised, the actual number was reckoned to be at least twice this figure.[29] Their occurrence both in Kent and beyond had also been mapped, showing the densest distribution in the centre of the county between the Medway and the Stour, with a particular concentration south east of Maidstone.[30] Although it has always been recognised that other types of house exist – notably the end jetty which some believe evolved at an earlier date than the Wealden[31] – little attention had been paid to distinguishing them in detail, sorting out their relationship with the aisled hall or the Wealden, or charting their evolution and their distribution. It was not, for example, generally recognised that many of the houses built in or after the late 14th century did not conform to either the Wealden or end-jetty types discussed above. Thus it was imperative to obtain, through systematic survey, a clearer picture of what medieval buildings existed in the county, in terms of their types, their dates, their size and their distribution.

The result of the survey was to make clear that different parts of the county have rather different medieval houses remaining. This is true with respect to their dates, their density and their quality. This fact had already been recognised by both Rigold and Everitt, although neither had pursued the matter in any detail.[32] But it has played little part in informing the work of most social and economic historians. Documentary evidence for the development of Kentish society in the Middle Ages is patchy. Most historical work has of necessity been undertaken on the estates of major ecclesiastical institutions, for the survival rate of their documents is greater than that of the laity. Consequently, for the period before the mid 16th century far more is known of the economic circumstances of the north and east of the county than of the less well-documented centre and west of Kent. Even where the documents survive they do not answer all the questions, for they were written for specific purposes and leave large sections of medieval life untouched. Buildings, or a lack of them, may supply evidence for economic prosperity and social structure which is unattainable by other means. It is beyond the scope of this book to do more than link the distribution of surviving buildings with some of the better-known aspects of the county's historical development. But the patterns are striking enough to suggest that once building evidence has been quantified and illustrated, it could and should be used as an important source which in part can fill what is otherwise a gap in our knowledge.

# 1 Historical background

## Geology and topography

Kent is composed of a series of geological and soil formations which extend in narrow bands across the county from west to east, each band giving way to the next in rapid succession (Figure 3).[1] Starting from the north coast, alluvial marshland is followed by various Tertiary deposits forming the north Kent plain where London clay, brick-earth, sand and gravel create fertile soils well suited to arable crops, and rich pasture lands. Although the dip-slope of the North Downs extends north towards the coast, the chalk on the lower parts is overlaid with clay and sand resulting in good soils, and these also occur in the three

river valleys which cut through the Downs: the Darent at the western edge of modern Kent, and the more important gaps created by the Rivers Medway and Stour further east (Figure 4).

The chalk Downs, largely covered by clay-with-flints, are dissected by dry valleys; here the soil was extremely difficult to work before the advent of modern machinery, so rough pasture and woodland abounded. The south-facing chalk escarpment drops steeply to the Vale of Holmesdale, a shallow valley extending from the chalk to the lower Greensand and incorporating a narrow band of Gault clay which gives rise to soils of variable quality, many of them fertile. To the south, the lower Greensand forms a less

*Figure 3 The geographical regions of Kent.*

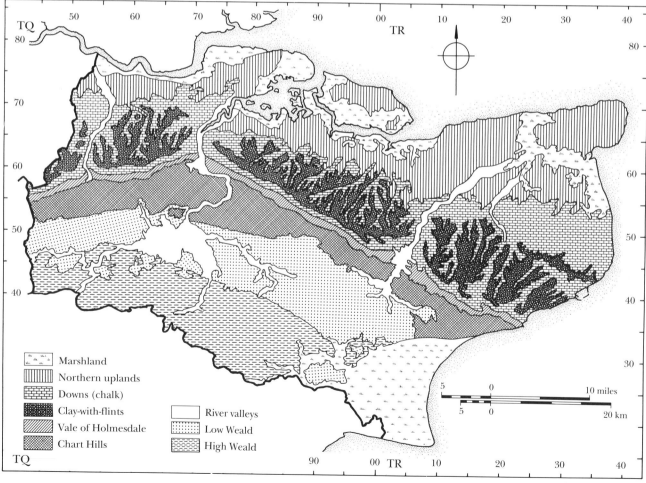

Marshland
Northern uplands
Downs (chalk)
Clay-with-flints
Vale of Holmesdale
Chart Hills
River valleys
Low Weald
High Weald

10

prominent line of hills than the Downs, usually known as the Chart Hills or ragstone hills. This range is most extensive to either side of the Medway gap, narrowing as it runs east and west. At its northern edge the region has coarse-grained sandstones giving rise to light soils which are often covered by heath; further south lie the Hythe Beds which are composed of a hard, sandy limestone called Kentish ragstone, which tails off to a softer sandstone in the west. The Hythe Beds, and a narrow band known as Atherfield Clay to its south, constitute another fertile belt crossing the county from west to east.

Below the ragstone scarp of the Chart Hills lies the low Weald or Vale of Kent, a wide flat valley largely underlain by heavy clay. It is wet in winter and dry in summer, and until the turnpike roads were built in the 18th century, it was notoriously difficult to traverse. Heavy clays compounded by bad drainage resulted in mediocre farmland, but in some central areas the solid geology is covered by alluvium and brickearth, particularly associated with the Medway and its tributaries, and here the soils are more productive. Further south the land rises to the hilly, high Weald, where both clay and sands are dissected by numerous small streams resulting in deep, narrow valleys. Neither the terrain nor the soil make this an easy area to farm; woodland has always been extensive and fields are small. Finally, to the south east of the Weald lies the large area of Romney Marsh where a changing coastline and alluvial deposits give rise both to excellent pasture and to marsh.

A brief summary of the main features of this east–west banding takes no account of the extraordinarily wide variety of soils, frequently resulting in extremely localised conditions. Nor do geological maps make apparent the important – but less easily defined – north–south divisions of the county. West, centre and east become clearer when a land-use capability map is consulted.[2] In the first place it is apparent that there is far less highly graded land west of the Medway than east of it. Second, low and high Weald divide into three, the divisions lying approximately along the line of the Medway, and on a line separating Headcorn in the centre from Smarden to the east; the central section of this region, from the Medway to Headcorn, has a higher land-use capability than do the sections on each side. Finally, there is, overall, more high-quality land in east Kent than elsewhere, notably on Romney Marsh and in the lowlands to the north of the Downs. Modern land use may not accurately reflect medieval land use, but it is certainly a pointer. This may particularly be the case in Kent where so much of the county was enclosed at an early date and the medieval landscape survives to a greater extent than is usual.[3] As we shall see, both topography and modern land use are guides to the disposition of medieval buildings.

*Figure 4 Relief and drainage of Kent.*

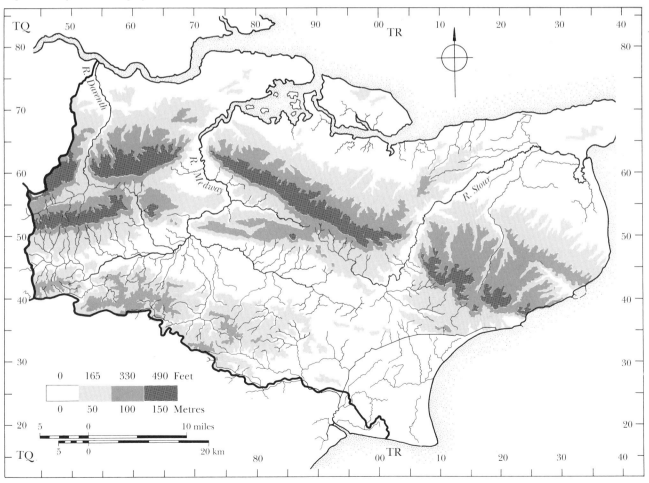

# The regional distribution of wealth

Analysis of the distribution of wealth in medieval England is a difficult subject; suitable assessments are rare and widely spaced in date, and there were numerous exemptions and variations in the accounting which make comparisons between areas, and between data of different periods, somewhat unsatisfactory.[4]

## Late 13th and 14th centuries

From the late 13th and early 14th centuries the taxation of Pope Nicholas IV, of 1291, and the lay subsidy of 1334, have both been used to provide a picture of the country's wealth just before the Black Death.[5]

In terms of ecclesiastical wealth per square mile it seems (with various caveats) that at that time Kent was the sixth wealthiest county in England.[6] Given the presence of the estates of the Archbishop of Canterbury and the Bishop of Rochester, and of a number of prominent monastic houses, this is hardly surprising. But Kent was a large county and its ecclesiastical wealth was not evenly distributed. At the time of Domesday, ecclesiastical manors were concentrated to the north east of the county, and this concentration remained unchanged throughout the Middle Ages. Studies of individual ecclesiastical estates allow us to examine their wealth in more detail. The richest ecclesiastical of all was the Archbishop, and it was those of his manors which went to make up the bailiwick of Wingham, in the fertile arable and pasture lands of Thanet and the extreme north east of the county, which brought in the highest revenues. This was followed by the estates of the eastern bailiwick of Aldington, which included much of Romney Marsh. Archiepiscopal manors further west and south, both in Kent and beyond, were less wealthy. Before the late 14th century the profits came largely from direct farming of the demesnes; later they were maintained through the establishment of profitable leases.[7]

Christ Church Priory, Canterbury, was not only the wealthiest religious house in the county, but the second (later the third) wealthiest in England.[8] The distribution of the arable wealth of its manors in the 14th century is graphically illustrated by A Smith, whose published map shows that the largest estates again lay to the north and east, followed by those in the Vale of Holmesdale, with smaller properties in most other areas.[9]

North and east Kent were not totally dominated by ecclesiastical possessions. Despite the considerable holdings of the Church, this part of the county also supported a large number of secular estates. After the Conquest nearly 200 manors and other lands, formerly in the hands of many minor landholders, were granted to the King's half-brother Odo, Bishop of Bayeux. These were scattered throughout the county, and many, including the smaller number of holdings granted to other laymen, lay in the same areas as the ecclesiastical and monastic estates.[10] Following Odo's final disgrace in 1087, his property was redistributed among a variety of less prominent men, whose lands were often widely dispersed, and some of whom held no more than a manor or two.

This pool of secular lands was an important source for the later medieval holdings of the gentry in the county.

These later gentry estates originated in a number of ways. Some were properties held directly from the Crown, others were knights' fees on both secular and ecclesiastical estates.[11] However, such estates were not all held by rural landowners, for by the late Middle Ages many wealthy moneyers from Canterbury, and traders and merchants from the ports of north and east Kent, also had property in the countryside. The level of early 14th-century lay prosperity in this area is suggested by the lay subsidy assessment of 1334.[12]

The 1334 lay subsidy was levied on movable goods, not on landed wealth, but it is generally accepted as a reasonable indicator of the distribution of lay wealth before the Black Death. Nonetheless, it cannot be used uncritically. Throughout England an unknown proportion of people were deemed to have incomes below the taxable minimum, but in Kent there were additional exemptions. All property within the Cinque Ports was excluded, and the property of those who were termed 'men of the Cinque Ports', and of the Canterbury moneyers, was exempted, no matter where it lay. However, such property, outside the towns, was assessed even though no charge was made, and this record provides some idea of the extent and wealth of Cinque Port men and of moneyers in the rural areas.

Most of the published distribution maps of the 1334 subsidy include these nominal assessments, with the result that the lay wealth of Kent per square mile ranks eighth in national terms.[13] Details of the published maps, compiled to illustrate different points, vary, but all agree in showing that the highest yielding area extended along the north coast, from Sittingbourne eastwards.[14] This was followed by a large part of the eastern downland behind Sandwich and Dover (being Cinque Ports, their assessments were totally excluded), and by Maidstone and its surrounding region. Most of western and the rest of eastern Kent fell into a third band. The centre, particularly the Weald, but also the area as far north as the crest of the Downs, fell firmly into a fourth category which had assessments among the lowest in England.

The separate listing of men of the Cinque Ports and of moneyers shows that a high proportion of wealth, particularly in the east of the county, lay in their hands. When their assessments are removed, much of east Kent, particularly round Dover and Sandwich, is no wealthier than the centre of the county. Even though some of this moveable wealth may have been generated by trade, it is likely that it also stemmed, like that of the Church, from the profits of land.

From the early 14th century onwards recurrent and devastating economic and social problems were caused by bad weather, poor harvests, sheep disease and human mortality, of which the Black Death was only the worst manifestation. The resulting depopulation, higher wage levels and higher prices for the products of animal husbandry led both lords and peasants to turn much of their land from arable to pasture, and were instrumental in deciding landlords to lease their demesnes.[15]

## 15th and 16th centuries

In the early 15th century, sheep disease and the difficulties England experienced with foreign trade resulted in sheep farming, wool production and the prosperity of ports, which depended on the wool trade, coming under threat. However, the demand for wool picked up again in the last quarter of the century, when there was a relatively steady increase in cloth manufacture and export.[16] The economic problems of the 15th century had a significant effect on landlords and on the poorer members of society, which is indicated by falling population figures and tenant numbers. They did not, however, work to the disadvantage of all, and many of the better off among the peasants were able to turn the situation to their advantage and start accumulating sizeable holdings.[17] By the early 16th century, when the Tudor lay subsidies provide the next comparable assessments of lay wealth, there is no sign that the wealthy in the north and east of Kent were worse off than they had been two hundred years before.

The Tudor subsidies began in 1512 and continued through the 16th century. Unlike the 1334 subsidy, people were assessed not only on moveable goods, but also on annual income from land, or on wages, the tax being levied on whichever yielded the greatest revenue to the Crown. As with the earlier subsidy, none of the assessments are straightforward to use, but it has been estimated that those for 1514 and 1515 are the most reliable for purposes of comparison between the two periods.[18] The overall assessment of 1515 shows that Kent had moved up the league table of lay wealth, from the eighth to the fourth richest county in England.[19] Since none of the 16th-century subsidies included assessments for the men of the Cinque Ports, the real lay wealth of the county should have been even greater.

The only detailed work to have been undertaken on the Tudor subsidies which includes analysis of the Kentish material relates to that of 1524/5.[20] Although in some counties this subsidy may be a relatively reliable source regarding both levels of wealth and numbers of taxpayers, there are major problems with the Kentish documents. Information relating to certain areas is missing altogether; for some, totals survive but no details, for others details but no totals. This means that although the yield, mostly broken down into hundreds, can be estimated, evidence for the basis of the assessment, and whether it was paid by a small number of wealthy men or a larger number of the less prosperous, is frequently missing. In addition, the assessments for the men of the Cinque Ports were not included at all. All this does not mean that the returns are useless, but that the results are partial and must be used with caution, particularly in comparisons with the 1334 lay subsidy.[21]

What detailed evidence there is relates largely to the east of the county and to a small area around the Hoo peninsula.[22] This shows that the hinterland of Dover and Sandwich, as well as one or two other small parts of the county, had more taxpayers per square mile than most other areas of England. Considerably fewer men paid in the extreme north east of the county, and fewer again in Romney Marsh. Overall assessments of the yield for each region are available for most of Kent, and indicate that, with the exception of the extreme west and south east, the whole county paid more than 50 shillings per square mile, which is among the highest of any part of England.[23]

The greatest yields, of 72 shillings per square mile, lay along the central section of the north coast, so that in terms of lay taxation this region, where the Church was not greatly in evidence, remained the wealthiest in the county throughout the Middle Ages. In the north east the yield was down to between 58 and 65 shillings per square mile, although, as analysis of the 1334 subsidy showed, the exclusion of the men of the Cinque Ports must have distorted the figures in this area so that the real wealth was probably considerably greater. Despite this, studies in the tenurial history, discussed below, suggest that wealth was substantially redistributed in this area during the late 14th and 15th centuries, resulting in lay prosperity being concentrated increasingly in fewer hands.

The most striking aspect of the 1524 subsidy is the new prosperity which is apparent in central Kent. Yields of 55 to 69 shillings per square mile were collected through most of the central Weald, Chart Hills and Vale of Holmesdale, areas where assessments had been lowest in 1334.[24] By the mid 16th century the wealth of this central and southern region is well attested. It seems likely that it was closely related to a newly developing prosperity among those sections of the peasantry who were able to benefit by the gradual withdrawal of the great northern landlords from their outlying lands, and the consequent opportunities afforded to those with initiative.

By the late Middle Ages the Weald's most valuable resource was its timber and firewood, and in the east of the region this could be transported by water for sale and use elsewhere. From the 13th century, the Archbishop and the religious houses were constantly in dispute with their tenants over the illegal felling and disposal of timber, the tenants finally gaining the upper hand, and receiving the timber rights in return for rent.[25] But this was not the only source of tenant wealth in the 15th and early 16th centuries. Tanning, and later iron working, developed in the western Weald. Broadcloth production was centred on Cranbrook. Mixed farming was practised throughout, with sheep particularly prominent towards Romney Marsh and a strong emphasis on cattle rearing in the Cranbrook and Benenden areas. In many cases income from more than one of these sources was relied upon. But the extent to which this picture can be projected backwards is less clear.[26] Although clothworkers were first settled in Cranbrook in 1331, little is known about the industry before the 15th century.[27] Various mid 15th-century references to the shipment of raw wool and fleeces to Essex and to the production of Kentish woollen cloth have been found, but sheep farming faced a lot of problems in the early part of the century, and wool prices were at their lowest in the 1440s and 1450s.[28] They picked up in the 1460s, although the major increases did not come until the last two decades of the century.[29] Meanwhile evidence for the Wealden broadcloth industry is sparse before the 1560s.[30] Similarly, although cattle farming was clearly big business by the mid 16th century it is uncertain how far back specialist farming may have occurred.[31] The absence of relevant documentation, together with a lack of detailed work on surviving documents, hinders interpretation. Where research has occurred there is some indication that the prosperity began some time before the end of the 15th century. In Plaxtol, which formed part of the Archbishop's manor of Wrotham, lying on the edge of the Chart Hills and the low Weald to the west of the Medway, references to graziers, butchers and tanners occur from the 1480s onwards, occasionally phrased in such a way as to suggest that the families concerned were already well established.[32] By the 1490s, both here and more centrally in the Weald, heriots were commonly paid in the form of cattle.[33]

Romney Marsh is a region where evidence of change between the subsidies is confused by lack of 16th-century details concerning the men of the Cinque Ports. In 1334, the assessment per square mile, including men of the Cinque Ports, was relatively high.[34] But when their assessments are removed, a great variation is apparent between the hundreds, ranging from high figures in the Folkestone and Hythe area to extremely low ones in the centre of the Marsh. It is probable that such variations may be accounted for by the presence of a few very wealthy people.[35] In 1524 the yield was among the lowest in the county. Although this total must have been depressed by the exclusion of the men of the Cinque Ports and their property in the surrounding region,[36] it is likely that changes had taken place. In the 15th century, flooding had caused the landlords major problems, probably encouraging them to turn from arable to pasture farming. By 1500 much of the Marsh was used for grazing and many of the less wealthy had lost their livelihood.[37]

It is even more difficult to grasp what was occurring in west Kent, partly because the documentation is scarce and partly because little work has been done. Despite its proximity to London, the west of the county appears to have been the least economically advanced region. The soil was poor,[38] the Archbishop's demesnes were let for far less than those of either east Kent or Sussex,[39] and apart from the area immediately adjacent to London, the subsidies of 1334 and 1524 are consistent with each other in showing the lowest assessments and yields in the county: the new prosperity which was apparent in the central Weald by the early 16th century is far less marked to the west of Goudhurst, where yields of only 38 to 42 shillings per square mile were recorded. This suggests that the Weald did not develop in a uniform manner.

# Population trends

Regional prosperity and density of population were not necessarily synonymous. The problems of estimating total populations and assessing demographic trends in the Middle Ages are well known, and estimates for the population of Kent are as imprecise as any.[40] By the late 14th century, when the medieval population was considerably reduced from its peak in the 13th or early 14th century, the Poll Tax of 1377 netted 56,557 people over the age of fourteen.[41] From this it has been suggested that the total population of the historic county lay in the region of 90,000.[42]

The next time that an overall figure can be obtained is in the mid 16th century when a number of surveys of households and communicants were undertaken in the diocese of Canterbury.[43] On the basis of these it has been suggested that the population of the whole county was between 80,000 and 85,000.[44] Possibly this figure is on the low side, for although the population of England generally continued to decline during the first half of the 15th century, it is normally suggested that by the early 16th century the numbers were back to late 14th-century levels.[45] In Kent such an assumption is supported by evidence from forty-four parishes, for which both the number of tax payers in 1377 and the number of communicants in 1557 is known. Since poll-tax payers were over fourteen years of age, and communicants usually fifteen or more, the figures are generally reckoned to be comparable.[46] In the late 14th century the taxpayers in these parishes numbered 6,566; in the mid 16th century there were 7,910 communicants, indicating a rise of 20 per cent.[47] Since the parishes lie within a limited area of central Kent, there may be some doubt as to how far the results are representative of the county as a whole. However, while twenty-four of these parishes showed an increase in population, the other twenty showed a decrease, suggesting considerable fluctuation. Even so, it is unlikely that the county as a whole was out of step with the sample to the extent that there was an actual decrease – although the overall increase may have been less than 20 per cent. From the mid 16th century the population certainly was rising, and by 1603 the total, again calculated from the number of communicants, has been reckoned as 130,000.[48]

Whether accurate or not, county estimates of this sort conceal the fact that there are likely to have been variations in growth and decline in different regions of Kent. These are not easy to chart, both because of the long gap between 1377 and the mid 16th century, and because the evidence for each period is so partial.

In 1377 figures for all five lathes exist. Most, but not all, of these are broken down into hundreds, and in some cases even into parishes. At that time the densest populations lay in the central section of the north coast and in the Maidstone area, followed by the rest of the north coast and much of the central inland region, including stretches of the Medway and Stour valleys, the Vale of Holmesdale, the Chart Hills and the low Weald. For Romney Marsh only the total population for the lathe of Shepway survives, but averaged out this indicates a reasonably high density. On the other hand, in the neighbouring section of the eastern high Weald, another single figure for seven hundreds suggests that the Cranbrook area was the most sparsely populated in the whole county. This was followed by relatively low numbers in most of west Kent, including the western Weald, and in the eastern section of the Downs behind Dover.[49]

Comparison of the 16th-century population with the late 14th-century evidence is difficult. No detailed mid 16th-century surveys are known for the diocese of Rochester, which roughly covers all Kent west of the Medway. Even in Canterbury diocese evidence is partial, so that at the later date some of the most detailed information survives for the high Weald and Romney Marsh, where the earlier figures were very generalised. Archdeacon Harpsfield's Visitation of 1557 provides household and communicant numbers for much of the centre of the county, but excludes most of the area east of Canterbury and north of Folkestone. In 1563 another survey lists households throughout the diocese. However, there are severe discrepancies between some of the 1557 and 1563 totals, and it is likely that the earlier and less complete set is the more reliable.[50]

In 1557 the greatest density of population lay in the high Weald and in small groups of parishes around Maidstone and Ashford in the centre, and Sittingbourne (or Milton) and Faversham along the north coast. This contrasts with low densities in and around Romney Marsh, in much of the rest of the north and, in so far as the evidence exists, further east in the county. Although the absolute numbers in the 1563 survey may be suspect, the general picture is similar to that of 1557, and adds the information that the far east of the county contained relatively fewer people by this time.

Lack of evidence means that the situation in west Kent remains shadowy. In 1377 the west generally was fairly sparsely inhabited. For the mid 16th century, work on parish registers suggests that the western Weald continued to be less densely populated than the central area.[51] This was still the case in 1676 at the time of the Compton Census. By then, and possibly long before, pressure from London had spilt over into that part of Kent closest to the capital. But the influence of London never seems to have reached far into the rural areas of the county.[52]

Overall, it can be inferred that there was a movement of population from north and east to centre and south, and to some extent this reflects the increasing wealth of the central part of the county which was revealed by comparing the 1334 and 1524 lay subsidies. However, and perhaps not surprisingly, the changes in population are more marked than the changes in wealth.

# Landholding and tenure

There is seldom a simple correlation between areas of known wealth, however created, and the building of surviving houses. It is possible for areas with high assessments of wealth to contain many people who paid small amounts, or a few who paid more. Thus the generality of men in rich agricultural regions might be burdened with tenurial and social obligations which militated against the accumulation of enough wealth for building fine houses. It is equally possible for those who lived on more marginal land to be less burdened or less dependent on agriculture, and therefore to have higher disposable incomes. Such factors almost certainly played their part in medieval Kent. In order to explore these issues it is necessary to know more about manorial conditions in the county and their effect on the tenantry. Unfortunately this is no easy task.

Kent may be subdivided into a number of geographical regions, and the colonisation of the county, broadly speaking, followed the topography. The earliest settlements lay along the north coast, in the Vale of Holmesdale and in the river valleys linking the two. The original manorial centres were established in these regions, and all other parts of the county were at first dependent upon the communities of those areas. By the time of the Conquest, the outlying lands, which originally had served as detached pastures for their parent estates, were permanently settled, and in some regions, notably on the Downs, had become totally independent. However, the Wealden and marshland territories in particular remained economically important to their parent manors, which attempted to retain control over them for as long as possible. Effectively this meant until the 14th century, although nominally their overlordship continued until much later.[53] The result was that many manors in Kent were not located wholly in one area but had land scattered in several topographical regions.[54]

## Tenure

On the great estates a sizeable proportion of land was held in military tenure, by knight service. It has, for example, been calculated that one-sixth or one-seventh of the estates of the Archbishop and Christ Church Priory was held in this way throughout the Middle Ages, while some sixty-four of Odo of Bayeux's manors were enfeoffed at the time of Domesday.[55] The majority of these military tenures lay in north and east Kent and in the Vale of Holmesdale.

The type of tenure usually associated with peasants in Kent is gavelkind. It now seems to be agreed that this was not as universal as was once suggested, but it was nonetheless of considerable importance. Gavelkind was a free tenure: men were personally free and could dispose of their land at will, but owed both rent and a number of obligations to the lord. These were normally light, and the difference this made to the position of peasants in Kent as opposed to Sussex has been noted. By the 14th century the distinction between those who held by military tenure and gavelkinders and between gavelkinders and bondmen seems, in fact, to have been blurred. Many at the upper levels of society held land by both military tenure and gavelkind, and in some cases those whose land was largely in gavelkind became as important as those who held by knight service. At a lower social level peasants frequently held both gavelkind land and bondland.[56]

For our purpose the most important aspects of gavelkind tenure were partible inheritance, the rule dividing property equally between all sons, and the freedom to sell or bequeath land at will. It was once considered possible that partible inheritance in Kent in the 13th and early 14th centuries led to the 'descendants of a common ancestor, living in one large house or in a group of adjoining houses and holding a domain in common and undivided'.[57] If this had occurred, it could have had significant implications for the design and development of dwellings, even though the majority of surviving houses are of later date. But in fact the buildings themselves provide no evidence of this, and, despite the way some documents are worded, historians have tended to reject the view that joint tenure of an inheritance was common.[58]

An alternative view, that partible inheritance led to the creation of ever smaller and less viable units, has also not found favour. In the first place, the incidence of several male heirs dividing property is not as high as might be supposed. Furthermore, the second aspect of gavelkind, the freedom to dispose of land at will, seems to have resulted either in a man acquiring enough property to divide into viable holdings amongst his heirs, or, if the inheritance was too small, in the disposal of uneconomic fragments.[59] In many parts of England there is evidence of an intensely active land market in the later Middle Ages, and Kent was no exception.[60]

## Landholding

It was hoped, at the start of this project, that it might be possible to correlate the size and type of medieval houses with the size of holdings. This has now been done in Sussex, where it has been suggested that houses with ground-floor areas of 70–150 sq yd (58–125 sq m) can be associated with tenements of 50–125 acres, with larger tenements able to support larger houses.[61] The same may have been true in Kent, but it has not been possible to verify the hypothesis because of the uncertainties raised in studying the documents.

Detailed studies of a number of manors in Kent, where a full range of documentary sources are available, have disclosed a considerable amount of information about the possible sizes of holdings in terms of rent paid, the prevalence of an active land market, and some detail about the topography of the manors, at least at their centres.[62] As elsewhere in England, tenant numbers dropped progressively through the 14th and 15th centuries, and this led to a high level of stratification, with a few coming to hold a larger proportion of the land. It was from among the latter that the farmers of the demesnes were often drawn. Alterations in the composition of the tenantry seem to have varied in different parts of the county. Stratification was greatest in the north and east, where the drop in tenant numbers was most acute. In central Kent the changes appear to have been less extreme, with fewer outstandingly wealthy tenants and more in the middling range.[63]

To date, almost all documentary work has been done on ecclesiastical estates where central administration and continuity of ownership until the Dissolution led both to the creation of better archives and to their survival. Secular estates tended to change hands more frequently, and there was little incentive to preserve manorial records. Thus very little work has taken place on manors in lay hands, and it is as yet unclear whether the circumstances of the tenants, particularly in the late 14th and 15th centuries, were similar.[64] As we shall see, the house evidence suggests that there might have been differences.

This is not the only problem. Manorial documentation was compiled primarily to supply the lord of the manor with information concerning his income and rights. The documents therefore seldom produce the type of data needed to understand the situation of individual tenants.[65] It was not always necessary for the lord to record the precise location of land which produced rents; nor the size of the holding, as opposed to the amount of rent; nor what type of land a person held. In a county where many manors had outlying lands, lack of this type of information makes it extremely difficult to understand the nature of the tenements. There are signs that the active land market went hand in hand with the practice of sub-letting, a level of activity which went largely unrecorded in manorial documents. Finally, some tenants certainly held land of more than one manor.[66] All this combines to make it virtually impossible to assess the true size of the tenants' holdings.

Initially it was hoped to include some work on manorial documents to back up the building surveys. Various sources, such as account rolls, rentals and court rolls, were examined for both ecclesiastical and secular estates. But it very soon became apparent that unless detailed and painstaking research was undertaken on individual manors, very little of value would emerge. To undertake the task in any way that would usefully contribute to a county-wide survey of medieval houses was beyond the brief of this project.

# The gentry of Kent

## Emergence of the gentry

One issue which has not so far been addressed in this chapter is the background to the emerging gentry class of the 14th and 15th centuries, and the distribution of the gentry within the county. It is generally recognised that Kent was not a county of high-ranking gentry.[67] At the time of the Conquest, the great landowners were the King, the Archbishop, the religious houses – notably Christ Church Priory – and Odo, Bishop of Bayeux; to these may be added four other lay tenants-in-chief whose holdings were relatively small. After Odo's disgrace his lands, which had been formerly in many hands, were again widely distributed, so that, by the late 11th century, a pattern of minor landowners was established, particularly in parts of the north and east.[68]

Very few noble families had their main estates in Kent, even though many held land there, and few of the knights' fees which were created on the estates of the tenants-in-chief grew to any size, except for the holdings of the Clares who held the Lowy of Tonbridge from the Archbishop.[69] Over the next three centuries the importance of feudal tenure gradually diminished, and in its place there emerged by the late 14th century a new gentry class who sometimes held their lands by knight service, and sometimes by gavelkind.[70] In Kent, as elsewhere in England, status, wealth and office were of greater significance to these new men than was the form of their tenure.

In a recent thesis on the Kentish gentry between 1422 and 1509, P W Fleming identifies some 275 families of unequivocally gentry status. Of these only 6–11 per cent had members who had been knighted; a higher percentage of families included esquires, but between 56 and 66 per cent were simple gentlemen, with the proportion rising towards the end of the period.[71] Thus during the 15th century the majority of the Kentish gentry were not of high status, but parish gentry who were locally important but played little role in county affairs. The difference in status and lifestyle between this group and the emerging yeomen who formed the upper strata of the peasantry was probably small, and it is likely that considerable association and movement took place between gentlemen, yeomen, merchants, tradesmen and those who had careers in administration or law. To some extent the practice of gavelkind in Kent, although increasingly circumvented by the gentry, helped to maintain fluidity between one class and another, as brothers set themselves up on small estates. Certainly many of the gentry families came to have numerous branches, not all of whom might strictly count as being of gentry status.[72]

## Distribution of the gentry

The distribution of gentry estates in Kent was not evenly spread throughout the county. The densest distribution lay on the fringes of London and in the Stour valley to the east. This was followed by the Medway valley, and the central and eastern part of north Kent. The areas of lowest density were on the Downs and in the high Weald, followed by the low Weald and Romney Marsh.[73] But within this distribution lay another. From the late 13th century, the main seats of the more important gentry families, those whose most prominent members ranked as knights and esquires and tended to hold the major county offices, were primarily located in east Kent. The Stour valley was a favoured area, as were the northern lowlands of central and eastern Kent. These were regions of fertile arable land where many of the large ecclesiastical manors were located, and where the wealthiest lay estates lay cheek by jowl with the accumulating property of the Canterbury moneyers and Cinque Port merchants. Society, as in all arable areas, tended to be ordered and hierarchical, and labour a necessary commodity. One would expect this to be reflected in the surviving buildings.

The high density of less important gentry families in north-west Kent is largely accounted for by the proximity of London. There is plenty of evidence to indicate the desire of Londoners for country estates, and while the wealthiest among them frequently bought property at considerable distances from the capital, the countryside nearest to London was popular with those who had less to spend.[74]

A far smaller number of obviously recognisable gentry families occur in the low and high Weald, including the area where the documents suggest a marked change in wealth and population between the 14th and 16th centuries. The Weald was primarily a region of pastoral farming, valuable timber resources and expanding occupa-tions of a diverse nature. But it was by no means uniform, and the east and west Weald developed rather differently in the centuries after the Conquest. The value of timber, combined with ease of access and transport, meant that the eastern half remained under the control of the great northern landlords for as long as possible; when the change came it was the tenants who profited, and this part of Kent was probably the one where social distinctions between the gentry and wealthy yeomen were least clearly defined.[75] The west, on the other hand, was much less easily accessible, and the major landowner, the Archbishop, granted out estates from an early date. The most important of these was the grant of the Lowy of Tonbridge to the Clares. They later augmented this, and in their turn created knights' fees to fulfil their obligations to the Archbishop. The result was that a feudal system came into being which had more in common with north Kent than with the rest of the Weald.[76]

By the 14th century a number of manors and small estates had been established, mostly along the Medway. Many of these were very small, and their holders do not always seem to be recognised among the ranks of the gentry.[77] Yet they almost certainly had a profound effect on the development of the region during the 14th and 15th centuries. The fact that there is a marked difference in the surviving building evidence of the east and west Weald may be due in part to their presence.

# 2 Houses of the early and mid 13th century

The study of high-status domestic buildings of the 13th and 14th centuries is a relatively neglected subject. It began with the publication of the first volume of Turner and Parker's *Domestic Architecture in England* in 1851,[1] and although it was continued in this century through the work of Margaret Wood and others, there is still a great deal to be done.[2] Because such buildings are widely dispersed and few in number, and frequently survive in fragmentary form, their affiliations are often national rather than local, and they have tended to be neglected by students of vernacular architecture. Few have been subjected to recent and rigorous investigation and recording, and when they have, perhaps during the course of restoration, they have often been found to be more complex in their planning and building history than the published literature suggests. It is clear that there is scope for a full-scale review of the subject, as some recent writers are well aware. But this can hardly be done from the existing literature, and a great deal of new fieldwork would be required to form the basis of a revised assessment.

In this project, a number of early domestic buildings in Kent were recorded, although the self-imposed limits of the project meant that neither castles, archiepiscopal palaces, nor any of the Templar manors were included, although they may be referred to in discussion. Attention concentrated on rural domestic buildings, and began with the surviving remains of three stone houses, and the interpretation of their original function. Luddesdown Court, Luddesdown, possibly of the 1220s or 1230s, and Nettlestead Place, Nettlestead, and Squerryes Lodge, Westerham, both of which are likely to have been built in the mid 13th century, have all been interpreted as first-floor halls.[3] At Nettlestead Place, an exceptionally fine vaulted undercroft has a much altered first floor with no original details remaining, while a further range may retain an early outline (Figure 6). Far more survives at Luddesdown Court and

Squerryes Lodge. In the former, three two-storey ranges of some size still have evidence of roof construction, window seats, medieval decoration and early fireplaces (Figure 7). In the latter, two ranges of two storeys remain, one lit by a plate-traceried window (Figure 5b). Doorways in both buildings provide some clues as to layout and circulation. Given the size and splendour of the surviving structures, it is hardly surprising that they should have been interpreted as complete houses, with the main room designated a first-floor hall. But at Nettlestead Place this interpretation has not been accepted by all commentators. The site, still entered by a later medieval gatehouse, was large, and it has been suggested that what survives may only have been a chamber or solar block serving a detached hall of which all trace has gone.[4] Since the ground-floor area of the main range is the largest of these three buildings, Nettlestead Place is the test case, and it is perhaps appropriate to begin by re-examining the evidence for first-floor halls generally, before considering how best to interpret the Kentish remains.

## First-floor halls: a re-examination of the evidence

Recently, M W Thompson has presented the first-floor hall as an aristocratic introduction from the Continent at the time of the Conquest, replacing the native English ground-floor hall at the highest social levels, particularly in castles and palaces.[5] On the other hand, an alternative view, that the first-floor hall was rare, and that the function of many two-storeyed ranges has been misinterpreted, has been propounded by Blair.[6]

The issues are extremely complex, and a full discussion of them lies beyond the scope of this book. It is undeniable that first-floor halls are common in keeps and castles. In Kent this includes both major castles, such as Dover and Rochester, and smaller sites like Eynsford Castle or Walmer Old Manor House.[7] Outside this context the situation is much less clear cut. Throughout England, a number of great first-floor rooms remain in bishops' palaces, such as Winchester, Norwich, Wells and Lincoln. In the past these were thought to be first-floor halls which were replaced later by ground-floor, aisled halls, but recently doubts have been expressed.[8] At Canterbury, Lanfranc's presumed hall may have been on the first floor, although it has not always been interpreted this way.[9]

In fact, it is no longer possible to be certain about the function of these early ranges, and the view that first-floor halls were once fashionable but later superseded is increasingly hard to sustain: ground-floor halls in bishops' palaces were being erected as early as the 12th century at Old Sarum, Wiltshire, Farnham, Surrey, and Hereford, while proven first-floor halls continued to be built well into the 13th century and later at Wells, Somerset, St David's, Dyfed, and Southwark, London.[10] In royal palaces, evidence for 12th or 13th-century first-floor halls is scarce. The only certain example is the Lesser Hall at Westminster, and the documents do not support the view that further examples once existed of which all trace has gone.[11] In the late 12th century it seems likely that Henry II went so far as to erect an aisled hall at Saumur, when it was the custom in France for royalty and the nobility to have their halls at first-floor level.[12] This strongly suggests that he was building according to recognised English practice, and that the term hall at this time denoted an aisled ground-floor hall, of the type described by Alexander Necham in the 1190s.[13]

In fact one may wonder whether in England there was any real element of choice for unfortified rural residences. Necham writes as though, by the late 12th century, the normal hall was understood to be aisled and at ground-floor level. During the 13th century the layout of this ground-floor hall became standardised.[14] It was entered by opposed doorways at one end of each long wall, and two or three further doorways in the adjacent gable wall led to service rooms and perhaps to a passage to a detached kitchen. The hall was heated by a central open hearth which was situated away from the entrance, towards the upper or dais end which was where the owner sat. A further doorway at that end usually gave access to private rooms beyond.

This arrangement of elements was repeated, with minor variations, throughout the Middle Ages, suggesting that people had a very clear idea of how a ground-floor hall should function. The large number of doorways, which allowed entry from the exterior and access to other parts of the house, indicates that the room was the focal point of the dwelling, used by all the household. The precise layout, with external and service doorways set away from the private end of the hall, suggests a hierarchical arrangement of space in which people of different status had their allotted places. That this plan was all but universal after the 12th century, from palaces to the smallest surviving open-hall houses, is a measure of how deeply embedded this sense of hierarchy must have been.

Presumed or proven first-floor halls, on the other hand, are arranged rather differently. Only occasionally are they replicas of ground-floor halls transposed to an upper storey, as occurs at the 14th-century Bishop's Palace, Southwark.[15]

Opposed entrances were rare, the services lay elsewhere, the fireplace was enclosed on a side wall, and the inner chamber was variously located. Lack of direct access to services, and often of an obvious position for the dais, suggests far greater privacy and a rather different function. It seems possible that all houses required a ground-floor hall in order for the household to function properly, but that in larger establishments a second, somewhat more private, public room was also required. At Rochester Castle, for example, the King had an upper hall in the keep, but there was a second hall in the bailey, a pattern which was repeated in several castles and bishops' palaces.[16]

As Thompson suggests, where two 'halls' survive, as they do at Lincoln, the upper one may have been designated by 'the portmanteau term camera' and was probably used for more private official functions.[17] The fact that the upper hall is often the earlier of the two has created the impression that it was superseded by the ground-floor hall. However, at Winchester, Hampshire, and perhaps elsewhere, the storeyed range probably accompanied an earlier ground-floor hall, and it was this early hall which was superseded by the new ground-floor hall which survives today.[18]

## Chamber blocks

In rural situations where the buildings cater for individual households, surviving storeyed stone ranges are less likely to have had the function of a hall and frequently can be interpreted as chamber ranges accompanying timber ground-floor halls which have gone. Although this view is beginning to find favour, it is not easy to prove beyond doubt, partly because the documents do not make this distinction plain, and partly because there is as yet very little confirmation available from excavated sites, which is where conclusive evidence for the layout of rural sites will ultimately be found.

A number of storeyed stone ranges have never been interpreted as first-floor halls. It has always been accepted that by the 13th century some open halls had two-storeyed ranges attached to them which contained subsidiary accommodation. Apart from royal or episcopal palaces, one may cite Warnford, Hampshire, Appleton Manor, Berkshire,[19] and Much Wenlock Priory and Chelmarsh Hall, Shropshire,[20] as well as the late 13th-century example of Old Soar, Plaxtol, in Kent. All of these have clear and unambiguous evidence for ground-floor halls attached to two-storey chamber blocks.

## Detached chamber blocks

There is a second group of two-storeyed stone ranges which are generally accepted as chamber blocks, despite the fact that there are no signs of contemporary halls. Some have two doorways in one long side and can be interpreted therefore as service wings which lay at right angles to halls that have been replaced. These include buildings such as Little Chesterford Manor, Essex, Swalcliffe Manor, Oxfordshire, and Hambledon Manor, Hampshire.[21] Squerryes Lodge, Westerham, in Kent belongs with this group. It has two doorways side by side opening into two

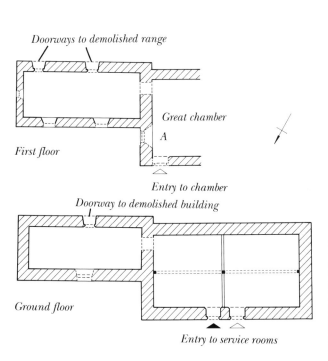

Doorways to demolished range

Great chamber

A

First floor

Entry to chamber

Doorway to demolished building

Ground floor

Entry to service rooms

a

b

Figure 5 Squerryes Lodge, Westerham: a) Plan of ground floor (below) and partial plan of first floor (above); b) Blocked first-floor window at A on plan (BB/8758).

ground-floor rooms, with a large chamber above lit by a plate-tracery window in one gable wall (Figure 5). However, the interpretation of this group is not quite as clear cut as might be supposed.

At Swalcliffe Manor, the two doorways imply that the lower-end wing (now rebuilt) was of standard form, but the wall in which they lie is separated from a later 14th-century hall by straight joints in the stonework. Whether the wing stood free or was attached to an earlier hall is not clear. At Little Chesterford Manor, Essex, where the wing is also only a generation or two earlier than the present aisled hall, the two 'service doorways' are of different sizes and set far apart, suggesting the range did not begin life as a normal service wing; in addition, it appears that the first floor originally may have been reached by an upper doorway at one end of the wall towards the hall, a feature which is repeated at Squerryes Lodge.[22] A first-floor doorway opening directly into the open hall at the lower end and reached by stairs within the hall occurs at Oakham Castle, Leicestershire, where the great width allows room for it beneath the roof of the hall; but this would hardly have been possible where an attached hall was smaller, and possibly both aisled and timber framed. At Squerryes Lodge, there is not enough room for a normal hall to join at right angles, since the land starts to rise sharply less than 15 m from the side wall of the

stone block. Thus this range and that at Little Chesterford are likely either to have served as first-floor halls, or to have been chamber blocks which were completely detached from their ground-floor halls. While the latter theory cannot be proved, it seems the more likely hypothesis, for it is more logical to see the present arrangement resulting from rebui'ding an earlier ground-floor hall than to presume that the function of the original stone range changed abruptly, and in a short space of time, from hall to chamber block. This may sound like special pleading, but since there is evidence that detached chamber blocks were built throughout the 13th century, it should not be dismissed out of hand.

In royal palaces, hall and *camere* were frequently detached. Excavation has made this clear at Clarendon, Wiltshire, where the apartments of the King and Queen remained distinct from the hall and from each other through the 13th century;[23] the same is suggested by the numerous orders, issued throughout the 13th and 14th centuries, for pentices to link the chambers and other ranges in several royal houses.[24] In ecclesiastical palaces, documentary evidence is less explicit, prompting the continuing discussion over the function and nomenclature of detached ranges with large first-floor rooms. However, in Kent the accepted chamber range at the Archbishop's

Palace of Charing, in its present form possibly originating in the late 13th century, lay at a considerable distance from the hall, and appears never to have been linked to it by anything more than what has been described as a corridor.[25] In Oxfordshire the chamber of the bishop's manor of Harwell remained separate from the hall until the late 14th century.[26]

Detached chamber ranges were not, however, confined to the dwellings of kings and bishops, although the extent to which this was common practice is difficult to assess.[27] If a surviving range was completely free standing and the associated buildings have gone, it can only be judged by those aspects of its layout, structure and architectural detail which are indicative of function. In many cases the remains are too fragmentary or too amorphous to allow conclusions to be reached. Nonetheless, evidence is gradually coming to light which suggests that some storeyed stone ranges should be interpreted as detached chamber blocks, and that their halls lay a little distance away and were often timber framed.

The evidence comes in two forms. First, some sites have been excavated which contain a number of disparate buildings whose functions can be postulated. Second, some surviving storeyed ranges have enough detail remaining for interpretation as a hall to be unlikely. Among the excavated examples the most convincing is probably the manor house of Penhallam at Jacobstow, Cornwall, where a late 12th-century two-storeyed stone range appears to have been a chamber block associated with a detached ground-floor hall of which all trace has gone.[28] The old hall was replaced in the 13th century by a stone hall built a little distance away but attached to the storeyed range by a subsidiary structure. The chamber block was raised over a timber-joisted undercroft and heated by a wall fireplace which lay off-centre, perhaps indicating division into two rooms. This is the kind of range which, in surviving buildings such as Boothby Pagnell Manor, Lincolnshire, has often been interpreted as a first-floor hall with integral solar.

Unfortunately, no other excavated example is as complete as Penhallam. At Wharram Percy, North Yorkshire, a stone building of two storeys has been identified as a chamber block of the late 12th century, but in this instance the identity and location of the accompanying hall are in some doubt.[29] At Alsted, Surrey, a very small 13th-century, two-storey stone range was probably associated with a timber building whose remains were too fragmentary for satisfactory elucidation. In c 1300 the latter was replaced by a recognisable ground-floor hall and solar whose erection necessitated the destruction of all but one wall of the earlier stone range. Here the evidence strongly suggests that the first complex contained a free-standing timber hall and detached stone chamber block.[30]

Some surviving storeyed ranges have details which imply they were not the first-floor halls they were once assumed to be, but are more likely to have formed a detached component in a larger complex whose hall has gone. In Shropshire, the earliest surviving storeyed block at Stokesay Castle and the free-standing tower at Wattlesborough are likely to have have been accompanied originally by timber-framed halls. Another example is the manor house of Donington-le-Heath, Leicestershire, probably of the late 13th century. The present, large first-floor room, heated by a central wall fireplace of 16th-century date, and lit by windows in the gable walls, was formerly divided into two

rooms, each entered independently through doorways in one of the long walls whose fair faces were toward the exterior of the building.[31] The opposite long wall has two further doorways leading to smaller ranges behind. This circulation makes no sense as a complete house, but could be interpreted as two first-floor chambers each with its own entrance and its own set of inner and more private rooms.

An even more conclusive example is Little Wenham Hall, Suffolk, also built in the late 13th century. This has often been cited as a classic instance of a first-floor hall,[32] but there are two glaring inconsistencies. The first floor contains one large room and an extremely fine chapel which leads straight off it, an arrangement far more appropriate for a chamber than a hall; if it was a hall, the only possible chamber accommodation is a poky room on the floor above the chapel. In a house of such quality, the absence of suitable private accommodation is inconceivable at this date, and it is far more likely that the whole range formed the chamber block of a larger house. The external walls indicate that an attendant hall must have been detached, and the shape of the site suggests it lay on the same alignment as the surviving range, not at right angles, an arrangement which might have occurred at Squerryes Lodge, Westerham.

In Kent, Rigold convincingly argued some years ago that the stone range at Temple Manor, Strood, built between 1228 and 1245, should not be interpreted as a first-floor hall as had previously been assumed. It is known that in 1308 the Strood property contained a hall, chapel and *camera* as well as subsidiary buildings. Rigold believed that the surviving stone range, with vaulted undercroft and two chambers above, was the *camera* used by the Knights Templar both as a residential unit and probably for transacting business. Archaeological evidence indicates that the hall mentioned in 1308 must have been detached from the stone range, and since its site was not located during excavation, it probably lies outside the boundaries of the property currently in the guardianship of English Heritage.[33]

Temple Manor was not a normal domestic dwelling, but its layout, with stone *camera* or chamber block completely detached from a ground-floor hall, is not dissimilar to the other buildings discussed here. In each case there is plenty of room on the site for further buildings. But proof that what survives are chamber blocks will only be forthcoming when more examples have been excavated and the sites of the presumed hall ranges identified. Until such time all theories remain at the level of speculation.

# Nettlestead Place and Luddesdown Court

It is against this tentative background that the remains at Nettlestead Place and Luddesdown Court must be considered. The first point to be made is that the main rooms in each are extremely large for private chambers. The internal ground-floor area of Nettlestead Place is 102 sq m, and at Luddesdown Court the largest chamber on the first floor is 95 sq m, with the additional rooms making the overall area even larger. Little can be deduced at Nettlestead Place, since the remains are limited to the vaulted and undivided undercroft (Figure 6a). This, however, indicates that the range stood free on both long sides and at its west end. The first-floor walling has largely disappeared except on the south side where two projections have been interpreted as latrines (Figure 6b).[34] The total destruction of the other three walls at first-floor level means that there is no evidence of doorways, fireplaces or subdivisions, and their whereabouts can be no more than speculative. By the 15th century the upper floor is likely to have been subdivided and entered via an external staircase at one angle, which served both the main range and the smaller adjoining range, which was possibly later. If the projections are original and really are latrines, then the range may have been divided from the start, but the western one, which is centrally placed, conceivably could have contained an extremely large chimney stack. In fact, the presence of latrines, the absence of internal stairs and the undivided nature of the undercroft suggest that this was not a first-floor hall but an unusually large chamber block.[35]

At Luddesdown Court far more survives. Three first-floor rooms in three ranges lie above massively joisted lower rooms providing 158 sq m of accommodation (Figure 7). As far as can be seen, the lower rooms were not subdivided at first. On the first floor, the main chamber is heated by a central wall fireplace which may have been added or rebuilt in the early 14th century. The room was probably always entered by an external doorway at the east end of the range, and there is no evidence for secondary stairs between the floors. At the west end a doorway leads to another smaller chamber at right angles which was also heated, by a corner fireplace. Beyond this is a narrower range with what appears to have been a latrine block at the end. Surviving doorways between the ranges suggest that the whole structure is of one build. Both the larger chambers had scissor-braced roofs and were decorated with medieval, possibly 13th-century, wall paintings.

Two facts in particular might be used to support the theory that Luddesdown Court was a first-floor hall. Although very little original fenestration remains, it is clear that there were windows on all three of the free-standing walls, and therefore that a ground-floor hall would have had to be detached. Since so much accommodation survives, it may seem like special pleading to suggest that at one time there was yet more. Second, the main range at Luddesdown

Court, at 95 sq m, is larger than any of the currently accepted chamber blocks on secular sites (apart from Nettlestead Place), although larger chambers survive in some ecclesiastical complexes, for instance the abbot's house at Battle Abbey, East Sussex, or the Old Deanery, Salisbury, Wiltshire.[36]

On the other hand, several arguments can be advanced against the interpretation of the main room as a first-floor hall: it is smaller than Nettlestead Place and not significantly larger than the contemporary *camera* at Temple Manor, Strood (86 sq m); a lack of subdivision in the main undercroft and of any evidence for internal communication between the floors puts this out of line with the arrangements which Rigold postulated for first-floor halls;[37] and finally there is the matter of what accommodation would have been appropriate to the status of the owner.

Surviving houses of the 12th and 13th centuries have seldom been studied with the status of their owners or builders firmly in mind.[38] Recently it has been remarked that first-floor halls did not extend far down the social scale, but how far down has never been established.[39] It is a truism that all surviving stone dwellings of this date were built for people of high status, but the social differences between such people, and whether their needs and expectations in terms of accommodation varied, have not been explored. The hypothesis that first-floor halls were confined to aristocratic levels may be countered with an alternative theory: that the higher the social status, the more likely the patron was to require grand chamber accommodation in addition to the hall. It was also more likely that the house reflected, in reduced form, the arrangement of royal palaces in which, as the 13th century progressed, every important member of the family or the retinue came to have a suite of rooms comprising at the very least a chamber and a wardrobe, and often more. The emphasis given to the position of the hall has tended to push consideration of the amount and quality of the chamber accommodation aside.

## Status of builders of early houses

In Kent, Luddesdown Court, Nettlestead Place and Squerryes Lodge were all built for families of baronial status, or closely connected to such families. During most of

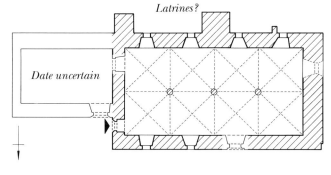

*Figure 6 Nettlestead Place, Nettlestead: a) View of undercroft from the east (BB91/2689); b) Plan of undercroft.*

*a*

*b*

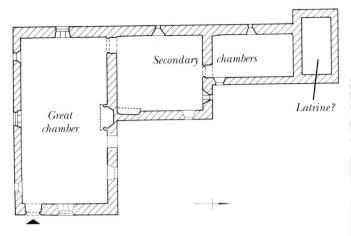

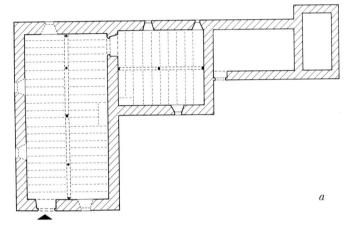

*a*

*b*

*Figure 7 Luddesdown Court, Luddesdown: a) Plans of first floor (above) and ground floor (below); b) View from south west. Almost all the window openings and much of the flintwork have been renewed (BB90/8720).*

the 13th century, the manor of Luddesdown was held by the Mountchesneys who held half of the Honour of Talbot in Swanscombe which owed thirty knights for the service of Rochester Castle. The family held several manors in Kent, as well as land in other counties. Warine de Mountchesney, the most likely builder of the surviving house, paid 2,000 marks for his inheritance in 1213. He married Joan, daughter of William the Marshall, Earl of Pembroke; and his daughter, also Joan, married William of Valence, half brother of Henry III.[40] When he died in 1255 he left an estate estimated at 200,000 marks, and Matthew Paris lamented the passing of one of the noblest, wisest and richest men in the kingdom.[41] Thus Warine was no normal lord of the manor, but a member of the nobility in the close circle of the King.

Luddesdown Court lies on one of the family's smaller Kentish manors, tucked into the chalk hills, and why they should have built a large and well-decorated house there is unclear. The quality of the detailing suggests it was actually used as a family residence, and it is possible that it was used as a hunting lodge. Hunting was a favoured activity among several baronial families in Kent, the most eminent example being the Clares at Tonbridge who established two large parks, the North and South Frith, just to the east of Tonbridge.[42] The building evidence in no way contradicts such a suggestion, for one of the closest documentary

parallels to Luddesdown Court is the hunting lodge at Woolmer, Hampshire, built for Edward I in 1284–5, where a stone chamber block, incorporating two fireplaces, two wardrobes and a chapel, was combined with a timber-framed hall, kitchen and other buildings – exactly the arrangement suggested for Luddesdown Court.[43]

Nettlestead Place was built for the family of de Wahull of Odell. Their main estates lay outside the county in Bedfordshire and elsewhere, but they held one and a half knight's fees of the Clares at Nettlestead and Pembury.[44] By 1291 the property seems to have passed to the Pimpes,[45] who were a knightly family of county stature through the 14th and 15th centuries. Again, why the de Wahulls, who hardly seem to figure in Kent apart from holding this property, should have erected a house of such obvious magnificence so far from the centre of their barony is intriguing.

The third mid 13th-century house studied in connection with this project, Squerryes Lodge, Westerham, was part of the manor of Westerham held by the de Camvill family as tenants-in-chief.[46] The de Camvills were an important baronial family in Lincolnshire in the late 12th and early 13th centuries, but virtually nothing is known of their position in Kent except that they were probably related by marriage to the de Crevequeurs of Leeds Castle.[47]

Thus the three earliest surviving houses were all built by families whose baronial connections lay mainly outside the county. Although their names are known, their role in Kentish society, and their reasons for building substantial houses where they did, remain obscure. Whether the pursuit of pleasure in the form of hunting provides a compelling enough reason for the presence of these houses remains open to question. If not, then historians must find alternative answers. By the end of the 13th century all three families had disappeared from the Kentish scene.

# 3 Ground-floor halls: late 13th and early 14th centuries

Excavation has revealed the long history of the ground-floor hall as the centrepiece of medieval dwellings, and throughout England examples of aisled halls survive at a high social level from the 12th century, such as the Bishop's Palace, Hereford, Farnham Castle, Surrey, and Oakham Castle, Leicestershire. But Kent is not well endowed in this respect, and the earliest surviving hall in the county is probably the partially preserved aisled hall of the Archbishop's Palace in Canterbury, which dates from the early 13th century.[1] The earliest ground-floor hall in the countryside to survive until recently seems to have been the unaisled hall, possibly of mid 13th-century date, at Court

Lodge, Godmersham, a manor of Christ Church Priory.[2] Both of these were built of stone.

In the course of this project some two dozen ground-floor halls dating from the mid 14th century or earlier were recorded.[3] Half were built of stone, the other half of timber. Although the earliest ground-floor halls about which we have information may have been of stone, stone houses in general are not necessarily earlier than timber ones. In fact, several of the timber buildings have 'archaic' structural features which suggest that they were erected before c 1300, whereas the majority of surviving stone examples are likely to date from the first half of the 14th century.

*Figure 9 Ratling Court, Aylesham. Partial reconstruction of aisled hall and open end bay. Later cross wing shown in outline. The shaded areas indicate timbers which survive and are visible.*

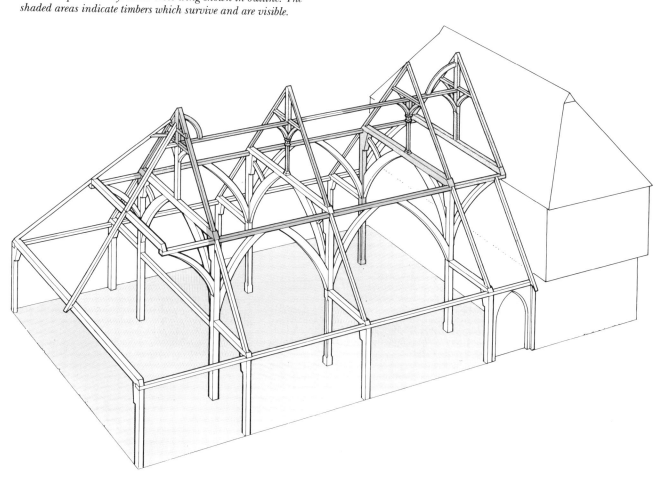

# Timber-framed halls

Dating the earliest timber buildings is difficult. As explained in Appendix 1, none of those with archaic framing which were sampled for tree-ring dating proved amenable to the treatment, and dating has had to be done by more conventional means. Only one example is well documented: Eastry Court, Eastry, was a manor of Christ Church Priory, and the serjeant's rolls for 1293–5 record the purchase of timber and stone, the demolition of an old thatched hall, and the payment to carpenters for raising the new hall and chamber. This late 13th-century hall was altered in the 14th century, when first the timbers had to be strengthened, and later the external walls were rebuilt in stone. Subsequent alterations culminated in the destruction of all but one truss (Figure 8).[4] Despite this, enough remains to provide some idea of the original aisled form, the style and structure of which place it among the earliest to survive in the county. It follows from this that the study of upstanding timber framing in Kent is likely to begin only in the last decade or two of the 13th century.

Aisled halls of somewhat similar construction to Eastry Court have been recorded at Eastling Manor, Eastling, Chilton Manor, Sittingbourne, and Bardingley Farmhouse, Sutton Valence, while rather more sophisticated examples survive at Newbury Farmhouse, Tonge, and probably at Ratling Court, Aylesham (Figure 9). In other early timber buildings the open truss was of unaisled form, as at Barnes Place, Hadlow (Figure 47), Little Moat Cottage, East Peckham (Figure 48), and Court Lodge, Fawkham (Figure 46), and occasionally the whole structure was built without aisles, as at Hurst Farm, Chilham (Figure 10). It is likely that most of the unaisled buildings were a little later in date than the aisled ones.

The earliest evidence of timber-framed halls from excavated house sites comes from very much the same period and produces the same range of evidence. Only two rural houses in Kent, Moat Farm, Leigh, and Pivington, Pluckley, have been fully revealed by excavation. To these one may add the house at Joydens Wood near Bexley, now in Greater London.[5] All three are dated by associated

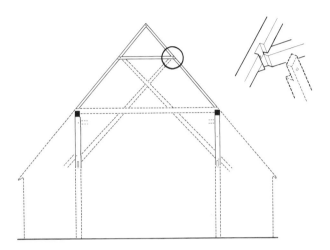

*Figure 8 Eastry Court, Eastry. Reconstruction of partially surviving truss at north end of open hall, and detail of the junction of scissor and passing brace, collar and rafter, shown from the other side.*

*Figure 10 Hurst Farm, Chilham. Partial reconstruction of open hall. The shaded areas indicate timbers which survive.*

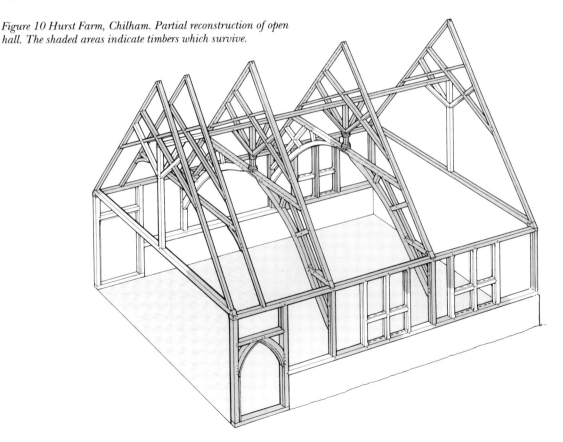

pottery to the late 13th or early 14th century. All were basically of aisled form, although they may not have had open trusses with free-standing arcade posts. The Joydens Wood house was probably of base-cruck construction, but the others may only have had single-bay halls without open trusses. This is reflected in their size: the hall at Joydens Wood, depending upon the interpretation, measures 72 sq m which is about the same size as the contemporary surviving houses, but that at Leigh (52 sq m) is smaller, and Pivington (31 sq m) is far smaller than any hall which survives until well into the 14th century.

## Stone halls

The majority of stone halls in secular and ecclesiastical manor houses date from the first half of the 14th century. On the estates of Christ Church Priory, building activity between 1285 and 1322 is documented in the so-called *Memorandum Book* of Prior Eastry, and this indicates that the priory was actively engaged in modernising and extending the buildings on its manors at this time.[6] Not all building work undertaken by the priory during this period was recorded in the *Memorandum Book*, and this includes the work at Eastry Court, known only from the serjeant's rolls;[7] but at Chartham in 1303 and Great Chart in 1313, the

*Figure 11 Mersham Manor, Mersham. View from south east, showing open hall with service end to the left (BB92/7740).*

construction of new stone halls is documented, and the buildings still survive. No mention in the *Memorandum Book* may indicate that the very similar halls remaining at Mersham Manor, Mersham (Figure 11), and Copton Manor, Sheldwich (Figure 18), were not built until after 1322, and stylistic details make dates between *c* 1320 and *c* 1340 most likely. At much the same time, St Augustine's Abbey was also improving building on its property, with new work taking place on the granges at Minster and Salmestone in Thanet. Possibly this outburst of building activity arose in part from the imposition of the Statute of Mortmain in 1279, which limited the acquisition of new property by religious institutions. Instead, they may have been encouraged to spend money improving what they had, including the erection of new and substantial buildings on their estates.[8]

The dates of the majority of surviving secular stone houses are not substantially different. The only remaining stone-built aisled hall is at Nurstead Court, Meopham, dated by tree-ring analysis to *c* 1309* (Figure 12), although another may have existed at Gallants Manor, East Farleigh, where the cross wing has produced a tree-ring date of *c* 1322*. Hoad Farm, Acrise, has similarities to Mersham Manor and Copton Manor, and Battel Hall, Leeds, is comparable to Ightham Mote which is known to have been erected in the 1330s or early 1340s*. Penshurst Place was built in the 1340s, and somewhat similar dates, towards the mid 14th century, are likely for two stone rectories, at Cliffe-at-Hoo (The Rectory House) and Southfleet (Old Rectory or Southfleet Rectory, now known as Friary Court and Old Friary).

*Figure 12 Nurstead Court, Meopham. View of demolished end, with hall and services, from the north east. (Reproduced courtesy of the British Architectural Library, RIBA, London).*

## Differences between stone and timber halls

The nature of the relationship at this time between timber and stone, and between aisled and unaisled buildings, is by no means easy to define. In the first place, judging from the buildings investigated in this project, there is a marked difference in the distribution of stone and timber framing (Figures 15 and 16). Stone buildings occur in a broad band across the county. They are situated either on the Downs, where chalk blocks and flint served as building materials, in Thanet where there was an outcrop of chalk, or on the Chart Hills where ragstone was available. When it mattered, stone for building could be carried considerable distances in the Middle Ages: it clearly was for churches, and wealthy people might move it for domestic buildings as well, particularly if water transport was available. In 1330/1 Christ Church Priory shipped Folkestone stone for Eastry manor house from

Folkestone to Sandwich, whence it was transported over land, and in 1322/3 a new chamber at Mersham was built with materials brought several miles over land from Great Chart.[9] But this is unlikely to have been a very common occurrence, and stone was probably not normally shifted over long distances. Elsewhere houses were built of timber. Although much of Kent was wooded, suitable trees were less common in parts of the north and east, so timber also was moved by water, particularly from the dens of the western Weald, via the port of Smallhythe near Tenterden.[10]

Leaving aside the regional aspect of materials, it appears that stone always had a certain social cachet. By the 14th century the grandest houses, such as Penshurst Place and almost all those built by clergy or religious institutions, were wholly or largely of stone. In the 13th century the issue is complicated by the question of first-floor halls: if the two-storeyed ranges of the 13th century were first-floor halls, then halls of high status were built of stone from an early date. But if they were chamber blocks, then it is likely that the accompanying halls were of timber, and that stone was used only for the more prestigious parts of the dwelling. Whichever way those houses are interpreted, it seems likely that timber was the normal material for rural halls until around 1300 when a number of patrons, by reason of rank or wealth, changed to building halls of stone.

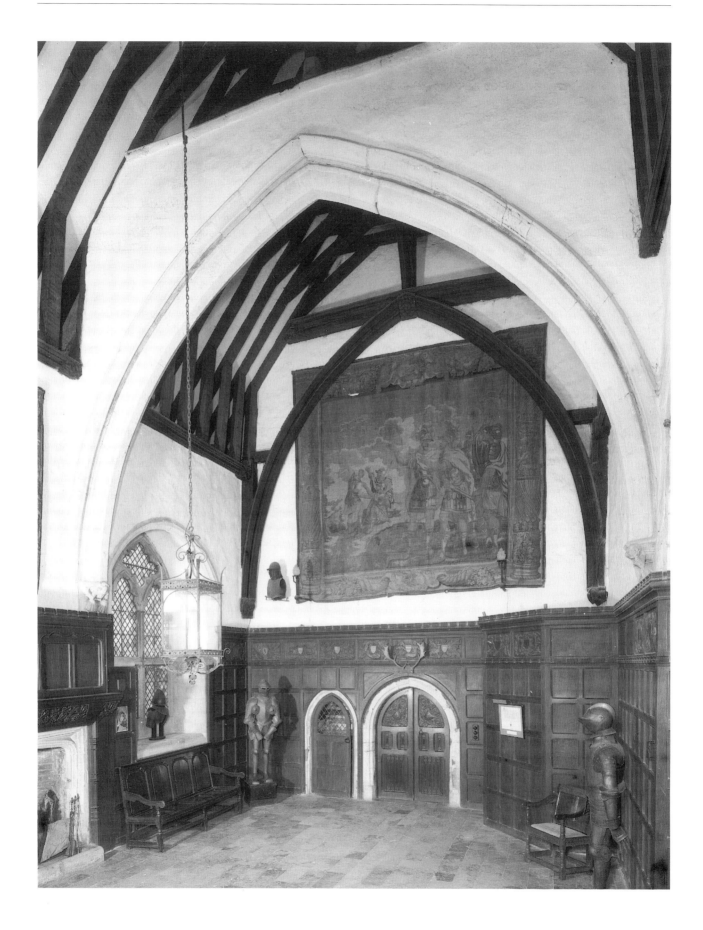

This did not mean that stone halls were larger than timber ones. On the contrary, below the level of Penshurst Place and the Archbishop's palaces, six of the seven largest halls in Kent dating from this period were built of timber.[11] This suggests that quality and size were not synonymous. Aisles, which were the normal means of spanning great widths, were avoided in stone halls, so that only at Nurstead Court was stone used for a large aisled hall of exceptional quality (Figure 12). Elsewhere, and particularly in houses of ecclesiastical origin, quality or status was sufficiently indicated by the use of stone; and fine details, such as traceried windows, seem to have been of greater importance than size alone.[12] This is not, however, to suggest that early stone houses were small. Not only do they frequently include extensive chamber accommodation, but their halls were all over 46 sq m in area.[13]

All this suggests that stone and timber may have been used at this time by clients of different status with different priorities. The earliest surviving timber aisled halls are almost certainly earlier in date than most of the stone halls, and it is likely that they represent the tail end of a long tradition which, at the highest level, was in the process of being superseded. There is a distinct possibility that houses such as Luddesdown Court and Squerryes Lodge once possessed ground-floor halls which were probably aisled; and, because these no longer exist, it can be inferred that they were built of timber. Without positive evidence from excavation, such a statement may appear contentious. Yet it is otherwise difficult to account for what occurred. For by the early 14th century, aisling was going out for all houses of quality. Even among those built of timber which were large and fine enough to survive, new ways had been found for getting rid of the main defect of aisled structures – that is, the free-standing posts in the middle of the open hall. And by about 1300 people who could afford to do so abandoned the timber tradition altogether and went in for new unaisled halls of stone.

# The form and layout of the hall

Whatever its size and material, the area of the open hall was divided into a number of bays. In aisled buildings, the divisions are structurally and visually obtrusive, and in most unaisled timber buildings they are still prominent since the main roof trusses tend to be carried on tie beams and posts with large arch braces linking the two. In two stone buildings, Ightham Mote and Battel Hall, the division is formed by a stone arch (Figure 13), a feature otherwise known only in the hall at Mayfield in Sussex. But in many stone buildings the bays were notional, with roof trusses of uniform scantling. Such was the arrangement in the halls of most of the Christ Church Priory manor houses, and at Hoad Farm, Acrise; and something like the same effect was achieved at Penshurst Place where the crown posts and tie beams of the roof are so far above the ground that they are relatively inconspicuous to people below.

Most halls were of two bays, but larger halls had three. Sometimes there were three more or less equal bays, as at The Deanery, Chartham, and Hurst Farm, Chilham (Figure 10), but occasionally the bay at the lower or entrance end was much narrower and probably partially closed by a spere truss as at Bardingley Farmhouse, Sutton Valence, Court Lodge, Fawkham, Ratling Court, Aylesham (Figure 9), and Southfleet Rectory (Figure 14). The same arrangement was also implied by the excavations at Pivington, Pluckley. In other early buildings it is possible that low speres or screens unconnected with the roof construction performed the same function of dividing the entrance passage from the hall proper. Evidence of these remains at Hamden, Smarden, and low speres have been postulated in the excavated hall at Joydens Wood.

In some cases the screens passage may have been entered via a porch. Penshurst Place has a fine two-storey stone porch of the 1340s, and the roof structure of Ightham Mote indicates an abutment above the entrance which can

*Figure 13 (opposite) Ightham Mote, Ightham. View of open hall looking towards service end, showing stone arch of central open truss (BB86/7698).*

*Figure 14 Southfleet Rectory, now Friary Court and Old Friary, Southfleet. Long section through hall and cross section through upper-end wing, from the west.*

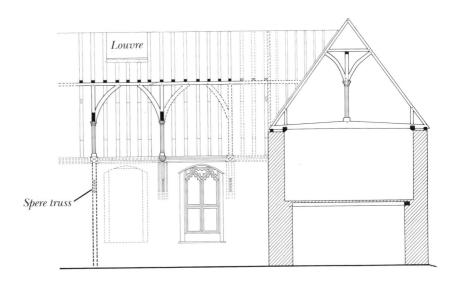

29

only have been a storeyed porch, presumably of timber since no external trace remains. Storeyed porches must have been rare, but lower ones may have been common; many excavated buildings have evidence for projections in front of the entrance, as at Joydens Wood and at Alsted in Surrey and Bodiam in Sussex.[14] One actually survives at Hamden, Smarden, and mortices suggest that an earlier porch preceded the present brick one at The Plestor, Borden, although it is unlikely that the doorway which carries the evidence is contemporary with the earliest aisled hall for which fragmentary evidence survives. At Hurst Farm, Chilham, the original doorway remains beneath a later porch, and its fine state of preservation suggests that it was protected from the start. Thus porches may have been standard features of houses, but their almost total destruction implies they were not normally very substantial.

Surviving buildings provide few clues as to the arrangement at the dais end of the hall. Evidence for fixed benches and, exceptionally, for canopies above the end wall, is clear only in later houses; nevertheless, the presence of an extra tie beam not far from the upper-end wall at

*Figure 15 The distribution of stone houses of the 13th and early 14th centuries investigated by the RCHME project.*

Court Lodge, Great Chart, and of a complete crown-post truss in the same position at Southfleet Rectory (Figure 14), might have been connected with some construction to distinguish this end of the hall.

Within the hall, the open hearth normally lay towards the dais end. At Penshurst Place it remains just to that side of the main truss, and a similar hearth position has been revealed in all the excavated halls. Louvres for the escape of smoke from the open hearth rarely survive. Where there is evidence for their former presence, as at Southfleet Rectory, The Deanery, Chartham, and Hamden, Smarden, they lie towards the entrance end of the hall, presumably to allow smoke to drift up and away from the dais end. Unfortunately, all structural evidence for louvres has often been destroyed by the insertion of a chimney stack in the same position. This may be what occurred at Copton Manor and Ratling Court. But whether all halls had them is not certain. In some cases no chimney stack was inserted and no evidence for a structural louvre can be seen. At Ightham Mote traces were apparently discovered in the 1860s, although the evidence has now gone.[15] Nothing, however, remains to suggest a louvre in the surviving lower bay of the roof at Mersham Manor, and this is often the case in later buildings, even large ones such as Godinton Park, Great Chart, built in the late 14th century.

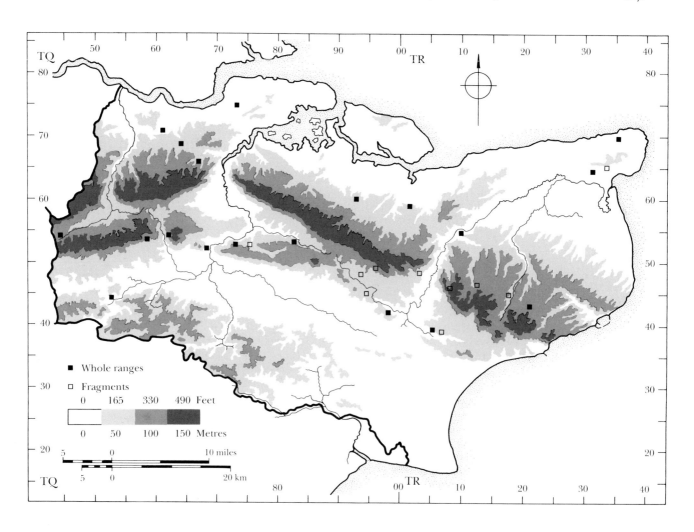

The upper end of the hall was lit by full-height windows, sometimes one to each side, sometimes two, and several examples remain in stone houses. Most of them had simple traceried heads to the lights, and halls with low side walls may have had gabled windows, as survived until recently at Court Lodge, Godmersham, and still exist at Nurstead Court (Figure 12). The precedent was probably set by the 13th-century hall at the Archbishop's Palace, Canterbury.[16] In timber buildings, and particularly aisled ones, the hall windows have almost always been destroyed, so the evidence for windows remaining at Hurst Farm, Chilham (Figure 10), is a rare survival from this early period.

## Builders of stone houses

Substantiating the claim that the choice of stone or timber had a social significance is not easy, for information about the builders of surviving late 13th and early 14th-century secular houses is patchy. Some of the more complete stone houses are reasonably well documented. Nurstead Court was the centre of the manor of Nurstead which owed service for the defence of Dover Castle as part of the barony of Horton Kirby. It was held by the knightly de Gravesend family who produced three bishops in the late 13th and early 14th centuries. The house, which was built in c 1309*, is likely to have been erected for one of the secular members of the family, Sir Stephen de Gravesend, who had accompanied Edward I to Scotland and was a knight of the shire in 1311.[17]

Southfleet Rectory was probably built for Thomas of Alkham, rector from 1323 to 1356 and chancellor of the diocese of Rochester.[18] The Rectory House, Cliffe-at-Hoo, was another valuable benefice and was a peculiar of the archbishopric of Canterbury; during the first half of the 14th century the living was held by a succession of rectors who were all men of considerable distinction holding high church offices both within Kent and elsewhere.[19] Finally, Sir John de Pulteney, wealthy merchant, financier, lord mayor of London and landowner in many parts of the country, had Penshurst Place built after receiving licence to crenellate in 1341.[20]

However, in other cases, evidence of who was in possession of secular properties when the new stone houses were built is less easy to discover. There appear to be no means of tracing who held Hoad Farm, Acrise, or Battel Hall, Leeds, in the early 14th century. The same is even true of Ightham Mote, Ightham, for its association with Sir Thomas Cawne, who has always been considered the builder, is only documented from about thirty years after the 14th-century house was erected, and his family circumstances at his death in c 1372 suggest that he is unlikely to have been old enough to have been building Ightham Mote as early as the 1330s.[21] Likewise the ownership of Old Soar, Plaxtol, is unknown in the late 13th century when the surviving chamber and chapel ranges were built. Later, the property was held by the Culpeper family, but there is no record of their tenure there before the early 15th century.[22] Even when, as at Gallants Manor, East Farleigh, the family ownership is known, the precise circumstances often remain vague. The land upon which Gallants Manor was built was acquired by the Culpepers of Preston Hall, Aylesford, in 1319.[23] It is unclear, however, which of the

Culpepers built the house in c 1322*, or what their relationship was to the rest of the family.[24]

Figure 15 illustrates the distribution of stone houses, of the mid 14th century or earlier, investigated in the course of this project. It distinguishes between the twenty or so buildings of which at least one complete range survives, and those houses where the former existence of an early stone structure is indicated by fragments ranging from short stretches of wall to vaulted undercrofts beneath later and unrelated timber structures.[25] Half a dozen of the twenty or so buildings with substantial accommodation surviving were built by Christ Church Priory or St Augustine's Abbey, and are situated in the eastern half of the county where much of the land belonging to the major ecclesiastical institutions lay. Indeed, with the exception of Hoad Farm, Acrise, there appear to be no unfortified rural stone dwellings of secular origin in east Kent of which considerable parts of the fabric remain. On the other hand, in mid and west Kent some eleven secular stone houses remain upstanding. Two of them, Newbury Farmhouse, Tonge, and Battel Hall, Leeds, lie in the middle of the county. The rest are situated west of the Medway, and these include the earliest houses of all. This is in marked contrast to the distribution of the fragments from demolished stone houses, most of which have been found in the eastern half of the county.[26]

The reason for the pronounced westerly weighting of surviving early secular dwellings is not easy to understand. As discussed in Chapter 1, despite the large amount of Church land in east Kent, the north and east of the county also contained many secular manors. In addition, this region had the highest assessment of lay wealth in the early 14th century. Out of fifty-eight families who supplied sheriffs and knights of the shire between 1272 and 1340, thirty had their main seats east of a line drawn north–south through the centre of the county from Sittingbourne to Tenterden, while only nineteen lay west of that line.[27] This underlines the predominance of the gentry in east Kent during this period. In the circumstances, it might not be unreasonable to suppose that most of the early surviving houses, which are likely to have belonged to those of knightly or gentry class, would have been situated in this region. But, as indicated above, the majority of buildings with considerable 13th or 14th-century work still remaining are situated in west Kent.

Two possible explanations for this apparent contradiction come to mind, although at present neither of them can be said to provide the complete answer. The first is that the distribution of county office holders is a red herring rather than a clue, and the rank of families associated with the surviving houses in west Kent was socially superior, or at any rate different, to those whose lands and houses lay to the east. If so, their houses ought to have been grander than those of their eastern fellows and perhaps had a better chance of survival. One or two pieces of evidence seem to point in this direction. The only surviving houses discussed here whose owners are known to lay claim to baronial connections are the three earliest: Luddesdown Court, Nettlestead Place and Squerryes Lodge. Moreover, two of the grandest 14th-century houses were built by families who likewise had extensive contacts beyond the confines of the county. Sir Stephen de Gravesend, who may have built Nurstead Court, was a knight of the shire in 1311, and his family was somewhat unusual in supplying two bishops of

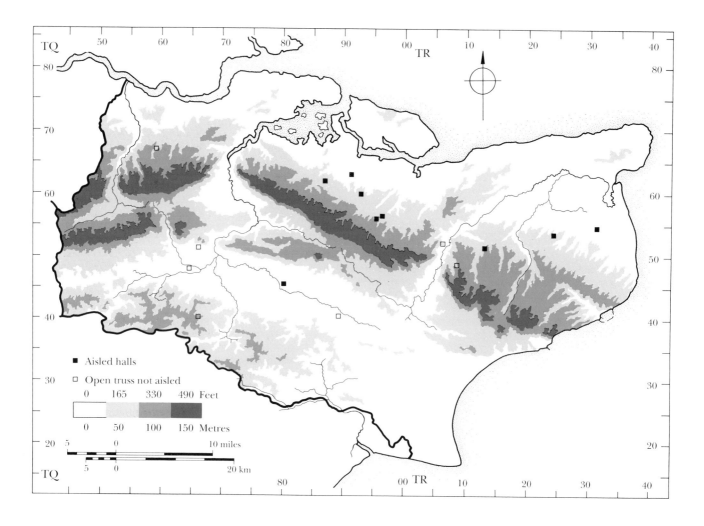

*Figure 16 The distribution of timber houses of the 13th and early 14th centuries investigated by the RCHME project.*

London and one of Lincoln in the late 13th and early 14th centuries. Meanwhile, Sir John de Pulteney of Penshurst Place, who held no county office but enjoyed royal patronage, had lands throughout the country, and was given the highest individual assessment in Kent in the lay subsidy of 1334. The orbit of these men was national rather than county based, and as discussed in Chapter 2, some of these families may have come to Kent primarily for purposes of recreation.[28] The fact that their families do not always figure among the lists of county office holders may imply greater rather than lesser status. The surviving structures at Old Soar, Ightham Mote and Battel Hall suggest that their builders must have been people of substance, and it is difficult to believe that their associations with these properties would have gone unrecorded if they had belonged to the upper strata of the county gentry. It is therefore worth raising the question whether they too belonged to wealthy families with few local affiliations, for this might account for the puzzling lack of information pertaining to them.

The second explanation for the difference in survival between east and west has nothing to do with the original owners of the buildings, but centres on the probability that later events led to more rebuilding in the east. This theory

is difficult to verify without detailed work on the later buildings, but perusal of the statutory lists and the *Buildings of England* is promising.[29] There were fifty-eight families identified as supplying sheriffs or knights of the shire between 1272 and 1340, and there are still identifiable buildings of some kind at the main seats of twenty of them. Two, or 33 per cent of the total in the western half of the county, are post-medieval in date; eleven, or 79 per cent in the east, were largely rebuilt after the 16th century.[30] The superficial nature of the research and the small number of houses involved in this sample hardly constitute proof, but 15th-century and later evidence conclusively demonstrates the continuing profusion of gentry in east Kent and the high status of some among them.[31] It seems likely therefore that the marked absence of medieval gentry houses in east Kent was due as much to later rebuilding as to any real difference in the pattern of building at the time. If the fragmentary remains of the stone undercrofts at Boughton Court, Boughton Aluph, and Dean Farm, Elmsted, are anything to go by, some impressive secular houses were built in east Kent in the period leading up to the Black Death.

# Builders of timber-framed houses

The distribution of the early timber-framed open halls investigated in this project is somewhat different to that of the stone houses. As Figure 16 indicates, they are to be found mostly on the northern slopes of the Downs or in the low Weald, with a few outliers in the Stour valley and the high Weald. The buildings fall into two categories. In the first are fully aisled halls, almost all of which lie north of the scarp of the Downs and have some elements of 'archaic' framing; in the second, with a more southerly distribution, are quasi-aisled or unaisled halls, some of which have base crucks and few 'archaic' features. Typologically the aisled halls are the earlier, although chronologically it is likely that there was at least some overlap between the two groups.

Apart from the Christ Church Priory manor house at Eastry, all the surviving timber-framed buildings are likely to have had secular origins. But even greater obscurity surrounds their builders than those who erected stone dwellings in this period. According to Hasted, four of the most 'archaic' structures – Newbury Farmhouse, Chilton Manor, Hurst Farm and Ratling Court – were accounted manors and held by eponymous families at the turn of the 14th century.[32] Despite this, the Chiltons and the Newburghs are elusive characters who cannot be firmly identified in 13th or early 14th-century records, and the history of both properties only begins to clarify in the later 14th century when these families were extinct. There is somewhat more detail about the other two. Hurst was held as a knight's fee of the Honour of Chilham, one of the baronies owing castleguard service at Dover Castle. In 1346 the heirs of John de Herst held the fee in Herst, Syberston and Felborough, indicating that land was held beyond the immediate vicinity of Hurst. By the mid 14th century Hurst was coupled with Murston, and the Herst family had disappeared.[33] Ratling Court, Aylesham, was originally held as a knight's fee of the Archbishop by tenants called 'of Ratling', their tenure being traceable back at least to the late 11th century. In 1171 Ratling Court was assessed at only £5 per annum so it cannot have been a very extensive holding. The Ratlings can be followed through the 13th and early 14th centuries, but before the end of the 14th century the property had become part of a larger estate held by a better-known family.[34]

The small size of many of the knights' fees on the Archbishop's estates has been noted,[35] and the evidence of Hurst Farm and Ratling Court suggests that some of the earlier medieval timber houses may have been associated with such relatively small estates, held by shadowy families at the very bottom of the knightly class. These houses mostly lie in the north and north east of the county, in the region where the old manorial centres were situated, and where many small feudal estates lay side by side with the larger properties of the men who held county office. It was also the area where the highest assessments of lay wealth in the subsidy of 1334 were to be found. The combination of all these elements helps to explain why the earliest timber-framed buildings are largely confined to the northern part of the county.

Houses in the more southerly group plotted on Figure 16 belong in a slightly different category and are largely situated in the western low Weald. Only Bardingley Farmhouse, Sutton Valence, has an 'archaic' aisled hall of the kind found in north Kent. The rest are 'quasi aisled'. Three of them certainly have base crucks, and there may have been another. To this group can be added three more very small base-cruck structures in the Weald, two in Yalding and one in Speldhurst, which may date from the first half of the 14th century, but which have not been plotted on Figure 16 because their lack of archaic features and small size make it more likely that they were built somewhat later in the century.[36] Most of these buildings have modern names, but three have been traced: Old Cryals, Brenchley (not a base cruck), Barnes Place, Hadlow, and Hamden, Smarden.

According to Hasted, Old Cryals was held in the mid 13th century as half a knight's fee by the eminent de Criol family of Ostenhanger from Alicia de Waltham. She in turn held of the Clares, earls of Gloucester, who themselves held the Lowy of Tonbridge from the Archbishop. However, in the early 14th century, possibly before the present house was built, the de Criol estates passed via an heiress to Sir Richard Rokesle, and subsequently, together with Ostenhanger itself, they went with another heiress to the wealthy Poynings family.[37] All the families involved were of high status and the evidence of the other houses discussed suggests that Old Cryals was not the sort of dwelling such families would normally have built for their own occupation. This raises the question of whether the property was used by them, administered by an agent, or sub-tenanted, questions to which there is at present no satisfactory answer.

Barnes Place was also held of the Clares of Tonbridge. It seems to have been one of a number of small manors and estates which the Clares are known to have created along the Medway and its tributaries in the 13th century. Barnes Place itself was an estate which was probably held by substantial peasant freeholders. When the family emerge into the record in the late 15th century, they are on the verge of becoming gentry, augmenting their holdings by purchase, and mixing with local gentry and London trade.[38] The third house, Hamden, Smarden, is only traceable because in 1362 John Hamden left a perpetual endowment of 6s per annum to the bell-ropes of Smarden parish church 'out of his land called Hamdens'.[39] What kind of a man he was, or what kind of tenure he held by, is not known. It is possible that he held by gavelkind, but since it is not clear which manor his lands formed part of, it would be unwise to speculate. Nevertheless, in some sense it is likely that he belongs in the same category as the Barnes family. In other words, although such people may have been as well off financially as their counterparts who built the aisled halls of the northern plain, the chances are that they were not holders of military tenures stretching back for several generations. Instead, they may have belonged to a newly developing class, hovering between the gentry and the peasantry, the forerunners of the later class of prosperous yeomen. Their timber buildings, of a different form to the northern aisled halls, are perhaps the first of the wealthy peasant or yeoman dwellings which emerge into the record in some numbers shortly after the Black Death.[40]

# 4 Subsidiary accommodation: late 13th and early 14th centuries

The hall range may have been the most important room of the medieval dwelling, but it never stood alone. All the houses considered so far had some subsidiary accommodation, although its full extent and precise form frequently cannot be determined. This is particularly true of timber buildings whose ends are universally fragmentary and difficult to interpret. It therefore seems best to begin by considering the subsidiary accommodation of stone houses and those of mixed stone and timber construction.

It has been claimed that before the late 14th century, no distinction was made between the high and low ends of the hall.[1] However, the Kentish evidence suggests that this was not the case, and that by *c* 1300 the house plan was fully developed at both ends of the hall, with clearly distinguished upper-end and service accommodation. Of fourteen houses of stone, or a mixture of stone and timber, and dating from the period *c* 1280–*c* 1350, ten have upper ends remaining beyond the dais end of the hall, and only one has no evidence surviving because the hall and all that lay beyond it has gone.[2] Six houses still have lower or service ends, and three more have evidence for structures at the lower end which have been demolished.[3] Thus, wherever the evidence survives, it is clear that houses had subsidiary rooms at both ends, and both documents and surviving remains suggest that their functions were already specialised.

## Building and documentation on Christ Church Priory manors

### *Documentary evidence*

Documentary evidence for the type of subsidiary accommodation which might be expected in manor houses of *c* 1300 comes from the *Memorandum Book* of Prior Eastry.[4] Since this concerns the manors of Christ Church at a time when they were run by the Priory, and monastic manor houses might not have required the same accommodation as secular ones, the evidence should be treated with caution. However, the five surviving stone Christ Church Priory houses which have been studied appear to have had very similar accommodation to the seven known secular examples and the two rectories. There may have been differences of precise function, but this does not seem to have affected the overall form. Thus before discussing the evidence of the buildings themselves, it is appropriate to consider the Christ Church Priory documentation.

The *Memorandum Book* lists building work done on the Christ Church Priory estates between 1285 and 1322, although in fact no work is dated after 1318, and we know that not all work undertaken on the manors was recorded in this central account.[5] Over seventy entries relate to domestic building on twenty-two manors in Kent, and it is these which have been analysed. Most of what was done is preceded by the word *novus*, although occasionally repairs and extensions to existing accommodation are specified. There are several entries for the majority of manors over the thirty-three year period, and it is clear that some of them received extensive attention. This tended to occur in two or more campaigns spaced at intervals of several years. Nowhere does an entry for a single year suggest the building of a complete house, ie hall, private apartments, chapel, kitchen and services. Equally there are few entries for individual items. To illustrate this one may look at the work which took place at Chartham. A new gatehouse was built in 1292 (together with fencing, the cost was 67*s* 3*d*), a new chapel with a new stone garderobe was erected in 1302 (£38 10*s* 0*d*), a new hall with two stone chambers and fireplaces and other appurtenances in 1303 (£70 18*s* 9*d*), a new kitchen and dairy in 1304 (£60 17*s* 8*d*, including a barn) and finally a new garderobe in 1305 (£6 17*s* 9*d*). The cost indicates that most of the building at Chartham was substantial and probably of stone, as was indeed specified in two instances. Presumably no more building was done after these campaigns until Prior Chillenden spent considerable sums in renovation at the end of the century.[6]

Two campaigns costing more than £60 were exceptional, but one of this magnitude and another costing more than £40 occurred at Monkton and Great Chart, while a number of manors had one or more campaigns of around £30 as well as several less costly ones. At Copton and Mersham, extensive stone remains indicate major undertakings of the early 14th century but only minor work is recorded in the *Memorandum Book*, which may mean that the main building took place after 1322.

A closer look at the Kentish entries in the *Memorandum Book* raises some interesting and important points concerning terminology and room usage. Apart from the hall, the rooms named were chambers (eighteen examples), solars (sixteen), chapels (twenty-two), garderobes (fifteen), a variety of service rooms (five) and cellars (three).

## Solars and chambers

The first question concerns the use and meaning of the terms solar and chamber. These terms may have been roughly equivalent, analogous to the modern drawing room, lounge, sitting room or living room. Since the *Memorandum Book* was written by a single scribe, presumably faithfully copying the work of different hands from differing sources, this is a possibility, but a closer look at how the two terms were used suggests that they may indicate accommodation in different places and with differing functions.

In 1853 Parker pointed out that the term solar, in addition to referring to the main private chamber, was often used for a room above outbuildings.[7] More recently, in analysing a late 13th-century survey of buildings erected on various manors by Southwark Priory, Blair proposed that the solar might indicate a complete and integral cross wing, including the rooms on the ground floor.[8] Both suggestions are relevant to the Christ Church Priory document, but neither entirely explains the way the term was used in this case.

Out of the sixteen entries for solar, three occur in association with stables or a cattlehouse, totally dissociated from other domestic rooms. This is compatible with Parker's suggestions that the term could be used to designate an upper room in an outbuilding. But in other cases the solar certainly lay within the main house. In five instances a solar was built 'with' a new hall, and in three it was combined with service rooms.[9] None was heated. One of these last examples is likely to survive at Court Lodge, Great Chart, for which an entry for 1313 records a new hall with pantry and buttery, and solar above (Figure 17). The shell of the present building indicates the tripartite division of the lower end, with a central passage to a detached kitchen separating two service rooms, and with an upper room above. When the architectural evidence is put alongside the documentation, there can be little doubt that the solar here was the upper room next to the hall and above the service end.

Chambers were often also associated with halls: five of the eighteen examples are mentioned 'with' halls in the same way as solars. But there were differences. In three

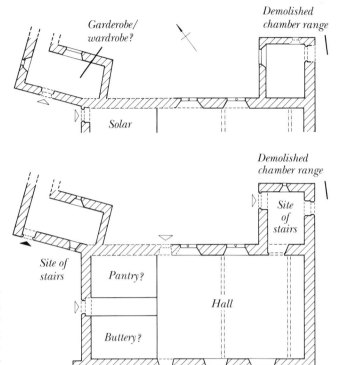

*Figure 17 Court Lodge, Great Chart. Plan of ground floor (below) and partial plan of first floor (above).*

cases the chambers were heated by fireplaces, and in six instances they were built 'with' chapels (as opposed to two solar/chapel combinations). In addition, the average cost of work which included a chamber was £27, whereas the average cost of work including a solar was only £19. These facts together suggest that the chamber was normally a grander, better-appointed room than the solar.

Chambers are also found in outbuildings, although the two examples mentioned specify particular users, ie the monks' chamber and the servants' chamber. In fact chambers, unlike solars, sometimes acquired qualifying words, so that there was a *camera armigerorum* at Adisham and a *camera maiora* at Chartham. In addition, there are two instances of lower chambers (*camere basse*) and one of a chamber in the garden. Only once is a service room, a larder, possibly associated with a chamber, although an early 15th-century document describing accommodation at Salmestone Grange, Margate, which belonged to St Augustine's Abbey, refers to the chamber over the pantry and buttery, ie like the solar at Court Lodge, Great Chart.[10]

From this it appears that the term chamber was usually applied to a room of some standing. In several cases it seems to indicate the great or best first-floor room at the upper end of the house next to the chapel, and to have been the only heated room in the house other than the hall. The only contemporary room surviving in this position is at Copton Manor, Sheldwich (Figure 18), but it was, unfortunately, not referred to in the *Memorandum Book*. However, at Court Lodge, Great Chart, ground and first-floor doorways in the small extension at the upper or south-east end of the hall probably led from the surviving 1313 hall and solar range to the earlier and now demolished building of 1311 which, according to the *Memorandum Book*, contained a chamber with a chapel and garderobe. It is odd that the rooms at the upper end of the hall, on which so much money was spent, have more frequently been destroyed in Christ Church Priory manor houses than in other early buildings. This may be fortuitous, but one explanation might be because this suite, with heated chamber, chapel and garderobe, was reserved for visitors, whether monks or not, and was never part of the day-to-day accommodation. Even when the manors were farmed out in the later 14th century, perhaps these best rooms were little used and therefore fell into disrepair long before the rest of the house.

In addition to describing the upper-end first-floor room, the term chamber was used for other 'living' rooms, whether upstairs or down, often identified by adjectives indicating for whose use they were reserved. There is no evidence that the term chamber was used in the *Memorandum Book* to indicate a separate block with a special function of the kind proposed for Temple Manor, Strood. In comparison with the chamber, the solar seems to have been smaller, unheated and situated at the lower end of the hall. Possibly it was the room used by the resident official, the serjeant.[11] Solars also occurred above outbuildings where they presumably indicate simple upper rooms of domestic function; exactly what this entailed is not clear, but they might have been where tenants who worked on the manor, or visited from other manors, were accommodated.

*Figure 18 Copton Manor, Sheldwich: a) View from the north; hall and lower end (BB89/1804); b) Plan of ground floor and partial plan of first floor.*

a

*Figure 19 Mersham Manor, Mersham. Hall and lower end: plan of ground floor and partial plan of first floor.*

## Garderobes

Two further terms frequently used in the *Memorandum Book* were chapel and garderobe. The first is self-explanatory, although its relationship to the rest of the accommodation is not always clear. The second is another word which causes considerable confusion. Today garderobe is normally used as a euphemism for latrine. But in medieval times it meant wardrobe, an inner chamber, closet or storage room which might or might not contain a close stool or lead to a latrine. The latrine itself seems to have been called a *camera privata* or privy chamber, a term which later came to have other meanings. In royal houses it was sometimes used for a lower room, but it could equally well lie on the first floor; it was usually allied to other rooms and formed part of a suite of accommodation.[12]

The Christ Church Priory evidence fits the picture obtained from royal accounts. Only three of the fifteen entries for garderobes are on their own, the rest are combined with chambers (two), chapels (three), chambers and chapels (two), solars (four) and a cellar (one). In the existing buildings it is not easy to identify such rooms, largely because they were likely not

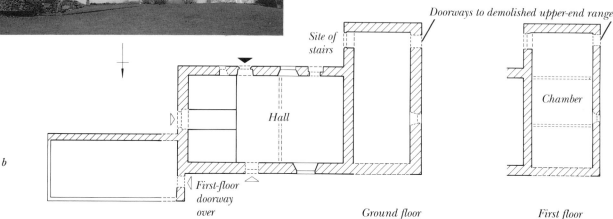

b

to be part of the main range but to form extensions or projecting wings which have since been demolished. Possibly a garderobe/wardrobe projects beyond the solar at Court Lodge, Great Chart (Figure 17). This range seems to have been added to the main building and is not mentioned in the *Memorandum Book*; it is of two storeys and has evidence suggesting a latrine projecting from its east wall. The similarly placed range at the lower end of Copton Manor, Sheldwich, might have been a wardrobe (Figure 18), although its larger size may indicate a complete chamber block, possibly one where the first-floor function would have been described by a qualifier such as knights' or servants'. Extensions to the surviving accommodation are also indicated by doorways in the wall of the chamber wing at Copton Manor and the room over the lower end at Mersham Manor, Mersham (Figure 19). At Copton Manor, openings on both floors suggest a substantial range which might well have accommodated a wardrobe, although, as it is likely that there was also a chapel attached to this end of the house, the doorways may have led to extensive further accommodation. At Mersham Manor, the much smaller doorway is visible only on the first floor and may indicate not a complete range but only access to a small latrine. Lack of precise architectural evidence makes the identification of such features no more than conjec-

tural, and one is left in the same position as Margaret Wood who knew that the wardrobe was an important room but was often unable to find evidence for it in surviving buildings.[13]

# Upper end accommodation in stone houses

## *Layout and circulation*

Most writers on Kentish buildings have emphasised the prevalence of the unitary roof over medieval houses, that is to say, single ranges in which the chamber accommodation lay in line with the hall under an overall roof.[14] In fact, there was at all periods far more variety than has commonly been supposed, and cross wings in the early stone buildings, particularly at the upper end of the house, were commoner than ends-in-line. At Old Soar, Plaxtol, probably built in the 1280s or 90s, the high-end chamber lies in a two-storey wing with further ranges leading off it (Figure 20). Similar wings, usually with evidence for subsidiary ranges, survive at the upper ends of Newbury Farmhouse (Figure 21), Copton Manor, Penshurst Place and Southfleet Rectory, as well as at Ightham Mote where the wings, despite being constructed partly of timber, relate more closely in size and layout to

*Figure 20 Old Soar, Plaxtol. Ground and first-floor plans of chamber and chapel ranges.*

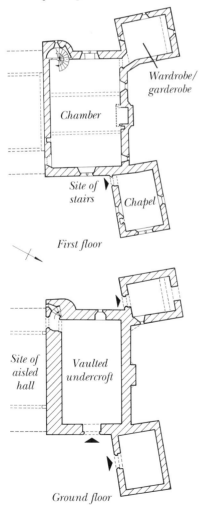

*Figure 21 Newbury Farmhouse, Tonge. Ground-floor plan of aisled hall and upper-end cross wing.*

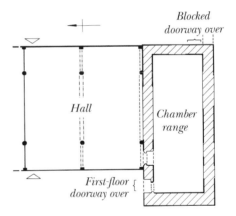

*Figure 22 Ightham Mote, Ightham. Reconstruction of medieval house, showing, from left to right, two solar ranges with chapel behind, open hall and suggested reconstruction of porch, services and kitchen.*

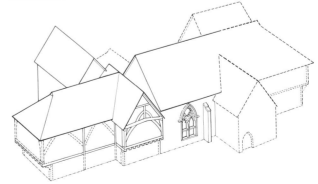

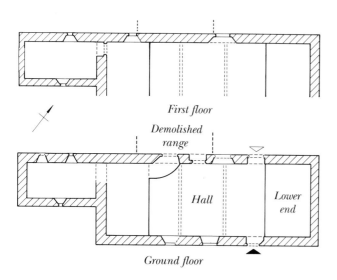

*Figure 23 Hoad Farm, Acrise. Plan of ground floor and partial plan of first floor.*

stone than to timber buildings (Figure 22). The arrangement of doorways at Court Lodge, Great Chart, and Mersham Manor indicates that they also are likely to have had similar wings. Only Nurstead Court, Hoad Farm, Acrise (Figure 23), and Battel Hall, Leeds (Figure 24), have confirmed ends-in-line, and all of them have, or had, secondary ranges extending the main core of the building by additional accommodation.

However they were arranged, the hall and chamber elements varied in their degree of integration. Despite being physically united, there were still, in some cases, recollections of the distinct and disparate units of accommodation which

*Figure 24 Battel Hall, Leeds. Hall and upper end: plan of ground floor and partial plan of first floor.*

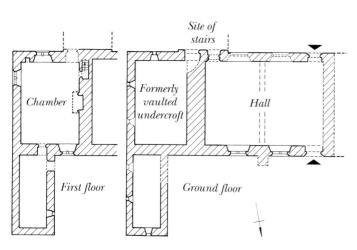

*Figure 25 Old Soar, Plaxtol: a) Interior of chamber, looking towards corner where way through to chapel has been created (BB89/1927); b) Chamber and chapel ranges from south east (BB89/1944).*

are likely to have prevailed throughout the 13th century. This is well illustrated at Old Soar (Figures 20, 25). At first sight the three ranges, containing chamber, chapel and wardrobe with latrine at first-floor level, seem to provide the type of *en suite* accommodation discussed on the Christ Church Priory manors. But in fact all is not so clear. The entrance in the end wall of the hall leads directly to newel stairs from which, in a most awkward manner, one may either enter the undercroft or ascend to the great chamber. The main undercroft is also reached from outside, and the other ground-floor rooms can only be reached from the exterior. On the first floor the wardrobe wing is entered from the chamber by an original doorway, but the entrance to the chapel has been crudely broken through at a later date, so that originally one could only reach the chapel from an external staircase and doorway. There was, therefore, very little communication between the various parts, and the ground-floor functions of the subsidiary wings may have had nothing to do with what went on above them.

Old Soar is likely to have been built in the late 13th century, but even in the 14th century direct access between all rooms at the upper end was not always possible. At Battel Hall and Hoad Farm secondary wings were separated from the main range by thick walls, and, as at Old Soar, there is little sign of original internal communication at ground-floor level. At Ightham Mote, where the ground-floor plan is largely lost, it is clear that access to both levels of the chapel range was only from the stair wing and not from the upper-end rooms at all. In most houses the main ground-floor room was reached from the hall via a stair lobby. Original doorways in the end walls of the hall indicate direct access only at Nurstead Court and at the two rectories (The Rectory House, Cliffe-at-Hoo, and Southfleet Rectory). But by the early 14th century intercommunication was increasing. At Copton Manor, where both floors of the wing were reached from a stair projection, doorways on the opposite wall led at each level to a further range, which has since been demolished, and at Southfleet and Cliffe-at-Hoo rectories rear extensions are only separated from the upper-end rooms by thin partitions, which implies that internal access was likely.

## The form and use of ground-floor rooms

It is impossible to ascertain precisely the functions of the ground-floor rooms at the upper end of the house. The documentary evidence supplied by the *Memorandum Book* is very little help in this respect since it seldom refers to any rooms below the chamber, although they obviously existed. This in itself may indicate that they had no specialised function but were used for storage and to elevate the chambers above. In three cases the room below the great chamber was vaulted – at Old Soar, Penshurst Place and formerly at Battel Hall, Leeds. Elsewhere the ceilings were probably of timber. A slight uncertainty over the form of the ceilings arises because nearly all have been renewed, in many cases being reset at a higher level. This is most clearly seen at Copton Manor, Sheldwich (Figure 26), where rendering on the west front of the wing has

been removed to reveal original doorways and windows, those on the first floor set somewhat below the present floor level.

At Newbury Farmhouse, Tonge (Figure 27), the position of original ground and first-floor doorways also proves that the ceiling between the floors has been raised by 0.3–0.4 m, and steps down from the floor level in the hall may indicate that the ground floor in the wing has

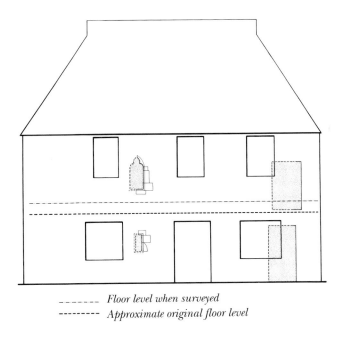

------- *Floor level when surveyed*

-------- *Approximate original floor level*

*Figure 26 Copton Manor, Sheldwich. West elevation of cross wing indicating original openings (shown shaded) and former level of first floor.*

*Figure 27 Newbury Farmhouse, Tonge. Long section through hall and cross section through upper-end wing, indicating original first-floor level (shown by broken lines below later floor).*

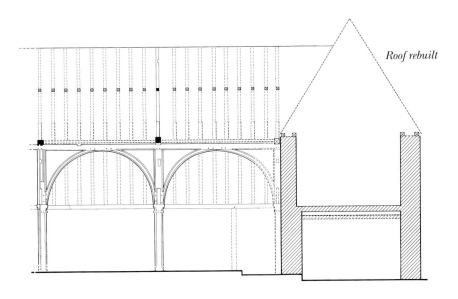

*Roof rebuilt*

been dug out by up to 0.4 m as well. Although the increased height in this case may be as much as 0.8 m, the difference was usually only 0.2–0.5 m.[15] It was, however, enough to change the character of the room.

The original ground-floor windows have often been masked or destroyed, but such evidence as there is suggests that most ground-floor rooms were poorly lit. At Old Soar, two of the ranges had only slits which supplied little more than ventilation, and the room below the chapel had no windows at all, any light having to be provided through the open door. It is possible that other houses also had no ground-floor fenestration in some of the smaller ranges, although it is often difficult to prove this today since they have almost all had later windows inserted. Where the original windows survive, they are small single lights of rectangular form. Few of these are now in use, but evidence of their shape and size can be seen at Copton Manor, Battel Hall, The Rectory House, Cliffe-at-Hoo, and Hoad Farm, Acrise.

The lack of direct access between hall and ground-floor room at the upper end of most houses, the presence of vaulting or the low height of the ceilings, and the inadequate fenestration all combine to suggest that the ground floors of these upper ends were not designed as dwelling spaces, but were probably used for storage. They required considerable adaptation to turn them into acceptable living accommodation after the Middle Ages.

## First-floor chambers and chapels

The great chamber at the upper end of the house was raised above this low ground-floor room. It was usually substantial and of considerable height, and was probably

*Figure 28 Battel Hall, Leeds. Fireplace in chamber (BB90/10301).*

finely detailed, although little of this tends to survive. Several examples still have their roofs, with scissor braces at Copton Manor, and two or more bays of crown posts at Old Soar, Southfleet Rectory and Ightham Mote. The windows might have decorative hood moulds and be provided with window seats, and occasionally evidence for stone wall-cupboards remains. All these features can be seen at Old Soar, but they also occurred elsewhere, for example at Southfleet Rectory and Battel Hall.

The chamber was sometimes, if not always, heated by an enclosed fireplace. As already discussed, fireplaces in the Christ Church Priory manor houses may have been confined to this room, and this accords with the surviving architectural evidence. A fireplace is known to have existed in the upper-end chamber at Court Lodge, Godmersham, on the wall shared with the hall.[16] A very fine example survives in the same position at Battel Hall (Figure 28), and a chimney and mutilated fireplace remain on the external wall at Old Soar. Although it cannot be proved, the present fireplaces at Ightham Mote, Penshurst Place and Southfleet Rectory probably occupy the same positions as earlier ones.

The chapel, if one was present, was also more likely to be situated at the upper than the lower end of the house. This is suggested both by the documentary references in the Christ Church Priory *Memorandum Book*, and by the few remaining examples. Lack of evidence for a chapel has been remarked upon at Penshurst Place, and Kent has sometimes been thought of as a county with few private chapels.[17] However, the existence of up to 200 possible manorial chapels is known from various sources, the majority of which were secular in origin.[18] Few of these chapels survive today, and some of them, such as Burleigh Chantry and Pett Chapel, Charing, are so fragmentary that their date, their relationship to the manor house they served, and even their positive identification as chapels (as opposed to ruined chamber blocks) is unclear from the surviving architectural evidence. Two of the survivors, at Newlands Chapel, Charing, of the late 12th century, and Horton Manor, Chartham, of *c* 1300, were at ground level and appear to have been detached from other buildings; but others lay within or next to the house.[19] The only two which remain within the group of buildings currently under discussion, at Old Soar and Ightham Mote, are on the first floor and form part of the main accommodation at the upper end of the house. In both instances they occupied separate wings off the main chamber, although in neither case is there evidence of direct access from the chamber to the chapel.

Some private chapels, like that at Charney Bassett, Berkshire, clearly were entered only from the chamber.[20] This could even be true in royal residences, for at Rochester in 1254, after years in which people apparently passed through the king's chamber to reach the chapel, a flight of external steps was ordered to be made to provide separate access.[21] This amenity seems to have been a feature of Little Wenham Hall, Suffolk, where the chapel could be entered either from the main room, or by a small doorway opening from a newel stair. When the main door was closed, internal windows between the chamber and chapel allowed people in the chamber to participate in the services in privacy.[22] At Ightham Mote the chapel was originally reached only from the stairs and not from the chamber, but, as at Little Wenham, a window between the two permitted the occupants of the chamber to be seated by the fireplace and watch what was going on next door. The same may have been

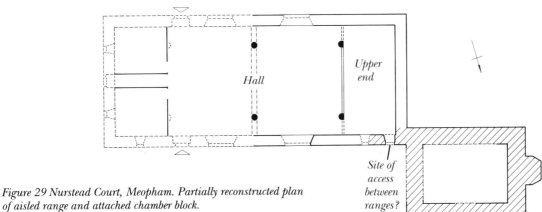

*Figure 29 Nurstead Court, Meopham. Partially reconstructed plan of aisled range and attached chamber block.*

true at Old Soar, where there was just room for a squint, which would have been destroyed when the wall was broken through to allow access between chamber and chapel. A squint also seems to have been provided at Hornes Place, Appledore, in the late 14th century, although the total demolition of all the buildings on that side of the chapel makes it impossible to deduce the precise arrangement.

In some noble households of the 15th and early 16th centuries, everyone was bidden to attend mass.[23] But whatever the habits prevailing a hundred years earlier among families of slightly less elevated status, the fact that communion only had to be taken by the laity once a year meant that the service in chapel only needed to be seen and heard. Thus lack of direct access between the chapel and private chamber may have been perfectly acceptable; indeed, it was probably seen as positively desirable to exclude the officiating clergy and other members of the household from the chamber.[24] The arrangement in monastic manor houses could well have been different, but for this there is in Kent no evidence.

## Nurstead Court

There has been one notable omission in this discussion of upper-end accommodation, for Nurstead Court, built in *c* 1309*, has hardly been mentioned so far (Figure 29). The reason for this is that Nurstead Court, alone of all the Kentish stone houses of *c* 1300, had no first-floor accommodation above the inner room at its upper end. The chamber here was open to the roof, and the only surviving first-floor accommodation lay in a separate and earlier block which could be reached from one corner.[25] Very little survives of this earlier building, which has been compared with the three-storeyed tower at Stone Castle and the earliest remains at Lympne Castle.[26] Its height is not known, but it probably contained only one room on each floor, the lowest level forming an undercroft partly sunk into the ground. The status of the de Gravesend family makes it highly unlikely that they would have been satisfied with such meagre accommodation to accompany such a grand and finely detailed hall. The whole arrangement is so out of keeping with developments elsewhere in the county that one cannot help wondering if what remains is only part of a house: a hall with accompanying service and inner rooms, plus an earlier building of unknown function; to which should be added a complete range of residential accommodation which has

now vanished. In other words, Nurstead Court still has, at a later date, the hall which houses such as Luddesdown Court and Little Wenham have lost, and they have the well-appointed chamber block which is missing at Nurstead Court. If so, it is probable that the chamber block was detached. As argued above, this does not seem an impossible arrangement even for the early 14th century. On the other hand, and as will be shown, open inner ends to open halls were not unknown in timber-framed houses of this period.

# Lower-end accommodation in stone houses

## *Layout and circulation*

Unlike the upper-end accommodation, that at the service end of surviving stone houses frequently lay in line with the hall, continuing under the same roof. This was the case in all the Christ Church Priory manors for which there is evidence, except for Chartham, and it also occurred at Nurstead Court, Hoad Farm, Acrise, and most probably Ightham Mote and Southfleet Rectory. Lower-end wings are known only in three stone buildings: The Deanery, Chartham, Penshurst Place and Gallants Manor (Figure 30), although, if the interpretation of

*Figure 30 Gallants Manor, East Farleigh. Ground-floor plan of lower-end cross wing.*

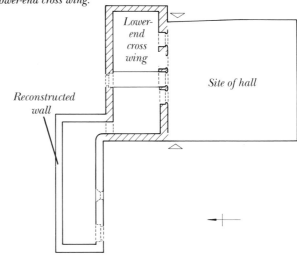

*Figure 31 Court Lodge, Great Chart. Exterior of lower end of hall with external doorways to kitchen passage and first-floor solar (top left and bottom centre of the hall range, both now serving as windows). On the left is an added wing with two external doorways; that on the first floor is now blocked (BB70/7342).*

Squerryes Lodge is correct, then a detached lower-end wing was built there during the 13th century. Elsewhere evidence for the form of the lower end has gone.

The fact that the end often lay in line with the hall did not necessarily mean that the accommodation was limited. Although there is no evidence for more than a single main bay at Nurstead Court and Hoad Farm, Acrise, extra two-storey ranges were attached to the lower ends of several Christ Church houses, eg Court Lodge, Great Chart, Copton Manor and Mersham Manor, and may also have occurred beyond the wings of Penshurst Place and Gallants Manor.

In some cases the wall between hall and lower end has doorways indicating a division into three, with outer doorways to two service rooms and a central one leading through to a detached kitchen. These existed until the 19th century at Nurstead Court (Figures 12, 29) and can still be seen at Penshurst Place and Gallants Manor. Several of the main ranges under unitary roofs had internal timber partitions which have gone, taking the internal doorway evidence with them, as at Court Lodge,

Great Chart, where a stone doorway (now a window) centrally placed in the external wall shows that the buttery and pantry, mentioned in the *Memorandum Book*, were separated by a passage to a detached kitchen (Figures 17, 31). The Rectory House, Cliffe-at-Hoo, like Squerryes Lodge of the previous century, only had two service doorways, suggesting that the kitchen was reached from the rear doorway to the hall. At Ightham Mote (Figure 13) only two doorways survive today, although the larger size of the doorway placed centrally in the end wall of the hall may indicate that there was a triple grouping originally.

The removal of timber partitions meant that small units of ill-lit and unheated space could later be turned to larger, heated rooms. In some cases, particularly where the services lay in a cross wing, this may have gone hand in hand with raising low ceilings, as indicated by redundant corbels to carry a low cornice at Squerryes Lodge. But the height of blocked first-floor doorways at Court Lodge, Great Chart, and Mersham Manor, Mersham, shows that in other buildings, notably those where the end lay in-line, the ceilings were always at their present level.

Bearing in mind the evidence of the *Memorandum Book*, which suggested that specialised service rooms were more likely to occur in conjunction with the less well-appointed solar than with the grander chamber, one can perhaps begin to see a pattern emerging: the first ground-floor rooms to have specialised functions were the buttery and pantry at the lower end of the house, and possibly they were given reasonable height earlier than the rooms at the upper end. This extra height in turn meant that the solar above was less impressive than the great chamber, which tended to lie in a wing at the upper end over a low undercroft. The evidence is slight and must not be pushed too far. Some houses had well-appointed cross wings at their service ends, and at Copton Manor, one of the few where both ends survive and where blocked windows and doorways indicate the original ceiling levels, there is no sign that the ground floors were of different heights at either end. But the combination of the documentary and much of the architectural evidence suggests that there was a general trend in that direction.

## The first floor: access and accommodation

Evidence for the stairs to the chamber or solar over the services is fragmentary. At Court Lodge, Great Chart, access to the upper floor was clearly by an external doorway in the gable wall, and since the additional

*Figure 32 Hamden, Smarden. Plan and sections after Rigold 1967a. The plan is half the scale of the sections.*

chamber block at this end also had an external first-floor doorway, there may have been a single set of stairs and timber gallery to serve both ranges (Figures 17, 31). This means that the solar at Court Lodge was totally separate from the hall and upper-end accommodation. Possibly the same arrangement occurred at Copton Manor, where signs of external doorways to the secondary wing at the service end may indicate that outside stairs and gallery gave access to the first floor of the main range as well as to the wing (Figure 18). The dispersed accommodation at the lower ends in these two Christ Church Priory houses is not dissimilar to the arrangement at the upper ends of houses such as Old Soar. But at The Rectory House, Cliffe-at-Hoo, and at Gallants Manor, doorways at the rear of the lower-end hall wall look as if they may have led to internal stairs; unfortunately the service end of The Rectory House has gone, and at Gallants Manor the joists in the wing are not exposed, so no break for the stairs is visible.

As discussed above, in those houses with wings at the upper end and lower ends-in-line, the room over the services, which was perhaps the solar, was the less impressive of the two. However, where the lower end lay in a wing, the chamber was certainly no mean room. At Penshurst Place it may not have been so large as the one at the upper end, but it was still lit by a window with fine

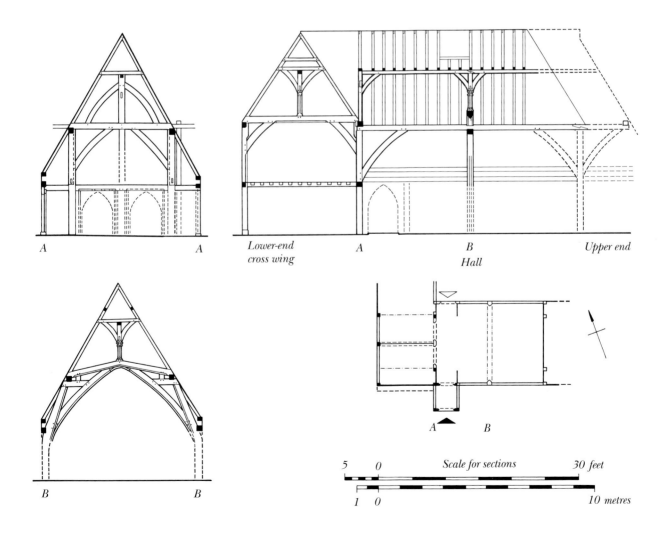

A           A

*Lower-end cross wing*    A      B     *Upper end*

*Hall*

B         B

A    B

5    0     *Scale for sections*     *30 feet*

1   0           *10 metres*

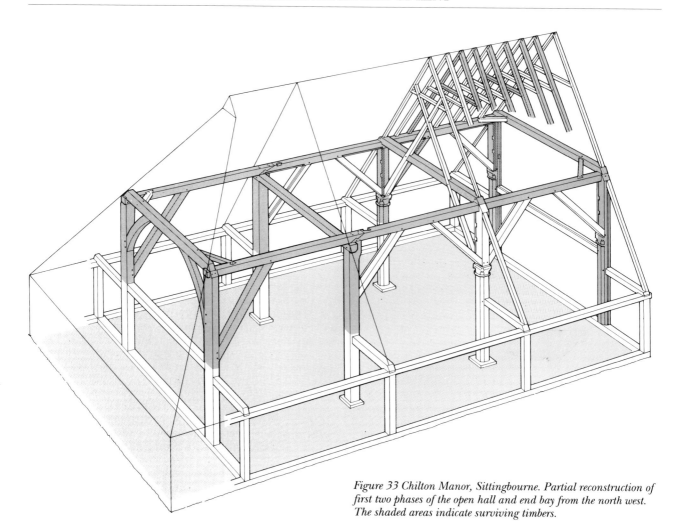

*Figure 33 Chilton Manor, Sittingbourne. Partial reconstruction of first two phases of the open hall and end bay from the north west. The shaded areas indicate surviving timbers.*

tracery decoration, and at Gallants Manor a well-detailed crown-post roof remains above. This wing was actually timber framed over a stone ground floor, but despite the mixed materials, it was, like those at Ightham Mote, very similar to wings of the same period which were built wholly of stone.

## Subsidiary accommodation in stone houses: conclusion

The importance of subsidiary accommodation in houses of stone, or mixed stone and timber construction, built before the mid 14th century, is clear. It was provided at both ends of the hall, and always included upper chambers, either attached to the hall or, at Nurstead Court, set at one remove. First-floor rooms at the upper end tended to be grand, whilst ground-floor accommodation at the lower end was already specialised and domestic. Both ends usually had more than one range, often set at odd angles, and the rooms were not necessarily linked by internal communication. The impression given is that units of accommodation which had once been disparate, were gradually being drawn together into the integrated plan of the later Middle Ages, and that as

this occurred, so the individual components began to acquire their habitual functions.[27]

## Subsidiary accommodation in timber-framed houses

Subsidiary accommodation in wholly timber-framed houses is of an entirely different order. In the first place, very little of it has managed to survive and, secondly, where timber ends do remain, they appear to be quite unlike the equivalent parts of stone houses. The evidence comes in three forms: cross wings, ends-in-line and signs of the former existence of structures which have since been replaced. These will be dealt with in turn.

### *Cross wings*

Original timber cross wings from this period are extremely rare, and two of them are associated with stone buildings: the lower-end wing of Gallants Manor, of *c* 1322*, is timber framed on the first floor; likewise the two upper-end wings at Ightham Mote, of the 1330s*, were built more or less simultaneously with the stone hall and chapel there, and had timber framing above ground-floor walls which were partly of stone. The only other surviving examples are the lower ends of Hamden, Smarden (Figure 32), usually assigned to the second quarter of the century,[28] but which is possibly a little later; and the lower-end wing at Eastry Court, which seems to be contemporary with a partial rebuilding of the hall, perhaps in the 14th century.[29]

## Evidence for secondary rooms in single-range structures

Elsewhere what little evidence remains for private accommodation indicates ends-in-line, not wings. At Chilton Manor, Sittingbourne (Figure 33), datable to the 13th century by its archaic framing techniques and the apparent use of volute caps to the arcade posts, two bays of a 13th-century hall survive. To the north is a third aisled bay, which may be secondary and the result of a 14th-century reconstruction. This could have been part of the hall or it may have formed a second room beyond the hall, with an additional aisled end beyond that. Ambiguity over the function of bays next to the hall sometimes occurs elsewhere. At the excavated Moat Farm, Leigh, the archaeological evidence is insufficient to ascertain whether the three bays formed a single-bay hall with separate bays at either end, or a two-bay hall and one separate bay.[30] Outside Kent the same kind of uncertainty seems also to apply to the very large aisled hall excavated at Park Farm, Salehurst, Sussex,[31] and similar problems of interpretation have arisen over some of the surviving houses in the Vale of White Horse, Oxfordshire.[32] In the latter it seems likely that an end bay may sometimes have formed a separate room without being completely partitioned off from the hall, and this may be what happened at Chilton Manor.

It is difficult at Chilton Manor to be sure which end of the hall was which; but the fact that the roof timbers are faced to the north suggests that that was the upper end, and the problem bay to the north was an inner room beyond the dais. In other houses enough of the hall, or of its later medieval arrangement, remains for a more certain identification of upper and lower ends. At Ratling Court, Aylesham (Figure 9),

where a spere truss marks the service end, the roof has signs of a hip beyond a closed truss at the upper end of the open hall, proving that the range continued for another, separate, bay. The position of features such as windows, doorways and spere trusses shows that the arcade plates of the aisled hall continue into the upper end at Dormer Cottage, Petham (Figure 34), and the lower end at Court Lodge, Fawkham. At Hamden, Smarden, a scarf in the arcade plate at the upper end of the hall suggests that there was an upper end-in-line there too (Figure 32). This, however, is about the sum total of evidence for partially surviving subsidiary accommodation in timber houses built before c 1370.[33]

## The form of early timber ends and the reasons for their disappearance

The scarcity of surviving ends does not mean that timber halls were built to stand alone. Several houses have signs that some kind of structure originally lay beyond the hall, although it was clearly not a continuation of the same range. At the lower end of Barnes Place, Hadlow, an exposed arcade post has a groove, suggesting a plank partition; it was set towards the hall face, which indicates that the wall was not external. But there is no evidence that the aisled structure continued, and it is therefore likely that the original lower end was separately framed. Similar kinds of evidence imply that timber ranges of independent construction already existed, or were intended, in other houses.[34] Several of these were rebuilt as cross wings during the Middle Ages, but unfortunately there is no evidence for their original form. In other early timber houses too little of the end walls of the hall remain for any firm deductions to be made about what might have lain beyond.[35]

The almost complete destruction of early timber ends suggests that it was virtually impossible to adapt them to suit later needs. If so, in this respect they must have been somewhat different from their counterparts in stone houses. The fragments that survive are not wholly conclusive, but they suggest that subsidiary accommodation in early timber buildings was either open to the roof, or had low ground floors which could only be used for storage.

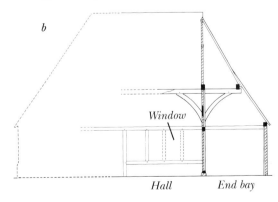

a Figure 34 Dormer Cottage, Petham: a) Exterior from the west (BB87/1933); b) Long section of surviving timbers of east arcade and east wall showing part of open hall and upper-end bay.

b

Window

Hall          End bay

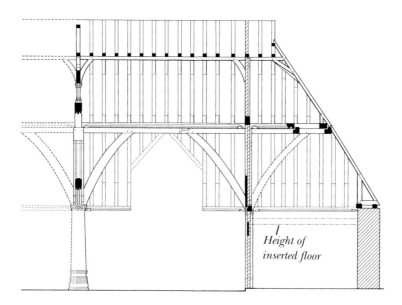

*Height of
inserted floor*

*Figure 35 Nurstead Court, Meopham. Long section through part
of hall and upper-end bay, from the north.*

Evidence for in-line ends occurs only in aisled halls. The
most complete survival, the two phases of Chilton Manor, is
difficult to interpret because nothing but the central frame of
the aisled structure remains. That the aisle walls should have
been replaced is hardly surprising, but the lack of evidence
for internal partitions and floors suggests that these were
minimal, and that the north end bay may have been open to
the roof. This could have been true for all houses with signs
of in-line ends. We know that the hipped end bays of
Nurstead Court were originally open, and that a floor was
only inserted, at least at the upper end, in the later 14th
century (Figure 35). The sheer size of Nurstead Court made
this possible, but most wholly timber-framed aisled halls were
considerably smaller. Their intrusive arcade posts, arcade
plates, braces and end tie beams meant that the only usable
first-floor space was above the central section. Where the roof
was hipped, which was probably the norm and certainly the
case at Ratling Court and Dormer Cottage, head room would
have been severely restricted by the three sloping roofs.

Given these circumstances, it can be inferred that no in-
line ends in timber aisled buildings were designed to have
upper chambers. At a later date, when provision of first-
floor accommodation was seen to be desirable, the result
was the complete rebuilding of nearly all such ends. The
only early aisled house, other than Nurstead Court, where
the whole hipped end survives and an upper floor has been
inserted, is the tiny Dormer Cottage, Petham, in which the
central section of the end bay provides just enough room
for a small cupboard.

Differences in status between stone and timber dwellings
have already been considered in Chapter 3, and one of the
ways in which these seem to have manifested themselves was
in the provision of subsidiary accommodation. Nonetheless,
social distinctions are unlikely to have been so extreme as to
have led to stone houses having two two-storeyed ranges, and
timber ones nothing but open bays, and it has usually been
assumed that south-eastern timber houses of the late 13th
and early 14th centuries did have at least one two-storeyed
component.[36] In fact it is likely that hipped open bays only
occurred when the end bays were constructed at the same
time as the hall itself, and few houses have contemporary
bays at both ends of the hall. In most of the examples
discussed, they were only found at the upper end.

What happened at the service end is altogether more
puzzling. Whatever form the accommodation took, it was
clearly perceived as inadequate before the end of the Middle
Ages, for it was replaced by sizeable service-end cross wings in
a number of cases. Yet such evidence as there is does not
suggest that the original ends were too small. In fact, contrary
to the tendency in stone houses, it is possible that the service
end was larger than the upper-end bay. This is implied by the
surviving arrangement at Hamden, Smarden, which has only
a bay at the upper end and a whole wing at the lower end; by
the excavated evidence at Pivington and Joydens Wood, in
which the lower ends were clearly the larger of the two; and
possibly by inference from the later 14th century, by which
time several houses had service-end cross wings, an
arrangement which appears to have been so well established
by then that it is likely to have had forerunners.

If lower-end wings were common in the early 14th
century, then the reason for their replacement was not

primarily concerned with size, even if the late medieval wings which took their place were even larger. Instead, one suspects it concerned their form and structure. It has been argued that many stone wings, usually at the upper end, had low and poorly lit ground floors which were later modernised by having their ceilings raised. While this was a relatively simple alteration in buildings with stone walls, it was much more difficult in timber-framed ones. In fact, it was easier to rebuild than to adapt. Evidence for exceptionally low and inconvenient ground-floor ceilings is forthcoming in buildings of the late 14th century and will be discussed in Chapter 6. No comparable evidence exists for timber buildings of this period, but it is difficult to see what other reason there could be for sweeping away so

completely all trace of early service-end accommodation in timber buildings.[37]

If this deduction is correct, it implies that stone and timber buildings evolved in different directions. The reason for this may have to do with social status, which had the effect that those who built timber houses required only one two-storeyed element, whereas those who could afford stone had two. Where only one was possible, it made better sense to place it at the lower end. The position of the first-floor chamber was, after all, less critical than the position of the service rooms. As will be seen, there is plenty of later evidence to indicate that the upper ends of timber buildings were never emphasised in the way that they had been in the earliest stone houses.

# 5 Construction and roofs: late 13th and early 14th centuries

A discussion of construction in the earliest surviving Kentish houses must begin with evidence of a very fragmentary nature. Even when substantial parts of early stone buildings survive, their roofs have often been completely replaced, leaving little or no evidence of their original form. In timber buildings, apart from the wholesale demolition of ends or wings referred to in Chapter 4, walls have often been rebuilt in solid materials, and internal timbers removed to provide larger or higher rooms in houses whose internal layout has changed. Thus between the 13th and the mid 14th centuries, evidence for analysis is provided by only a small number of complete buildings together with fragments of others. As is so frequently the case in studies of this kind, it is difficult not to give undue emphasis to these relatively scanty remains in an attempt to unravel the developments of this formative period.

No simple typological sequence of the earliest structures can be charted. Before the mid 14th century four different, even if related, typological groups are identifiable which can be arranged only roughly in chronological sequence. In the first place there is a group of timber buildings with 'archaic' construction: that is, using passing braces and other laterally disposed timbers, with early jointing techniques, and without benefit of any longitudinal roof members. A second group, which is not perhaps wholly dissimilar to the first, in that the roofs still have no longitudinal members but rely on simple scissor braces, collars or, occasionally, crown struts, is confined to stone buildings. Several of these structures are reasonably well dated, and the question of their chronological relationship with buildings in both the first and the third group needs considering. Houses in the third group

may be timber framed or stone. Their main characteristic is the introduction of some kind of longitudinal roof member – normally a collar purlin – in conjunction with a supporting crown post or king strut; at the same time they retain lateral roof stiffening of early form, or have timber scantling or details which suggest a relatively early date; those structures that have timber frames are frequently still aisled. Fourthly, and not always readily distinguishable from houses in the third group, are those buildings in which base crucks or other methods of clearing the open hall of free-standing arcade posts are introduced.

These types of structure had all made their appearance in Kent before the mid 14th century, but finding precise dates and sorting out the chronological sequence are not easy, particularly since it is clear that the different forms overlapped in time. Some of the buildings had stone walls, some timber; the material is likely to have influenced the form of the roof, and the choice of material was itself probably determined by considerations of wealth, status or even geographical situation.

## Early wall construction and interrupted sills

Evidence from excavated sites in Kent shows that from the late 13th century, timber-framed walls were being constructed on stone ground walls, and aisle or arcade posts were being placed on padstones. No sign has been found of buildings early enough or primitive enough to have been built with

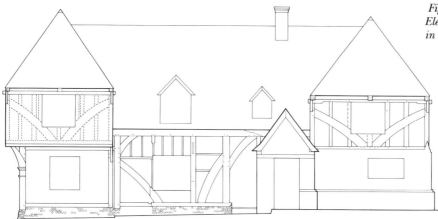

*Figure 36 Lower Newlands, Teynham. Elevation of west wall showing interrupted sill in cross wing and at end of hall range.*

*Figure 37 6 Adelaide Cottages, East Farleigh. Reused post with evidence for former lapped timber (BB87/1371).*

# Timber-framed aisled halls and passing braces

Surviving remains suggest that one or two of the earliest remaining timber buildings originated sometime in the mid 13th century, but that most examples only date to the latter part of the century. Precise dating is difficult for, in the absence of tree-ring dates, the documented date of 1294/5 for Eastry Court is the only firm date available. There are virtually no buildings in Kent with early structural techniques: even where archaic forms of bracing were used, some of the joints are of the mortice-and-tenon variety, and evidence for lap jointing alone remains only in a few timber structures: at Cogan House, Canterbury, secret and open notched lap joints are used with passing and duplicate braces in an aisled building which, it has been suggested, may even date from before 1238.[6] At The Plestor, Borden, and 6 Adelaide Cottages, East Farleigh (Figure 37), single timbers showing evidence for braces with lap joints survive in otherwise rebuilt open halls. Passing braces were used at Eastry Court (Figure 8), Eastling Manor (Figure 38a), Bardingley Farmhouse, Sutton Valence, and Newbury Farmhouse, Tonge (Figure 38b), and in each case these were lapped at their upper ends but tenoned at the base. The first two

*Figure 38 Partially reconstructed cross sections of open trusses: a) Eastling Manor, Eastling; b) Newbury Farmhouse, Tonge.*

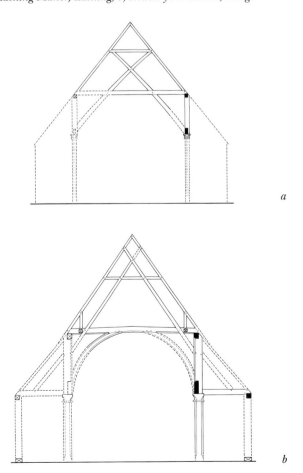

*a*

*b*

earth-fast posts, such as those for which fragmentary evidence has been revealed in Hertfordshire and East Anglia.[1] The free-standing arcade posts of very few early structures survive down to the base, most having been cut away and underbuilt with solid walling at a later date, but padstones or stylobates show up in excavations, and those arcade posts which still remain to the bottom were supported in a similar manner, as at Nurstead Court in the early 14th century.[2]

In most early timber buildings the external walls have been replaced, but where they remain, timber sill beams are supported on low walls of packed stones. However, there is evidence to suggest that the main posts sometimes passed across these sills to a padstone below, the sills being tenoned into the posts at either side. Three excavated sites, at Moat Farm, Leigh, and Pivington, Pluckley, Kent, and Park Farm, Salehurst, Sussex, seem to show evidence of this construction in the late 13th or early 14th century,[3] and a much later example still survives at Lower Newlands, Teynham, built in *c* 1380* (Figure 36). There, all the main timbers, except for the posts of the open truss, run past the sill beam. It is possible that the same arrangement occurred at Hurst Farm, Chilham, one of the few early 14th-century houses with surviving external walls (Figure 10). In this instance, the main posts of the two open trusses are carried on high sill beams, but the only fully visible corner post, which also serves as a door jamb, runs past to a lower sill at ground level. On the other side of the doorway, the high sill beam was tenoned into the door jamb.[4] This form of construction with 'interrupted' sills is normally associated with northern England,[5] but it may once have been a far more widespread technique which, in the south east, had been superseded before the end of the 14th century.

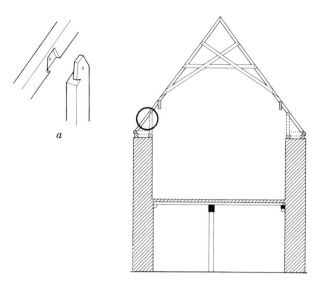

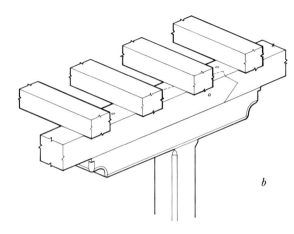

*Figure 39 Luddesdown Court, Luddesdown. Cross section of surviving truss in rear range: a) Detail of junction of rafter and ashlar piece in rear range; b) Samson post, bolster, spine beam and joists below main chamber.*

examples may be the earliest: in them the braces are tapered,[7] and braces and collar overlap at the top and are pegged to the rafters with a single peg. In all cases the braces are interrupted by the arcade posts, so that, where they were needed, separate braces spanned the aisles.

Most of these houses have nearly straight timbers of square section. Newbury Farmhouse is unusual in having arch braces below the passing braces, and in these being both curved and moulded; in addition a flying cornice supported the ashlar pieces, and the spandrels were originally infilled with boarding, all features which make this building rather more sophisticated and richly detailed than the others. The overall appearance of its cross section is not dissimilar to Almshoe Bury, Ippolitts, Hertfordshire, dated on the basis of its dog-tooth ornament to the mid 13th century.[8] However, dog-tooth ornament has recently been

dated as late as 1292/3* at Warbleton Old Rectory, Sussex, and it therefore may be possible to place the construction somewhat later in the 13th century.[9]

Certainly in Kent, the use of mortice-and-tenon joints, and the date of 1294/5 for Eastry Court, tend to suggest that the earliest aisled halls are not early in national terms. Apart from Cogan House, Canterbury, no aisled timber buildings have been found so far whose structural details can be compared to Old Court Cottage, Limpsfield, just over the border in Surrey, which has been assigned to the mid 13th century.[10] The temptation to push the earliest remains too far back should be resisted unless the case can be proved, for if, as seems likely, the next group of timber buildings dates only to the turn of the century or even later, a gap is created which, despite the small numbers involved, is somewhat unlikely. Certainly the burden of proof lies with those who seek earlier dates.

*Figure 40 Collar-rafter roofs: a) The Deanery, Chartham. Hall range; b) Old Soar, Plaxtol. Chapel; c) Ightham Mote, Ightham. Chapel.*

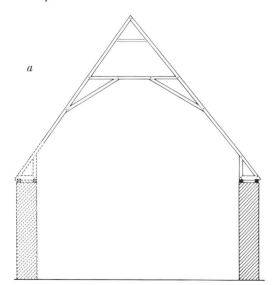

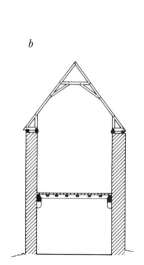

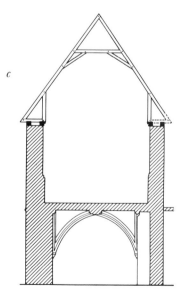

# Early roof construction in stone-walled buildings

## *Roofs with lateral members only*

Stone buildings do not call for the same roof construction as timber ones. None of Kent's stone houses, with the exception of Nurstead Court, is aisled, and there is therefore no occasion for main trusses with roof timbers extending below tie-beam level. Instead, the trusses are confined to the roof itself, so that over-timbering in the form of passing or duplicate bracing was not appropriate. Thus the longer roof members of the timber buildings were reduced to simple collared rafters, or to scissor braces which, instead of occurring only at the main trusses, took the place of the intermediate collar-rafter trusses and occurred throughout the length of the roof.

One of the earliest roofs for which evidence remains may be a fragment at Luddesdown Court, possibly built in the 1230s. The stone gables of both the main range and the smaller wing at right angles to it have residual traces of former scissor-braced trusses, and one mutilated truss survives against the gable wall of the smaller range (Figure 39). It consists of a simple pair of scissors with a collar, and evidence for former ashlar pieces. All the timbers are lapped and the ashlars were jointed with notched laps.[11] Secret notched lap joints apparently occur over the eastern part of the archdeacon's house (monastic larder) in Christ Church Priory, Canterbury, but have not been found in any rural houses.[12] In addition to the roof timbers, the floor joists at Luddesdown Court suggest 13th-century timber construction. They are lodged on massive spine beams, carried on samson posts which are scarfed in an unusual and not fully visible manner, with face-halved scarfs with sallied and probably under-squinted

butts. This sort of construction suggests a date in the 13th or possibly early 14th century.[13]

Scissor braces and simple collar-rafter roofs over stone buildings continued to be used over a long period (Figures 40, 41). At Chartham in 1303 the Christ Church Priory manor house, now The Deanery, had a roof of collar-rafter form with soulaces, and double collars in the area where the louvre may have been situated. Collars and soulaces also occur in the smaller range at Squerryes Lodge, perhaps, though not necessarily, dating to the mid 13th century, and in the smaller ranges of later houses such as the chapels of Old Soar of *c* 1290 and Ightham Mote of *c* 1342*. A very similar roof to that at Luddesdown Court, combining scissors and collars, is to be found over the earliest section of the hall range at Minster Abbey, Minster in Thanet, formerly a grange of St Augustine's Abbey. At Mersham Manor and Copton Manor, both Christ Church Priory manor houses, and Hoad Farm, Acrise, all probably built in the late 1320s or 1330s, scissor braces with no collars were used throughout the surviving ranges, those at Copton Manor (Figure 41a) lying over three ranges of markedly different size.[14] This suggests a relatively indiscriminate use of these simple roof types, although scissors alone, with no collars, may continue slightly later than the roofs with scissors and collars combined.

One other roof type without longitudinal stiffening occurred in early stone buildings in Kent. This was the crown-strut roof in which vertical posts were set at bay-length intervals between tie beam and collar. A roof of this form survives over the refectory of the Blackfriars, Canterbury. Money for building, including supplying timber for roofs, was obtained between 1237 and 1259, and it has been suggested that the basic form of the roof dates back to this period.[15] Outside Canterbury two examples were erected around the turn of the century. One lies over what may have been the great chamber of St Augustine's grange at Salmestone, dating either to the late 13th or very

*Figure 41 Scissor braces and crown struts: a) Copton Manor, Sheldwich. Scissor braces over hall; b) Court Lodge, Great Chart. Crown strut of open truss in hall.*

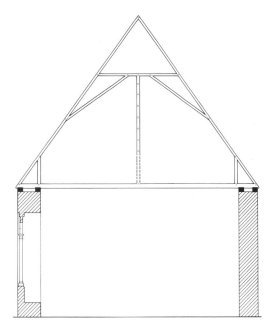

*a*

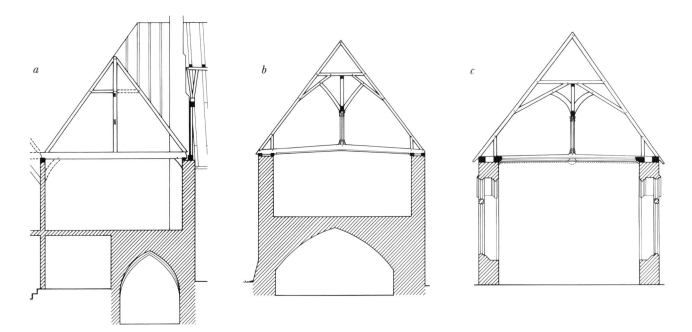

early 14th century. The other is over the hall of the Christ Church Priory manor house of Court Lodge, Great Chart, firmly dated to 1313 (Figure 41b).[16] Despite the fact that both buildings are rural, they belong, like so many of the scissor-braced and collar-rafter roofs discussed above, to the milieu of the great religious establishments in Canterbury, and may well have been built by the masons and carpenters employed there.

## King struts, crown posts and the introduction of longitudinal roof timbers

The date and means by which both vertical and longitudinal roof members first came to be used in England have long been debated. The questions concern both the possible influence of continental, particularly French and Flemish, buildings on English roofs during the 13th century, and the diffusion and development of roof types within England itself. These issues relate not only to buildings beyond the confines of Kent, but also to ecclesiastical as well as secular roofs.[17] Research during this project has not obviously contributed to the debate over ultimate origins, but it has revealed further information pertaining to the use and possible dates of the various forms in the late 13th and early 14th centuries within the county.

It has been suggested that a small group of Canterbury buildings dates to the third quarter of the 13th century.[18] The two most important are the 'Guest Hall' of St Augustine's Abbey and the 'Table Hall' of Christ Church Priory. Both have king-strut roofs with central posts rising to the apex of the rafters and a longitudinal timber or collar purlin tenoned into the posts, supporting the collars; at St Augustine's Abbey the ordinary trusses have double collars, at Christ Church Priory they are scissor braced. The king struts themselves are variously and elaborately braced to other timbers. Free-standing king struts, however

*Figure 42 King struts and crown posts: a) Salmestone Grange, Margate. King strut in timber range at south end of 14th-century hall; b) Old Soar, Plaxtol. Crown post above main chamber; c) Salmestone Grange, Margate. Crown post over chapel.*

handled, are not particularly common, and most of those which have so far come to light lie in south-east England, with a concentration in and around Canterbury. They almost certainly date to the first quarter of the 14th century or earlier, but whether they originate as early as the third quarter of the 13th century is perhaps open to question. Documentary evidence tends to support a date before 1283 for the building of the Table Hall, although the moulding profile of the timber wall plate and tie beam is more consistent with very late 13th or early 14th-century work.[19]

*Figure 43 Nurstead Court, Meopham. Crown post of open truss in hall.*

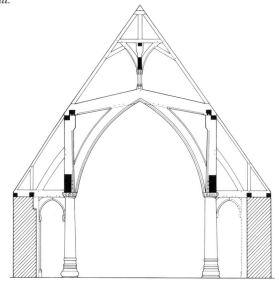

*Figure 44 Early crown posts and king struts: a) Old Soar, Plaxtol. Open truss over chamber, late 13th-century crown post (BB89/1938); b) Nurstead Court, Meopham. Crown post of open truss over hall, c 1309\* (BB64/1930); c) Hurst Farm, Chilham. Crown post of open truss over hall, early 14th century (BB86/713); d) Ratling Court, Aylesham. King strut over hall, early 14th century (BB90/5442); e) Gallants Manor, East Farleigh. End crown post over chamber, c 1322\* (BB86/3963); f) Court Lodge, Fawkham. Crown post of open truss over hall, early 14th century (BB89/10302).*

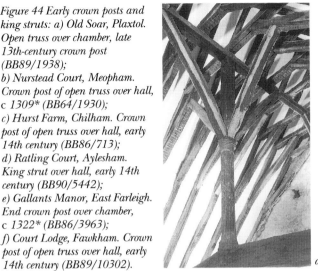

*a* *b* *c* *d* *e* *f*

At St Augustine's Abbey, the erection of the Guest Hall is undocumented and it can be dated only by an argument which takes the surrounding dated buildings into account, a procedure which can lead to a date in the 1260s, though the inference is by no means certain. Other members of the group are more likely to have been constructed around 1300. The chapel roof of the Eastbridge Hospital, Canterbury, which shares some characteristics with that over the Table Hall, has received a very tentative tree-ring date of c 1301.[20] In the course of the RCHME's work in Kent, only one new king-strut roof came to light. It is actually in an originally timber-framed building, but is closely related to the Canterbury group, lying over the earliest extant range of Salmestone Grange (Figure 42a). Dating is uncertain, but it is clear that the roof precedes the crown-strut roof over the 'great chamber' and that both roofs predate the chapel of 1326.

The final type of roof used over early stone buildings was the crown-post roof, in which a vertical post set upon a tie beam carried a longitudinal member or collar purlin which in turn supported the collars of the other trusses. Unlike the king strut, the post stopped short beneath the collar purlin. Normally it had a moulded cap and base and was braced to the collar purlin and to the collar or to soulaces beneath the collar. While it is obvious that surviving king-strut roofs preceded the vast majority of crown-post roofs, the original relationship between the two is still unclear. It

is generally agreed that the earliest known crown-post roofs in England are those over the Old Deanery, Salisbury, Wiltshire, and Manor Farm, Bourn, Cambridgeshire, both probably of the 1260s or 1270s.[21] A scattering of others have been claimed for the last two decades of the century, including one or two in Kent. There seems no reason to dispute the accepted date of c 1290 for the crown posts over the stone chamber at Old Soar, Plaxtol (Figures 42b, 44a) and, as discussed below, the crown post in the timber aisled hall at Ratling Court, Aylesham, has been dated to the last quarter of the 13th century.

The plausibility of this sort of dating for early examples has recently been reinforced by the tree-ring date of 1292/3\* for the timber-framed Old Rectory, Warbleton, East Sussex, where, although the crown post of the open truss has gone, evidence of its former presence remains.[22] In Kent itself the earliest crown post for which there is a tree-ring date is that at Nurstead Court of c 1309\* (Figures 43, 44b), where a second vertical timber rises above the collar of the open truss to a small yoke in a manner reminiscent of some of the king-strut roofs. Other relatively early examples, all set above stone or stone and timber ranges, are in the cross wing of Gallants Manor, East Farleigh, of c 1322\* (Figure 44e), in the chapel of Salmestone Grange (Figure 42c), consecrated in 1326, and in the hall and chamber ranges of the Old Rectory, Southfleet, and Ightham Mote, the latter built in the 1330s.

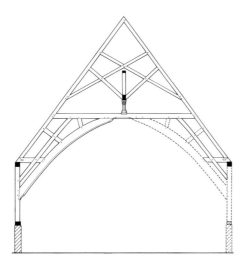

*Figure 45 Hurst Farm, Chilham. Open truss in hall with extended arch braces and crown post and scissor braces above.*

# Crown posts and king struts in timber buildings

One or two wholly timber-framed buildings with crown-post roofs may also date back to the years around 1300. Ratling Court, Aylesham, which combines king struts and crown posts within its aisled hall, has been claimed for the last quarter of the 13th century but could as easily date from the first decades of the 14th (Figure 44d).[23] The high braces from the king struts at the ends of the hall down to the collar purlin echo similar braces at both the Table Hall and the chapel at Eastbridge Hospital. On the other hand, at Hurst Farm, Chilham (Figures 44c, 45), which is an unaisled building, long arch braces rise to a raised tie beam, an arrangement which, like the use of a truncated tie beam with duplicate bracing below, is not dissimilar to features found at the Old Rectory, Warbleton, East Sussex. This roof also combines the crown post with scissor braces, a feature which is not common, although it occurs in one or two other houses, such as Old Cryals, Brenchley, and the reused roof over the open hall at Lynsted Court, Lynsted. Hurst Farm may well date to the decades to either side of 1300, the other examples are possibly a little later.[24]

Elsewhere crown-post roofs which show no such obviously 'early' characteristics are perhaps more likely to have been constructed in the 14th century. The crown post of the open truss at Court Lodge, Fawkham (Figure 44f), has a prominent jowl to one side of the collar purlin. This feature has been dated to the 13th or very early 14th century,[25] but nothing about the rest of the structure at Court Lodge (Figure 46) would suggest a date before 1300.

# The relationship between crown posts and king struts

That crown posts were known in Kent by the last decade of the 13th century and were relatively widely used in the first half of the 14th has been common knowledge for a long time. But what was perhaps not clear before was the extent to which the carpenters of the great religious houses in Canterbury avoided this form of roof for domestic ranges. The earliest domestic crown posts in the county all occur in secular buildings or over the halls of rectories. Despite the fact that nearly twenty domestic roofs of late 13th or early 14th-century date erected by Christ Church Priory and St Augustine's Abbey survive, both within Canterbury and the surrounding area, not one has crown posts until the chapel at Salmestone Grange, Margate, of 1326, and that is the only exception.[26] Later, in the years around 1400, both establishments used crown posts quite extensively, but by that time they were ubiquitous throughout Kent.[27] This suggests that a new dimension can be added to the discussion of king-strut and crown-post roofs in Kent and perhaps elsewhere, for it indicates not just that there was a surprising lack of interest in king-strut construction by other builders, something which was noted by Hewett,[28] but that the Canterbury workshops went their own way and themselves showed an even more surprising lack of interest in the new developments taking place elsewhere.

It is historically probable that some of the large and important buildings in Canterbury were erected earlier than the generally smaller buildings with crown posts found elsewhere, and, as the existence of domestic crown posts in Kent cannot be proved before the last decade of the 13th century, it is likely that some of the surviving king-strut roofs are earlier in date. But since crown posts are known elsewhere in England from the 1260s or 70s, and since no constructional development from king strut to crown post is visible in the roofs of the Canterbury workshops, no simple typological or chronological sequence can be charted within the county.

The Canterbury religious houses had numerous continental contacts, so the case that has been made for foreign influence on their roof carpentry is quite plausible.[29] But as far as one can tell, the stimulus to use crown-post construction in Kent is likely to have come from another direction. Two other possibilities come to mind. The first is the potential influence from crown-post roofs over Kentish churches, whose dates have not yet been studied in detail; and the second is the influence of earlier domestic buildings elsewhere in England, notably London. Since the London buildings have all gone, the matter of sources remains unresolved. But, whatever the case, Canterbury craftsmen took no part in this and continued to employ other roof types, often without longitudinal stiffening, throughout the first third of the 14th century. In the end they too adopted the crown post, but not until long after it was in general use throughout the south east.

# Base crucks and quasi-aisled construction in timber buildings

If the dating of Hurst Farm, Chilham, to the years around 1300 is correct, it indicates that some people were at that date already finding ways of constructing wide timber-framed halls without aisles. Hurst Farm, with a span of 8.5 m, is wider than the majority of aisled halls. In this case the building is totally without aisles, and is unique for its

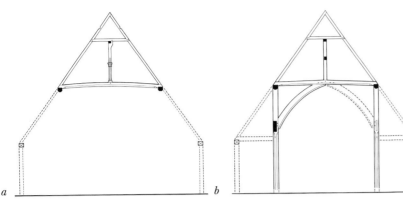

*Figure 46 Court Lodge, Fawkham. Cross sections in hall: a) Open truss; b) Spere truss.*

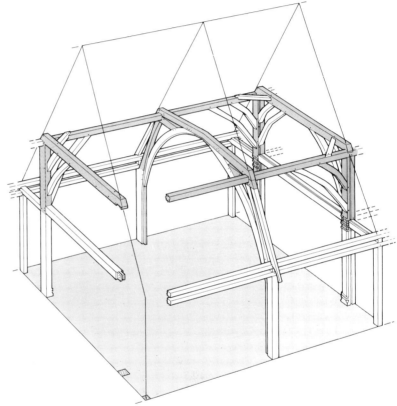

*Figure 47 Barnes Place, Hadlow. Reconstruction of base-cruck hall. The shaded areas indicate those timbers which survive, although the timbers of the base-cruck truss itself have been reused in a different arrangement (see* A Gazetteer of Medieval Houses in Kent *for measured drawing of existing truss).*

width, although another relatively early example of a slightly narrower undivided hall remains at Old Cryals, Brenchley. Elsewhere the closed trusses were still aisled, but the incentive to get rid of the arcade posts from the open truss led to a succession of experiments. At Court Lodge, Fawkham, an aisled spere truss reduced the length of the main hall area, so that the crown post and tie beam of the open truss could simply be carried by the arcade plates without further support below (Figure 46). Later, around 1400, a couple of buildings are known which replaced the arcade posts by extended arch braces to the external walls; these will be discussed in Chapter 7. But these were exceptional solutions. The normal way of removing free-standing posts from a two-bay hall was by means of base crucks, in which the open truss is formed by curved timbers that span the aisles and rise to the arcade plates.

The date of origin of base crucks and the question of whether they are related to true cruck construction has been debated on many occasions.[30] As is well known, no true cruck trusses have been found as far east in England as Kent. However, the number of known base crucks is growing slowly, as is the number of small, cruck-like members which occur at the ends of upper storeys to carry half-hipped roofs. The latter form appears to be essentially of 15th-century or later date, and will be discussed in Chapter 7. But the earliest examples of the former date to around 1300.

The earliest building of base-cruck construction so far discovered in Kent is probably Barnes Place, Hadlow. This has been considerably altered but enough remains to allow a reconstruction of the original form (Figure 47). The central truss had double tie beams clasping the arcade plates, and these plates and the tie beams of the end trusses were strengthened by massive paired braces. The present crown-post roof above may be an insertion of *c* 1400; if so, the form of the original upper roof is unknown.[31] The scantling of the timbers, the surviving details, and particularly the use of double ties and paired braces, suggest affinities with early buildings elsewhere, and in particular those of base-cruck construction such as West Bromwich Manor House, Staffordshire, recently tree-ring dated to *c* 1273*.[32] While there is no compelling reason to date Barnes Place quite so early, it was probably erected in the late 13th or very early 14th century.

Other buildings of base-cruck construction are more difficult to place. Tree-ring dating has, for a number of reasons, proved impossible, and since the form certainly continued well into the 15th century, a cautious approach to dating base crucks would be wise. Hamden, Smarden (Figure 32), has been assigned to the second quarter of the 14th century. The central truss, with double tie beams and blocking pieces, is not entirely dissimilar to Barnes Place, although other features, including the presence of a contemporary cross wing and the details of the crown-post trusses, might suggest a somewhat later date. Little Moat Cottage, East Peckham (Figure 48), could also have originated in the first half of the 14th century, but other examples are less easily datable; the small size and close proximity of buildings such as Burnt Oak and Nightingale Farmhouse, both in the hamlet of Benover in Yalding parish, may mean that they were not constructed until late in the 14th century, although they are unlikely to be later than that. These will be discussed further in Chapters 6 and 7, alongside those whose structural or stylistic details imply dates well into the 15th century.

At the moment only about half a dozen houses of base-cruck construction have been found in the county which could date from the 14th century; to which may be added the excavated house at Joydens Wood. However, this type of construction may have been commoner than is now supposed. The three-bay hall at Crundale House, Crundale, has closed trusses of aisled form and an open truss which is likely to have formed a spere. The central truss is marked only by a tie beam carrying the arcade plates above it in reversed assembly. The beam is embedded in a partition, and there are no signs of mortices below – certainly there are no pegs for braces to free-standing arcade posts. It is possible that this indicates a truss of base-cruck construction. If so, it raises the possibility that wherever open trusses have been removed from halls in which closed trusses were aisled, base crucks might have been used. It has, for example, been assumed that the central truss of Dormer Cottage, Petham, was of fully aisled form.[33] Probably it was, but since no evidence for its original arrangement is currently visible, this cannot be proved, and the alternative cannot be ruled out.

The three earliest firmly identified base crucks, at Barnes Place, Hadlow, Little Moat Cottage, East Peckham, and Hamden, Smarden, have been included among the quasi-aisled buildings illustrated on Figure 16 and discussed in Chapter 3. To these could be added three more, in Yalding on the Medway and Speldhurst on the Sussex border, which have not been mapped because they may be slightly later in date. All six lie in the Weald of south-west or central Kent. It is true that the postulated base cruck at Crundale House is

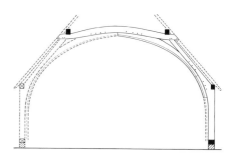

*Figure 48 Little Moat Cottage, East Peckham. Partial reconstruction of base-cruck truss in open hall.*

in the Stour valley, and that at Joydens Wood lies in north-west Kent, but these unconfirmed examples apart, it is not until later, in the 15th century, that base crucks occur in the north or north east of the county. This is in marked contrast to the distribution of early aisled halls.

## The origins of base-cruck construction

It has been noted that in England generally base crucks are normally associated with those of high rank.[34] Stone-walled examples were often built by barons or wealthy religious establishments, and in Kent the hall of Cobham College falls into this category. Among timber-framed structures many were manor houses or rectories. But, in Kent at least, those who opted for base crucks were not exactly the same sort of people as those whose halls were fully aisled. As discussed in Chapter 3, early aisled halls occur in the more highly manorialised northern part of the county, on estates whose feudal origins probably go back to the Conquest or beyond. In contrast, the earliest base crucks may not have been associated with manor houses and are found in areas where the estates are likely to have been granted relatively recently. This is perhaps given support by the postulated example at Joydens Wood, where the excavations revealed no evidence of any building preceding that which may have been constructed with base crucks. The implication appears to be that on sites such as Ratling Court, Aylesham, whose history can be traced back to the 11th century, those who built the present aisled halls were either constricted by the presence of earlier buildings, or hidebound by the conventions of their long ancestry; whereas the new men who erected Barnes Place, Hadlow, or Hamden, Smarden, may have been building the first structure on the site, unhindered by any physical or psychological burdens from the past.

Considered on their own, these observations tend to support the view that base crucks emerged late, rather than the view that their history stretched back several centuries.[35] In purely Kentish terms, it is tempting to see their origins entirely outside the cruck tradition, and simply as part of the development of aisled halls: at very much the same time as the first base crucks appear, other halls, often on sites which are likely to have been established for a long time, were beginning, at least at the open truss, to be spanned by alternative constructions without aisles. Although it is unclear why some people chose base crucks, and others used extended arch braces, or spere trusses and unsupported tie beams, all these solutions seem to be experiments in overcoming the structural predicament encountered when removing intrusive arcade posts from the centre of the aisled hall. The idea that base crucks were used to modify aisled halls is not new. The question is whether this is the result of one long-standing tradition intruding upon another, or whether it represents independent invention. It is a thorny problem which cannot be solved in terms of Kent alone, but it is worth noting that in this county at least new structural forms, such as extended arch braces, were

invented at this time. It is difficult to see why base crucks alone should be considered outside the context of other solutions.

In the late 14th century, structural methods received a radical shake up as new ways of creating open halls were devised, and the necessity for aisling of any kind disappeared. Both fully aisled and base-cruck structures continued to be erected for a long time, but they became old-fashioned and out of favour with anyone who aspired to be up-to-date. Their later history was largely confined to smaller houses in certain parts of the county.

# 6 The evolution of the late medieval house

All the surviving evidence suggests that not much house building took place in the mid 14th century, that is from the 1340s to about 1370. A number of houses can be dated to the first third of the 14th century, or have characteristics in common with those which can be dated to that time, and tree-ring dating conclusively proves that many more were erected in the last third of the century. However, very few can be ascribed to the intervening period with any degree of confidence.

New houses start appearing again around 1370, but there are differences between these new houses and those that remain from the early 14th century. In contrast to the earlier period, building in stone had virtually ceased, and the majority of new houses were timber framed. New types occur, which no longer used aisles or base crucks in their construction. For the first time in timber buildings, storeyed accommodation at the ends of the hall remains as frequently as the open hall itself, and the location and density of the survivors contrast markedly with the earlier pattern of distribution.

These new types have sometimes been presented as if they emerged fully formed. That there were differences between them and what went before is indicated by the fact that they have survived where their predecessors have not. But whether this means that they were the first houses to have the potential to last indefinitely is another matter. It is argued below that they are most likely to have developed from structures built of timbers which were sturdy enough to guarantee a long life so long as they remained acceptable to the taste of later generations and were left alone. In the event they were found wanting, and most of them, whether they preceded or were contemporary with the new types of timber-framed house, have been demolished. However, enough evidence for them remains for their form and the reasons for their replacement to be discussed. The houses which now constitute the bulk of late medieval domestic architecture in the county were nearly all the result of new initiatives which made their appearance in the late 14th century or soon after. These can be classified by date, type and size, the three headings being so closely connected as to suggest that they reflect differences in the resources and requirements of their owners. As the variations are critical to any understanding of historical development, they will be examined in some detail.

## Late medieval house types

The new types are all variants on a common theme, that is a house with an open hall in the centre and private rooms at either end. Earlier houses had contained this same basic accommodation, but there were differences. The most important of these were the replacement of the aisled or quasi-aisled form by single-span construction, and the general introduction of sizeable first-floor chambers at each end of the open hall. Where the subsidiary accommodation lay within the same range as the hall, the second of these changes could not have taken place without the first, and it brought with it the heightening of the external walls in both the storeyed accommodation and in the hall itself. Once this was accepted, the way was open for buildings to be designed in new ways. The results may be classified by type. Since the number and layout of rooms in each type remain remarkably standard, classification might be thought to be entirely cosmetic, but in fact the differences are more than superficial, for the types are distinguishable by size and by date, suggesting that they were not chosen arbitrarily but had some social and economic significance.

Figure 49 illustrates the types which were found at this time. The first (Figure 49a and b) was the hall and cross wing, in which the subsidiary accommodation lies in separate ranges placed at right angles at one or both ends of the hall. The earlier form (Figure 49a), with a low hall and hipped wing or wings, almost certainly developed from earlier timber buildings. But by the late 14th century the hall was no longer aisled and the wing or wings had two full storeys. Figure 49b illustrates the form of cross-wing house with a higher hall which became commoner as the 15th century progressed. The wings might occur at one or both ends and were sometimes gabled. The cross wing is not a form normally associated with Kent, but it was, in fact, extremely important, used in nearly a quarter of the county's surviving medieval buildings. The rest of the identifiable types lie under a single, overall roof with the ends placed in line with the hall. This arrangement has always been considered quintessentially Kentish.[1] Within the overall form houses can be classed by whether the end bays projected at the front (Wealdens, Figure 49c and d), at the ends only (end jetties, Figure 49e) or not at all (unjettied, Figure 49f). In addition to the illustrated examples there are other houses, again forming about

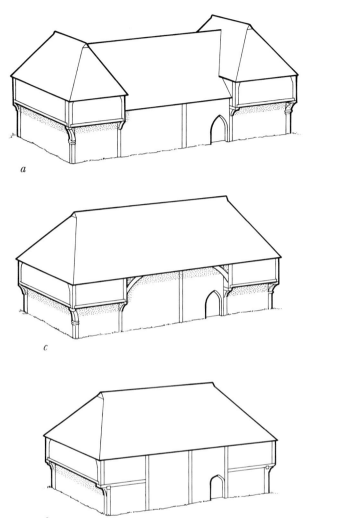

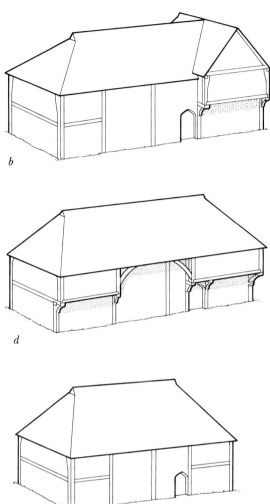

*Figure 49 Simplified diagram of types of late medieval house. The detailed arrangements may be variously combined: a) Hall and two cross wings, with hipped roofs; b) Hall and gabled cross wing, with upper end in-line; c) Wealden house, jettied to front and ends, with entry into hall; d) Wealden house, jettied to front only, with entry into passage overshot by lower-end chamber; e) End-jetty house, jettied at both ends; f) Unjettied house.*

a quarter of the total, in which only the hall survives, or else the remains are too limited to be classified.

The contrast between the many late medieval examples which fall readily into well-defined categories, and the fragmentary and inconclusive remains of subsidiary accommodation in timber houses of the 13th and first half of the 14th centuries, is so striking as hardly to need emphasis. It is therefore appropriate, before discussing any of the new types in detail, to begin by asking how and why new house forms emerged and whether they retain any sign of what preceded them.

## The partial survival of houses

It is important to realise that the homogeneous timber-framed house was a rarity, at least before the very end of the Middle Ages. None of the rural houses built in Kent before the Black Death has survived as anything more than a fragment, and even when building began again in earnest few houses were constructed in a single campaign. More than half the houses recorded in the course of this project contain more than one phase. This does not mean that they were simply enlarged later on, although that sometimes happened, but that the earliest surviving section was formerly part of a larger whole. Sometimes what has gone was probably contemporary with what is left, but since so many houses are now of two, three or even more periods, it is likely that piecemeal building was almost the norm, and that parts were replaced as and when necessary. It follows that we are seldom looking at the first building on the site, merely the earliest extant component left from a continuous sequence of reconstruction. Multi-phase construction became rarer as time went by, but it applies to over 70 per cent of all houses whose earliest phase dates from the late 14th or early 15th century, and only declines thereafter when more houses were completed in a single campaign. Some of those whose first surviving phase was erected around 1400 were updated before the Middle Ages were over; others appear not to have been modernised until the late 16th or 17th century or even later.

The question of whether the earliest houses surviving in any number within a region are the first substantial and permanent buildings to have been put up has been discussed by a number of writers. In recent years the view that earlier structures must have been flimsy or impermanent has been questioned.[2] Once timber walls were built on stone foundations rather than with earth-fast posts, impermanence is likely to have been caused by inadequate construction of the superstructure rather than by deterioration from ground level upwards. In some parts of the country, solid foundations and long-lasting peasant buildings have been claimed from the 13th century onwards.[3] Thus it is necessary to ask whether large numbers of buildings have vanished in Kent which could have survived and if so, what they were like and why they were replaced.

One of the features noted about timber houses built before the mid 14th century was the selective way in which they survived: considerable evidence exists for open halls, but almost none for ancillary accommodation. In the late 14th and 15th centuries surviving structures are more varied. Out of seventy-one houses of which part can be dated between *c* 1370 and *c* 1440, eleven have hall ranges surviving alone; fourteen had wings or ends remaining without their halls; and two consist of cross wings added to earlier open halls, the form of whose original secondary accommodation is unclear. In all other cases the hall survives with at least one subsidiary end, although only nineteen appear to be complete dwellings of a single period. The partial nature of the survival of the majority suggests the piecemeal replacement of earlier ranges. Very few have any trace of the structures which were rebuilt, so the question of whether these were solid or flimsy, permanent or impermanent, is not easily resolved.

However, this is not true in all cases, and an accumulation of evidence of varying kinds implies that a large number of well-built structures may have been swept away because they became redundant. The signs are that this was not something which happened at one particular moment, for the parts which were demolished dated from the 15th century as well as from earlier periods, and they were replaced both during and after the Middle Ages.

Until the new types of house with higher external walls and upper storeys became generally available in the later Middle Ages, timber-framed houses, even if solidly built, were likely to have a number of features which came to be seen as handicaps when expectations changed, and these reduced their chances of survival as complete entities. Some houses had only one such defect, some two, others as many as three; and few if any of the latter are likely to remain today. Clearly, when the houses were built, these features were not handicaps. The shortcomings became apparent only with changing demands, perhaps already during the Middle Ages, but more often not until later. There were several critical periods for the survival of a house on its road to the present day.

## The insertion of first floors in low open halls

One problem, which only became apparent after the Middle Ages, surfaced with the desire to put an enclosed fireplace into the open hall. The insertion of the chimney, which was quickly followed by the floor dividing the hall into two storeys, led to greater warmth, created an additional chamber and enabled communication right across the house at first-floor level. This change took place in almost all surviving medieval buildings, but it did not happen overnight. Open halls began to be superseded by fully storeyed ones in the early 16th century, and the flooring over of formerly open halls probably began shortly

*Figure 50 Double aisled halls with one aisle later removed to create a vertical wall for first-floor windows: a) Lacton Manor, Westwell. Section through hall; b) Bardingley Farmhouse, Sutton Valence. The new front wall after demolition of the original aisle (BB86/1249).*

*a*       *b*

*Figure 51 Old Hall, Petham. A low hall and single-storey upper end, with lower-end cross wing (BB91/2704).*

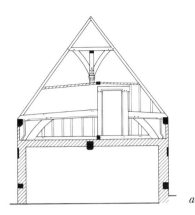

*Figure 52 Lower Newlands, Teynham: a) Cross section through open truss after insertion of first floor; b) West elevation (BB86/5423).*

after. But the change to fully two-storeyed dwellings took a long time to complete.[4] Most remaining medieval houses in Kent are tall enough to incorporate an upper floor without difficulty, but it is here contended that there were once many others in which this change was not possible.

Until the late 14th century most houses appear to have been aisled or quasi-aisled. Unless they were of considerable size, they presented overwhelming problems when the need for a first floor arose, for if the tie beam of an aisled hall was too low to pass beneath after the first floor was inserted, then use of the new first-floor space was at worst impossible and at best severely restricted. Only the taller and larger aisled structures were probably worth retaining: in sizeable aisled halls the first floor could be lit by removing one aisle, thus disposing of a useless triangle of roof space and creating a vertical wall in which to put windows. This alter-ation affected aisled halls of all dates (Figure 50). Occasionally the aisle walls were totally rebuilt. This might be done by narrowing and consequently heightening the aisles, as at Ratling Court, Aylesham, and Barnes Place, Hadlow, a practice which was apparently common in Essex;[5] or by removing both aisles and arcades altogether and heightening the old external walls, as occurred at Divan Court, Eastling, where the only sign of the former aisled hall lies above the tie beam in the roof over the central span. All these are sizeable houses with high-set arcade plates; but not all solidly built aisled or base-cruck halls were as large as this. Houses in which the tie beams were lower, like Dormer Cottage, Petham (Figure 34), and Nightingale Farmhouse, Yalding (Figure 56), were virtually impossible to adapt. At Dormer Cottage the open truss and all that lay to one side of it has gone, leaving only a minute first-floor room over the hall, with a cupboard beyond the surviving closed truss. At Nightingale Farmhouse everything except one base-cruck truss has been demolished or rebuilt. Very few other aisled halls as tiny as this have survived, but whether they were always rare is another matter.

Halls did not have to be aisled for the addition of a first floor to be awkward, as can be demonstrated by illustrating what happened to other low halls, mostly of rather later date. The Old Hall, Petham (Figure 51), and Lower

Newlands, Teynham, of c 1380* (Figure 52), are unusually complete houses in which first floors were inserted into low open halls. At Old Hall the problem was overcome by removing the tie beam of the open truss, cutting off the base of the crown post and jacking up the remains on an inserted collar. At Lower Newlands the solution was to cut through the tie beam and support the cut ends on the jambs of a new doorway. In this case the open truss was the only part to cause a problem, because the crown posts at the end of the hall were supported on high wall plates to the wings. A similar arrangement occurred at the cross-wing end of Old Hall, Petham, but at the upper end, where the inner bay was originally open, separate stairs were required when a chamber was inserted. This was not very convenient for the occupants and is not often found today.

Yet it is seldom that more than one truss was ever cut through, suggesting that when that was necessary, an alter-native solution was found which solved the problem without the risk of destabilising the structure. It is noticeable that several surviving houses with very low tie beams have been divided into two occupations, for example at Hill Crest and

Kent Cottage, Staplehurst, of *c* 1389*, and Peartree Cottages, Loose (Figure 53). In neither case is it known when this occurred, but the fact that it was unnecessary to cut away at least one of the tie beams may indicate that the division was contemporary with or earlier than the insertion of the floor. This is not to suggest that dividing

*Figure 53 Peartree Cottages, Loose. Low hall divided into two occupations on line of open truss; the further end, to the right, has been largely rebuilt (BB92/15194).*

*Figure 54 Harts Farmhouse, Molash. Former open truss against chimney stack which now forms the end of the house (BB88/8022).*

the house was a solution to the problem, only that where this happened it may have prevented more radical measures such as total or partial demolition. In a number of houses with low halls only one bay survives, the second bay and all beyond it being demolished. Usually the open truss remains against a chimney stack added against the newly created gable wall, as at Harts Farmhouse, Molash, of *c* 1466* (Figure 54), where subsidiary accommodation is provided in a tall cross wing of the same date as the hall. At Southenay Cottage, Sellindge (Figure 55), the focus of the house shifted to the surviving end which was rebuilt and enlarged in the 16th century.

In all these adaptations the original range was just high enough for it to be worth preserving. But in some houses this was not the case. At Nightingale Farmhouse, Yalding (Figure 56), a base-cruck truss remains at the rear of a later chimney stack. The original wall plate, at 2.1 m high, lies only just above the later floor level, and this, together with the slightly higher arcade plates running the length

*Figure 55 Southenay Cottage, Sellindge: a) Cross section through low open truss showing added chimney stack; b) View from north west showing chimney stack, now forming the end of the house (BB86/2845).*

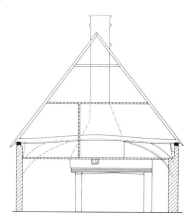

*a*

*b*

of the open hall, made straightforward insertion of a first floor impossible. From the moment the decision was taken to insert the floor and build a timber stack, the old hall structure was doomed. The upper-end accommodation, of unknown form, was rebuilt as a wing destroying the closed truss of the hall; the arcade plates were removed, the walls heightened and the roof completely renewed. Later the front wall was totally rebuilt and raised again, and an even taller wing was added beyond the cross wing. But the fact that the inserted chimney utilised part of the open truss, and that the lower end of the house was demolished so that no way through was required, allowed the base-cruck truss to survive. About half a dozen fragments of this sort have been found. Often they were once part of a closed truss from one end of the former open hall which was left behind to support a wall or a chimney as the range first to one side, then the other, was rebuilt.[6]

*Figure 56 Nightingale Farmhouse, Yalding: a) Cross section through base-cruck truss, formerly in centre of open hall, with added timber chimney; b) Exterior of present house with former base cruck and timber chimney in the gabled sliver to the right. The hall range has been heightened (twice), and a wing added to the left (BB88/3749).*

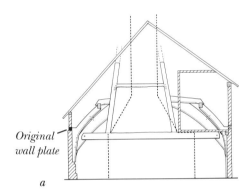

*Original wall plate*

*a*

*b*

*Figure 57 Rype Cottage, Lydd. A low single-aisled open hall. One end was originally lofted over, the other may have been open (BB87/8244).*

## The heightening of low halls with open ends-in-line

The second handicap which early or low buildings faced was the growing desire for adequate subsidiary accommodation. As discussed in Chapter 4, despite the fact that two-storeyed chamber ranges were common in early stone houses, very few ends or wings survive in timber houses in Kent erected before the late 14th century. In the late 14th and early 15th centuries the situation changed. Many houses were built in which halls and ends survive together, and in addition a number of ends or wings remain without their contemporary halls. The earliest surviving cross wings are usually tall and often well detailed, as at Old Moat Farmhouse, Chart Sutton (Figure 103a), where a fully two-storeyed wing of *c* 1377* was jettied on three sides, had a crown-post roof, and quarter-round mouldings to all the main timbers on the first floor, including the original window frames. A number of

*Figure 58 Ashby Cottage, Westbere. A rare survival of a low open hall. One of the end bays was also open, the other was originally lofted over (BB92/14337).*

wings of this quality were built around this time; among them, a three-bay wing which replaced an older end to the early aisled hall at Chilton Manor, Sittingbourne; in this case we may infer that the old end was already perceived to be inadequate. As already suggested, one reason for this was that many early ends lay in line with the hall and were aisled, hipped and open to the roof, a combination which it was peculiarly difficult to update without rebuilding.

Open ends-in-line continued to be built during the 15th century. In some cases they occur in aisled buildings which, when they were as low as Rype Cottage, Lydd (Figure 57), could be just as awkward to adapt as their predecessors. Others were not aisled. Survivors range from the Old Hall, Petham (Figure 51), where it was just possible to create a small chamber, to Ashby Cottage, Westbere (Figure 58), which had a single-bay open hall, an open end, and an end which was originally lofted over. Ashby Cottage was probably only built *c* 1500, and is an extremely rare but valuable survival of a house which never had a first floor inserted in either the hall or the open end bay. Although

*Figure 59 The heightening of low open halls: a) Well Cottage, Detling. Cross section showing heightened walls and reset roof; b) The Old Farmhouse, Speldhurst. The original posts and wall plates (to the left) remained when taller posts and new wall plates were added (BB89/9806).*

Hearth area of inserted smoke bay

*a*

*b*

hardly any houses of this sort remain today, it seems likely that the arrangement was once common, and its existence indicates that some at least of the houses with open bays and wall heights of only 2 m – 3 m were well built and perfectly capable of survival, provided they were kept in good repair or were not pulled down to make way for something more commodious.

It was possible to heighten the walls of a low building without destroying all of the original, and this occasionally happened. Sometimes new and taller posts were added at each end to carry a higher wall plate, as in the hall at The Old Farmhouse, Speldhurst (Figure 59b). Otherwise short lengths of new post were set on the old wall plate to support a new one above, as occurred throughout Well Cottage, Detling (Figure 59a), and at The Dragon House, Smarden, as well as in a short stretch of the rear wall of Nightingale Farmhouse, Yalding. Either way the roof had to be rebuilt, even if the timbers were reused, as at Well Cottage. Very few examples of such updating have been found, and it seems that it was usually considered less trouble to rebuild the house altogether.

## The problem of low ground-floor rooms in storeyed ends

A third handicap concerns the possibility that some of the earliest two-storeyed timber-framed ranges had chambers set above such low undercrofts that it was considered necessary to alter them before the end of the Middle Ages. At Coppwilliam, Staplehurst (Figure 60), a single-aisled hall with a contemporary two-storeyed cross wing has been dated 1370/1*. The building has lost its original roof and with it any evidence for a second end or wing, and it has been cased in brick. Both in the former open hall and in the surviving storeyed end, the ground-floor ceilings are only 1.7 m, or 5½ ft, high. However, in the wing the ceiling seems to have been raised from an original height of 1.3 m, or just over 4 ft. If this interpretation is correct then the ground floor of the wing could never have provided normal living or service accommodation, and was probably used for storage. The wing was jettied, certainly to the front and possibly to the side as well, which means that before the introduction of brick walls to take new joists, it was virtually impossible to heighten the ceiling without rebuilding the entire wing.

The example of Coppwilliam raises the possibility that other early timber houses may have had storeyed ends whose ground-floor height was so low that the rooms beneath functioned only as undercrofts. This is the only house so far found in the county with clear evidence for a ceiling height as low as 1.3 m. But an equally low undercroft has been found at The Cottage, Aston Tirrold, Oxfordshire, which has been tree-ring dated to the late 13th century,[7] and in Kent this may be the reason why almost no timber cross wings built before the late 14th century survive. A number of later medieval houses had ground-floor ceilings of 1.5 m – 1.7 m which were heightened subsequently. These ranged from poor, low buildings such as Rype Cottage, Lydd, or Ashby Cottage, Westbere (Figures 57, 58), where the increased height meant that the original loft which lay at one end was dispensed with altogether, to higher quality examples like The Fleete House, Smarden,

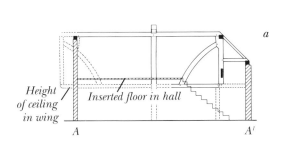

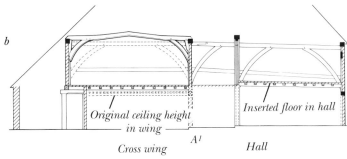

*Figure 60 Coppwilliam, Staplehurst: a) Long section of cross wing, and b) long section of hall and cross section of cross wing, showing the exceptionally low original ceiling level in the cross wing.*

and Divers Farmhouse, East Sutton (Figure 61). Here very low ground-floor rooms persisted in fully fledged end-jetty and Wealden houses. At The Fleete House the lowest ceiling, of approximately 1.5 m, lay in an unjettied end, and it was not too difficult to raise the joists while retaining the timber walls. At Divers Farmhouse, which is a Wealden formerly with jetties to the front and to one end, both storeyed bays had ceiling heights of about 1.7 m which could not have been raised until the external walls were rebuilt in brick in the 17th century.[8] It seems likely that the difficulties faced in heightening jettied construction before the walls were rebuilt in brick may have led to many timber-framed ends with exceptionally low ground-floor ceilings being totally demolished and replaced.

## The implications of partial survival

Most of the houses discussed above were altered only in the 16th century or later. Demonstrating that low open halls, or low storeyed ends, were found wanting after the Middle Ages is a different issue from proving that such buildings were replaced by loftier open-hall houses as early as the 15th century. This affects the origin of the Wealden, for unless it can be shown that Wealden houses superseded earlier solidly built dwellings, then the theory that the first surviving structure on a site – eg a Wealden – is the first permanent house to have been built there is hard to refute.

Several of the recorded 15th-century open halls were erected against earlier ends, and since these ends clearly never stood alone, they must have accompanied earlier halls which were replaced later. At The Blue House, East Sutton (Figure 62), a Wealden hall and upper end of *c* 1468* was added to an earlier cross wing, probably dating from the early 15th century. A similar cross wing and Wealden sequence occurred at Tudor House, Chislet

*Figure 62 The Blue House, East Sutton. Cross wing (to left) and added Wealden hall and upper end of* c *1468* (BB87/8268).*

*Figure 61 Divers Farmhouse, East Sutton. Long section indicating original ceiling levels in end bays.*

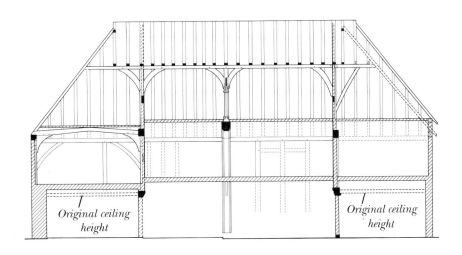

*Figure 63 Spoute House, Plaxtol. An end-jetty house built in two phases: right-hand end, c 1424\*; hall and left-hand end, c 1445\* (BB87/1089).*

(Figure 69a). In other instances the earlier end was not a wing but lay in line with the new hall. At Hadley House, Smarden, the old end had an aisle at the rear; at Spoute House, Plaxtol (Figures 63, 68j), a jetted lower-end bay of *c* 1424\* had a hall and upper-end bay added in *c* 1445\*, and similar sequences can be found elsewhere.[9] Occasionally, as at Biddenden Green Farmhouse, Smarden, the new open hall lies between two ends or wings which date from a generation or two before. In none of these instances is there any trace of the earlier open halls, which suggests that they were structurally separate from, and therefore probably earlier than, the surviving ends.

To discover what these earlier halls were like, one is thrown back on putting the different pieces of evidence together and asking what is most likely to have occurred. In examples such as Chilton Manor, Sittingbourne, and Ratling Court, Aylesham, cross wings dating to the late 14th or 15th century were added to earlier aisled halls which still survive. The quality of these wings is little different from that of other cross wings whose medieval halls have disappeared without trace, and it is extremely unlikely that late 14th-century wings such as those at Rooting Manor, Little Chart, or Exhurst, Staplehurst, were added to halls of lesser quality than those at Chilton Manor or Ratling Court. But these wings are among the largest to survive, and both

house names and documentary evidence suggest that the buildings were above the status of average farmhouses. However, there is evidence that at least in some parts of Kent, as in the parish of Chart Sutton, similar buildings were erected by yeomen or wealthy peasants.

In Chart Sutton three early two-bay cross wings survive, at Old Moat Farmhouse of *c* 1377\*, at Dunbury Farmhouse of *c* 1400, and White House Farmhouse, probably built in the first third of the 15th century. At White House Farmhouse, the hall was rebuilt in the 16th century and the only clue to its earlier form lies in mortices on the corner posts of the wing, which seem to indicate where the wall plates of a low hall were once housed. At Old Moat Farmhouse the open hall, which was either earlier than or contemporary with the surviving wing, was also rebuilt in the 16th century, but its rafters and collars were reused over the new hall range; they show that the previous hall had crown posts with a separate king strut above the collar of the central truss, in a manner not dissimilar to the much grander version surviving at Nurstead Court. This implies that a hall of some consequence, which may have been aisled, was replaced.

At Dunbury Farmhouse an enigmatic single-aisled hall of earlier date than the wing remains; neither its date nor its precise form are clear, but for present purposes this hardly matters. The important point is that it precedes the wing and its timbers are as solid as those of the next phase. In addition to these early wings the parish contains the earliest known Wealden house, at Chart Hall (formerly Chart Bottom) Farmhouse, dated 1379/80\*, and the surrounding

66

parishes of Staplehurst, Sutton Valence and East Sutton also have a number of early houses.[10] They include an archaic aisled hall at Bardingley Farmhouse, Sutton Valence, as well as several late 14th or early 15th-century buildings in which halls and ends survive together and in isolation. Although the majority are larger than average for the county, none of them, with the exception of Exhurst, Staplehurst, is likely to have been of manorial status.

Given the exceptional quality of the surviving work of the late 14th and early 15th centuries in this area and the clear evidence of substantial early halls at Bardingley Farmhouse, Dunbury Farmhouse and Old Moat Farmhouse, it is difficult to imagine that the owners of any of these houses were making do with impermanent structures for their now demolished ranges; this includes The Blue House, East Sutton (Figure 62), where the hall which served the cross wing of the early 15th century was rebuilt as a Wealden as early as c 1468*.

As will be discussed later, the evidence from this part of Kent is of a slightly different order from that found elsewhere in the county since far more medieval houses of high quality remain. But this, in fact, is an important part of the argument. It may well be that the poorest medieval houses in the county, buildings such as Southenay Cottage, Sellindge, or Ashby Cottage, Westbere, replaced impermanent structures of which all trace has gone: the work has not yet been done which can prove or disprove this point. However, given the evidence of the rebuilt low open halls and low storeyed ends discussed above, it would be quite remarkable, not to say unmedieval, if the larger houses, such as the Wealdens, made this transition from impermanence in one go. The various strands of evidence combine to suggest that a much larger number of low houses once existed, both low halls with storeyed wings, and low ranges including open halls and open-end bays, than survives today.

The signs are that many such structures were solidly built with timbers which were no less substantial than those of surviving dwellings, and there seem to be no purely structural reasons why such buildings could not have survived; however, there are several reasons why they may have been found inadequate by the better-off among the yeomanry or peasantry. Few of them will have been complete dwellings of a single date, and at some point in the continual see-saw of piecemeal rebuilding which had undoubtedly taken place, the transition from impermanent to permanent had been made. When this happened we still cannot surmise, but it is here suggested that this change did not immediately precede the invention of the new forms in the late 14th century.

As early as the late 14th century the limitations of some of the older structural forms were recognised, and experiments were being made with two new types of design. In the first place taller cross wings with more commodious ground-floor accommodation were added to update low hall ranges. This catered for the new requirements most easily, and was probably the earliest solution, but it often resulted in the destruction of the old-style hall range in the 16th or 17th century when it proved impossible to adapt. The second and more novel solution, most readily accepted where circumstances required most if not all of a house to be rebuilt, was to raise the height of the wall plates to incorporate both a high open hall and a fully two-storeyed end under a single overall roof. This led to a higher hall than before and to the introduction of the standard types of medieval house, the

Wealden and the end jetty, which are now considered to be so essentially Kentish. Unforeseen by their builders, these houses proved easy to adapt to later living standards with plenty of room for inserting first floors and even attics. As a result there was little reason to rebuild them in toto.

The new types became popular only gradually, and the vast majority were not built until the second half of the 15th century. As we shall see, Wealden and end-jetty houses together account for over half the surviving open-hall houses built after c 1370, but it is unlikely that they formed such a high proportion of the houses built during the Middle Ages;[11] throughout the 15th century it is almost certain that these new designs lay alongside a far larger number of less impressive, low dwellings. Some of these may have been impermanent, but many must have been just as well built, and some had been partially updated by the addition of tall cross wings. The subsequent discussion, in which numbers, types and dates of surviving medieval houses are analysed, is necessarily concerned with the implications of what survives. It is difficult to bear in mind the many buildings which have disappeared, but unless this is done, our picture of late medieval housing in Kent will be distorted.

# The pattern of late medieval development

By the end of the survey of medieval houses in Kent, records of 477 buildings, judged to date from after about 1370, were available for examination. Among the total were a number of fully two-storeyed buildings as well as some designed for special purposes, and others which were fragmentary survivals of uncertain form. However, 379 of them were open-hall houses, and these have been analysed from various points of view to obtain a picture of the development and distribution of buildings in the county dating between c 1370 and c 1540. Not all the houses are relevant to all the calculations. Some are virtually undatable and cannot be used to plot developments through time. Others have more than one phase, each of which can be used for different purposes. In addition, a number of houses which were not recorded at all have been included on occasion: for example, a Wealden to which access was refused may be used for statistical purposes relating to numbers of surviving medieval houses, or to the distribution of Wealdens, but it has to be excluded from those concerned with the date or size of houses. Thus the number of buildings which occur in the following figures varies. Fully floored houses and special-purpose buildings have been excluded. The number of two-storeyed houses recorded is not large, and no systematic coverage of them was attempted, so analysis of their introduction and distribution is necessarily sketchy and is dealt with separately.

## The chronology of surviving houses

In order to discuss the development of open-hall houses in the later Middle Ages, it is necessary first to address the question of dating. This was done by using tree-ring dated buildings to provide a framework within which to assign dates to all other buildings. The evidence of the tree-ring dates is fully discussed in Appendix 1. In order to be able to chart changes over time, each building, or phase of building, was given a date range, usually of forty years or less, although this was by no means always feasible. Those structures which could be assigned a forty-year date range were then, for the purposes of calculation, given a mid date, and this is the one that has been used for all calculations in which date plays a part.

The first of these, illustrated in Figure 64, plots the incidence of building by decade. The actual number of usable buildings is 378; but since some houses were of more than one date, major structural phases have been enumerated separately, bringing the number of examples on the diagram up to 405. The darker shade on the diagram has been used to indicate those houses recorded in the sixty parishes in which survey work was concentrated. When all reservations have been taken into account, the results from these parishes are less random than those from elsewhere. Thus they have been shaded separately, and it is likely that the pattern they reveal is a more accurate reflection of what was occurring than the total sample from the whole county. It is obvious that giving buildings apparently precise dates by means of mid dates is bound to produce inaccuracies. Nonetheless, provided no results are taken as absolute, this is the clearest way to demonstrate change over time.

After the complete absence of new buildings dating from the mid 14th century, Figure 64 shows that new houses from *c* 1370 start to survive again. The absolute numbers in each decade may not be enormous, but the difference from the earlier situation is noticeable enough to be significant.

*Figure 64 The numbers of open-hall houses. The diagram illustrates the number of recorded houses, or phases of houses, built in each decade between 1370 and 1549.*

However, in the early 15th century numbers, far from increasing, levelled off or, if the buildings from the sixty parishes, which provide the most accurate reflection of development, are viewed in isolation, actually declined, a situation which lasted until the 1440s or 1450s. It has been suggested that the survival pattern of buildings is not so much a reflection of building activity at the time as of later developments, and that once buildings of a particular type were introduced they should increase in strict proportion.[12] Thus, despite the possible replacement of many low-walled houses at a later date, the number of houses surviving in Kent should have increased steadily after *c* 1370. Although it would probably be incorrect to place too much reliance on the fine detail of Figure 64, the evidence from the sixty parishes contrasts so markedly with these expectations that the possibility of there being a genuine reduction in the number of new houses built in the first half of the 15th century has to be given serious attention.

The slackening of pace coincides with the very period when the change in the design of houses was starting to occur. Figure 65 plots the temporal distribution of the different types of open-hall house built after *c* 1370. Since the numbers are not large enough to be broken down by decade, they have been divided, using mid dates, into five 34/35 year periods. In this diagram, buildings in the sixty surveyed parishes have not been distinguished. In the first of these periods, houses with cross wings, or houses where open halls survive alone, predominate, and comparatively few of the newer high-walled types were built. In the second period the new types begin to outnumber the old, although many of these are not in the sixty intensively surveyed parishes. The change is not unexpected, particularly when later developments are taken into account, but it sheds no light on the overall reduction in numbers in the early 15th

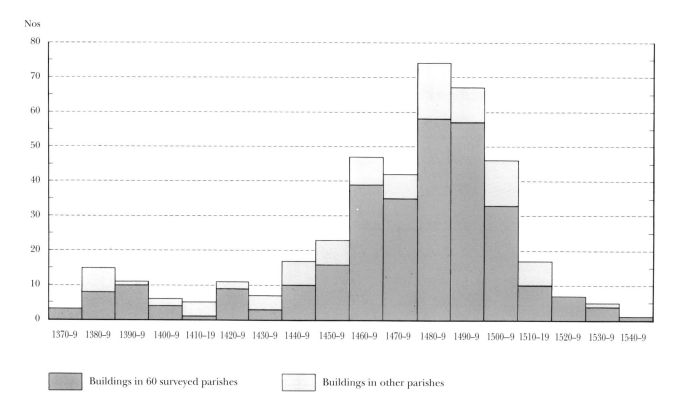

Nos

Buildings in 60 surveyed parishes          Buildings in other parishes century which was so clearly revealed in Figure 64. Whether halls and cross wings were replaced by new-style medieval houses or by post-medieval ones, the actual number of surviving medieval houses might have been expected to increase not diminish. This suggests either that after a short outburst of activity in the late 14th century, few new houses were built before the mid 15th century, or that if they were, they still took the form of the smaller, lower dwellings which were so prone to destruction after the Middle Ages. Although detailed historical discussion has been left until Chapter 12, it is worth remarking here that both possibilities imply that money for fine buildings remained in short supply during the agricultural and economic depression of the 15th century, recovery from which started only in the second half of the century. Not until this time did the new types of house come into their own.

The proliferation of new or better houses seems to have gathered pace after about 1450, and the pattern of Figure 64 and the fact that several buildings turned out to have tree-ring dates in the 1460s may indicate that although revival was already in the air, the upturn really took off in that decade. From then until the first decade of the 16th century there is a definite increase in the number of surviving medieval houses. Figure 64 shows the totals peaking in the 1480s and 90s, and this would remain true even if some buildings have been wrongly dated by a decade or so.

In the early 16th century the diagram shows a dramatic fall in numbers back to the levels of the mid 15th century and earlier. Previous writers have dated some splendid

*Figure 65 The incidence of different house types. The diagram indicates the number of different house types recorded in five periods from 1370 to 1545.*

open-hall houses into the second or third decades of the 16th century.[13] However, tree-ring dating suggests that these dates should be revised. Some of the finest houses which were thought to come at the very end of the open-hall tradition were actually built as early as the 1480s, and by the end of the first decade of the 16th century they were being superseded by fully storeyed dwellings. In part this was a regional development, for although fine open halls ceased to be erected in some areas, rather less impressive ones were still being built elsewhere, almost up to the mid 16th century. Yet few late examples survive.

The introduction of storeyed halls does not, however, seem to be an adequate explanation for the rapid decline of the open hall as illustrated in Figure 64. Although no systematic attempt was made to count or analyse newly built, early 16th-century, two-storeyed dwellings, they were recorded whenever they were found. These included houses like Court Lodge, Linton, of *c* 1506*, and Little Harts Heath, Staplehurst, of 1507*. But such early examples were rare. Fully storeyed buildings of later 16th-century date seem to be commoner than earlier ones, and the final impression was of a genuine drop in the total number of new houses built, just as there had been a century earlier.[14]

## The dating of different house types

Figure 65 illustrates the effect of the introduction of the new, high-walled houses from the late 14th century onwards. The only type which can be dated to the late 14th century with confidence is the Wealden house. The Wealden has frequently been considered as the ultimate expression of the medieval house contained within a unitary roof, and has usually been presented as later than

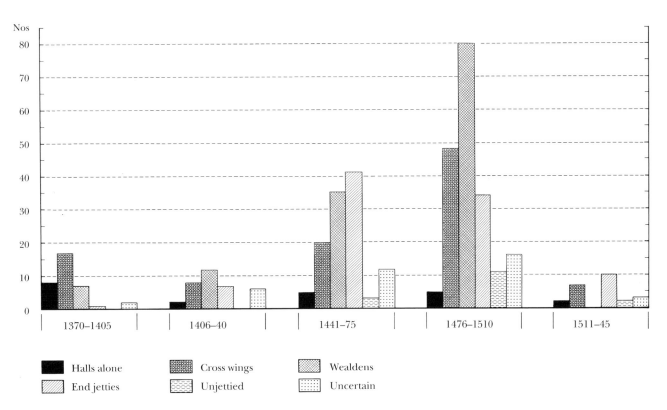

Legend:
- Halls alone
- End jetties
- Cross wings
- Unjettied
- Wealdens
- Uncertain

*Figure 66 Chart Hall Farmhouse, Chart Sutton (1379/80\*). An early Wealden house. Evidence survives for former upper-end bay to left (BB90/363).*

the simpler end-jetty form.[15] However, if the dating suggested here is correct, then the first surviving Wealdens in Kent are likely to precede the first surviving end-jetty houses. The problem of dating is complicated by the 'rogue' tree-ring dating of The Old Farmhouse, Hadlow (discussed in Appendix 1), but this example apart it seems clear that recognisably 'early' features, such as jointing techniques, unusual structural methods or early forms of moulding, are all absent from the first end-jetty houses, but are found in a few of the Wealdens.

The earliest firmly dated Wealdens in Kent are Chart Hall Farmhouse, Chart Sutton, of 1379/80\* (Figure 66) and West Court, Shepherdswell with Coldred, of *c* 1399\*, both exhibiting a number of 'early' structural and decorative details. The earliest end-jetty houses on the other hand have none of these features and the first tree-ring dates are somewhat later. One end of Spoute House, Plaxtol (Figure 63), dates to *c* 1424\*, and Wenhams and Thistles, Capel, is dated *c* 1431\*. No end-jetty houses visited by the RCHME were arguably much earlier in style or structure, and it is difficult to resist the conclusion that end jetties were developed three or four decades later than their Wealden counterparts. Despite this, Figure 65 suggests that

by the mid 15th century the two forms were equally prevalent, that the Wealden became dominant in the late 15th century, but that the end-jetty form of open-hall house lasted longer. This may be explained by the fact that the kind of well-off people who had the money to build Wealdens were later the sort who first wanted the new fully storeyed dwellings.

The number of houses in the unjettied category is small, and the type emerges at a relatively late date, none being datable before the mid 15th century. Only a small proportion of the houses whose type cannot be identified are datable. Most of them have evidence for a hall and contemporary end; and, since they never have evidence of front jetties, they are seldom likely to have been Wealdens, the majority probably being flush-walled buildings of end-jetty or unjettied form.

The need to distinguish between different house types is not simply a matter of classification for its own sake, but because the various types developed differently and tended to be different in size. Studies elsewhere have also organised houses according to size, and these have implicitly, if not always overtly, included type.[16] The number of medieval houses recorded for this project made it possible to examine the two aspects together, and the matter was tackled in two ways. In the first place, overall area and the areas of the various components of the house were analysed, and in the second the types were considered in relation to their height.

## The relationship between size and type of house

Figure 67 defines houses by type, date and size. Because so many houses had more than one phase, the calculations include both fully and partially surviving houses, and are based on the median area measurements for each section of the house. In order to draw on the largest possible sample, each part has been treated separately, and the representative house has been compiled from the aggregate of each part. In fact these proved remarkably similar to the median total areas of fully surviving houses.

The first point to note is the relatively large size of Kentish houses. In much of England the ground-floor area of peasant houses ranged between 42 and 59 sq m, but in Kent the median size of almost all timber-framed houses is larger than this.[17] The median ground-floor area of the 184 single-phase dwellings was 79 sq m, with 84 per cent of them being larger than 60 sq m; in fact, Figure 67 indicates that only a handful of unjettied and uncertain buildings of the early 16th century consistently had less than 60 sq m of ground-floor accommodation. Since the majority of houses had some two-storeyed component, the actual floor space was considerably larger. Kent is not unique in this; it applies to the south east generally. A table illustrating the size of Sussex houses built before the mid 16th century indicates that 173 or 80 per cent of houses below mansion house level have more than 60 sq m of ground-floor accommodation, and the same is true of 155 or 58 per cent of medieval houses recorded in Surrey, where it is recognised that houses were usually smaller.[18]

The second point about the overall ground-floor areas shown in Figure 67 is the difference in size between the different types of house. Those with cross wings were consistently larger than Wealdens, which in turn were larger than end-jetty houses. The fact that end-jetty houses are smaller than Wealdens gives added weight to the argument that they

emerged later, for it is generally accepted that large houses do not develop from small ones. Those in the unjettied and uncertain categories are more varied, but correspond most closely to end-jetty houses, suggesting, as mentioned above, that most of the houses of uncertain form were built with flush front walls, whether jettied at the ends or not.

Despite the differences in absolute size, the four house types which lay under unitary roofs – Wealdens, end jetties, unjettied and uncertain – show remarkably similar trends over time. Both Figure 67, and Figures 68–70, which illustrate simplified plans of actual examples, indicate that all four types diminished in size between the late 14th and the early 16th centuries. In Wealdens, the median overall ground-floor area was reduced from 99 to 82 sq m; in unjettied buildings the reduction was from 79 to 52 sq m. This is not to say that large houses were not erected at later dates; four of the seven largest Wealdens recorded dated to the period 1476–1510, but these resplendent houses were outnumbered by many others which brought the median size down to a lower figure than in earlier periods.

Since, as a rule, more smaller houses survive as time went by, the impression has been created that the size of open halls gradually diminished in relation to the rest of the house.[19] The number of medieval buildings recorded in Kent allows this hypothesis to be tested. It was noted in Hertfordshire that the living area of most open halls was roughly square, with only the site of the opposing doorways and screens passage extending this to a rectangle.[20] Figures 68–70 indicate that halls were of similar proportions in Kent. This meant that in houses with unitary roofs, the size of the hall was more or less fixed by the width of the building, so that without substantially elongating the end bays, the proportion of the parts would remain fairly standard. Figures 67, 68 and 69 show that the end bays were

*Figure 67 The sizes of different types of house. The diagram compares the median ground-floor areas of different house types, divided into five periods from 1370 to 1545.*

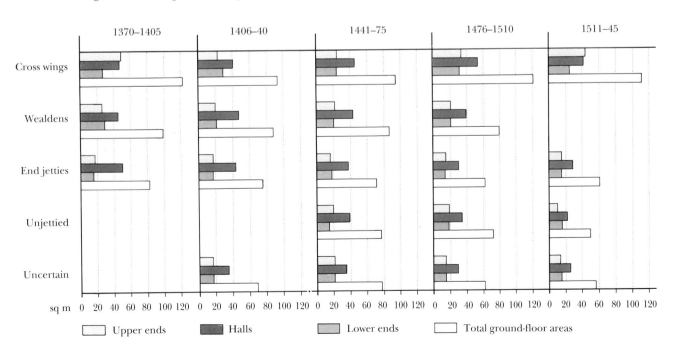

*Figure 68 Simplified house plans. Late 14th and early 15th-century houses: Halls only: a) Henikers, Sutton Valence, c 1364\*; b) Parsonage Farmhouse, Aldington, c 1385; c) Walnut Tree Cottage, East Sutton, c 1401\*. Hall and cross wings: d) Lower Newlands, Teynham, c 1380\*; e) Hill Crest and Kent Cottage, Staplehurst, c 1389\*; f) Bartons Farmhouse, Plaxtol, c 1383\*. Wealdens: g) Chart Hall Farmhouse, Chart Sutton, 1379/80\*; h) West Court, Shepherdswell with Coldred, c 1399\*; i) Vane Court, Biddenden, c 1419\*. End jetties: j) Spoute House, Plaxtol, c 1424\* (service end), c 1445\* (hall and upper end); k) Wenhams and Thistles, Capel, c 1431\*; l) Belks, Otham, c 1440.*

not noticeably increased in size, although a few of the larger, late Wealden houses, like Tong House, Eastling (Figure 69e), had contemporary wings constructed at the rear. Despite occasional exceptions of this sort, the open hall accounted for 45–58 per cent of the ground-floor area of unitary roofed dwellings throughout the Middle Ages. Within this narrow range, houses of the mid 15th century or earlier all had halls whose median size occupied 49 per cent or more of the ground-floor area; the halls of those built in the early 16th century took up 48 per cent or a little less of the overall space – a difference which is almost too small to count as a decrease.

The one type of house which did not conform to the overall trends was the cross-wing house. For one thing, the

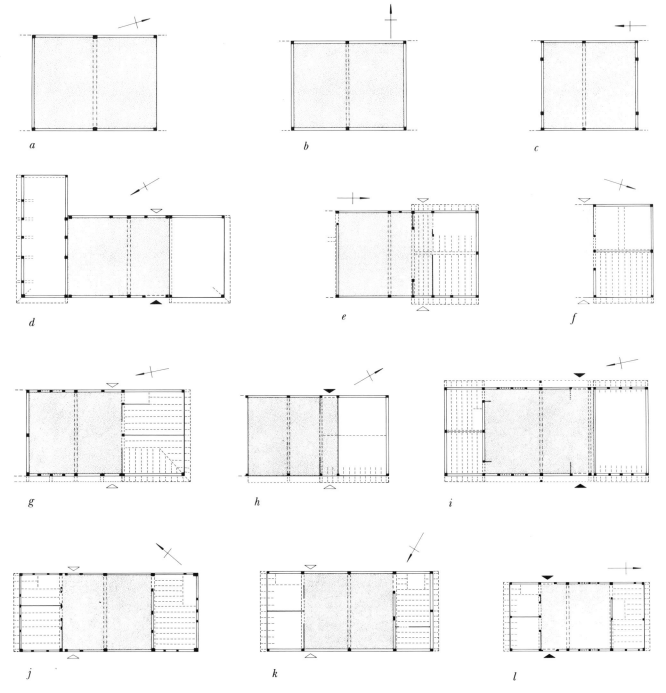

a

b

c

d

e

f

g

h

i

j

k

l

proportion of the hall to other ground-floor rooms was always smaller, for it never occupied more than 36–45 per cent of the total ground-floor area. Because the hall and ends lay at right angles to each other, the width of one did not have to dictate the size of the rest, so a much greater variation in relative sizes was possible. Not many cross wings survive with contemporary halls, but all the signs are that the relationship changed significantly as time went on. In the late 14th and first half of the 15th centuries, the wings hardly ever projected in front of the hall. As the examples in Figure 68d–f illustrate, they lay flush with the hall at ground level, with only the jettied first floor projecting above. Some houses, however, had wings projecting at the rear, as at one end of Lower Newlands in c 1380*. This might occur at either end but was commoner in upper-end wings in the late 14th century, which accounts for the higher median area of this end and helped to contribute to the high overall area of cross-wing houses. Large wings of this sort became less common during most of the 15th century. Instead, many smaller wings were built (Figure 70b), often surviving without their halls, probably because they represented an easy and relatively cheap way of updating an earlier house whose low open hall was replaced at a later date. Where hall sizes are known they are not exceptionally large, but the overall size of house remains high because the area given up to subsidiary accommodation was above average.

In the late 15th century a new class of cross-wing house emerged. With the exception of the biggest of the late 14th-century wings, these were larger and grander than any timber houses previously built, and for the first time a number of them (Figure 70c–e), like Stoneacre, Otham (Figure 142), Court Lodge Farmhouse, Southfleet, and Old Standen, Benenden, project at the front as well as at the rear. As in the late 14th-century group, the upper-end wing was usually the larger of the two, but the relatively large size of both wings led to the proportion of the hall to the subsidiary accommodation remaining low. However, the absolute size of the hall was higher than it had been in the mid 15th-century examples.

It may be objected that the owners of these very large dwellings are hardly likely to have been of the same social rank as those whose buildings lay under a unitary roof, and that their houses should not be considered together. However, the problem of disentangling those of gentry status from those who were not is fraught with difficulty, and it was decided at this stage to treat all timber-framed houses together. The extent to which gentry and non-gentry houses can be separated is a problem that will be postponed until Chapter 11. For the moment it is simply important to note that late cross-wing houses were of a somewhat different order from either earlier cross wings or houses of other kinds.

*Figure 69 Simplified house plans. Late Wealdens and end jetties: Wealdens: a) Tudor House, Chislet, c 1465 (Wealden hall and upper end added to earlier service wing); b) Shieling Hall, Langley, c 1500; c) Luckhurst, East Sutton, c 1490*; d) West Hoy Farmhouse, Smarden, c 1500; e) Tong House, Eastling, c 1505 (integral rear wing). End jetties: f) Symnel Cottage, Aldington, c 1460*; g) Manor Cottage, Speldhurst, 1508/9*; h) Dennes House, Waltham, c 1525.*

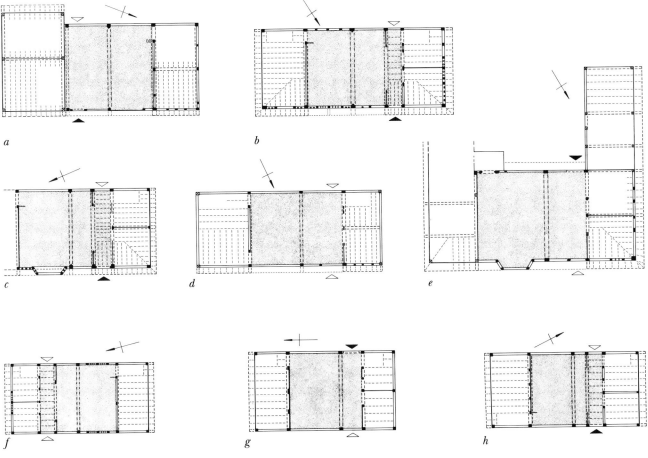

## Single-ended houses

The discussion so far has made no reference to single-ended houses. Rather it has been assumed that every complete medieval dwelling consisted of an open hall and two blocks of secondary accommodation, one at each end. The reason lies in the lack of positive evidence that purpose-built single-ended houses were ever built. Uphousden Farm, Ash next Sandwich, probably of the late 14th century, and Country Fair and Light Horse (94, 96 High Street), Edenbridge, of *c* 1410*, are rare examples where the precise placing of subsidiary timbers and the weathering of an outer wall suggest that the hall originally stood free at one end. But before the early 16th century such instances are very few and far between. Many houses have only one bay or wing of subsidiary accommodation now remaining, but where the construction of the opposite wall of the hall is visible, it nearly always indicates that it was formerly attached to or covered by another range which has been removed. Weathering at this point is seldom found; even when it occurs, as in the late 15th century at 4, 5, 6, 7 Belle Vue, Sellindge, the provision for an original internal doorway from the hall to the room beyond and the early date of the

*Figure 70 Simplified house plans. Late cross wings: a) The Barracks, East Malling and Larkfield, c 1445; b) Harts Farmhouse, Molash, c 1466*; c) Stoneacre, Otham, c 1500; d) Court Lodge Farmhouse, Southfleet, c 1480 (service wing), c 1515 (hall and upper-end wing); e) Old Standen, Benenden, c 1505.*

addition suggest that a further bay was intended from the start, even if it was not actually built for some time. In the 16th century a few small single-ended houses were found, as at Little Laverall, Speldhurst, of *c* 1533*. The probate inventories, which survive in some numbers from 1565 onwards, describe houses which may have been of this form; but by and large there is little evidence for two-cell dwellings among the remaining open-hall houses in the county.

## The height of houses

From a certain point in the project, it became apparent that not only were there variations in size between different types of house, but also variations in height. As a result, height measurements were always taken thereafter. Unfortunately, as they had not been noted in every house, the number of relevant buildings in the earliest and latest periods was too small to divide into five house types and five periods. Instead the buildings have been divided into the three groups into which the information on sizes most naturally falls, and into three periods of seventy, fifty and fifty years. The median heights are tabulated in Table 1.

Throughout the Middle Ages, the elevation of two-storeyed wings in cross-wing houses remained consistently higher than that of Wealdens, which in turn remained higher than the amalgamated group of end-jetty, unjettied and uncertain houses. The differences are considerable, 0.3 m – 0.6 m separating each category. But within each

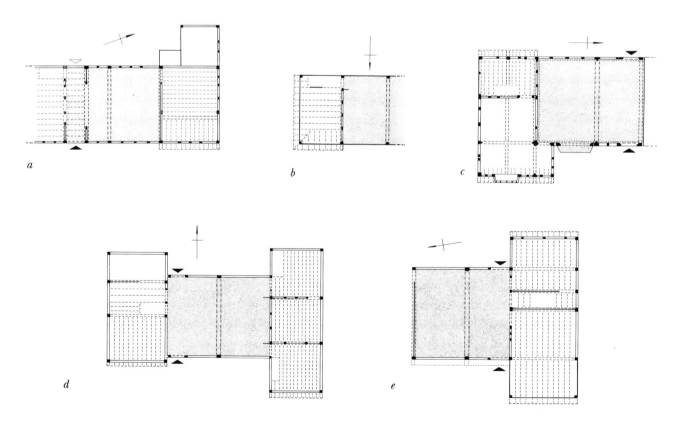

a

b

c

d

e

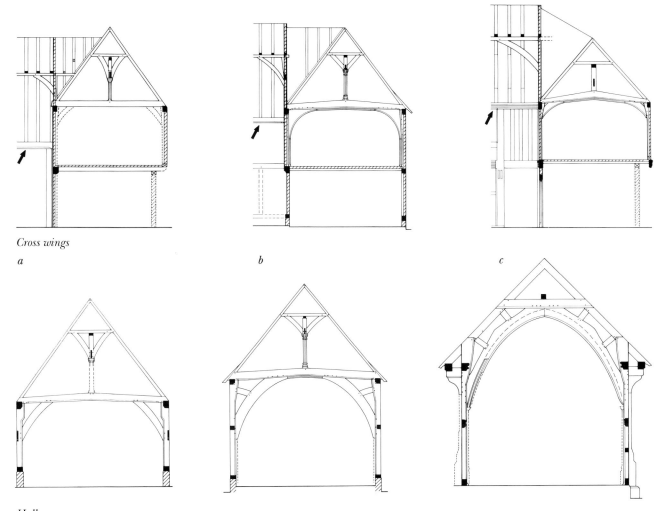

Cross wings

a                 b                 c

Hall ranges

category the heights remain more or less static over time. On the other hand the figures for the hall ranges of cross-wing houses present a markedly different pattern. At the turn of the century these were substantially lower than the halls of buildings under unitary roofs. By the second half of the century, they had risen by over 0.7 m to above the height of Wealden halls, and by the early 16th century by another 0.25 m, which meant that they were considerably higher than the halls of any other type of house. An illustration of the effect of this, using an example from each period, is shown in Figure 71. It seems likely that as the new types of

*Table 1 Median heights of different types of house (heights in metres).*

| Types | No. in sample | 1370–1440 | 1441–90 | 1491–1540 |
|---|---|---|---|---|
| Cross-wing houses: halls | ( 35) | 3.40 | 4.15 | 4.40 |
| wings | ( 48) | 4.49 | 4.49 | 4.59 |
| Wealden houses | ( 76) | 4.15 | 4.10 | 4.29 |
| End-jettied, unjettied and uncertain houses | (103) | 4.00 | 3.70 | 3.75 |

*Figure 71 Comparative heights of halls and cross wings at different dates. In the cross-wing sections, an arrow indicates the height of the hall wall plate: a) Lower Newlands, Teynham, c 1380\*; b) The Barracks, East Malling and Larkfield, c 1445; c) Riseden Hall, Goudhurst, c 1505.*

house became commoner during the 15th century, so those who chose to build contemporary hall and cross-wing ranges, perhaps in order to gain the benefit of larger subsidiary accommodation, also altered the proportions of their halls in line with the prevailing style of unitary roofed dwellings.

Thus the distinction in height between the three main categories of house, and the changes which occurred between c 1370 and c 1540, seem to be closely allied to the development in the area of different house types. The combined evidence suggests that the design of houses was closely connected with people's means and requirements, and therefore probably with their social and economic position. That the size of house might vary according to wealth or status is unsurprising; that this might affect the design as well is perhaps not always borne in mind. However, another dimension, that of geographical distribution, needs to be taken into account before conclusions are drawn. This aspect will be considered in Chapter 10.

# 7 The construction of late medieval houses

The new house types of the 15th century, which are what make the surviving medieval buildings of Kent so remarkable, depended upon the ability of carpenters to erect high-walled halls and jettied upper storeys. Initially this must have been brought about by a cultural change, which meant that people wanted to live in halls uncluttered by intrusive timbers and to conduct a significant part of their lives on the first floor, as the well-to-do had been doing in stone houses for a long time. But the new desires required new structural forms to make them feasible. This chapter discusses construction in general terms, and concentrates on those aspects which are useful in evaluating chronological development, and may lead to a greater understanding of the interaction between the form of house and the type of structure. Technical analysis of construction, and the most important structural features of medieval houses, are examined in detail in *The House Within*.

## Late aisled and base-cruck construction

Despite the fact that timber halls without aisles were known by the late 14th century, it seems that both fully aisled and quasi-aisled buildings continued to be erected. As discussed in Chapter 6, many of these are likely to have disappeared. Those that remain are often difficult to date. Unfortunately, tree-ring dating was only successful in one instance, either because the houses were not built of oak, or because the timber was too fast grown. However, some of the buildings luckily have details which may be dated by other means, and the combined evidence suggests that aisled construction continued to be employed throughout the 15th century.

The archetypal aisled hall erected around 1300, with double aisles and two full bays, seems to have ceased to be built by *c* 1370; certainly no examples of later date were identified during the project. Possibly such buildings, with their inconvenient central truss, were particularly susceptible to total destruction; but since they survive from earlier periods, and since later aisled halls of reduced form were found in some numbers, the total lack of evidence for them may indicate that they had been superseded by the end of the century. Halls of two full bays were still built, but in all surviving instances the free-standing arcade posts of the open truss were replaced by other forms of construction. This had occurred before in some early 14th-century houses, either using base crucks, as at Barnes Place, Hadlow, or

extended arch-brace construction, as at Hurst Farm, Chilham. The later examples may be seen as successors to these, and tend to be found in much smaller buildings.

Extended arch-brace construction in later buildings was identified in only two houses: at Walnut Tree Cottage, East Sutton, of *c* 1401*, and Church Farmhouse, Newington next Sittingbourne (Figure 72).[1] Although in the use of extended braces and raised tie beams, they bear some resemblance to

*Figure 72 Extended arch braces at the open truss: a) Church Farmhouse, Newington next Sittingbourne. Cross section; b) Walnut Tree Cottage, East Sutton (BB86/1294).*

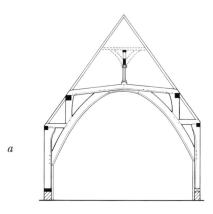

*a*

*b*

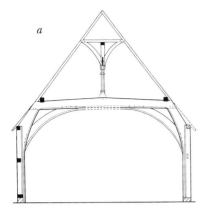

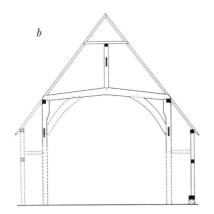

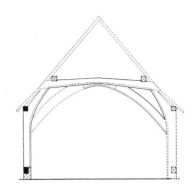

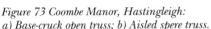

*Figure 73 Coombe Manor, Hastingleigh:*
*a) Base-cruck open truss; b) Aisled spere truss.*

*Figure 74 Burnt Oak, Yalding.*
*Base-cruck open truss.*

the earlier Hurst Farm, the two later houses have the odd feature of truncated arcade posts at the central truss standing on the backs of great braces. Base-cruck construction was probably a commoner method of removing the free-standing arcade posts. No examples could be tree-ring dated, and where the base crucks survive alone, precise dating is impossible. But at Coombe Manor, Hastingleigh (Figure 73), lack of any early structural details, combined with the late style of the crown post of the open truss and the possibility that the walls were close studded, suggest a date well into the 15th century; and in Yalding parish the close proximity and relatively small size of Nightingale Farmhouse (Figure 56) and Burnt Oak (Figure 74) imply yeoman or peasant dwellings which are more likely to date from after *c* 1350 than before.

Although two-bay halls ceased to be constructed with two aisles, a reduced version in which only the rear aisle remained went on being built through much of the 15th century. An early example, probably dating to the late 14th century, occurs at the Tudor Lodge Gift Shop and Peacock Antiques, Chilham (Figure 75a). This is a Wealden house whose front was of normal Wealden form, formerly with a full-height hall window and well-lit upper chambers. At the back, the house was aisled, with a single free-standing arcade

post to the open truss of the hall.[2] The structural and stylistic details of other single-aisled buildings, such as Well House, Selling, and Skinners House Cottages, Chiddingstone, indicate that they are later in date.[3] Two examples were found in which the arcade post at the rear of the open truss was replaced by a base cruck: at Bannister Hall, Borden (Figure 75b), where the hall has service-end doorways with four-centred heads leading to a contemporary cross wing, and at Old Well House, East Peckham, where a single base cruck is inferred but not proven (Figure 86b). The latter house is of end-jetty form, and at one end of the hall the surviving arcade post is raised on a cross beam (Figure 77c). The details of both buildings suggest that they were only built in the mid or second half of the 15th century. Similarly late dating has been proposed for at least one single-aisled base cruck in Sussex.[4]

A second means of reducing the obstruction caused by the arcade posts was through shifting the open truss to the position of a spere truss separating the entry bay from the hall proper. Genuine spere trusses, combined with open trusses to form three-bay halls, had never been particularly common in Kent. They were used occasionally in the 14th century or earlier, as at Bardingley Farmhouse, Sutton Valence, and later examples occur in quasi-aisled halls where

*Figure 75 Single-aisled buildings: a) Tudor Lodge Gift Shop and Peacock Antiques, Chilham. Open truss of single-aisled Wealden house; b) Bannister Hall, Borden. A single-aisled hall with a base-cruck open truss and four-centred doorways to the service-end cross wing.*

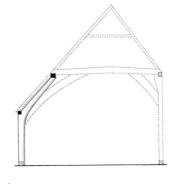

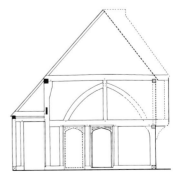

*a*

*b*

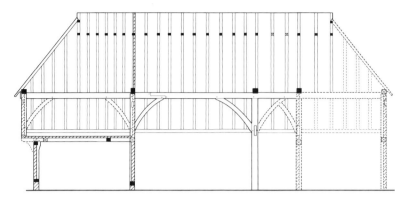

*Figure 76 (above) Lacton Manor, Westwell. Long section; the braces in the short passage bay survive on the other side of the hall. Original form of reconstructed end unknown.*

*Figure 77 Single-aisled, single-bay, open halls: a) Allens Hill Farmhouse, Cliffe-at-Hoo. Closed truss separating open hall from chamber and passage bay; the four-centred doorways to the services lie in the partition on the far side of the passage; b) The Cottage, Anvil Green, Waltham. Single-aisled hall with clasped purlin roof and arcade post supported on cross beam; c) Old Well House, East Peckham. Arcade post of aisled hall supported on cross beam (BB89/4812).*

the arcade posts of the central truss have been removed: Coombe Manor, Hastingleigh, combines a spere truss with base crucks, and Fairfield House, Eastry,[5] may have had a 'floating' tie beam to the open truss, unsupported by posts, in an arrangement similar to that found at Court Lodge, Fawkham (Figure 46). In these instances the spere truss provided additional solid support for the long arcade plates and roof above, allowing the living area of the hall to remain unobstructed. But in some smaller halls the same effect was achieved by placing the open truss itself over the division between hall proper and passage. It thereby acquired the function of a spere or screen and blurred the distinction between open and spere trusses. Coppwilliam, Staplehurst (Figure 60), and Lacton Manor, Westwell (Figure 76), are among a group of houses of this form, some of which were distinguished by unusual arcade bracing in the passage bay, the reduction in length resulting in one brace joining the other instead of rising to the arcade plate.[6]

A further way in which free-standing arcade posts were removed in aisled buildings was by reducing the hall to a single open bay. This occurred when the screens passage was overshot by the lower-end chamber. At ground level the plan was similar to those in the previous group, but a fully closed truss separated the passage from the single hall bay and more chamber space was thereby gained at the lower end. In all the examples found so far, as at Allens Hill Farmhouse, Cliffe-at-Hoo, and The Cottage, Anvil Green, Waltham (Figure 77a and b), the house was also only single aisled, so that the advantages of a higher front wall were likewise available.

## Dating of aisled structures

There is a natural tendency to place all aisled structures early, but the evidence suggests that most of the houses discussed here date well into the 15th century. Allens Hill Farmhouse, like Bannister Hall, Borden, has four-centred doorheads; and similar doorheads together with close-studded framing indicate a late date for Fairfield House, Eastry. Where the roofs survive they are usually of crown-post or collar-rafter form, but at The Cottage, Anvil Green, Waltham, an original crown-post roof, for which there is evidence in the lower-end bay, was replaced in a second single-aisled phase by a spindly,

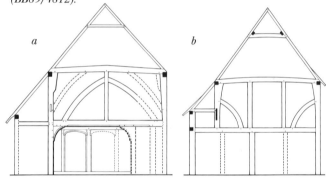

*a*  *b*

*c*

but smoke-blackened clasped-purlin roof without queen struts or wind braces (Figure 77b). Although this is not precisely datable, it is likely to have been constructed in the 16th century rather than earlier. Several of the buildings were not truly aisled in that there were no free-standing arcade posts, and those in the closed trusses were raised up on cross beams.[7] Two examples of this arrangement are illustrated, from The Cottage, Waltham, and Old Well House, East Peckham (Figure 77b and c).

Finally, aisles are also found in fully floored buildings. At Harts Farmhouse, Molash, of *c* 1466*, an aisle at the rear of a two-storeyed cross wing housed the stairs to the upper floor. Such an arrangement is perhaps more akin to an outshut, but at Old Selson House, Eastry, single-aisled construction was used for a two-storeyed hall heated by a fireplace backing on to a through passage and single service room. Both the form and the details suggest a date well into the 16th century. That the house was aisled, rather than having a rear outshut, is indicated by the fact that both ground-floor rooms run from front to back, the arcade posts being embedded in the cross walls and only obvious on the first floor.

On the whole the later the aisled building, the smaller and more reduced in form it is likely to be. But one late example seems to have been of surprisingly large size and high status. The actual hall of Campion House, Benenden, has been replaced, and all that is left are two arcade posts which are structurally part of the lower-end cross wing (Figure 78). This contains two service rooms at the front beneath a two-bay chamber spanned by a crown-post roof; at the back is an attached kitchen heated by a smoke bay. All the details suggest a date of *c* 1500. The body of the aisled hall might have been earlier, but the integral arcade posts with evidence for the position of the hall arcade plates suggest it was contemporary. Nothing is known about the form of the hall, but its width implies that it was sizeable, and the details of the wing indicate a house of some quality. If aisled halls of this sort were still being built around 1500, it is puzzling that no other trace of them has so far come to light.

Evidence for late aisled structures has gradually been accumulating elsewhere in the south east, examples dating from the late 15th and early 16th centuries being cited in Essex, Suffolk and Sussex.[8] Many of the buildings have only single aisles, but one of the latest, from Depden, Suffolk, has double aisles as well as a spere truss of similar form to those found in several of the Kentish examples.[9] Since many of these buildings were relatively small and often rather less well built than their larger contemporaries, it is likely that they are the rare survivors of a once numerous class.

# Jettied construction

The new types of house which evolved in the late 14th century were almost all dependent upon jettying, in which the upper floor of a storeyed structure oversailed the one below on one or more sides. For this reason it is relevant to investigate the history of the jetty and consider the moment when it first occurs in Kent.

Until recently it was not possible to prove that jettied construction in England occurred before the 14th century. But newly discovered evidence from documentary sources and surviving buildings now shows that jettying was known in

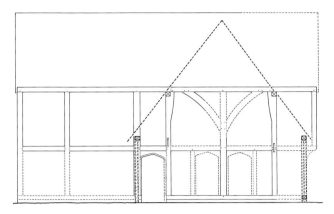

*Figure 78 Campion House, Benenden. Elevation of cross-wing wall showing evidence for former aisled hall; broken line indicates outline of original roof.*

the 13th century. It is possible that the technique was introduced from the Continent, although the dating sequence in different countries is not easy to establish; and it may have been used in towns before spreading to the countryside. In London, jetties appear to have been present as early as 1244, when they were said to be causing a nuisance to passers by,[10] and evidence for jetties in a surviving 13th-century house has been discovered in Bury St Edmunds, Suffolk.[11] In rural buildings the jetty at York Farm, West Hagbourne in the Vale of White Horse, Oxfordshire, has been tree-ring dated to *c* 1285, and other Oxfordshire examples have dates in the early 14th century.[12] In Essex, the jetties in the cross wings at Tiptofts, Wimbish, and Wynter's Armourie, Magdalen Laver, have been dated variously between the late 13th and the early 14th centuries.[13]

In Kent no such early examples have come to light. As discussed in Chapter 4, few late 13th or early 14th-century timber-framed houses have surviving evidence for the precise form of their private accommodation. It is frequently impossible to tell whether houses had end bays or cross wings, and whether these were two storeyed, let alone whether they were jettied. The first building with clear evidence of jettying is probably the stone and timber east–west solar range of Ightham Mote, dated to *c* 1330*.[14] It is possible that jetties were also used in the stone and timber wing at Gallants Manor, East Farleigh, of *c* 1322*, and the timber-framed wing of Hamden, Smarden, which was built sometime in the mid 14th century. But visible jetties in rural Kent date only to the last quarter of the 14th century, by which time the formative stages of the construction were long since passed. The first examples appear at much the same moment in both cross-wing and Wealden houses, the earliest dated ones lying in Chart Sutton, at Old Moat Farmhouse, a cross wing of *c* 1377*, and Chart Hall Farmhouse, a Wealden of 1379/80*, although it is almost certain that a slightly earlier instance occurred at Coppwilliam, Staplehurst, in 1370/1*. In fact, since known unjettied buildings are considerably later, it is possible that all storeyed accommodation in timber building in Kent was jettied at this time. If so, this might imply that the technique had a long history in the county. But too little is at present known of the earlier examples to allow a sensible analysis of its origin and development.[15]

# Wealden construction

## *Development of the Wealden*

In the late 14th century, a number of developments were afoot which, when they came together, helped to lead to the invention of the Wealden. In the first place there was a movement away from aisled construction, and the beginning of the heightening of the hall walls. This can be seen in a number of late 14th-century buildings where the halls survive alone. In some, like Walnut Tree Cottage, East Sutton, of *c* 1401*, and Church Farmhouse, Newington next Sittingbourne, quasi-aisled construction still occurred (Figure 72), but others dispensed with aisles altogether, as at Henikers, Sutton Valence, of *c* 1364* (Figure 80a), and Parsonage Farmhouse, Aldington.

The second development was the increasing importance of storeyed subsidiary accommodation. Instead of low open ends or chambers lying over low storage undercrofts, one or both of which forms may account for the destruction of the subsidiary accommodation in the houses mentioned above, the bays at the ends of the hall were evolving specialised functions which entailed building two full storeys. The obvious way to accomplish this was by erecting cross wings, and examples such as Lower Newlands, Teynham, of *c* 1380* (Figure 52) show that this is precisely what happened.

Such developments affected far more of the country than Kent, but there they were associated with a third, strictly Kentish, phenomenon, whose presence was critical to the evolution of the Wealden. This third factor was the Kentish tendency to place buildings under hipped, monospan roofs. This was no new invention. The first surviving unitary roofs date from around 1300, Nurstead Court of *c* 1309* being the most famous example. In the late 13th and early 14th centuries they were used over many stone ranges, as at Copton Manor and Mersham Manor, and were probably ubiquitous in timber-framed buildings. They occurred over the unfloored end bays of large houses such as Ratling Court, Aylesham, and Chilton Manor, Sittingbourne, and they were almost certainly also common over smaller buildings such as Dormer Cottage, Petham, even though few such buildings have survived. So strong was the desire to use hipped roofs that, except in the far west of Kent, they were normal even when the structure took the

form of a cross wing, as at Lower Newlands, Teynham, and Old Hall, Petham (Figure 51) – buildings which would never be mistaken for cross-wing houses north of the Thames, where gabled wings predominate. In these two examples the wings are obvious because the halls have low walls. But as aisles were abandoned and the walls of the hall became higher, allowing taller windows to light the hall, the hip over the wing meant that the visual distinction between hall and wing disappeared. In these circumstances it is not difficult to see how the idea of placing a single roof over the entire building might arise. It must have been cheaper and easier to construct a single roof than to place separate hipped roofs over several ranges.

If these suggestions are correct then it seems likely that the Wealden developed directly out of the cross-wing house. This hypothesis is supported by the fact that in the late 14th century cross wings and halls surviving on their own outnumber Wealdens in Kent (Figure 65), and by the fragmentary evidence relating to earlier houses, which indicates that wings already had a history in timber building. In fact, the junction of hall to wing and of hall to Wealden end, and the method of forming the jetties, were often handled in a similar manner. In addition, as will be discussed in Chapter 8, the arrangement of the first-floor chamber in Wealdens was sometimes treated as if it lay in a wing. Thus the jump from one design to the other was not as great as might be imagined. It consisted primarily in how to resolve the structural problem created in Wealdens by having a single wall plate running from one jettied bay to the next across an open space, which meant that its centre point had to be carried on a tie beam supported by a post on a different plane.

The precise date and location of the invention of the Wealden are matters of debate.[16] It is likely to have started more or less fully formed, and probably did not appear before about 1370. The earliest dated example is Chart Hall Farmhouse, Chart Sutton, of 1379/80* (Figures 66, 79), which lies within a few miles of Henikers, Sutton Valence (Figures 68a, 80a), and Walnut Tree Cottage, East Sutton (Figures 68c, 72b), where different experiments relating to spanning halls without aisles were taking place at the same time. Possibly Wealdens were invented in this part of Kent, although it must be acknowledged that those examples

*Figure 79 Chart Hall Farmhouse, Chart Sutton. Long section and cross section of early Wealden house, 1379/80*.*

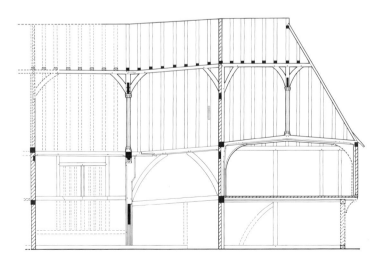

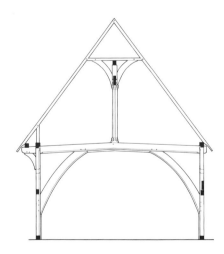

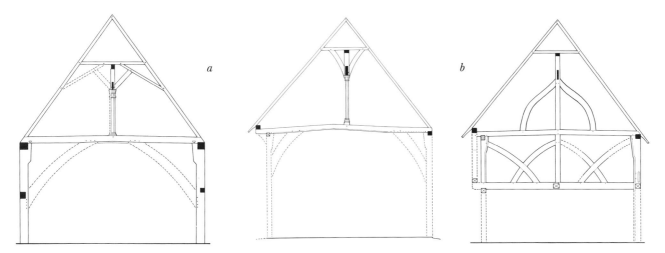

*Figure 80 Cross sections of early houses: a) Henikers, Sutton Valence, c 1364\*, open truss; b) West Court, Shepherdswell with Coldred, c 1399\*, open and closed trusses (latter shown from chamber to indicate assembly of jetty).*

which are likely to date from the late 14th century or the first decade of the 15th are widely distributed throughout the county and into eastern Sussex.[17]

## Structural details of Wealdens

Although the forward jettying and overall roof which define the Wealden are present from the start, some of these early examples show hesitancy over certain details of construction, together with abnormal methods of jointing timbers together. Reversed assembly, in which the wall plate rests on top of the tie beam instead of being carried between post and tie, was commonly used for the central truss of Wealdens. It provided an obvious way of supporting the flying plate across the face of the hall, for the tie beam of the open truss protruded beyond the hall wall and supported the plate at the half-way stage.

Reversed assembly at the front had implications for the rear of the house, and was often repeated in order to keep the wall-plate height the same as the flying plate. This specialised use of what, in other contexts, is usually

considered an 'early' structural feature, recurs throughout the history of the Wealden house. But in the first Wealdens of the late 14th or very early 15th century, it was sometimes crudely handled and used in other parts of the building as well. At Chart Hall Farmhouse (Figure 79) and Uphousden Farm, Ash next Sandwich, one or more of the main posts were turned sideways so that the pronounced jowls formed better supports for the wall plates and tie beam. The arrangement in these two houses is uncommon, if not unique, and in later Wealdens this ungainly method of carrying the horizontal timbers was modified in favour of alternative solutions to the structural problem. Normally, reversed assembly was used only for the open truss, but at West Court, Shepherdswell with Coldred, of c 1399\*, the closed truss at one end of the hall was constructed the same way (Figure 80b). These are small points, but they suggest that around the turn of the century, Wealden construction was still in the formative stage. Another sign of immaturity may be that, as discussed above, at least one Wealden dating from around 1400 has been found with an aisle at the rear.[18]

The structural details of later Wealdens were handled with more assurance, but the houses were never built to a standard design, as can be seen in Figure 81 which illustrates the open trusses of two of the finest surviving

*Figure 81 Cross sections of large Wealdens: a) Manor House, Benenden, c 1400; b) The Old Palace, Brenchley, 1485\*.*

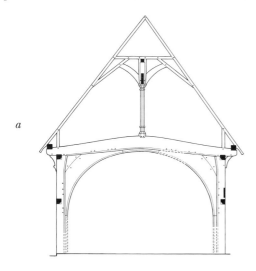

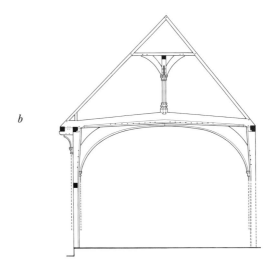

Wealdens. The Manor House, Benenden, of *c* 1400, is jettied to front and rear, necessitating flying plates, carried on an extended tie beam, at both sides of the hall. The Old Palace, Brenchley, of 1485*, has high-springing arch braces, as found in most late open halls, and details such as colonettes accentuating the open truss. The flying plate here is clasped by a bracket below the tie beam, and the roof has the unequal slope which occurred when the crown post was set centrally to the hall rather than to the roof itself. The problem of joining the hall and the storeyed ends could be solved in a number of ways, and some of the most commonly encountered variations are discussed in *The House Within*.[19] The *raison d'être* of the Wealden – placing an open hall and storeyed ends which were jettied to the front under a single roof – ceased to apply when houses started to be two storeyed throughout. Only one fully two-storeyed Wealden was certainly identified during the survey, at Little Harts Heath, Staplehurst, built in 1507*. It is one of the earliest two-storeyed houses to have been found, and was presumably erected at a time when the implications of fully storeyed dwellings had not been completely assimilated.

## End-jetty houses and end 'crucks'

It was argued in Chapter 6 that small size, relative simplicity and late tree-ring dates combine to suggest that end-jetty houses are a later development than cross wings and Wealdens, and not the precursors of the latter as has often been assumed.[20] One reason for placing end jetties early was that a number of them have curved timbers, sometimes called upper crucks or end crucks, resting on the jetty at the end of the storeyed bay and carrying a small half hip to the roof.[21] Upstreet Cottages, Lyminge, and Old Kent Cottage (formerly Frogholt), Newington next Hythe, are previously published examples.[22] One example, Burnt Oak, Benover, in Yalding parish, occurs in a quasi-aisled structure which has base crucks in the hall. At first sight this seems to fit the idea of early dating well, but further examination reveals that the end crucks lie in a separate and secondary building phase. Two phases are also found in other examples, at Tolhurst Farmhouse, Smarden (Figure 82), and Well

*Figure 82 Tolhurst Farmhouse, Smarden. Cruck-like timbers at the east end of the house.*

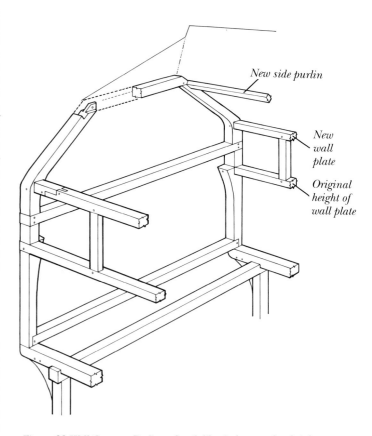

*New side purlin*

*New wall plate*

*Original height of wall plate*

*Figure 83 Well Cottage, Detling. Cruck-like timbers used to heighten the end wall.*

Cottage, Detling (Figure 83). It is sometimes difficult to work out which phase came first, but at Well Cottage the evidence is unambiguous: an original, low house was heightened by the addition, above wall-plate level, of cruck-like timbers carrying a new and higher wall plate which supported a new half-hipped roof. Finally, two pairs of end crucks occur at either end of Summerfield Farmhouse, Staple, in a fully two-storeyed house which is likely to date to the late 16th or even 17th century.[23]

A common feature of all houses with end crucks is an unusually low wall height. End-jettied or unjettied houses were, as discussed in Chapter 6, considerably lower than Wealden or cross-wing houses, their wall plates averaging 3.8 m from the ground. But those which had end crucks (six in all) were considerably lower than this. None had wall plates higher than 3.2 m and the average, at 2.26 m, was far lower. Contriving to insert a first-floor chamber into a house this low and then lighting it was extremely difficult, particularly if the roof was hipped in the normal Kentish manner. It is hardly surprising that methods were evolved to raise the height of the end wall, thus changing the hip to a half hip. This allowed room to move around in and provided a vertical wall for a window. In these circumstances curved cruck-like timbers provided an excellent means of support for the collar. That some of these houses were built in two phases may imply the replacement of earlier single-storeyed ends; but at Well Cottage the jettied upper storey was already there, although the first floor can

| Roof types | 1370–1405 | | 1406–40 | | 1441–75 | | 1476–1510 | | 1511–40 | | |
|---|---|---|---|---|---|---|---|---|---|---|---|
| | Nos. | (%) | Nos. | (%) | Nos. | (%) | Nos. | (%) | Nos. | (%) | Total nos. |
| Collar-rafter | 3 | (8%) | 6 | (17%) | 18 | (16%) | 43 | (21%) | 14 | (26%) | 84 |
| Crown-post | 34 | (92%) | 30 | (83%) | 94 | (84%) | 150 | (72%) | 29 | (54%) | 337 |
| Clasped-purlin | | | | | | | 11 | (5%) | 10 | (18%) | 21 |
| Butt-purlin | | | | | | | 5 | (2%) | 1 | (2%) | 6 |
| Totals | 37 | (100%) | 36 | (100%) | 112 | (100%) | 209 | (100%) | 54 | (100%) | 448 |

*Table 2 Chronological incidence of roof types in timber-framed buildings.*

have been no more than a loft. Dating, as always, is imprecise. But the fact that end crucks tend to occur in two-phase buildings, and that some among them can be shown to be late (when half-hipped roofs had perhaps begun to be used in other contexts), together with the small size and relatively poor quality of the houses in which they occur, all suggest that they belong to the later 15th century or later.

# Late medieval roof construction

Roofs are frequently the only part of medieval structures to survive intact, and even when the roof has gone, or where it is not accessible, it is often possible to deduce its original form from peg holes and mortices in the tie beams below. Thus surprisingly few houses have roofs of totally unknown form. Just as house types can be used to reveal the progress of building through the late Middle Ages, so also can roof types which vary in date, in distribution, and in the kind of house with which they were normally associated. It is therefore worth analysing their occurrence in some detail.

## Crown-post roofs

Although early examples of crown-post roofs are scattered throughout England, the form became paramount in the south east during the 15th and early 16th centuries.[24] During the course of the project in Kent, 75 per cent or 337 out of 448 visible roofs datable after *c* 1370 were found to be of crown-post construction.

Table 2 compares the development of various roof types found from the late 14th century onwards. It only includes those which could be dated with some degree of confidence. In the late 14th century, 92 per cent of all roofs were of crown-post form. In later periods, with the increase in surviving collar-rafter roofs and the introduction of side purlins, the proportion of crown posts drops, and is successively 83 per cent, 84 per cent and 72 per cent. But only in the first half of the 16th century did the proportion (as well as the actual number recorded) drop significantly to only 54 per cent. Crown posts were, without doubt, the roof type *par excellence* for open halls in Kent, and although they

continued to be used in the earliest floored buildings, their popularity speedily declined. The latest firmly dated domestic example is over the two-storey hall range at Bartons Farmhouse, Plaxtol. The date is *c* 1548*, and the crown post is a plain affair with no cap and only two-way braces to the collar purlin.

Until the introduction of the side purlin in the late 15th century, anyone who wanted a smart roof over his open hall went in for a crown post. Of 127 Wealden houses in which the roof type was recorded, only three had roofs other than crown posts. All are late buildings with side-purlin roofs. On the whole, therefore, the latest Wealdens still clung to the traditional crown post even after other roof types were available. Crown posts were, of course, found in other kinds of building. Table 3 shows that 75 per cent of all cross-wing houses and just over 60 per cent of both end jetties and miscellaneous buildings were roofed in this way. However, the fact that the crown post can be associated most consistently with Wealdens, followed by cross-wing houses, is an indication of its prevalent status throughout the 15th century.

Despite the fact that Kent has some of the largest, best-built and well-appointed timber medieval houses in England, it is not a county renowned for the use of decoration. The profusion of mouldings associated with late medieval Suffolk is missing, and even in comparison with Sussex, timber detailing was relatively plain. It is perhaps in this context that the whole-hearted adoption of the crown post should be seen. Decoration of a crown-post roof was normally confined to a moulded cap and base, possibly supplemented by simple mouldings to the main posts and their braces. Around 1500 a few of those people who built the largest and best timber-framed houses seem to have wanted more elaborately decorated roofs, introducing new roof types not previously associated with Kent. But on the whole the crown post appears to have suited the plain taste of people in Kent.

During the 200–250 years of its use, the crown post underwent little in the way of structural or decorative development. As the analysis of tree-ring dated examples in

*Table 3 Roof construction in different types of buildings.*

| Roof types | Cross wings | | Wealdens | | End jetties | | Miscellaneous | | Floored halls | | |
|---|---|---|---|---|---|---|---|---|---|---|---|
| | Nos. | (%) | Nos. | (%) | Nos. | (%) | Nos. | (%) | Nos. | (%) | Total nos. |
| Collar-rafter | 20 | (18%) | | | 30 | (34%) | 31 | (29%) | 3 | (14%) | 84 |
| Crown-post | 80 | (75%) | 124 | (98%) | 53 | (61%) | 68 | (64%) | 12 | (57%) | 337 |
| Clasped-purlin | 4 | (4%) | 2 | (1.5%) | 4 | (5%) | 6 | (6%) | 5 | (24%) | 21 |
| Butt-purlin | 3 | (3%) | 1 | (0.5%) | | | 1 | (1%) | 1 | (5%) | 6 |
| Totals | 107 | (100%) | 127 | (100%) | 87 | (100%) | 106 | (100%) | 21 | (100%) | 448 |

*Figure 84 Crown posts of the late 14th century and after:*
*a) Old Moat Farmhouse, Chart Sutton, c 1377\* (BB90/2534);*
*b) West Court, Shepherdswell with Coldred, c 1399\* (BB88/6709);*
*c) Country Fair, Edenbridge, c 1410\* (BB89/9826);*
*d) Noah's Ark Farmhouse, East Sutton, c 1456\* (BB87/6279);*
*e) Old Gilwyns, Chiddingstone, c 1460 (BB86/4427);*
*f) Symnel Cottage, Aldington, c 1460\* (BB88/4854);*
*g) Street Farmhouse, East Sutton, c 1495 (BB89/357);*
*h) Cobrahamsole Farmhouse, Sheldwich, 1508\* (BB91/6810);*
*i) Manor Cottage, Speldhurst, 1508/9\* (BB90/2601).*

Appendix 1 illustrates, it is not always easy to distinguish early from late examples; the diagnostic features which exist tend to be common to all kinds of timber construction, not just to crown-post roofs. Between the late 13th and the early 14th centuries, there was a move from elongated timbers of slight scantling to heavy timbers of considerable size. Crown posts of the 14th century can usually be distinguished by the almost square braces which rise to collar and collar purlin (Figure 84a), but by the second half of the 15th century these tended to become thin and plank like. During the 14th century braces might rise to soulaces (Figures 80a, 81a), or even to the rafters, rather than to the collar. Soulaces disappear in the early 15th century, although they came back in some of the more elaborate roofs of *c* 1500 (Figure 84g). The changes in the decoration of cap and base were slight and sometimes confusing. A number of dated examples are illustrated in Figures 84, 151 and 152, and are discussed in Appendix 1. By the 16th century the roof had ceased to be a focus of decoration, and most 16th-century crown posts have completely plain posts accompanied by spindly, and often numerically reduced, bracing. As has been remarked, Kent was old-fashioned and conservative in clinging to the crown-post roof for so long,[25] and this conservatism seems to have led to a lack of interest in developing any refinements which lend themselves to being categorised by date.

## Collar-rafter roofs

It is generally thought that simple collar-rafter roofs are either 'early' or 'late' in date, and surviving examples certainly fall into two categories of entirely different date and kind. As discussed in Chapter 5, a number remain from the late 13th or early 14th century; they occur in large stone buildings, often over subsidiary ranges of relatively narrow width. As the crown-post roof grew in popularity during the 14th century, and its use spread down the social scale, the collar-rafter roof seems to disappear. As Table 2 shows, very few roofs of this form have been found in timber-framed buildings dating from the late 14th century. They became progressively commoner from the early 15th century, but even in the early 16th century, they only account for about a quarter of all roofs recorded.

The reason for this pattern of survival may be connected with the perceived status of collar-rafter roofs and of the buildings over which they were used. They never occur over Wealden houses. They are sometimes found in dwellings with cross wings, both over halls and over wings, but the majority, some 72 per cent of recorded examples, were used over such end-jetty or unjettied houses, as at Old Well House, East Peckham, or Pimphurst Farmhouse, Bethersden (Figure 85), or over buildings of uncertain function or miscellaneous form, including several possible kitchen ranges.[26]

The majority of these buildings are small. As Figure 67 shows, the median ground-floor area of Wealdens was always well over 80 sq m; that of end-jetty houses in the period 1406–75 was 76 sq m, dropping to 64 sq m thereafter. However, the median size of complete houses with collar-rafter roofs was consistently smaller: before 1475 it was 68 sq m, afterwards going down to 62 sq m. The same distinctions are apparent if heights are compared. Heights to the level of the wall plate are available for some 272

ranges, shown in Table 4. They are separated into those relating to main ranges and those pertaining to cross wings, and it is clear that the lower the structure, the more likely it was to be spanned by a collar-rafter roof: 61 per cent of all

*Table 4 Collar-rafter roofs in late medieval buildings.*

| Wall heights | Collar-rafter roofs | Other roofs | Collar rafters as percentage of all roofs |
|---|---|---|---|
| Main ranges | | | |
| Less than 3 m | 11 | 7 | 61% |
| 3 m – 4 m | 32 | 80 | 29% |
| Over 4 m | 2 | 95 | 2% |
| Totals | 45 | 182 | |
| Cross wings | | | |
| Less than 4 m | 4 | 4 | 50% |
| 4 m – 5 m | 5 | 24 | 17% |
| Over 5 m | 0 | 8 | 0% |
| Totals | 9 | 36 | |

*Figure 85 Collar-rafter roofs: a) Old Well House, East Peckham (BB89/4815); b) Pimphurst Farmhouse, Bethersden.*

main ranges of less than 3 m high had collar rafters, and combining main ranges and cross wings, 34 per cent of all roofs lying over ranges less than 4 m high were of this form. In contrast, a total of only 7 out of 134 ranges with higher walls was roofed this way. Thus as the wall height rises, the incidence of collar rafters drops sharply.

All these figures tell the same story: later collar rafters were used over small, low buildings, and there is a clear correlation between size and this simplest of roof types. One can perhaps go further and suggest that the reason why this roof type is not found in the late 14th and very early 15th centuries is directly related to the size of the buildings in which it occurs. It is unlikely that the form disappeared and was reinvented fifty to sixty years later; instead, it is perhaps more likely that it was superseded as a desirable roof type by anyone who had enough money to afford a crown post. Thus it probably remained in use for buildings too utilitarian or too poor and small to have escaped destruction. Not until the second half of the 15th century do such buildings start to survive in any numbers, and with them survive their collar-rafter roofs. Probably there had been an unbroken sequence of construction throughout the 14th and early 15th centuries, but today only the later examples are still there to be seen.

## Collar-rafter roofs with crown struts

Among the collar-rafter roofs are fourteen examples with crown struts, that is with centrally placed vertical struts rising from tie beam to collar but without carrying a collar purlin in the manner of a crown post. At first sight these have the same form as the 13th or early 14th-century crown-strut roofs of the Canterbury environs which were discussed in Chapter 5, and it has recently been suggested that somewhat similar roofs found in timber-framed buildings in Sussex and Surrey were related to the earlier examples.[27] In those counties several have been dated to the 14th century or even earlier, and it is therefore worth examining their occurrence in Kent.

Twelve of the fourteen crown struts are found in open-hall houses, but of these only one, at Old Well House, East Peckham, definitely lay above an open truss (Figure 86b). In several houses the open truss has been destroyed and one cannot be sure what form that took, but in five cases the crown struts were clearly confined to closed trusses only, sometimes because, as at Oast Cottage, Sheldwich (Figure 86c), the hall only occupied a single bay. A second point to make concerns the types of house in which they occur. For they are not found in Wealdens, nor in hall and cross-wing houses, but only in end-jetty houses, such as Tolhurst Farmhouse, Smarden (Figure 86a), and Plantation House, Eastling, or in houses which were probably of end-jetty form but now survive too partially to be categorised; two such examples remain in East Peckham, at Hale Street Farmhouse and Bush Farm Cottage.

In the light of the conclusions drawn from collar-rafter roofs in general, this strongly suggests 15th-century dates rather than earlier. This theory is reinforced by the fact that crown struts were also used at Mead Manor, Sturry, in a possible kitchen range dated to c 1465*, and again in some of the trusses at Rocks, East Malling and Larkfield, a fully floored building of uncertain purpose dated to 1507/8*

(Figure 90b). This is not to suggest that all crown struts date to the end of the 15th century or later, for a house like Handville Green, Waltham, has service doorways with two-centred arched heads, which are likely to date to the mid 15th century or even somewhat before.

Despite the fact that crown struts are not found in Wealdens and cross-wing houses, they seem to have been used only in relatively large buildings. Thus, although it was stated above that houses with collar-rafter roofs have a median ground-floor size ranging between 62 and 68 sq m, the eight open-hall houses in which both crown struts are found and the total ground-floor area is known, have ground floors ranging from 80 to 123 sq m. In other words

*Figure 86 Late crown-strut roofs: a) Tolhurst Farmhouse, Smarden; b) Old Well House, East Peckham; c) Oast Cottage, Sheldwich (BB89/9341).*

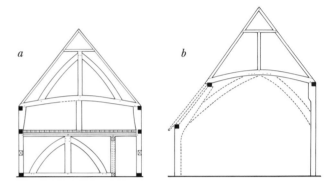

they are well above average. Not unnaturally the width of such buildings is also greater than average, and one may therefore surmise that the crown strut was used, usually in partition trusses, to reinforce what were otherwise over-large, unbraced roofs with no longitudinal stiffening. In fact, the strut may have failed to fulfil the structural role for which it was intended, but it is difficult to see its adoption in other terms. It shared neither the practical nor the decorative elements of the crown-post roof, but seems to have had a limited function in the largest of the relatively impoverished end-jetty, collar-rafter roof houses. As such it may have had little direct relationship with the 13th or early 14th-century crown struts, which also had a structural function but which, in Kent, were found only over high-status stone buildings and were only used for the open trusses.

## Side-purlin roofs

The side purlin was slow to makes its appearance in Kent. In some parts of England, the form had largely superseded the crown post in grander houses by the second half of the 14th century, but not in Kent. Side purlins occurred, in conjunction with crown posts, in the roof of Penshurst Place in the 1340s, but Penshurst Place can hardly be said to be typically Kentish and it had no successors in the county. Some early side-purlin roofs elsewhere in England are combined with great arch braces rising to high collars. But in Kent, even when such arch braces occurred, as in the halls of Ightham Mote and Cobham College, crown posts were inserted above, or, as at Starkey Castle, Wouldham, and Yaldham Manor, Wrotham, no longitudinal members were introduced at all.

These halls were constructed of stone, and utilitarian clasped side-purlin roofs over timber-framed open halls of lesser status remained virtually unknown until the late 15th century, when they appeared in a number of houses. It has been suggested that they were found first in the north west of the county and were an intrusion from Wessex, reaching the east of Kent only in the second quarter of the 16th century.[28] A group of clasped-purlin, queen-strut and wind-braced roofs certainly does emerge in the north west around the turn of the century, as at The Old Rectory House, Northfleet, Gravesend, of 1488/9* (Figure 87b), Dryhill Farmhouse, Sundridge, and Owls Castle, Meopham.

In Surrey, where systematic recording has taken place, it is clear that the number of clasped-purlin roofs in open-hall houses progressively declines from west to east;[29] but it is wrong to see this solely as a case of step-by-step diffusion, for recent research has shown that clasped-purlin roofs of more or less contemporary date were being erected in other parts of Kent. In the east of the county, two Wealden houses, Deanery Farm, Chartham, of 1496/7*,[30] and The Chequer Inn, Ash next Sandwich (Figure 87a), have similar roofs, and another occurs over a smaller and probably later open hall at Cottage Farmhouse, Upper Hardres. Since it is reported that a number of similar clasped-purlin roofs have now been found within the precincts of Christ Church Priory,[31] and since Deanery Farm at Chartham was built by the Priory, this may have been the immediate source for this eastern group.

All the examples discussed so far have queen struts and wind braces, but others, perhaps of later date, lack these features altogether. Dennes House and The Cottage, Anvil

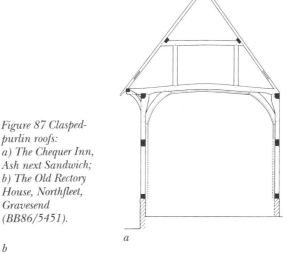

*Figure 87 Clasped-purlin roofs: a) The Chequer Inn, Ash next Sandwich; b) The Old Rectory House, Northfleet, Gravesend (BB86/5451).*

b

a

Green, Waltham, both probably dating to the third or fourth decade of the 16th century, have smoke-blackened roofs of simple clasped-purlin form. In north Kent, Sharp's House, Borden, had clasped purlins introduced to reinforce a crown-post roof; the new timbers are also smoke blackened indicating that the hall was still open, but the date of the alteration is probably some years into the 16th century. By the mid 16th century the side purlin had all but replaced the crown-post roof. Mid-century or later buildings have not been systematically studied during this project, but many clasped-purlin roofs were encountered, particularly in cross wings which were added to enlarge or update houses of earlier origin, such as Hurst Farm, Chilham, or Church Farmhouse, Newington next Sittingbourne.

The second type of side-purlin roof was the butt purlin, in which the longitudinal timbers were tenoned into principal rafters, rather than being clasped or carried between collar and rafter. This is often thought of as arriving even later in Kent, not being found in the east before c 1600. But although earlier occurrences of butt purlins are rare and specialised, their use was not unknown.

In other parts of England, butt purlins were found from the late 14th century onwards, but the earliest domestic example in Kent may be that over the hall of the stone-walled

'Meister Omers' in Canterbury, built by Cardinal Henry Beaufort in the 1440s. Shortly afterwards a similar form of roof was erected in the north-west transept of Canterbury Cathedral.[32] The date of the Meister Omers roof has not always been accepted, but there is no intrinsic reason why butt purlins could not have been used at this date, particularly in a building of high status and in Canterbury where, as discussed above, there was no strong adherence to the normal Kentish predilection for crown-post roofs.

Elsewhere in the county, late medieval butt-purlin roofs are later in date and, with two exceptions, confined to buildings of better than average quality. They are a feature of a small group of highly decorated arch-braced roofs erected in the years around 1500 or early in the 16th century, as in the cross wing at Rectory Park, Horsmonden, and the hall at the Star and Eagle Inn, Goudhurst (Figure 88). There is also one over the stone-built wing at Starkey Castle, Wouldham. At Hornes Place, Appledore, a richly moulded crown-post roof over the surviving cross wing formerly had butt purlins as well, but these have since been removed (Figure 89). A similar mixture of elements not normally found together occurs at Shakespeare House, Headcorn, where arch braces and butt purlins are combined with a central collar purlin, although here crown posts are omitted.[33]

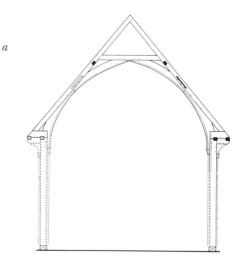

*Figure 88 Arch-braced roofs with butt purlins: a) Star and Eagle Inn, Goudhurst; b) Rectory Park, Horsmonden (BB86/2565).*

At much the same time, plain butt purlins were used in a few smaller buildings. In these there were no arch braces, but normal tie-beam trusses with the purlins butted instead of being clasped. At Farringtons, Edenbridge Bookshop (75, 77, 79 High Street), Edenbridge, a house of Wealden form, butt purlins occurred with queen struts and wind braces, and tree-ring analysis has produced a date as early as 1476/7* (Figure 90a). Rocks, East Malling and Larkfield, a fully storeyed and possibly non-domestic building, is also dated, to the years 1507/8*; it has two trusses with butt purlins and a third with the purlins clasped (Figure 90b). Vertical stability is provided by crown struts, and wind braces run from purlins to principals. Both of these roofs are really no more than variants of clasped-purlin construction and have little to do with post-medieval butt-purlin roofs. In these the purlins are staggered between the bays, so as not to weaken the principal rafter at a single point, and the common rafters are tenoned into the purlins rather than being laid upon their backs. Although it is clear that butt purlins were used in Kent earlier than has sometimes been suggested, they were not popular, and made little impact until they occurred in their post-medieval form in the years around 1600.

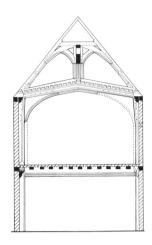

*Figure 89 Hornes Place, Appledore. An ornate crown-post roof formerly with butt purlins.*

*Figure 90 Simple butt-purlin roofs:*
*a) Farringtons, Edenbridge*
*Bookshop (75, 77, 79 High Street),*
*Edenbridge; b) Rocks, East*
*Malling and Larkfield.*

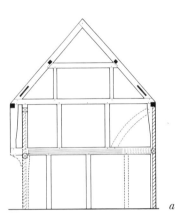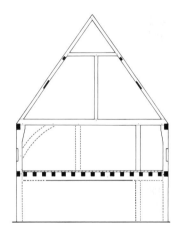

*a*      *b*

# 8 Form and function: the internal organisation of houses in the late Middle Ages

Early studies of vernacular architecture tended to concentrate on the evolution of house types or their structural elements, but more recently considerable attention has been paid to the social context of the buildings recorded. For the late 16th and 17th centuries, probate inventories have proved a rich source in helping to fill out the picture of how the various parts of dwellings were furnished and used. But for the Middle Ages no such handy source is available: in Kent very few probate inventories compiled before 1565 survive.

It has long been recognised that major changes occurred both to the form of houses and in living standards during the 16th century. The comments of William Harrison writing in 1577 vividly bring to life the comforts attendant upon the introduction of chimneys and window glass, not to mention the more general use of feather beds where straw pallets had been common.[1] Most surviving houses in Kent were already of an unusually high standard, but even so the replacement of the open hearth by a chimney, which led to the ceiling over of the hall, not only altered that room significantly but brought with it changes to the position of the entrance and to the form, position and importance of parlour, kitchen, services and main chambers above.

The evolution from medieval to post-medieval was by no means complete by 1565, but few houses described in the late 16th-century probate inventories appear to be wholly medieval in form. They are not, therefore, strictly comparable with the houses with which this book is concerned, and were not systematically studied in connection with this project. Transcripts of the first 103 probate inventories, all dating to the year 1565, which appear in the register of Canterbury Archdeaconry, have kindly been made available by Richard Harris, whose detailed analysis of them will be published in due course.[2] Information from these has been used where appropriate. In addition, a small number of late 15th and early 16th-century inventories from various other sources, mostly proved in the Prerogative Court of Canterbury, have been consulted. Information from other late 15th-century wills and inventories for the county has been taken from published sources.[3]

Manorial documents of various kinds can sometimes be valuable sources of information about house sizes and layout from the 14th to the 16th centuries,[4] but nothing of this kind has so far been found in Kent. Another approach has been to look at the incidental information included in the records of coroners' inquests;[5] but the difficulty with these lies in the fact that the information is haphazard, and can seldom be related to houses of particular size or status, so their value for present purposes is limited. In fact, no large body of documents exists which help one to understand how the medieval house worked, or from which changes over time can be charted, so the student is thrown back upon what the buildings themselves have to reveal. Although this may make the study of medieval houses appear somewhat impoverished in comparison with the study of early modern buildings. it also means that there is less need to reconcile buildings and documents and less temptation to force the buildings to fit the documents, instead of using them as sources in their own right.

Apart from size and plan, the most obvious source of information within the buildings resides in their architectural or decorative features. Unfortunately, as has been noted before, Kentish buildings are extremely sparing in their details.[6] There are none of the lavish displays found in parts of East Anglia, nor even the rich mouldings which occur in Sussex. Even so, a lot can be deduced about the way in which various rooms were used, and how this changed during the course of the later Middle Ages.

## The hall

In the 13th century, the surviving fragments of timber-framed open halls in Kent suggest that they were fairly utilitarian, with few signs of decorative features other than arcade capitals. During the 14th century, the growing predilection for crown posts meant that roof decoration was focused and small in scale by comparison with the displays achieved in the more elaborate side-purlin and wind-braced roofs of other parts of England. Below roof level, high-status houses had moulded surrounds to windows and doorways, but there is little evidence for other architectural decoration. This is not to imply that halls were bare and plain. In the first place they may have been painted: traces

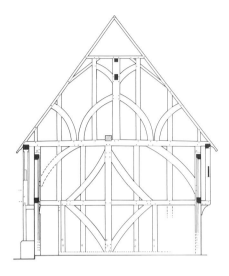

*Figure 93 (above) Manor House, Benenden.*
*Wall framing at the dais end of the open hall.*

*Figure 91 (left) Shieling Hall, Langley.*
*The open hall looking towards the dais end*
*(BB89/1295).*

*Figure 92 (below) Swan Street Farm, Charing.*
*The dais end of a formerly open hall, with*
*crenellated dais beam and projecting spere*
*(BB88/1719).*

of paint survive on the walls and timbers of large stone buildings such as Nurstead Court and Ightham Mote. In the second place they are known to have been adorned with hangings, as indicated in medieval manuscripts such as the Luttrell Psalter, which shows Sir Geoffrey Luttrell dining in his hall against the back-drop of a woven or painted cloth.[7]

Embellishment of the hall was not, however, confined to high-status stone houses. By the late 14th century, the average timber-framed house had at least some modest architectural detailing. It usually had a crown-post roof in which the capital of the open truss was carved, and the tie beam, arch braces and posts might also be moulded. The walls themselves were frequently decorated with symmetrically patterned bracing, particularly at the dais end (Figures 91, 92); although this is likely to have been partially covered by hangings in the manner of grander houses. In the 15th century many open halls were given a projecting, carved, cross beam above the fixed bench at the upper or dais end (hence the term dais beam), but examples are rare before the second decade of the 15th century. Even the Manor House, Benenden, the largest and most highly decorated early Wealden recorded in the survey (Figure 93), with a carved beam over its service doorways, had a plain beam

above the dais bench, the peg holes for which remain at the base of the wall. This suggests that in the late 14th and very early 15th centuries, the hanging in the hall may have been placed low down, right behind the bench, as shown in the illustration of Sir Geoffrey Luttrell. A hanging in this

*a*

*b*

*Figure 94 Dais speres: a) Yardhurst, Great Chart (BB89/4835); b) The Paper Mill, Benenden (BB89/5418).*

position has been reproduced at Bayleaf Farmhouse, an early 15th-century Wealden from Chiddingstone, now re-erected in The Weald and Downland Open Air Museum.

It is possible that at this time hangings were rare and expensive items, used in timber-framed houses only in the place of honour. Later, they seem to have become quite common, for there are many references to them in the probate inventories of the late 15th and 16th centuries, when they were not confined to the dais end but could be found 'round about the hall' as well as in other rooms.[8] As the 15th century progressed, the dais end of the hall frequently came to be distinguished in more architectural ways than hitherto, which must have meant placing the hangings higher up the wall, or on other walls altogether.

From about 1410, 60 per cent of all halls had carved dais beams projecting above the bench, and in halls of over 30 sq m the proportion was approximately 70 per cent, which implies that this was a status symbol. The profiles of these beams ranged from simple hollow chamfers and a single roll to more elaborate mouldings with multiple rolls and crenellated tops. A range of dated examples is illustrated in Figure 156. Nearly one-third of all houses with decorated dais beams also had short speres or screens projecting between the dais bench and the doorway to the parlour, and in many cases the moulding of the dais beam was continued along the top of the spere. Although few of these speres survive complete, mortices or mutilated

mouldings indicate their former presence. The two examples illustrated (Figure 94) from Yardhurst, Great Chart, and The Paper Mill, Benenden, are among those which remain intact, while at Swan Street Farm, Charing (Figure 92), the head of the spere survives, although the screen below has gone.

Canopies above the dais end have been found in various parts of England,[9] but in Kent only four are known at present; these are low canopies, placed directly above the

*Figure 95 The Old Flying Horse, Wye. The canopy above the dais-end bench (BB92/7713).*

*Figure 96 Smoke-blackened decorative plasterwork at Rugmer Hill Farmhouse, Yalding (BB88/2078).*

dais bench, thus allowing the upper-end chamber to overhang the hall. Three of the four are now only recognisable by the structural overhang, and any decorative effect has been destroyed; but the fourth, at The Old Flying Horse, Wye (Figure 95), has curved and painted panels forming a true canopy. Curiously, three of the examples occur in rectories or vicarages: at Northfleet, Otham and Westerham; while The Old Flying Horse lies near the church and may always have been connected with the

church and College at Wye. All of them are likely to date to the second half of the 15th century, and The Old Rectory House, Northfleet, Gravesend, has been tree-ring dated to 1488/9*.

Decoration at the dais end was not just confined to the projecting dais beam and spere. Many end walls were emphasised by symmetrically arranged bracing, sometimes positioned behind the dais bench, as at Swan Street Farm, Charing (Figure 92), but more frequently placed higher up the wall, as in Shieling Hall, Langley (Figure 91). About twenty late 15th or early 16th-century houses have close-studded framing behind the dais bench; this is usually found only at ground level, but very occasionally it also occurs on the upper part of the partition, as at Street Farmhouse, East Sutton.

Plasterwork between the timbers was often decorated with incised patterns. Only one certain example remains at ground level in the hall, at Rugmer Hill Farmhouse, Yalding, where a plain dais beam is accompanied by large panels of plaster incised with a herringbone pattern (Figure 96). The patterning runs from ground to roof, and its early origin is indicated by a heavy coating of soot towards the top. Elsewhere, combed plaster in circular patterns is commoner, like the panel illustrated from Church House, Loose (Figure 97). Whether patterned plasterwork was an alternative to hangings, or simply formed a background against which they could be placed, is not known.

Evidence for panelling is uncommon until after the mid 15th century. The earliest examples, from the late 14th and early 15th centuries, are indicated by no more than a groove under the dais beam implying the former presence of a boarded wall. This occurs in two aisled halls, at Dunbury Farmhouse, Chart Sutton, and Hazel Hill Cottage, Boughton Malherbe. It is only known in these houses because the underside of the dais beam is exposed, so it is possible that similar evidence is hidden elsewhere. Whatever the original numbers, these early boarded walls are likely to have been formed by lapped planks with feathered edges, not unlike the later 15th or 16th-century examples which survive at Yardhurst, Great Chart (Figure 94a), or Little Bursted Farmhouse, Upper Hardres (Figure 98).

*Figure 98 Little Bursted Farmhouse, Upper Hardres. Panelling behind the dais-end bench (BB87/1999).*

*Figure 97 Patterned plaster panel at Church House, Loose (BB89/7204).*

*Figure 99 Watermill House, Benenden. Evidence for the dais-end bench (BB91/21419).*

Towards the end of the century, from about the 1480s, panelling becomes more elaborate with the planks jointed into each other and decorated with raised linear mouldings, as at Shieling Hall, Langley, and at Watermill House, Benenden (Figure 99), where the position of the fixed bench is still clearly visible. One of the most elaborate survivals of all occurs at The Old Palace, Brenchley, where there seems no reason to doubt that the panelling is contemporary with the structure which was erected in 1485*.[10] Although later destruction has made it impossible to gauge numbers precisely, it is clear that panelling became fairly common towards the end of the Middle Ages. In the Rape of Hastings it has been estimated that about half the dais ends of surviving open halls were finished this way originally.[11] The ratio in Kent may have been much the same. About 20 per cent of all 15th-century halls had moulded lower-end beams above the service doorways. Some of these belong to the early years of the century, as at the Manor House, Benenden, but usually they were reserved for the finest houses of later date.

Fenestration also became the object of elaboration towards the end of the 15th century. The majority of halls, particularly those with low side walls, are likely to have been lit by plain mullioned and transomed windows as at Hazel Hill Cottage, Boughton Malherbe (Figure 111), but in some of the higher-walled houses the window projected as an oriel to give it greater emphasis. Evidence for early oriels remains in two of the large, early 15th-century Wealdens in Benenden – at the Manor House and The Moat – but they were far commoner around 1500 when a number actually survive, for example at Luckhurst, East Sutton, of *c* 1490* (Figure 100a), and Tong House, Eastling (Figure 69e). The window lights themselves might have decorated heads, ranging from simple arches, as found at The Old Hall, Sundridge (Figure 100b), to properly cusped tracery as at **Yorkshill Farmhouse** (Figure 100c), also in Sundridge. But that degree of ornamentation has seldom remained intact, and it was probably never common.

It might have been expected that more detail would have survived from the period around 1500 than from earlier years, since the later the date the less time the fabric has

*Figure 100 Windows in open halls: a) Luckhurst, East Sutton. A surviving bay window (BB92/14332); b) The Old Hall, Sundridge. A reconstructed hall window (BB88/3714); c) Yorkshill Farmhouse, Sundridge. The traceried head of a former hall window, now protected by an outshut (BB92/7726).*

had to deteriorate. Up to a point this may be true of paint, plasterwork and delicate details like window tracery, but the difference in time is not great; the destruction of most of these features probably only occurred after the Middle Ages, when taste changed and medieval buildings suffered indiscriminately, whatever their date of origin. If architectural details integrated into the fabric, such as patterned

*Figure 101 Street Farmhouse, East Sutton. Coving across the recessed hall, an applied rail below the chamber window, a moulded lintel over the doorway (at the far end) and a projecting moulded sill to the parlour window are all features of elaborate houses of c 1500 and later (BB91/6796).*

bracing and moulded beams, had existed in any numbers in the late 14th century, the evidence would be unlikely to have disappeared so completely. So, despite the possibility that more details will survive from a later than from an earlier date, the greater elaboration found in late 15th-century houses is probably an accurate reflection of the fact that greater sums of money were spent on decorating the hall as the century progressed.

Money was lavished on other parts of the house as well, notably the exterior of some of the finer houses, where moulded and crenellated lintels were placed over doorways, moulded rails applied between floors and under windows, and close studding used to emphasise the most important facades, as occurred at Luckhurst and Street Farmhouse in East Sutton (Figure 101). But more money was spent by more people on the hall than anywhere else, either inside or out. The major structural changes had taken place in the late 14th century, as walls were heightened, aisles removed and crown-post roofs introduced. Thereafter the basic frame and arrangement of the hall were fixed, and throughout the 15th century builders were primarily concerned to create more elaborate versions of an established type. Money went on ostentatious display in this, the most public room of the house, a fashion which can perhaps be seen as part of a desire to impress equals and inferiors alike. Interestingly enough the earliest ceiled halls, which in many ways reversed this trend, appeared in precisely those areas where the open hall had been given the most elaborate treatment a generation or two earlier. This architectural modification marked a major change in the way houses were used, which was closely bound up with the development of attitudes to comfort and privacy.

# Subsidiary accommodation

It has already been stated that little evidence for subsidiary accommodation remains from the early 14th century, but from c 1370 both wings and ends-in-line start to survive in profusion. Before the form and organisation of these parts

of the house are discussed, it is necessary to return briefly to Figures 65 and 67. Figure 65 shows that in the first period, from 1370 to 1405, more cross-wing houses than those with ends-in-line were built. These cross wings were distributed fairly evenly between the upper and lower ends of the house, but Figure 67 reveals that the average upper-end wing was far larger than the average lower-end one. A scaled-down version of this imbalance was reversed in the early 15th-century period. In Wealdens, on the other hand, the service end began by being the larger, although later the two ends tended to be much the same size as each other as in all end-in-line houses.

Very few late 14th-century houses have two surviving wings. Where they do, the upper end was larger, as at Lower Newlands, Teynham, of c 1380* (Figure 68d), or at least no smaller and of higher quality, as at Street Farm House, Borden. Paradoxically, where one wing and an end-in-line are contemporary, as at Hill Crest and Kent Cottage, Staplehurst, of c 1389* (Figure 68e), Peartree Cottages, Loose, or Old Hall, Petham, the wing lies at the lower end, with a small, sometimes even unfloored, bay at the upper end. This emphasis on the lower end in the majority of houses had already been apparent at Hamden, Smarden (Figure 32), and in the main dwellings excavated at Joydens Wood and Pivington.

Definition of status in terms of Kentish medieval houses is by no means straightforward, but it may be possible to detect a difference between the people who built those houses with upper-end cross wings and those with wings at the lower end. Where halls and upper-end wings survive together, as at Lower Newlands, Street Farmhouse, Borden, and Godinton Park, Great Chart, the halls are of 50 sq m or more, putting them in the category of the largest halls recorded in the survey. Occasionally, as at Chilton Manor, Sittingbourne, the late 14th-century wing was an addition to an even larger hall of earlier date. Several of these houses have traceable histories as manors or the centres of small estates. On the other hand, those houses in which lower-end wings survive with upper ends in-line have perceptibly smaller halls (35–50 sq m), and the histories of very few of them have entered the records. Since several of them lie in close proximity to other early buildings, they are likely to have been the homes of wealthy peasants or yeomen.

This permits the theory that late 14th-century timber-framed houses with upper-end wings were mostly built by people who were of superior social class or aspired in that direction. If these houses are set aside, then a second trend is discernible in which the lower end of somewhat smaller cross-wing houses is the more important of the two. This puts the latter in line with contemporary Wealdens, for of the seven Wealden houses dating to the period before 1405, all have lower ends surviving (while only four have upper ends); as Figure 67 shows, the lower ends tend to be larger than the upper ends.[12] Thus in buildings below the highest level, the lower end may have been the more important subsidiary area. However, although such a trend can be identified, the significance of such a small sample should not be over emphasised.

In the early 15th century some Wealdens survive with only their upper ends, and in Wealden and end-jetty houses of the later 15th century, there is no clear-cut pattern in favour of either end: in fact the two ends of the house were very similar in size. This is also true of cross-wing houses through the middle years of the 15th century when their proportions were little different from those of ends-in-line houses. It was not until nearly 1500 that subsidiary accommodation in cross-wing houses started to increase again, and in particular that the upper-end wing became markedly larger in relation to the hall. It is possible that this indicates a change of status among the builders, and that these did not belong to the same social class as those who erected houses of other kinds. This will be discussed further in Chapter 11.

## Solars, chambers and parlours

The question of which end of the house was the more important is another way of asking how the ends were used, both on the ground floor and above. Recent discussion has focused on the movement of the most important private accommodation from the first floor, where it undoubtedly lay in large stone houses of the late 13th and early 14th centuries, to the ground floor where the parlour had emerged in substantial farmhouses as the main private room by the mid 16th century.[13] It is obvious that the first-floor chamber was more important at Old Soar, Plaxtol, or Battel Hall, Leeds, where it lay above a stone-vaulted undercroft. It is likely that during the 14th century the owners of timber-framed houses followed the example of their superiors and made sure that they too had a fine chamber.

Although it was argued in Chapter 6 that a change from low storage rooms of undercroft form on the ground floor to higher 'living' rooms may have been responsible for the replacement of 14th-century timber-framed cross wings of the Coppwilliam type, this does not necessarily mean that the ground-floor parlour developed as early as the late 14th or early 15th century. In fact all the evidence suggests that it did not. Such a major change in the way houses functioned occurred only gradually, and where it was present, first-floor accommodation remained superior throughout the 15th century.

Since the service end in many late 14th and early 15th-century timber-framed houses tended to be larger than the upper end, and since at this time the first floor was seldom divided, it follows that the largest chamber often lay above the service end. In the same houses the ground floor at the upper end might be relatively insignificant, occasionally remaining open to the roof, as at Old Hall, Petham (Figure 51). Even if there were two storeys at the upper end, architectural and decorative details suggest that for a long time the ground-floor room remained unimportant in comparison with either of the chambers above.

Through most of the 15th century the ground-floor room at the upper end remained unadorned, the ceiling, for example, being formed by heavy, squared joists, unrelieved by chamfers or mouldings.[14] Even well-appointed and finely detailed Wealdens of the second half of the 15th century and later, such as Yardhurst, Great Chart, Brockton Manor, Charing, or Shieling Hall, Langley (Figure 102), have absolutely plain joists. Mouldings of any kind only seem to appear around 1500 when simple hollow chamfers occurred at Street Farmhouse, East Sutton, and a moulded main beam, still with simple rectangular joists, was used at Riseden Hall, Goudhurst.

Figure 102 Shieling Hall, Langley. Plain joists and moulded panelling in the parlour (BB89/1287).

It was the same with other aspects of decoration; even where the dais end of the hall was panelled, the parlour side of the wall remained plain. Shieling Hall, Langley, perhaps built in the 1490s, seems to have been a precocious and isolated example where the panelling was detailed on both faces. In a similar manner, no attempt was made to distinguish parlour windows until the very end of the 15th century, when a few houses were built with moulded sills or projecting oriels, as at West Hoy Farmhouse, Smarden, and Street Farmhouse, East Sutton (Figure 101); and windows occasionally retain moulded mullions and arched or traceried lights, as at Synyards, Otham. The houses which display such features are among those showing the greatest elaboration at the dais end of the hall. They tend to be the latest of that group, and the tentative nature and small scale of the changes suggest that even then the appearance of the hall was considered more important than that of the room beyond.

While it may seem natural for houses with large cross wings to have more than one room on the ground floor at the upper end, this is more surprising in ends-in-line houses which are traditionally considered to contain a single parlour. In fact the subdivided upper-end cross wing is a rarity before 1480, only three examples occurring in the survey, one of which incorporated a shop. On the other hand, ten upper ends-in-line were probably subdivided into two or more rooms before that. Although other parts of the house may have good detailing, as at Vane Court, Biddenden, of c 1419* (Figure 68i), subdivision of this sort

*Figure 103 Well-decorated chambers: a) Old Moat Farmhouse, Chart Sutton, c 1377\* (BB92/21712); b) Stoneacre, Otham, c 1500 (BB87/5645).*

meant small rooms which cannot have made impressive living spaces, underlining the impression that the room or rooms at the upper end continued to be of little consequence.

During the same period the main first-floor chamber remained the most important subsidiary room. In cross wings, as might be expected, it was often spanned by an open truss of crown-post form. At Old Moat Farmhouse, Chart Sutton, of c 1377\* (Figure 103a), not only were all the timbers of the open truss finished with quarter-round mouldings, but wall plates and window surrounds were

*Figure 104 False or transverse tie beams in the chambers of Wealden houses: a) Wardes, Otham. A tie beam with no crown post above (CL8854–12); b) The Rectory, Otham. The tie beam and crown post over the chamber, with the crown post of the former open hall visible beyond (BB86/4441).*

treated the same way. Chambers in later cross wings were frequently given similar emphasis. At Hornes Place, Appledore, the chamber in the early 16th-century wing has one of the most elaborate roofs in the county (Figure 89) and was clearly superior to the room below. At Rectory Park, Horsmonden, despite a parlour with moulded ceiling beams, the larger main chamber had a particularly fine roof (Figure 88b) which made it a far more impressive room than the parlour beneath. Other examples of fine chambers occur at Stoneacre, Otham (Figure 103b), and Old Standen and Campion House, Benenden. In several cases a large, decorated front chamber was reached from a smaller, plainer chamber which contained the stairs. Some of these are sizeable dwellings, certainly or very probably of gentry status. But this is unlikely to have been true of Old Moat Farmhouse in the late 14th century, or of the two Benenden examples a hundred years later. Interestingly, the surviving chambers in these three houses lie above the service end, whereas the others were at the upper end of the house.

Elaboration of first-floor chambers also occurred in Wealden and end-jetty houses. One way this was done was to introduce a structurally superfluous beam which looked like a tie beam but lay on the long axis of the house, spanning the chamber from hall wall to exterior. It divided the room into two as if by an open truss and, when combined with a hipped termination, it could create the false impression that the room lay within a two-bay cross wing. This was particularly true of those examples which had a crown post above, as at Chart Hall Farmhouse, Chart Sutton, in 1379/80\* (Figure 79), or The Rectory, Otham (Figure 104b). Normally, however, there was simply an arch-braced beam, usually cambered in the centre as at Divers Farmhouse, East Sutton (Figure 61) and Wardes, Otham (Figure 104a). Thirty-eight gratuitous beams of this kind were found in the survey, only six having crown posts above. Most of them are in Wealdens, although six occur in end-jetty houses. The earliest is probably Chart Hall Farmhouse, but the majority have mid dates after 1440. Although there are more such beams in upper-end chambers (twenty-three)

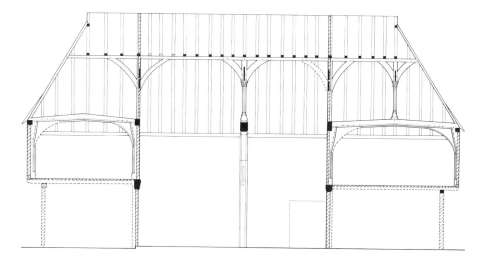

*Figure 105 Parsonage Farmhouse, East Sutton. Long section. Both ends of this Wealden house have transverse beams, although only that at the lower end has a crown post above.*

than in lower ones (fifteen), four of the six which carry crown posts are above the service end. At Parsonage Farmhouse, East Sutton, of *c* 1436* (Figure 105), both ends have transverse beams, but only that at the lower end has a crown post above.

Another feature which indicates the importance of the chamber is the presence of small first-floor doorways which are thought to have led to projecting latrines. The projec-

tions do not survive, but the doorways themselves and evidence for platforms and projecting chutes have been found, as at Rose Cottages, Yalding (Figure 106a), and Noah's Ark Farmhouse, East Sutton, of *c* 1456* (Figure 106b). An overhanging latrine of this sort has been reconstructed at Bayleaf Farmhouse from Chiddingstone, now in the Weald and Downland Open Air Museum.[15] In all, thirteen of these first-floor doorways have been noted, fairly equally distributed between cross wings, Wealdens and end-jetty houses. All the known examples are 15th century in date, and only two occur in houses likely to be earlier than *c* 1450. Ten of them are situated in upper ends, but only four are in houses with transverse beams spanning the chamber. Of these, one house, Yardhurst, Great Chart, had its latrine at the upper end and its transverse 'tie beam' at the lower end. The number of known examples is limited, but many others probably lie as yet undiscovered beneath later plaster and tile hanging. Since it is likely that the luxury

*a*

*Figure 106 Evidence for projecting latrines: a) Rose Cottages, Yalding. A small blocked doorway on the first floor once led to a projecting latrine (BB88/2665); b) Noah's Ark Farmhouse, East Sutton. Bracing in the end wall stops short for the jamb of the doorway to the former latrine; the doorway is now closed with vertical studs (BB87/9586).*

*b*

*Figure 107 Chamber window with traceried heads to the lights at Yardhurst, Great Chart (BB89/4842).*

*Figure 108 Rectory Park, Horsmonden; evidence survives for a projecting oriel with overhanging gable above.*

of a latrine would only be provided in a room of some importance, the presence of these doorways in late 15th and early 16th-century buildings testifies to the continuing status of first-floor chambers. This survey has not had occasion to consider later houses in detail, but a few examples of such doorways certainly occurred in fine 16th-century chambers, such as the two in the two high-quality chambers added to Peirce House, Charing, in the 16th century.

As in the hall, the fenestration of the chamber provided opportunities for embellishment. In so far as cusped or traceried lights survive at all, they tend to be found in halls or in first-floor chambers. This is the case in large cross-wing houses, such as Newington Manor, near Sittingbourne, or Rectory Park, Horsmonden, and also in smaller dwellings, as at Yardhurst, Great Chart (Figure 107), and The Thatched House, Smarden. Again, the survivors date from the second half of the 15th century or even later. Some of them are small side windows subsequently plastered over and forgotten, but evidence remains for larger, central projecting oriels which must have looked extremely handsome in their day. At Rectory Park, Horsmonden (Figure 108), for example, already noted for its roof, evidence for a large oriel at one end of the

chamber was revealed recently during restoration. Several other early 16th-century chambers have similar remains.

Painted decoration was briefly discussed in relation to halls, but some also survives in chambers. The late 14th-century cross wing at Chilton Manor, Sittingbourne, has tiny florets painted on the tie beam, while the crown post over the service end of Parsonage Farmhouse, East Sutton, of *c* 1436*, is coloured red. A red-painted crown post lies over the main chamber of the early 16th-century cross wing at Old Chilmington, Great Chart, although there the ground-floor joists are also red with a vivid black and white herringbone pattern on the soffits (Figure 109). Old Chilmington is a good example of the new, high-quality wings where it is not easy to tell whether the more important room lay upstairs or down, a state of affairs which seems to have become more and more common as the 16th century progressed.

An aspect of private accommodation which has not yet been touched upon is that of heating. The houses themselves reveal little sign of fireplaces in either parlours or chambers before the 16th century. It has been suggested that the stone stack built against the upper end of the Manor House, Benenden, with fireplaces on both floors, dates to *c* 1400, but this cannot be proved; in the absence of any other early examples, it seems more likely that it was a later addition.[16] Fireplaces definitely built with the house have not been found before the internal ones at Little Harts

*Figure 109 Old Chilmington, Great Chart. Painted beams and joists in the parlour (BB86/7122).*

*Figure 110 Tolhurst Farmhouse, Smarden. The skeleton of an end-jetty house in which the first-floor rooms lie largely in the roof space.*

Heath, Staplehurst, of 1507*, where they occur upstairs and down, and the external one heating the first-floor chamber in the service wing at Peirce House, Charing, which was probably built in the second decade of the 16th century. It is unlikely that even the best rooms in smarter houses were heated before the early 16th century.

Finally, the continuing importance of the chamber in the late 15th century is revealed by the isolated documents which survive. Since it was decided not to exploit 16th-century inventories, no systematic work on probate documents has been undertaken. However, about thirty-eight wills and inventories of the period 1461–1510 have come to hand which give some hints on room usage.[17] The term parlour seems to have been little used before 1490, although it occurs in two Tenterden wills, of 1467 and 1482. After that date it was found in several wills and inventories. But on the whole these appear to refer to new houses, as in a Cranbrook will of 1494/5 which mentions a new house with a parlour and buttery with 'next low chambers' and solars above, to houses in small towns, as in Cranbrook and Tenterden, or to houses which are undeniably grand, such as those mentioned in the will of Joan Hendle of Cranbrook and the inventories of William Brent of Charing and John Pympye of Nettlestead.[18] The latter were gentlemen and their houses were probably of the type represented by Rectory Park, Horsmonden, and Stoneacre, Otham, where both ground-floor and first-floor rooms were of some distinction. The fact that the term parlour is found in these contexts does not allow it to be inferred that such a room occurred in all farmhouses after 1490, and certainly not in those built fifty or a hundred years earlier. In several examples the house had a solar as well as a parlour, and the gentry inventories, where values are given, had goods of higher value 'in my Ladys Chambor' and the 'Gesten Chamber', which were probably on the first floor, than in the parlour below. Thus the combined architectural

and documentary evidence suggests that throughout the 15th century the best room in the best houses continued to remain upstairs.

The architectural evidence indicates that the emphasis on the first-floor chamber extended to quite a wide range of houses. Transverse tie beams, latrines and painted decoration occurred in medium-sized Wealden and end-jetty houses which were almost certainly built by yeomen or wealthy peasants rather than the gentry. Nonetheless the discussion has, of necessity, focused on the better-appointed dwellings, many of which lie, as Figures 103–108 indicate, in a relatively small section of central Kent. Below a certain standard, and in many parts of the county, there are no architectural or decorative details from which to deduce function; since terminology in documents is frequently ambiguous, the question of how the less wealthy used their subsidiary accommodation remains.

The documentary problem centres on the fact that in Kent the term chamber could be used for a ground or a first-floor room, while the latter could also be called a solar or a loft. Several of the documents dating before 1500 mention solars or solarium, and others refer to low chambers, base chambers or chambers beneath. These conjure up a picture of well-detailed solars lying over rather plain ground-floor rooms in the manner described here. Clearly not all houses were of this sort, but the ambiguity of the terminology makes it difficult to be certain of the arrangement in simpler buildings.

However, in 1565 enough probate inventories survive from a single year to provide a glimpse into a wide range of dwellings. Some of the same terms were still used, although by that date the term solar had disappeared and the parlour was much in evidence, indicating that changes in living styles were under way. Of the forty-four rural inventories which name rooms, the median value of those describing houses with unambiguous first-floor chambers (seven examples) was £182 15s, and that for houses with parlours (sixteen examples) was £158; for houses with lofts (nine examples) the median value was £78 16s, and for houses which *may* have been complete and had no first-floor rooms at all (fourteen examples), the median value was £29 15s. The median value for all ninety-four rural inventories was £25. These figures give an idea of the range of houses existing in 1565.[19]

It would appear that the majority of inventories in which rooms are named represent houses of above average quality. In terms of hierarchy, the evidence indicates at the top a number of high-class dwellings, which by now had both first-floor chambers (of the sort described in this chapter) and parlours below; then a slightly less favoured group with well-appointed lofts, perhaps typified in earlier houses by Tolhurst Farmhouse, Smarden (Figure 110); and finally houses with no evidence for first-floor accommo-

*Figure 111 Hazel Hill Cottage, Boughton Malherbe. Remains of an aisled hall with evidence of an open bay at the upper end (to right) (BB88/6955).*

dation at all. Most of these could have been low buildings with open ends of the kind identified in Chapter 6. It is unlikely that many have survived, but Hazel Hill Cottage, Boughton Malherbe (Figure 111), was perhaps a dwelling of this kind, with evidence for an open bay at the upper end. For several reasons it would be unwise to be dogmatic about the number of houses which fell into each category, but, as will be discussed in Chapters 10 and 12, there is reason to believe that in some parts of the county the surviving medieval dwellings may represent at least one-third of the total which existed in the mid 16th century. Almost certainly the number of houses rebuilt increases as one descends through the three categories, so that a higher proportion of those that were built with fully developed upper chambers, and later with parlours, may be expected to remain today.

## Service rooms

From the moment when service ends in timber buildings survive to be examined, the standard medieval arrangement of two rooms opening from the cross passage is evident, as can be seen in Figures 68–70. The vast majority of houses from the late 14th to the early 16th centuries were

*Figure 112 Gander Court Farmhouse, Staple. House formerly single storeyed throughout (BB88/3715).*

*Figure 113 China Court, Petham, c 1516\*. A late end-jetty house with formerly single-storey service end (to right) (BB87/8361).*

organised in this way, usually with a third doorway against the rear wall opening directly on to an internal ladder stairway to the chamber above. But a number of houses had service ends of slightly different form.

The first deviation from the norm occurred in houses which appear to have had an open bay at this end. Surviving examples of open end bays are not particularly common at either end of the house: fifteen houses have no evidence of original flooring in lower-end bays, as opposed to ten in upper ends. They are extremely difficult to date: Lacton Manor, Westwell (Figure 76), is one of a group of

reduced aisled buildings which were probably late; and Gander Court Farmhouse, Staple (Figure 112), has some framing which is not far off close studding, suggesting a mid 15th-century or later origin; but few of them have details susceptible of dating. None of them seems to originate in the period 1370–1405, but thereafter they occur throughout the later Middle Ages. At China Court, Petham (Figure 113), evidence of an open hearth, and therefore presumably of an open bay, at the lower end appears to belong to a period when alterations were made to the original build of *c* 1516\*. If the end bay was open to the roof it may have contained only a single room, although the space could have been divided by a screen at ground-floor level. Unfortunately, evidence for the doorway arrangement from the cross passage has not survived in any of the examples; as so often occurred, this was destroyed when the stack was inserted in the hall.

In open-hall houses with two-storeyed ends, an undivided service bay was rare. Where a house has not been remodelled too drastically, two clues may indicate whether the end was divided or not. The first is the presence of twin doorways from the cross passage; the second is a line of mortices on the soffit of the central beam or joist marking the position of the partition between the two service rooms. Since the doorway evidence has frequently been destroyed by the insertion of the chimney stack, and ceilings are often plastered, the evidence for subdivision is often lacking. However, some 180 houses have incontrovertible evidence for two rooms at the lower end. About thirty more with exposed joisting at the lower end have no sign of mortices for the central dividing partition. Despite this, a third of the latter have two doorways, and since two doorways strongly suggest two rooms, this implies that some partitions were not tenoned into the ceiling joists but were held in a less permanent manner.[20] In some cases the present anomaly may have resulted from reconstruction of the end bay, as at Church Farmhouse, Newington next Sittingbourne (Figure 114a), where three, not two, central service doorways now lead into a single undivided bay. But in other examples no such alterations are evident; at Symnel Cottage, Aldington, of c 1460* (Figure 114b), for example, the whole internal frame has been revealed, and while the mortices for the former partition between hall and service end are clearly visible to either side of the two doorways, there is no sign of others marking the longitudinal division of the end bay.

This means that any deductions made from a lack of partition mortices may be flawed, and if this half of the evidence is discarded, then only two medieval houses can be proved to have had a single unheated service room entered by a single central doorway.[21] One of them, Rugmer Hill Farmhouse, Yalding, has a unique form of doorway, the door itself apparently sliding sideways in a groove, like a window shutter. The other, where only the

hall wall survives, the service end itself having been rebuilt, is Searles, Speldhurst. Neither of these houses is particularly small; Rugmer Hill Farmhouse is a Wealden and Searles may have been another. Both date to the early or mid 15th century. In other parts of south-east England the single-room service end is apparently not unknown,[22] and it may be that there are other examples in Kent; but so far they have not been identified, although they certainly occur in early post-medieval dwellings, as at Old Selson House, Eastry.

The vast majority of houses undoubtedly had more than one lower-end room, and this causes immediate problems when it comes to reconciling buildings with documents.[23] Various 14th-century sources indicate that, at least at manor-house level, houses had both a buttery and pantry in the accepted fashion.[24] The architectural evidence implies that this was more or less true for all surviving medieval houses, right through the 15th century. But the later documents tell a different story. Only five of the probate inventories dating before 1510 are usable for this purpose. All had butteries, but only one, that of William Brent, gentleman, of Peirce House, Charing, had a pantry as well.[25] The 15th-century hall of his house has survived, but the service end was rebuilt, albeit still with two service

*Figure 114 Service-end doorways: a) Church Farmhouse, Newington next Sittingbourne. Three doorways now open into one room. Originally two service rooms were probably separated by a passage, leading to a detached kitchen. The end bay has been rebuilt (BB87/8196); b) Symnel Cottage, Aldington, c 1460*. Two service doorways must indicate that the end bay was once partitioned into two rooms (BB88/4866).*

a

b

*Figure 115 Peirce House, Charing. Elaborately carved doorheads of the service-end doorways indicate the high quality of this early 16th-century service wing (BB91/615).*

rooms (Figure 115), a generation or so later than the date of the inventory. The other inventories list only a buttery, and a heated kitchen which cannot have been one of these rooms.

Five inventories are not enough on which to base conclusions, but the same picture is revealed by the late 16th-century probate inventories transcribed by Richard Harris.[26] Of the forty-four rural examples with named rooms, twelve list butteries, none had pantries and only six had a second unheated service room which might have lain beside the buttery. These were variously termed: two houses had a second buttery, and the others had a milkhouse or a bunting house. All had kitchens which, with one exception, were clearly heated. However, the exception, together with five kitchens in houses where no buttery is listed, had no sign of either cooking or brewing equipment, suggesting that they may have been simple storage or preparation rooms and occupied the traditional position of the pantry. Three houses had chambers 'by', 'at' or 'behind the hall door', descriptions which fit the position of one of the medieval service rooms perfectly, and two of these contained beds.[27]

By 1565, when these probate inventories were drawn up, new houses were being built with single service rooms, and one cannot help wondering whether, even in the 15th

century, two service rooms were only the norm in high-class houses, such as that of William Brent. If so, it must have been recognised that the second room at the lower end of the house was available for a range of functions, and possibly the frequent lack of a fixed partition at this end was intended to allow flexibility of use. One possible function for a second room at one or other end of the house was to provide space for widows or other dependents. Wills, dating from the 15th century and later, frequently leave one or two rooms to the widow for life. The precise provision varied: some were given rooms in detached buildings, others had solars, and yet others were assigned 'base' or 'low' chambers; but if they later became elderly and infirm, it is likely they would have had to remain downstairs, whatever their husbands had intended for them. While new houses were almost certainly not built with designated widows' chambers, it is clear that finding room for them was a common problem.[28] At other times, alternative uses would be found for such rooms, possibly as service rooms of some kind. But it may be that anyone with enough money to build a large enough house allowed a 'spare' room for a potential variety of purposes. Looked at in this way, one can perhaps reconcile the ubiquity of two lower-end rooms in timber-framed houses with the lack of evidence for two designated service rooms in late medieval documents.

## Kitchens

Although very few medieval kitchens survive, documents suggest that specialised rooms for cooking were common throughout the south east, and there is no reason to suppose that Kent did not conform to the general trend. Five of the early probate inventories list kitchens, and many late 15th-century wills stipulate that the widow must be allowed access to the kitchen as well as to the hall. Twenty-one of the later 16th-century inventories used in this study list separate kitchens, although by then a few were apparently no longer used for either cooking or even brewing. In some cases it is clear that by that date cooking took place in the hall, either as well as, or instead of, in a kitchen – a fact which may reflect the way in which some houses were used in the later 16th century, with more time being spent in the parlour than previously, and the hall becoming more of a hall-cum-kitchen. In these circumstances many earlier kitchens may have taken on other functions.

Since detached kitchens became redundant, very few have survived, and those that do have often been heavily disguised. This makes them extremely difficult to identify

*Figure 116 Yaldham Manor, Wrotham. A timber-framed range with smoke-blackened roof beyond the lower end of the house may have been a detached kitchen.*

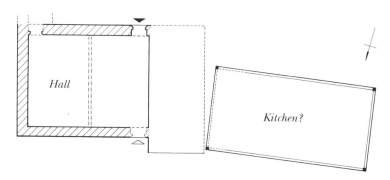

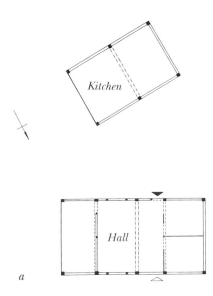

*Figure 117 Old Gilwyns and Gilwyns, Chiddingstone: a) A small range with smoke-blackened roof, set at a little distance behind the main house, is almost certainly the original kitchen; b) It has been converted to a separate dwelling, lying to the right, and in front of, the main house (BB86/4419).*

and study. It is not easy to gauge how many medieval houses had separate kitchens, nor to determine their precise form. Likewise the moment when indoor kitchens took the place of detached buildings is difficult to pinpoint.[29]

Large and early medieval houses certainly had detached kitchens and, although none survives, evidence for them remains in the doorways to kitchen passages leading through the service end from the hall, as at Nurstead Court, Meopham, and Court Lodge, Great Chart. Only one putative kitchen belonging to a late 14th-century stone house may be identifiable, at Yaldham Manor, Wrotham (Figure 116). There the service end of the house has been rebuilt, but just beyond, and lying at an angle to the hall, is an undatable range with a smoke-blackened collar-rafter roof. If it is a kitchen it is exceptionally large, and its off-axis alignment perhaps indicates an earlier origin. Possibly it did not start life as a kitchen even if it was later turned to this use. Unfortunately, because it is virtually featureless as well as unique, little can be made of it at present.

At Yaldham Manor, as in the earlier 14th-century houses, the detached building lay beyond the end of the house and could have been reached by a longitudinal passage through the service area. That a few later timber-framed houses had kitchens at one end is suggested by the presence of three service doorways, the middle one formerly leading to a central passage. This occurs at Church Farmhouse, Newington next Sittingbourne (Figure 114a), Chapter Farmhouse, Southfleet, and Gore Court, Pluckley.[30] However, it was not usual for timber-framed houses to have special access to the kitchen, which normally probably lay a short distance away opposite the rear doorway of the cross passage. Not many examples of this arrangement survive,[31] but among them is Old Gilwyns and Gilwyns, Chiddingstone (Figure 117), the kitchen having been turned into a separate dwelling (Gilwyns). Other probable examples where a kitchen may still remain within the curtilage of the original dwelling are Peirce House, Charing, and Reed Beds, Shoreham.

The simplest form of detached kitchen seems to have consisted of two bays, one of which was certainly open to the roof, the other possibly so, at least to start with. Both bays of the roof at Gilwyns are smoke blackened, and there is no sign of original ceiling joists in either bay. The same lack of evidence for flooring occurs in Reed Beds, Shoreham, although there the roof timbers are not visible. But most of the examples which are likely to date to the 15th century had only one open bay, the other being ceiled to provide a loft or chamber at one end. Laurel Cottage, Mereworth, may have been a kitchen; if so, the house to which it was related has gone. It is a two-bay structure, one smoke blackened, the other clean, which are the hallmarks of a kitchen; 16th-century and later additions and alterations have removed all trace of original flooring, but it is likely that the clean bay was of two storeys.

Mead Manor, Sturry (Figure 118), is considerably more sophisticated. Here a two-storeyed building of three bays now forms a complete dwelling in its own right. It has a

*Figure 118 Mead Manor, Sturry. A small two-storey range with integral smoke bay. It was probably not a complete dwelling and may have been an unusually elaborate kitchen.*

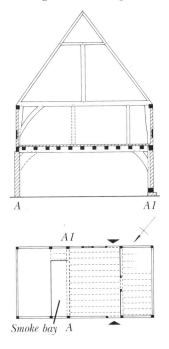

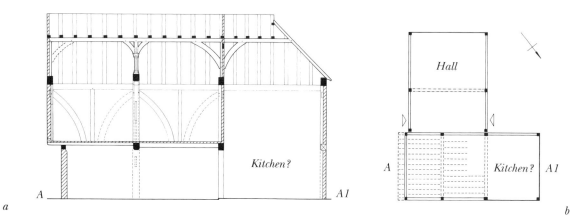

*a*

*b*

cross passage and single service room, as well as a main room heated by an integral smoke bay, only the latter being open to the roof, although smoke seems to have drifted freely above tie-beam level. The timbers have been dated to *c* 1465*, and, if this was always a house, then not only would it be unusually small for its date, but it would also be the earliest known two-storeyed hall heated by a smoke bay. Since Mead was always a manor, and this is manifestly not the manor house, it may be suggested that it was a subsidiary building, possibly a detached kitchen range serving the main house which has now gone. Because in both cases the postulated main dwellings have disappeared,

*Figure 119 Hever Brocas, Hever. A house with an open and heated bay at the rear of the cross wing which may have been an unusually early integral kitchen: a) Long section of wing, and b) plan.*

*Figure 120 Integral kitchens, heated by smoke bays: a) Long section, and b) plan of The Old Rectory House, Northfleet, Gravesend. The hall and kitchen are in a single range with evidence for an original outshut at the rear; c) Campion House, Benenden. Lower-end cross wing with kitchen at the rear.*

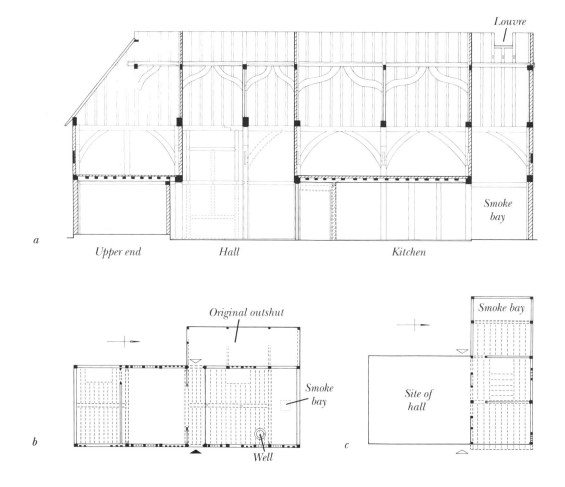

*a*

Upper end     Hall     Kitchen

*b*

*c*

neither Mead Manor nor Laurel Cottage can be firmly identified as kitchens, but evidence for partly floored three-bay kitchen ranges of 15th-century date has been found in Sussex, and two of the late 15th and early 16th-century wills refer to first-floor rooms over detached kitchens.[32] This suggests that partly floored buildings may be interpreted this way, and encourages the idea that activities other than cooking were beginning to be associated with kitchens – a first step on the path to integration.

Since kitchens were a fire hazard, the integrated kitchen forming part of the main house is usually thought of as a 16th-century development, not taking place until the hearth was no longer totally open. It is difficult to know when this change occurred, but a number of 15th-century houses had more than one room heated by an open hearth, and the function of the second needs to be considered. In two cases it is probable that the second room was a second open hall: at 13, 15, 17 New Street, Lydd, two mirror-image halls, each with a larger and smaller bay, and each with a two-storeyed bay at the end, abut each other in one long range; and at The Castle Inn, Chiddingstone, there appear to have been two two-bay open halls plus a third open and smoke-blackened bay, which might have been a kitchen.[33]

Apart from these two examples, a few relatively early buildings have open bays at the rear of wings in the position later occupied by integral kitchens. Hever Brocas, Hever, is perhaps the earliest (Figure 119). It has a three-bay lower-end wing of early 15th-century date, with the front two bays occupied by a fine chamber above an ostensibly undivided ground floor. Behind is a contemporary open bay with a smoke-blackened roof. Unfortunately, neither the doorways from the hall nor the ground-floor partition between the front bays and the open bay are visible, and the precise arrangement at ground level is unknown. But since the rear bay would appear to be too small for a normal hall, it is hard to resist the idea that it may have been a kitchen, in which case attached kitchens were somewhat earlier than previously has been supposed.[34]

By the end of the 15th century, the evidence for open bays with fireplaces, which almost certainly formed part of integral kitchens, starts to increase. In some cases the bay lay in a wing in the manner of the houses mentioned above, as occurred at Winkhurst Farm, Sundridge, re-interpreted as a kitchen wing since its erection at the Weald and Downland Open Air Museum.[35] In several others it lay at one end of the main range, as at Dryhill Farmhouse, Sundridge, and The Old Rectory House, Northfleet, Gravesend (Figure 120a and b), the latter dated to 1488/9*. In most of these the open bay was still of normal size, but at The Old Rectory House it was reduced to a narrow structural bay of smoke-bay proportions. Around the turn of the century small bays of this kind were being built as part of large cross wings containing one or two rooms at the front and a kitchen at the rear. A good example is Campion House, Benenden (Figure 120c), and another slightly later example formed part of the upper-end cross wing added to Lynsted Court, Lynsted, in 1517*.

*Figure 121 The Barracks, East Malling and Larkfield. The present attached kitchen to the left, heated by a large external stack, replaced an originally detached kitchen, necessitating the rebuilding of the service end of the house (BB88/5682).*

Finally a large number of kitchen wings, perhaps replacing earlier detached kitchens, were added to earlier houses. Occasionally they may have been wholly open to the roof, as at the Old Manor House, Chiddingstone. But most kitchen wings added to the rear of the services in the early or mid 16th century had small smoke bays at the far end. The evolution from detached to attached kitchen is neatly illustrated by The Barracks, East Malling and Larkfield (Figures 70a, 121), where three service doorways in the cross passage indicate the former existence of a 15th-century detached kitchen which was rebuilt in the late 16th century as an integral part of the house with a gable chimney stack. The service-end partitions were removed so that two of the three doorways and the rooms to which they led became redundant in the new post-medieval house.

Although the forms were various, the number of examples of kitchens for which evidence, whether detached or integral, survives, is not great. Excluding the kitchen ranges added in the 16th century, evidence was found for a former kitchen, or for a second hearth which may have served a kitchen, in about thirty houses. This gives us a very inadequate idea as to how common separate kitchens once were. In the Robertsbridge area of Sussex, one-third of all houses still had a separate kitchen in 1567, a date when the documents and the surviving houses suggest that some people of lesser status may have done their cooking in the hall.[36] In Hampshire, of 100 probate inventories dating between 1545 and 1558, 82 per cent had kitchens of some kind.[37] Probably the original number of specialised kitchens in the substantial medieval houses which remain in Kent was equally high, and we should visualise the great majority of survivors as once having had a detached kitchen, or later an attached kitchen adjoining the service end.

# 9 The demise of the open hall

In terms of the structure and function of medieval houses, the end of the Middle Ages was marked by the insertion of an enclosed fireplace and ceiling into the open hall, twin improvements which coincided with changes to the way dwellings were used. Typologically it is not difficult to chart this process. The first move was to reduce the two-bay open hall to one ceiled and one open bay, the latter containing both the open hearth and the cross passage. The next was to floor over the passage (unless it was already overshot, as in some open-hall houses), and to confine the lower part of the hearth by timber walls on three sides, so that it looked like a modern fireplace opening. A way across the rear was left at ground and first-floor levels, and the chute only encompassed the whole of a narrow structural bay in the roof. The third move was to increase the first-floor accommodation yet further by reducing the structural smoke bay to a non-structural tapering chimney stack, initially built of timber and later constructed of brick.

The trouble with this neat typological evolution is that it is not what happened in practice. The routes from the open hall with open hearth to the fully floored house heated by a brick chimney stack were many and devious. Not every stage occurred in every house, some of them in fact being extremely rare; and chronologically they did not necessarily occur in the expected order. Moreover, the whole process took a very long time to complete. The first changes in timber-framed buildings were already taking place in the second half of the 15th century, but fully two-storeyed houses and brick stacks were not universal until the 17th century.[1]

## The introduction of enclosed fireplaces and ceiled halls

### Early lateral stacks in open halls

In Kent, the first enclosed fireplaces may have been added to high-class stone open halls in the early to mid 15th century. At The Deanery, Chartham, a timber cross wing was built against the earlier hall, either in the late 14th century or some decades later in the 15th century.[2] The wall of the wing has red-painted timbers exposed to the hall, and it is clear that they have never been blackened by smoke, suggesting that the hall received an enclosed fireplace at the same time.[3] Since the hall roof timbers have

not been cut for an inserted chimney, it is likely that the stack was external, probably situated against the rear wall. This was the normal position for early enclosed fireplaces, as can be seen, at a later date, in the open halls of Ightham Mote and Cobham College.

In the second half of the 15th century, a few of the larger timber-framed open halls may have been intended to be heated by enclosed fireplaces from the start. Since in all cases the original heating arrangement has gone, its former presence is not always easy to prove. Old Wilsley, Cranbrook, is a large and well-appointed Wealden house with an absolutely clean, honey-coloured roof (Figure 122). It might be thought that the colour was the result of cleaning off the smoke deposit, but this treatment tends to leave a slightly darker shade of brown, and there is no trace of discolouration in the crevices between the timbers; both features lead to the conclusion that there never was an open hearth. The hall is now ceiled and heated by a brick chimney stack of *c* 1600, but its unusual position for a stack of that date, external to the rear wall, may indicate the site of an earlier and original stack.

Other open halls with clean roof timbers, which may have had enclosed fireplaces, occur at Bloors Place, Gillingham, and The Old Palace, Brenchley (Figure 81b), tree-ring dated to 1485*. In the latter there is no sign of a later lateral stack, although considerable rebuilding at the rear could have destroyed the evidence. The house has peculiarities which indicate that it may not have been a normal dwelling, but served some corporate or judicial function, and this raises the question whether it was ever intended to be heated at all. However, despite these uncertainties, it remains a distinct possibility that relatively high-class open halls of this period were heated by fireplaces with lateral stacks. Old Wilsley and The Old Palace were among the very best timber houses erected in the years just before 1500.

### Smoke bays in open halls

A few smaller timber houses with open halls also seem to have been constructed with enclosed fireplaces, but in these the fire lay within a structural smoke bay, placed internally on the longitudinal axis of the house. The clearest example, of early 16th-century date, is Church Farm, Bobbing, where a small bay between the cross passage and the open hall contained the hearth (Figure 123b). At ground-floor level, the opening, with a low timber bressumer, looks exactly like a normal fireplace, set against the front wall with a retaining

*Figure 122 Old Wilsley, Cranbrook. The roof over the former open hall has no evidence of smoke blackening (CL12101–17).*

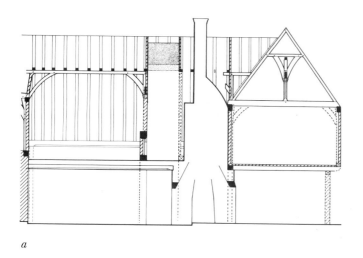
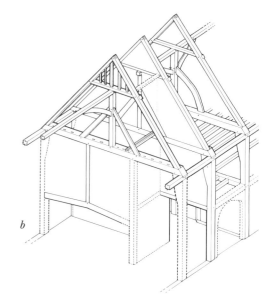

*a*

*b*

*Figure 123 Evidence for smoke bays in open halls: a) Lower Newlands, Teynham. The shaded area indicates the remains of a smoke bay introduced before the present floor and chimney were inserted into the open hall in 1603; b) Church Farm, Bobbing. Axonometric view of an integral smoke bay with passage behind it, possibly built when the hall was still open to the roof.*

wall on the other side of the fire, leaving room for a way through from one end of the house to the other. At Monckton Cottage and Heron Manor, Chilham, where the axial fireplace is again set within its own bay, the fact that the dais beam is partly masked by the ceiling shows that the latter, although not much later in date, was an afterthought. Enclosed smoke bays heating open halls have also been noted in Surrey.[4] Sometimes enclosed axial fireplaces may have been added to earlier halls which remained open. Such a sequence has been identified at Hundon, Suffolk, where a painting of the Agnus Dei on the inserted stack is cut by the later ceiling;[5] but without such explicit evidence, it is usually difficult to show that the fireplace was earlier than the flooring over. However, at Lower Newlands, Teynham (Figure 123a), smoke-blackened partitions in the

roof prove the former presence of a smoke bay, while the fact that the inserted hall ceiling comes half-way across this bay before being supported on a brick stack, dated 1603, implies that there were two phases of modernisation, the first of which left the hall open to the roof. If two-phased development of this kind happened elsewhere, the evidence for it was either not found, or has been lost.

## Partially floored halls and smoke bays

Usually the enclosing of the hearth and the ceiling of the hall took place at the same time. The least sophisticated arrangement was to leave one bay of the hall open. Very occasionally houses were actually designed this way, as at Little Bursted Farmhouse (Figure 124) and Walnut Tree Farmhouse, both in Upper Hardres, where the upper-hall bay and the cross passage were chambered over but separated by a completely open bay. These two houses are virtually unique among the sample surveyed in Kent, although the type is comparatively common in parts of

*Figure 124 Little Bursted Farmhouse, Upper Hardres. A purpose-built half-floored hall; the left half of the hall was chambered over from the start.*

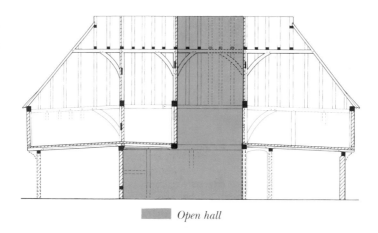

▨ *Open hall*

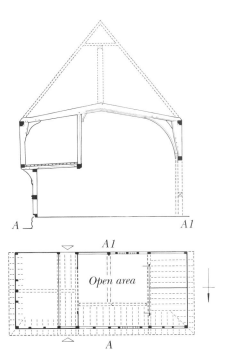

*Figure 126 Newlands Manor, Charing. When the open hall was reduced to a single bay, a 'gallery' was created along one side of the open bay; the white triangle indicates that this was partitioned off from the smoke-blackened part of the roof (BB90/14613).*

*Figure 125 Spong Farm House, Elmsted. Cross section and plan of an open hall with a gallery across the front, creating a continuous jetty.*

Sussex.[6] Nearby, at Spong Farm House, Elmsted, in 1520* (Figure 125) the matter was handled differently, with the rear part of the two-bay hall remaining open while a wide gallery, carried on a continuous jetty, was constructed across the front. Several houses of this form have been found in Hampshire, but the type seems to be rare in Kent.[7]

One ceiled and one wholly open bay are also not common among converted houses, although a few, such as King Post, Elham, and Whistlers, Cranbrook, may have been half floored in this basic fashion. The normal arrangement was to have a 'gallery' or floored area providing access between one end of the house and the other along the side of an enclosed smoke bay. This is likely to have been the case even where the longitudinal partition and ceiling joists of the linking piece have gone, as at Newlands Manor, Charing. No evidence for a linkage survives below roof level there, but diagonal lines between sooted and unsooted plasterwork on both lateral roof partitions indicate that a longitudinal partition must have separated the smoke bay from the 'gallery' (Figure 126). Although apparently rare in Sussex, inserted smoke bays of this type are common in Kent and Surrey.[8] Good evidence for the arrangement can be seen at Hever Brocas, Hever (Figure 132), Old Gilwyns, Chiddingstone, The Black Lion Public House, Southfleet, Sharp's House, Borden, and Lacton Manor, Westwell, to name but a few. An assessment of numbers is not possible for it seems likely that all trace frequently has been swept away.

## Timber chimneys

A typologically later, and in many cases probably also chronologically later, development was the insertion of a timber chimney. This looked exactly the same as a smoke

bay at ground-floor level, as indicated at Moat Farmhouse, Eynsford, but the flue tapered back towards the apex instead of rising straight up through the roof. Sometimes the fireplace area extended to the external wall, as at Belks, Otham, where the ground-floor walls were built of stone, and at Armada House, Charing (Figure 127), which was a

*Figure 127 Armada House, Charing. A surviving timber chimney in a two-storeyed house (BB87/8220).*

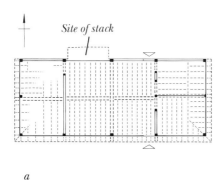

*Site of stack*

*a*

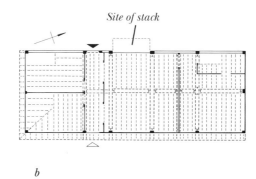

*Site of stack*

*b*

*Figure 128 Early two-storeyed houses which were probably heated by external stacks projecting at the rear: a) Court Lodge, Linton, c 1506\*; b) Place Farmhouse, Kenardington, 1512/13\*.*

two-storeyed building from the start; but often timber chimneys were altogether smaller and confined to the centre of the house, as in the example at Dormer Cottage, Petham, which was possibly inserted as late as *c* 1600,[9] or the more fragmentary and probably earlier remains at Barnes Place, Hadlow, Nightingale Farmhouse, Yalding (Figure 56), and Pimphurst Farmhouse, Bethersden. Whether the reredos was constructed of stone or made of timber and plaster is often unclear, but it is probable that many timber stacks, like the one at Nightingale Farmhouse, had no more than a well-plastered wall at the back.

## *Heating in early two-storeyed houses*

From the beginning of the 16th century, houses were being built which were designed to be of two storeys with enclosed fireplaces. An agreement of 1500 to build a three-cell house in Cranbrook specified that it was to be lofted throughout and heated by a chimney with two fires,[10] and although no surviving two-storeyed houses of quite such early date have yet been firmly identified, they certainly survive from a few years later. A number have been dated by tree-ring analysis, and these include Court Lodge, Linton, of *c* 1506\*, Little Harts Heath, Staplehurst, 1507\*, Rocks, East Malling and Larkfield, 1507/8\*, Place Farmhouse, Kenardington, 1512/13\* and Tudor Cottage, Lynsted, *c* 1514\*. Rocks is unusual and may not have been a normal dwelling, but the others are well-appointed houses which were fully two storeyed from the start. Court Lodge and Place Farmhouse are early continuous-jetty houses and seem to have been heated by external lateral stacks in the position suggested above for those late open halls with enclosed fireplaces (Figure 128).

A stack of unknown date with blocked-up fireplace remains in the correct position at Court Lodge, but at Place Farmhouse the original was destroyed and a brick chimney inserted in the cross passage in the 17th century. Evidence for the original cross passage and lateral fireplace position, gleaned from the framing of the rear wall and fragments around the present fireplace, would not have been forthcoming if the house had not been undergoing extensive

restoration when investigated. There is no firm evidence concerning the material of this vanished external stack; it may have been of brick or stone, although the total demolition of a solid chimney after only one hundred years is slightly odd, and the question arises whether it could have been made of timber. No external timber stacks have so far been found in Kent, but at Ticehurst, Sussex, the evidence for one remains on a gable wall, and it is quite possible that a feature of this kind could have been relatively common and yet vanished virtually without trace.[11]

These are not the only halls where postulating an external lateral stack solves the problem of how the hall was heated in the 16th century. At Wat Tyler's Cottage, Brenchley, built as a two-storeyed, continuous-jetty house in 1529/30\*, the internal fireplace is definitely a later insertion, and there are signs in the finishing of the rafter feet that something once joined the hall against its rear wall. A similar situation arose at Smallhythe Place and other 16th-century houses in Tenterden.[12] At Cooper Farmhouse, Pluckley, when the 15th-century open hall was ceiled in the mid–late 16th century, the joisting pattern allowed no space for an internal fireplace. The room is heated now by a small 19th-century brick fireplace built against the rear wall, but considerable reconstruction in the vicinity suggests that it replaces something earlier and larger. In none of these cases is there any visible evidence of the material which was used for the lateral stack.

Elsewhere, fireplaces lay internally on the longitudinal axis and their position is clearly marked by a structural bay of framing. At Rocks, East Malling and Larkfield, of 1507/8\*, Tudor Cottage, Lynsted (Figure 130), of *c* 1514\*, and Withers, Chiddingstone, the halls were heated by timber-framed smoke bays. At Little Harts Heath, Staplehurst, built in 1507\*, a fully two-storeyed house was still constructed in Wealden form with external decorative details akin to those of the later Wealden open halls of *c* 1490–1510 (Figure 129).[13] It has a small bay containing four fireplaces, heating the two ground-floor rooms and the chambers over, with original closets at the front and a passage at the rear. The fireplace openings are framed by timber studs, pegged to beams above, but the bressumers are not tenoned into these; instead they rest on brick jambs, and this, together with a lack of evidence for studding above the bressumers, shows that the stack was of brick from the start. The continued use of studding in such an

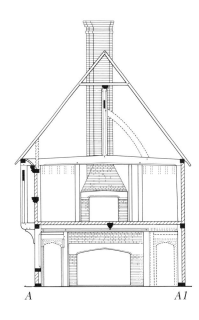

*a*                                                                                                    *b*

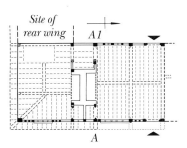

*Figure 129 Little Harts Heath, Staplehurst: a) Front elevation (BB92/7736), and b) cross section and plan of a two-storeyed Wealden house of 1507\*. Lack of evidence for studding across fireplace area indicates central stack was intended from the start.*

unnecessary way suggests that the builders were unfamiliar with brick and not quite sure of its structural advantages. This is not the only house with evidence for a brick stack in the early years of the 16th century, although none of the others exhibits the same hesitancy in using the new material.

The Priest's House, Smallhythe, Tenterden, probably built shortly after a fire of 1514, has an internal double brick stack. There are also fine early brick and stone fireplaces, rather awkwardly situated, in a small purpose-built bay at Town Farm Cottage and Town Farmhouse in Brenchley, which probably dates from much the same time.[14] The agreement to build the two-storeyed house in Cranbrook in 1500 specifies that Knockholt tiles were to be used for the roof, and the slightly ambiguous phrasing may mean that the chimneys were to be of the same material.[15] Certainly by 1513–14 repairs to Cranbrook parsonage included buying 2,000 bricks 'for amendyng the chimneye and ovenys'.[16] The wording suggests that an existing chimney was being rebuilt, and the quantity of bricks makes it likely that a brick stack was replacing a timber one.

# The organisation of two-storeyed houses

Several of these two-storeyed houses have transitional features which imply that they were experimental. In most of them there was originally no access right across the house at first-floor level, so that two stairs still had to be built in the medieval manner, one at either end of the house. Where the evidence survives, the cross passage and two service rooms usually remained in unaltered medieval form, and in many

new two-storeyed houses – as in the majority of conversions – the stack was inserted at the lower end of the hall, backing on to the passage. Sometimes, as discussed above, the fireplace was placed laterally. With both fireplace positions, the hall could continue to be used in much the same way as the open hall had been, with access at one end and the dais-end bench at the other. At Court Lodge, Linton, the upper end was still marked by a moulded dais beam, and Place Farmhouse, Kenardington, has a panelled dais-end partition.

Siting the fireplace between the hall and upper end, as occurred at Little Harts Heath, Town Farmhouse and The Priest's House, Smallhythe, must have entailed a complete re-organisation of space within the hall. How this was handled is unknown. Presumably the difficulties had to be measured against the advantage of a second room heated by a single stack. Most people at first seem to have opted in favour of the old arrangement, for the double upper-end fireplace was not common until the cross-passage entry was superseded by the lobby entry beside the fireplace. It has been suggested that this took place before 1526 at Cobbs Hall, Aldington, but as this seems only to be part of a once larger house, it is perhaps unwise to consider it the seminal building it has been made out to be.[17]

Despite reservations over the interpretation of Cobbs Hall, it is not impossible that the lobby entrance made its appearance at around this time. The present front entrance at Tudor Cottage, Lynsted, opens against a chimney heating

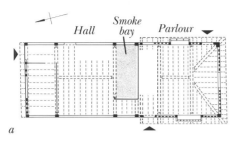

*Figure 130 Tudor Cottage, Lynsted: a) Plan, and b) front elevation of an early two-storeyed house of two periods. On the left is the hall of c 1514\* and on the right is the parlour of c 1528\* (BB87/4552).*

the parlour block which was added in *c* 1528\* to the rear of the smoke bay heating the hall of *c* 1514\* (Figure 130). When this house was recorded, every effort was made to establish whether the doorway originally opened into a cross passage and the chimney was inserted later; but no evidence was found to prove that any such alteration took place. It is therefore possible that this not very grand dwelling had a lobby entry as early as *c* 1528\*.

One of the notable features of the new two-storeyed houses is that they are among the first to show a marked improvement in the quality of the ground-floor room at the upper end, which was now almost certainly used as a parlour. At Place Farmhouse, Kenardington, the parlour ceiling joists received unusual attention for their date, and are certainly the most decorative in that house (Figure 131a). The same is true of the *c* 1528\* parlour added to Tudor Cottage, Lynsted. At Little Harts Heath, Staplehurst, the ceilings are the same in both hall and parlour, and the joists (Figure 131b) and window detailing are among the most elaborate to be found in early 16th-century houses.

Those houses with internal fireplaces away from the passage had parlours which were heated from the start. Possibly this occurred elsewhere as well. At Smallhythe Place a small external brick stack heated the second largest ground-floor room, in that case perhaps not a parlour but a special-purpose room; and there could have been an external stack against the gable wall of Place Farmhouse, replaced later by the present internal chimney. The structural evidence for such fireplaces is lacking, but since houses with internal upper-end stacks had brick fireplaces heating the parlour, it is possible that such an indulgence was not confined to them alone.

One consequence of providing a superior parlour below seems to have been that the chamber above became less important. Most of the new houses had very plain upper rooms, although in two cases the chamber over the hall was singled out for special attention. At Little Harts Heath it was not only heated but was lit by a fine window with a projecting moulded sill, decorated with incised plasterwork and spanned by a crown-post roof which is likely to have had a carved cap to the open truss (this has gone but even the end posts are not totally plain). One of the latest carved crown-post caps to be dated, to 1529/30\* (Figure 152q), remains above the hall chamber at Wat Tyler's Cottage, Brenchley. Of the six probate inventories of 1565 which specify a chamber over the hall, two, relating to wealthy households in Cranbrook and Tenterden, had the most valuable contents in this room.[18]

# The end of the open-hall era

That two-storeyed houses began to appear from 1500 onwards is clear enough, but it is equally clear that open halls continued to be built until well into the 16th century. Several late examples have been dated by tree-ring analysis. Some, like Little Laverall and Linkhorns Farmhouse, Speldhurst, of *c* 1533\* and 1540\* respectively, had small halls with a single open bay, but at China Court, Petham, of *c* 1516\* (Figure 113), the hall, though plain, was of two full bays, and at Hever Brocas, Hever, a two-bay hall with a crown-post roof was built as late as *c* 1532\* (Figure 132). Other, undated examples are likely to have been of similar or even later date. As will be discussed below, some of this distinction appears to be regional, with late open halls occurring only in certain parts of Kent.

Although in some areas high-quality houses were being built with two storeys shortly after 1500, there seems to have been a time-lag before conversions started to occur. Inserted ceilings and smoke bays or timber chimneys are not easy to date, and no examples have been tree-ring dated. No houses seem unequivocally to have been ceiled in the first two decades of the century, although no doubt a few were, and many may have been converted shortly after. Cooper Farmhouse, Pluckley, where the form of heating is uncertain, may be an early example, and others include the Old Manor House, Chiddingstone, and Newlands Manor, Charing, both of which have internal smoke bays. In Tenterden it is claimed that a majority of houses were ceiled by the time of the first probate inventories in 1565.[19] Unfortunately the 1565 inventories fail to produce an answer for the county as a whole, for although several list a number of chambers which are likely to have been on the first floor, only six specifically refer to a chamber over the hall. In fact architectural analysis suggests that many open halls remained open until the late 16th or early 17th century.

An interesting group of high-quality conversions occurs in the parish of East Sutton. Parsonage Farmhouse (originally of *c* 1436\*), Noah's Ark Farmhouse (*c* 1456\*), Divers Farmhouse and The Blue House (*c* 1468\*) all received expensive inserted ceilings with moulded main beams and sometimes moulded joists as well. The earliest ceiling of the group, probably of the mid 16th century, is that at Parsonage Farmhouse; the latest is The Blue House where one of the main ceiling beams is dated 1610. However, to judge by the plain chamfers of their main beams and thin scantling of their joists, as well as by the style of window mullions and

*Figure 131 Decorative joisting in the parlour: a) Place Farmhouse, Kenardington (BB92/14326); b) Little Harts Heath, Staplehurst (BB91/2715).*

a

b

fireplace openings, other local houses, such as Luckhurst (*c* 1490*) and Street Farmhouse may not have been converted until even later in the 17th century. Curiously, the rate of insertion in these East Sutton houses seems to be related to the order of the original building, the earliest houses receiving their ceilings first. Why this should be so is not clear. It may be a coincidence, but perhaps people were unwilling to undertake major conversions until routine maintenance was necessary, in which case the chronological order was likely to be maintained.

Evidence elsewhere in the county suggests a similar time-lag between purpose-built two-storeyed houses and conversions. It is not at all surprising that open halls which were erected only in the second quarter of the 16th century were not ceiled for some time, but other buildings were equally slow to follow the fashion. The possibility that Lower Newlands, Teynham, was left open until 1603, despite the insertion of an enclosed fireplace, has been mentioned already, and there are other examples where the ceiling or fireplace appears to be even later. At Peirce House, Charing, the placing of new stairs and the method of access to new chambers at one end indicate that considerable trouble was taken to leave the hall open during the 16th-century renovations; one part of it appears to have been ceiled sometime in the 17th century, but another part apparently remained open until demolished thirty years ago. How the hall was heated before the 17th century is unclear, but given the known gentry status of its owners it is possible that a lateral stack, of which all trace has gone, replaced the open hearth.

In another large and early dwelling, Hurst Farm, Chilham, half of the three-bay hall had been ceiled and heated by an axial stack by the early 17th century, but the other half appears to have remained open until 1714, this date being cut on one of the late-looking inserted ceiling joists. Thus, although the open hall was obsolescent by 1500 or soon after, houses with open halls nevertheless continued to be built until the mid 16th century, and there was no stampede to bring them all up to date.

Architectural evidence normally reflects social change, rather than anticipates it, but cause and effect are not necessarily clear-cut. In modern times it was central heating which made open-plan houses popular; the fact that the segregation of servants was no longer an issue was a *sine qua non*, but not an immediate cause. It may therefore be that in the Middle Ages, the need for the open hall among some sections of the community had ceased long before the room itself was changed. The trigger was the enclosed fireplace, which allowed the hall to be ceiled. That an extra chamber was created must have been a bonus, and one that could be turned to advantage, as demonstrated by those houses where it too received a fireplace, and therefore became the best first-floor room in the house. The process of modernisation began in about 1500, and the evidence suggests that, in line with developments elsewhere in England, the main impetus towards achieving fully two-storeyed dwellings came from the wealthier yeomen, not the gentry, whose larger halls were the last to relinquish their open form. This will be discussed further in Chapter 11.

*Figure 132 Hever Brocas, Hever, c 1532*. Long section and detail of roof of a very late two-bay open hall into which a smoke bay, A–D, was inserted. Later the smoke bay was itself replaced by a timber chimney, B–C.*

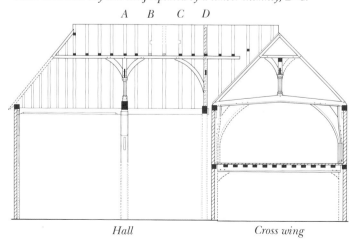

A   B   C   D

Hall

Cross wing

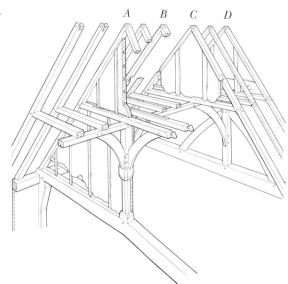

A   B   C   D

115

# 10 The regional distribution of late medieval houses

All students of regional architecture will be conscious of the way the style and construction of buildings vary between one county and the next. Few would confuse the standard timber-framed houses of Essex, Kent, Sussex and Surrey with each other. But regional distinctions within a county are more difficult to identify since the boundaries of change are seldom clear-cut. Documentary sources for Christ Church Priory show that the carpenters of the great estates were endlessly on the move, travelling long distances from one job to the next, and doubt has recently been cast on the concept of regional architectural differences within the county.[1] But the assumption that the distribution of house types was at the mercy of wandering carpenters – and in the last resort random – is not easy to sustain. Distribution of type and style is more likely to be determined by patronage, not craftsmanship. In the first place, Christ Church Priory carpenters presumably worked on Christ Church Priory properties and were not necessarily engaged on building houses for tenants or freeholders. Second, if there were regional concentrations of people with distinct social and economic priorities, it is at least possible that this might show in the relative density of different house types and sizes.[2]

When fieldwork for the project was complete, and assessment began, the sense of regional differences was so strong that initially the county was divided into six areas, the buildings from each being compared and contrasted under various headings. However, such an approach proved unproductive. It was soon clear that regional variations were far too complex for this kind of strait-jacket. There were no neat boundaries between regions, and critical differences sometimes existed between adjacent parishes or sub-regions, determined perhaps by local historical or geographical factors. For this reason the geographical unit for comparative purposes has remained the parish. Although it means that the patterns on the maps (Figures 133–141) are not always clear-cut, the larger regional differences can still be detected, while distinctions between small areas, which are unlikely to be random and certainly require explanation, would otherwise be lost.

Presenting the information in comprehensible visual form has not been easy. In all, the period after 1370 produced 480 recorded buildings or major phases of building, but the hundred or so located outside the sixty parishes were too random and too few to add anything useful to the overall picture. They were as likely to distort as to refine the pattern of geographical distribution. Only where the survey was systematic is there anything like an accurate correlation between houses and areas, although, where appropriate, the outsiders are mentioned in the text. Confining mapping to these parishes reduces the number to a maximum of 376, but this includes fragments, as well as several buildings which were not properly surveyed for one reason or another. As soon as it becomes necessary to extrapolate precise information concerning date, type, size or other factors, the usable sample is often considerably smaller, and becomes too small for more than one aspect to be plotted on a single map. However, by comparing one map with another a strong sense of regional development emerges, and this chapter seeks to identify the regional differences and relate the various strands to each other.

## The distribution of houses over time

Figures 133–137 illustrate the number of firmly dated open halls erected after *c* 1370. Houses, or major phases of building, were only included when they could be assigned a date range of forty years or less. This produced 305 examples which were divided by their mid dates into 34/35 year periods. The maps (Figures 133–137) are cumulative, each one illustrating new buildings in black and older ones in white, so that successive development in each parish and over the county as a whole can be traced.

### *Houses c 1370 – c 1405*

Houses dating to the first period, between *c* 1370 and *c* 1405, are plotted on Figure 133. They were found in only eighteen of the sixty parishes, and only four of these contained more than one example. The two parishes with three and four early houses are Chart Sutton and Staplehurst, which lie in the western part of the central low Weald and on the southern slope of the greensand of the Chart Hills. The impression of a definite concentration in this area is reinforced by buildings outside the designated parishes, for other early examples have been found in the vicinity, for example in Sutton Valence and Yalding. Apart from this cluster, which may extend westwards as far as Plaxtol, where there are two houses of late 14th-century date, most of the buildings which can be dated to this period are widely dispersed.

North of the Downs several parishes in central and eastern Kent contain isolated late 14th-century houses, and the picture could be supplemented by others from parishes such as Sittingbourne, Teynham and Lynsted, all in the central section of the northern plain. Comparison with Figure 16, which plotted the incidence of late 13th and early 14th-century timber-framed houses, indicates that the areas where late 14th-century houses occur are very much the same; this suggests a certain continuity, which in turn reinforces the claim that the pattern is not a matter of pure chance.

*Figure 133 Number and distribution of open-hall houses, or major phases of building, in the sixty surveyed parishes, 1370–1405. Only those houses are plotted which can be dated within a range of forty years or less.*

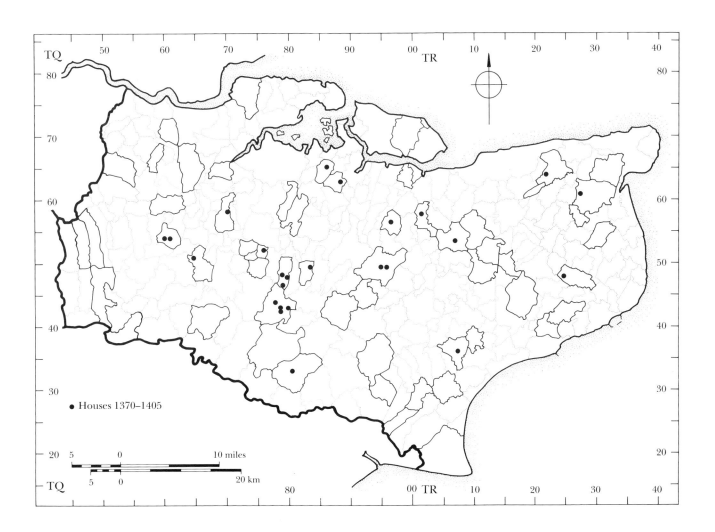

## Houses c 1406 – c 1440

Figure 134 indicates those houses believed to date between *c* 1406 and *c* 1440. They have been superimposed over the earlier distribution which allows the new buildings to be compared with the aggregate. As discussed earlier, the number of houses datable to this second period is not large, particularly within the sixty surveyed parishes. It is, however, noticeable that the greatest number were found in precisely the same low Weald and ragstone region as before, with only a few outliers further south and west. Again, the concentration within the surveyed parishes can be augmented by those from elsewhere, for a few houses dating before the mid 15th century were also found in the south-western parishes of Capel, Hever and Edenbridge. Not only were almost no early 15th-century houses discovered in the eastern half of the county, but very few occur anywhere north of the Downs. Indeed, it would appear that the building activity of the previous period, which was spread across much of north Kent, tailed off. Meanwhile a number of new houses continued to be erected in the western low Weald.

## Houses c 1441 – c 1475

Many more houses remain from the 1450s onwards. Those built in the mid and third quarter of the 15th century are illustrated on Figure 135, which shows open-hall houses with mid dates lying between 1441 and 1475. By this time far more of the county is covered. Fewer new buildings were found in Chart Sutton and Staplehurst, but considerable numbers were identified elsewhere in the low Weald and on

*Figure 134 Number and distribution of open-hall houses, or major phases of building, in the sixty surveyed parishes, 1406–40. Only those houses are plotted which can be dated within a range of forty years or less.*

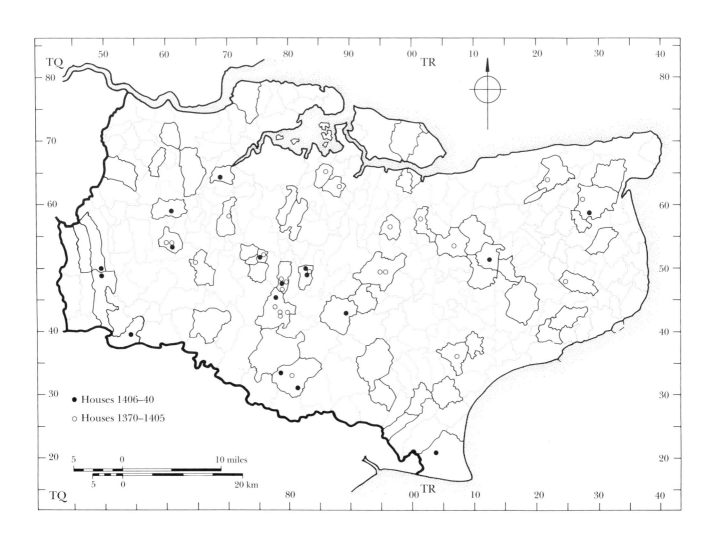

Legend:
- Houses 1406–40
- Houses 1370–1405

the greensand, with five or more occurring in Chiddingstone and Plaxtol to the west, and in Pluckley and Smarden to the east. In other areas, an unexpectedly large number seem to have been built in the northern parish of Borden near Sittingbourne, but otherwise they appear only sporadically north of the Downs, in the Vale of Holmesdale, the Stour valley, or the high Weald. In several parishes along the northern and eastern edges of the county, no buildings of this period were identified at all.

## Houses c 1476 – c 1510

The fourth map, Figure 136, illustrates the numerous open-hall houses built in the last quarter of the 15th century and the first decade of the 16th. It shows the rather generalised picture of Figure 135 filled out and expanded in selective ways. In some parts of southern central and western Kent, the number of new houses neither exceeded nor even matched the number built at earlier periods. This is particularly noticeable in the group of parishes lying directly south of Maidstone. On the other hand, activity seems to have intensified in certain areas. These include low Wealden parishes such as East Peckham and Smarden, as well as others in the Vale of Holmesdale, the Stour valley, on the Downs and the northern plain. At the same time, although the size of the parishes and the dispersal of settlements dilute the impact, this was the period when most surviving medieval houses in the parishes of the high Weald, such as Cranbrook and Benenden, were erected. No more than one or two houses were found in a number of parishes in north and east Kent, and nine of the sixty parishes still produced no closely datable late medieval houses at all. Most of these

*Figure 135 Number and distribution of open-hall houses, or major phases of building, in the sixty surveyed parishes, 1441–75. Only those houses are plotted which can be dated within a range of forty years or less.*

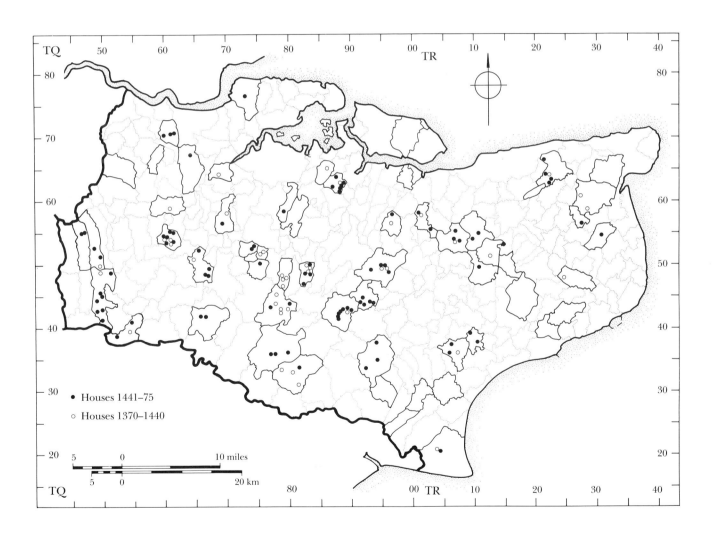

parishes lay along the north coast and in the rural parts of Romney Marsh. In a number of cases, houses survive in too fragmentary a condition for close dating, and they could not, therefore, be plotted on the maps. However, it is likely that the majority date to this period. They occur throughout the county, and in some cases would fill the gaps on Figure 136. Examples are Warden Manor, Eastchurch on the Isle of Sheppey, and The Woolpack Inn, Brookland on Romney Marsh.

## *Houses c 1511 – c 1545*

For the sake of clarity in the final chronological distribution map, Figure 137, the aggregate has been abandoned and only those open-hall houses dated after 1510 have been plotted. Not many were discovered – two lay in the centre of the county, but these are not enough to disturb the overall impression that new open-hall houses in the centre of Kent were few and far between, and that when new dwellings were put up, they were fully storeyed throughout. New open-hall

houses were only found in any number in the far west of the Weald and in a restricted part of the eastern Downs. The buildings tend to be simple and not easily datable, but several were sampled by tree-ring dating, and proved to have been erected well into the 16th century. Houses of this type were not often encountered outside the parishes of the survey.

## The distribution of house types

Before the historical significance of the pattern of survival can be discussed further, it is necessary to consider whether there is any connection between the chronological distinction and the various house types. The relationship between the date and type of medieval houses has been considered already in Chapter 6; if the conclusions reached

*Figure 136 Number and distribution of open-hall houses, or major phases of building, in the sixty surveyed parishes, 1476–1510. Only those houses are plotted which can be dated within a range of forty years or less.*

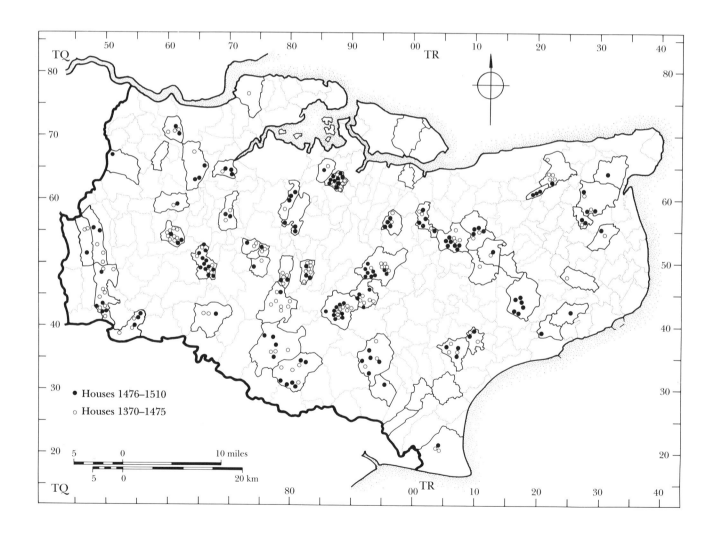

there are sound, it might be expected that different house types would have different distribution patterns across the county. However, as Figure 138 indicates, the picture is by no means straightforward.

On Figure 138, houses have been plotted by type, using only those examples in which type is clearly defined. The proportion of one type to another within each parish is illustrated, and the size of the circles provides a rough guide to the number of examples used. The actual number of medieval houses identified in each parish, classified by type and including those of uncertain form, can be found in Appendix 2. This method, though crude, produces a visual impression of relative density and distribution. Fifty-two of the sixty surveyed parishes were found to have closely datable late medieval buildings of identifiable type, and each of the three main categories – cross wings, Wealdens and end jetties –

*Figure 137 Number and distribution of open-hall houses, or major phases of building, in the sixty surveyed parishes, 1511–45. Only those houses are plotted which can be dated within a range of forty years or less.*

occurred in about two-thirds of them (thirty-six or thirty-seven out of fifty-two). The proportions of each varied considerably, but a number of interesting points emerge, especially if one considers those parishes in which a particular type forms 50 per cent or more of the identifiable buildings surviving.

In writing about Wealdens in 1963, Rigold rightly located the area where the largest number occur as lying in a square, east of the Medway and west of the Stour and Romney Marsh, comprising the Weald, the southern slopes of the ragstone hills and the Downs, and the plain to the north.[3] On Figure 138 this square includes, with one exception, all the parishes in which Wealdens both form 50 per cent or more of the house types and the large size of the circles indicates that eight or more buildings were used in the assessment. The parishes where the incidence of Wealdens is most striking are Benenden, Charing, East Sutton and Woodchurch, although sizeable numbers also occur in Borden and Chilham.

Rigold was well aware that other types of house could be found in this square and came to feel that the prominence of the Wealden had been somewhat overstressed, particularly in the Weald itself.[4] The proportions of the different types

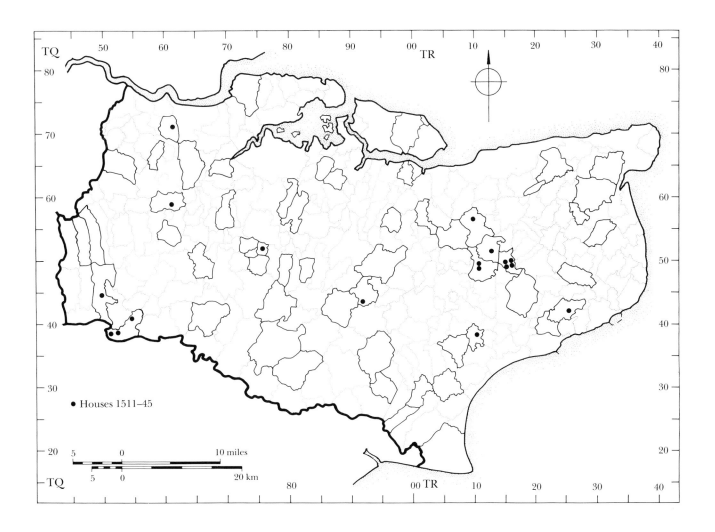

shown on Figure 138 help to put this into perspective. In no parish of more than seven examples do Wealdens form more than 70 per cent of identifiable houses, and within Rigold's square there are a number of parishes in which Wealdens are relatively insignificant. The large circles representing East Peckham, Chart Sutton, Staplehurst, Smarden and Pluckley are all dominated by other forms, and the same is true of several of the medium and small circles in this region.

Although there is no doubt that Wealdens are much more numerous in this central swathe than elsewhere, they actually constitute as large a proportion of the surviving houses in parts of east and even west Kent. In the east they account for 50 per cent or more of the houses in parishes such as Minster in Thanet, Ash next Sandwich, Shepherdswell with Coldred, Elham, Sellindge and Lydd, and the same is true of Southfleet, Eynsford and Sundridge to the west. Many of these parishes have very few medieval houses remaining, a matter to which it will be necessary to return. The points to stress here are firstly that, despite the conspicuousness of

*Figure 138 Proportions and distribution of the main types of open-hall house within the sixty surveyed parishes, 1370–1545. Houses whose form cannot be identified have not been included.*

Wealdens in the centre of the county, other forms are more numerous in many parishes, and secondly that Wealdens can form as large a proportion of the surviving total in other parts of Kent as in the central region.

It was Rigold's impression that the end-jetty house was dominant in the Weald itself.[5] The present project has only shown this to be the case in a few parishes, as indicated by the large circles representing East Peckham, Smarden and Pluckley and smaller ones representing East Farleigh, Linton (neither of these strictly speaking in the Weald) and Speldhurst. In other cases, as shown by the large circles for Staplehurst, Chart Sutton and East Malling and Larkfield, and the smaller one for Loose, the dominant type was the cross-wing house. Outside the central area no consistent pattern emerges; cross wings or end jetties are the common alternatives to Wealdens in north and east Kent, and end jetties or unjettied houses are prevalent in the west.

If one considers this map in relation to the chronological series, it becomes clear that cross wings predominate in the area of the earliest buildings around Staplehurst and Chart Sutton. In fact, though largely obscured by later houses on Figure 138, the majority of late 14th-century buildings in the north were also of cross-wing form. It is less easy to see a

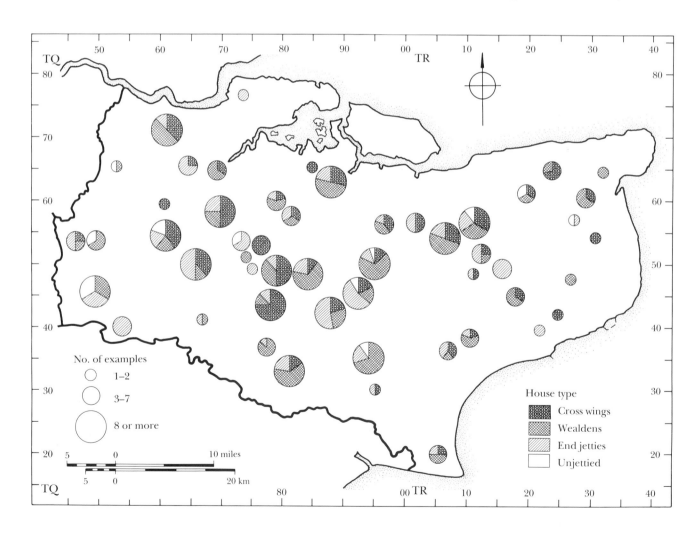

chronological peak for Wealdens. They are the predominant type in East Sutton, where houses were built steadily throughout the 15th century, in Charing where surviving houses date from the middle and second half of the 15th century, and in Benenden, Cranbrook and Woodchurch where most of the buildings date to the very end of the 15th century. Wealdens are most numerous in parishes where the settlement seems to be more widely dispersed (Figures 135, 136) – this is particularly noticeable in the high Weald and in Woodchurch – whereas the end jetty tends to be most prevalent in parishes such as East Peckham, Smarden and Pluckley where the majority of houses are late in date and more densely packed.

Parishes on the Downs and in west Kent appear to show a greater mixture both in types of building and in dates of erection. In Speldhurst in the western Weald, and in the eastern downland parishes around Upper Hardres, where open halls persisted into the 16th century, houses were nearly all of unjettied or end-jetty form. In parishes with large numbers of buildings of more varied date and type, such as Chiddingstone to the west and Chilham and Chartham in the Stour valley to the east, there is a distinct tendency for Wealdens to precede end jetties or unjettied houses, but the overlap in date is considerable. In the far east, the number of buildings surviving in any one parish is frequently too small for a pattern to emerge, but it is the case that the earlier buildings, such as Tudor House, Chislet, West Court, Shepherdswell with Coldred, or The Ship Inn and Uphousden Farm in Ash next Sandwich, are of cross-wing or Wealden construction, while the latest houses, such as Ashby Cottage, Westbere, Dane Farm, Hawkinge, or The Black Pig Inn and Gander Court Farmhouse in Staple have end jetties or are not jettied at all.

# The distribution of houses by size

A further issue to be explored is the distribution pattern of the marked variations in the size of houses. It was argued in Chapter 6 that there was a definite correlation between size of house and type of house, and it should therefore be possible in principle to translate a pattern of distribution by type into a pattern of distribution by size. The matter is, of course, complicated by the fact that most parishes in which more than one or two medieval houses survive contain several types of construction. Thus the first point to consider is the relationship between the sizes of different house types within a given area or parish.

It has been established already that the proportion of the open hall to the rest of the accommodation remained more or less constant in all ends-in-line houses throughout the Middle Ages, only cross-wing houses having rather smaller halls in relation to their total areas. This means that the size of the hall can be taken as an index for the relative size of the house; since hall areas are known for many houses in which the total accommodation cannot be calculated, the following discussion focuses on hall size rather than on house size.

In general, over the county as a whole, the open hall in cross-wing houses has a median size of 50 sq m, that for Wealdens is 43 sq m, for end jetties 35 sq m, and for unjettied buildings 34 sq m. When one examines the range of hall sizes within individual parishes, it becomes apparent that where the median size of Wealden houses is above that

for the county as a whole, as in Benenden (53.5 sq m), Woodchurch (48 sq m) or East Sutton (47 sq m), end-jetty houses are likewise larger than usual (42, 40 and 45.5 sq m respectively). Similarly, where the median size of Wealdens was below that for the county, as in Petham (41 sq m) or Southfleet (31 sq m), the end-jetty house was likely to be smaller (32 and 30 sq m respectively). Not unnaturally the ratios are not constant, and surprises can occur. In Plaxtol both Wealdens and end jetties have a median size of 38 sq m, and in Borden on the northern coastal plain the median size of Wealden halls is only 32 sq m, but the presence of one large and early end-jetty house brings that median up to 43 sq m. Nonetheless, there is a marked tendency for the size of house to be dictated not only by its type but also by its location.

This is demonstrated in a general way on Figure 139 which plots the distribution of houses according to hall size. The parishes have been divided into three groups: those in which the median size of hall is 40 sq m or more, those in which the median size is between 36 and 40 sq m, and those where it is less than 36 sq m. As on Figure 138, the size of the circle forms a rough guide to the number of halls represented in each parish. In some parishes the sample is noticeably smaller than the one occurring in Figure 138; this is particularly the case in those which are dominated by cross wings, for all too often the medieval hall has been totally or partially destroyed and cannot be measured. Parishes where this occurs include Staplehurst, Chart Sutton, East Malling and Larkfield and Chislet. Occasionally, as in Speldhurst and Sheldwich, many houses whose type is unclear have halls surviving, so the size of the sample, and of the circle, has actually increased.

Despite these problems the largest halls of all occur in thirteen parishes, of which five were dominated by cross wings, five by Wealdens and three in which there was a mixture. They are found mostly in parts of the low and high Weald and the centre of the county, and there are a few in north and east Kent. However, they are notably lacking over the whole of the west and north west of the county, even in parishes such as Southfleet, Halling, East Malling and Larkfield and Plaxtol where there was a high proportion of cross wings, or of cross wings and Wealdens. Parishes in which the median size of hall lay between 36 and 40 sq m are spread towards south and west Kent, with only a few outliers to north and east. They account for most of the high and low Weald and most of the surveyed parishes on the ragstone and in the Vale of Holmesdale, including Wrotham, Plaxtol, Thurnham, Detling, Charing and Pluckley. Finally, those parishes with a bias towards small houses have a predominantly northerly and westerly distribution, occurring on the Downs and on the northern plain right across the county, and on the ragstone and in the Weald to the west. In some cases the change from large to small is extremely abrupt. This is particularly noticeable in east Kent, between the houses of Chilham and Chartham in the Stour valley and those in the downland parishes to either side. An equally striking contrast is visible between the large houses of Staplehurst, East Sutton, Chart Sutton and Sutton Valence and the much smaller ones almost immediately to the west in East Peckham, East Farleigh and Loose.

When the different strands of information on date, type and size are put together, the variations begin to fall into place and the surviving pattern looks less and less random.

Houses of the late 14th and very early 15th centuries, as indicated in Figure 67, were larger than the majority of those built in the 15th century. They occur in clusters only in the western part of the central low Weald, and in isolation in the centre and eastern parts of north Kent, where early 14th-century timber-framed building had predominated. To start with, and following on from developments of the late 13th and early 14th centuries, cross wings were most numerous; however, several late 14th-century Wealdens were identified, and early examples in eastern Kent show that their distribution was widespread from the moment they first occurred.

During much of the 15th century cross-wing houses became smaller, and the gap in size between them and Wealden houses decreased. Given the quality of many Wealdens, it is possible that some people who were not over-concerned with size, but wanted the best that money could buy, turned away from the more old-fashioned design and chose Wealdens instead. They dominate most parishes where

*Figure 139 Median sizes of timber-framed open halls within the sixty surveyed parishes, 1370–1545.*

considerable numbers of large houses were erected in the mid and late 15th century, as in Chilham, East Sutton and Sellindge, and above all they occur in and near the central high Weald, in Cranbrook, Benenden and Woodchurch.

On the other hand, during the 15th century the numerous houses built in parishes such as Chiddingstone, Plaxtol and East Peckham to the west of the early buildings, and Smarden, Pluckley and Charing to the east, were smaller; here the dominant types were more likely to be cross wings or end jetties, although some small Wealdens occur in Charing.[6] In north-west Kent nearly all medieval houses are of relatively late date and small size. Most of the survivors are widely dispersed, although clusters occur occasionally, as in Southfleet, Halling and Borden. Where this happens the houses are often of Wealden form, and are among the smallest in the county. In the north east the picture is altogether more varied. Some early and sizeable cross-wing and Wealden houses remain, together with small and late examples of end-jetty and unjettied form; the greater disparity in date, size and type which is a feature of this region suggests that the builders may have varied more widely in their economic, and possibly social, status than the

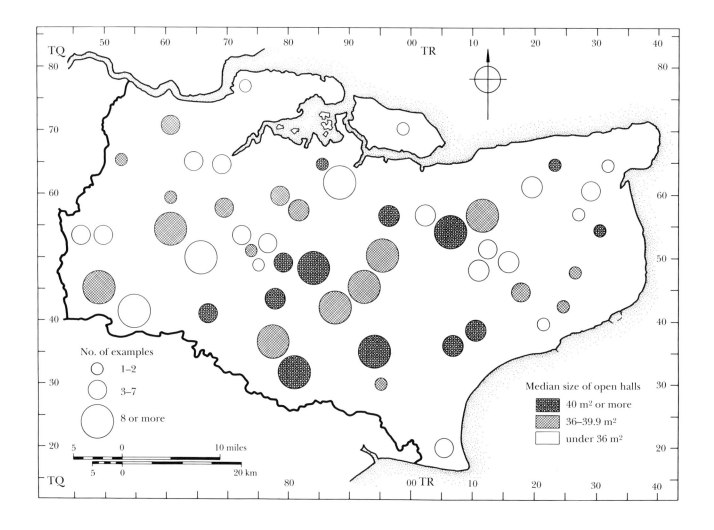

more uniform groupings in much of central and western Kent imply. Finally, there are parishes on the fringes of the county, notably on and near Sheppey, and in the rural parts of Romney Marsh, where no medieval buildings survive at all.

In some cases distinctions between regions are blurred because of more localised variations between sub-regions or even adjacent parishes. An example, which has already been noted, is the extraordinary early date and great size of buildings in the Staplehurst, Chart Sutton and East Sutton area. These stand out from the later buildings in the surrounding areas, all of which are far smaller. Sometimes striking contrasts are apparent even between one parish and the next. North of the Downs, the numerous small Wealdens and other dwellings of Borden do not appear to be repeated in the adjoining parish of Newington next Sittingbourne, where only two large cross-wing houses were found. An equally marked disparity, particularly in terms of numbers, emerges between Wrotham and Plaxtol, the former in the Vale of Holmesdale, the latter on the ragstone, but both originally forming part of the extensive manor of Wrotham. A less obvious but equally curious difference occurred between Cranbrook and Benenden,

with houses outside Cranbrook town being consistently smaller than those in rural Benenden. It is beyond the scope of this book to resolve the historical problems posed by such variations, but it would be wrong not to explore them further, and several of these contrasts are discussed in more detail in Chapter 12.

# The density of distribution

Although Figures 138 and 139 give a general indication of the number of houses forming the sample in each parish, they do not illustrate the actual density of survivors. A better impression of density is provided by the chronological maps (Figures 133–137), in which each building has been plotted as accurately as the scale allows. Figure 140 turns these examples, and others whose dates are too uncertain to appear on Figures 133–137, into numbers of open-hall houses per 1,000 acres. Up to a point, the greatest density

*Figure 140 Density of open-hall houses per 1,000 acres within the sixty surveyed parishes.*

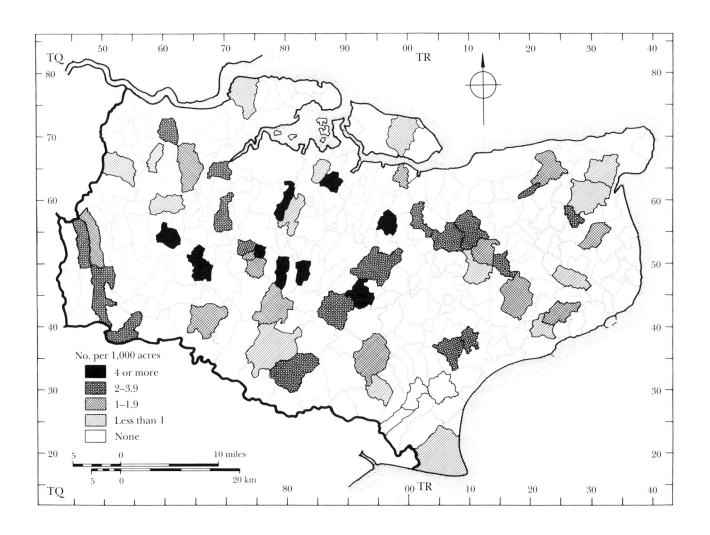

No. per 1,000 acres
- 4 or more
- 2–3.9
- 1–1.9
- Less than 1
- None

10 miles

20 km

occurs in those parishes with the largest number of survivors; but since parish size is now part of the equation, some of the largest parishes do not fall into the highest category. Those in which there are four or more medieval houses per 1,000 acres are closely grouped in the central and western part of the county.

In Essex a high density of surviving medieval buildings has been associated with parishes lying on the boulder clay.[7] To some extent the densest distribution in Kent lies on the greensand of the Chart Hills, but high numbers also occur in East Peckham, on the clay and alluvium of the low Weald and Medway valley, in Detling which is partly on chalk and partly on gault clay, and in Borden and Eastling which lie on the northern slopes of the chalk and on the fertile plain below. Thus all lie on reasonably fertile land, but precise geological or soil formation does not appear to be a paramount factor. Possibly of more significance is the fact that none of the parishes is large in size; in general there is a tendency for small parishes to have a higher density of medieval buildings than large ones. From this one might surmise a correlation between size of parish and size of holding, which in turn might be related to the date and

pattern of settlement, and the extent of the wastes, in different regions.

The second highest category, parishes in which between two and four buildings per 1,000 acres survive, spreads from one end of the county to the other, although fewer are found in the north east and in the high Weald. All the parishes with eight or more medieval buildings remaining are in these top two categories, with the notable exceptions of Staplehurst, Cranbrook and Woodchurch, which lie within the high and low Weald. The third and fourth categories are most marked around the fringes of the county, particularly in the north west, the north east and much of the high Weald.

To make any sense of the density of houses, the figures have to be related to the density of contemporary population, and this is not easy to do. As discussed in Chapter 1, assessments of medieval population or household numbers are neither plentiful, extensive nor wholly reliable. No surveys of the 15th or 16th century

*Figure 141 Surviving open-hall houses as a proportion of households recorded in 1557.*

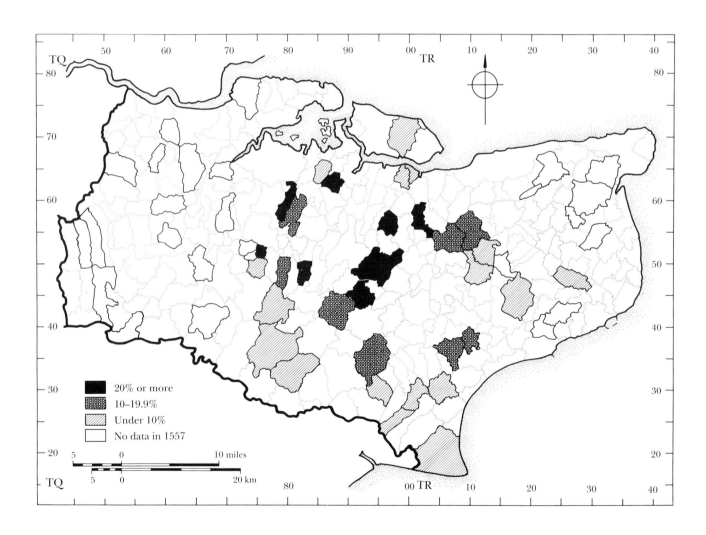

survive for west Kent, and for the centre and eastern part of the county, that is for the diocese of Canterbury, the earliest figures occur in two surveys, of 1557 and 1563, which enumerate communicants, or households, or both.[8] Unfortunately, the less complete survey of 1557, which only covers thirty-three of the sixty surveyed parishes, is probably the more accurate of the two. Since household numbers in the mid 16th century can be no more than a very rough guide to household numbers thirty to forty years earlier, and since the evidence assembled by the present project is restricted to open-hall houses, not to mention the added complication that the ecclesiastical parishes of the 16th-century surveys are not always identical with modern civil parishes, the chances of establishing a close correlation between houses and the numbers extrapolated from the documents are at best not high – and at worst may be positively misleading. But since this is the only means we have of estimating what proportion of the population lived in the surviving medieval houses, there is no alternative. Thus Figure 141 plots the number of surviving open-hall houses as a proportion of the households recorded in 1557. Although accurate interpretation is fraught with difficulties, a pattern of distribution emerges which is interesting enough to suggest that the exercise is worthwhile.

The parishes have been divided into three categories: those in which the surviving houses could have catered for over 20 per cent of the mid 16th-century population, those in which they served between 10 and 20 per cent, and those in which they account for under 10 per cent of the households recorded in 1557. The three Romney Marsh parishes in which no medieval houses were identified have been included in this latter category.

The complexities encountered when considering the meaning of these figures can be illustrated by examining the handful of parishes in which the number who paid the Poll Tax of 1377 and the communicants in 1557 can be compared. It so happens that both figures are available for most of those parishes in which the surviving medieval houses account for over 20 per cent of the households recorded in 1557, and it provides an opportunity to see how a rise or fall in the population affected the result. This group is concentrated in a relatively small area of central and northern Kent. In only three parishes, Borden, Eastling and Sheldwich, which all lie north of the Downs, do the houses represent more than 30

per cent of the mid 16th-century households. For Eastling and Sheldwich this is somewhat surprising, since the actual number of surviving medieval buildings there is not outstandingly high. The reason is that in these two parishes the population had fallen by nearly 40 per cent between 1377 and 1557, so the proportion of houses to households is exaggerated to the point of being misleading. This may not have been the case in Borden, where the absolute numbers of surviving medieval houses is considerably higher (see Appendix 2), but for that parish there are no detailed figures for 1377.

The situation in parishes south of the Downs is somewhat different, although the tiny parish of Loose where the population had also dropped by over 30 per cent is an exception. But in Detling, Charing and Pluckley the population had risen by between 36 per cent and 60 per cent. Since demographic trends suggest that the upturn is more likely to have taken place after 1520 than before,[9] it is probable that the proportion of houses to households in these parishes has gone the other way. In most of this central area south of the Downs, the surviving medieval houses could represent the homes of a sizeable part of the medieval population; certainly over 30 per cent and possibly much higher. Other parishes, where the population only rose or fell by under 10 per cent are Linton, Chart Sutton and Aldington; so in these Figure 141 may be reasonably accurate.

It may be thought that the problems outlined above are too complex to make Figure 141 meaningful. However, despite the reservations, it has its uses. Only through a map of this kind can one even begin to realise how large a proportion of the medieval population of Kent lived in houses which actually survive, and this provides a clue to their likely social and economic condition. It is of considerable importance to know whether the houses may have been inhabited by 30–40 per cent of the population, or by under 10 per cent. In fact, as is already apparent, the percentage must have varied in different regions. Chapter 12 will, among other things, attempt to tackle the problems of interpreting these proportions, notably in those parishes of the high Weald and in east Kent where, according to Figure 141, there was a very low ratio of houses to households; and also in west Kent, where no similar survey exists and it is even more difficult to form an idea of the status of surviving buildings.

# 11 Late medieval gentry houses

Little attempt has so far been made to isolate gentry houses from those of lesser status. In a book which is concerned to distinguish medieval houses by size and type, such indifference may seem perverse: in fact it is deliberate. Although it is self-evident that a vast gulf separates the grandest gentry houses from those of the majority of peasants, the problem of identifying the late medieval 'gentry house' in Kent is bedeviled by ambiguity. In the first place defining the gentry is no easy task; second, there is little evidence that they were erecting many new houses in the 15th century; and third it is not clear that as a class they can be associated with a particular type of house.

Dating, by dendrochronology and conventional means, has indicated that there is a hiatus in surviving houses in the mid 14th century. The obvious cause of this is the Black Death and the associated plagues and famine which occurred in the middle years of the century. Yet the houses which preceded this period were almost certainly all built by members of the landowning classes, and the severity of the problems which they experienced has been questioned.[1] It has been shown that the agrarian economy recovered quickly and remained profitable for much of the late 14th century. It might therefore be assumed that landlords could have resumed building in the 1350s or 1360s, and that a class of late medieval gentry houses could be identified with ease. But the evidence of surviving houses in Kent suggests that, despite the initial recovery from the mid-century troubles, landlords in the second half of the century ceased to put money into capital expenditure such as building in the way they had before. This situation appears to have prevailed through much of the 15th century as well, for there is little evidence among survivors for buildings on a par with the best which had been erected in the early 14th century. High-class houses remain rare until about 1500.

## Houses associated with the county gentry

During the late 14th and 15th centuries a few new stone houses were built for those of high status. Sir John Cobham received a licence to crenellate at Hever in 1383;[2] work was undertaken for Archbishop Bourchier at Knole after 1456;[3]
Sir Thomas Browne, Comptroller of the King's household, received a licence to crenellate Tonford Castle, Thanington, in 1448;[4] and Sir Humphrey Starkey probably rebuilt Starkey Castle in c 1500.[5]

Among the late 14th and 15th-century houses recorded for this project, hardly any were of stone. In the late 14th century, Yaldham Manor, Wrotham (Figure 116), was erected by the Peckam family who had emerged from a non-gentry background during the 14th century to a position of prominence in the county; members of the family became both sheriffs and knights of the shire in the late 14th and early 15th centuries.[6] Elsewhere new building tended to take the form of altering and enlarging earlier structures. The Hornes of Hornes Place, Appledore, who provided Justices of the Peace in the late 14th century, and sheriffs and knights of the shire in the 15th, added a stone chapel to what was probably a timber-framed house (now demolished).[7] At Ightham Mote, in the 15th century, the Hautes retained the hall and subsidiary ranges which had been built by another family, and simply added the gatehouse range and modernised the hall by refenestration and the insertion of an enclosed fireplace. Despite the fact that this list could be augmented, the number of surviving new stone buildings of this period is limited. In all cases those who built these houses belonged to families whose more eminent members were knights or esquires, and who held county office or even had positions at Court.

Prominent county families often built their houses of timber, but completely new buildings are likewise uncommon during most of the 15th century. An isolated and early example is the Manor House, Benenden (Figures 81a, 93), the largest Wealden so far identified in the county, which was probably built in the late 14th century. In the early 15th century the property belonged to a wealthy London lawyer, Sir William Brenchley, Chief Justice of the Common Pleas,[8] and it is just possible that he owned the house early enough to have been responsible for building it. Other timber houses whose families included knights or esquires among their number, or supplied sheriffs or JPs, are much later in date. Around 1500 the Ellis family built a new hall and parlour wing at Stoneacre, Otham (Figures 103b, 142),[9] and the Ballards erected a complete new dwelling at Horton Manor, Chartham.[10] At much the same time some older houses were updated by the addition of

*Figure 142 (above) Stoneacre, Otham. Hall and upper-end cross wing, c 1500 (BB87/5649).*

*Figure 143 (below) Peirce House, Charing. Early 16th-century service-end wing and porch-cum-stair turret added to an earlier open hall (BB91/608).*

finely decorated cross wings, as occurred at Hornes Place, Appledore (Figure 89), and Peirce House, Charing (Figure 143).[11] Most of these houses seem to have been the main residences of the families concerned, and are among the very best timber-framed buildings to survive from the turn of the century.

That so few new houses can be associated with the county gentry, or those who made their fortunes at Court or in London during the first seventy years of the 15th century, may be partly accounted for in a number of ways. One possibility is that where fine stone halls and subsidiary ranges had been erected in the 14th century, they remained adequate for their owners' needs throughout the Middle Ages. Later, when new types and styles of accommodation were required, many such houses were probably rebuilt. At all times the high-ranking gentry predominated in the east of the county, and this is where most of the surviving post-medieval gentry houses in Kent are to be found.[12] Thus continuing prosperity seems to have resulted in later generations rebuilding the seats they had bought or inherited. However, since the absence of new building is more marked in the first three-quarters of the 15th century than in the years around 1500, it is also possible that the economic and political uncertainties of the period, which made life particularly difficult for landlords, deterred many of them from spending their capital on new houses during that time.[13]

Throughout the 15th century a number of smaller and less elaborate houses were built which can be associated with high-ranking families but are unlikely to have been used by them as their main residences. Sutton Baron Hall, Borden (Figure 144), a late 15th-century Wealden, had been acquired by the Nortons in 1450/1. Sir John Norton was already an esquire in 1450, and the family came to hold considerable estates in the Sittingbourne and Faversham area, but it is doubtful whether any very prominent member of the family lived at Sutton Baron.[14] Ratling Court, Aylesham, was a timber-framed aisled hall of *c* 1300 to which a three-bay cross wing was added in the mid 15th century. By this time it is likely that the property had passed from the Ratlings to the Isaacs of Patrixbourne, and since later Isaacs retained their main seat in Patrixbourne, it is probable that Ratling Court was used by junior members of the family.[15]

The same sequence may be observed in other early houses where enlarged private accommodation was added after the property had passed from its original owners to more prominent families whose main estates lay elsewhere. Thus at Old Cryals, Brenchley, one end was rebuilt as a two-bay extension in the mid 15th century, probably when the house belonged to the Poynings of Ostenhanger.[16] A new three-bay wing was erected at Hurst Farm, Chilham, in the early 16th century, by which time the house, whose 15th-century history is obscure, may have been acquired by Thomas Darell, esquire, of Scotney.[17] Often, as in these instances, the precise sequence of events and the status of

*Figure 144 Sutton Baron Hall, Borden. A late 15th-century Wealden (BB92/30596).*

the house at the time of the addition are unclear, and the new work, while not negligible, was neither exceptionally large nor especially stylish.

Occasionally, the evidence points strongly in favour of a property being tenanted when the new work was undertaken. At Newlands Manor, Charing, the presence of a most remarkable chapel of the late 12th century suggests an early house of considerable quality, although who built it is unclear. What actually survives, at some distance from the chapel, is an unpretentious end-jetty house of late 15th-century date. In 1410 the manor had been acquired by the Darells of nearby Calehill in Little Chart, and it is difficult to imagine the surviving building as anything other than a tenanted farmhouse.[18]

## Houses of the lesser gentry

In addition to these houses, others were associated with families who, as far as can be ascertained, never rose above the ranks of the lesser gentry. An early example of this kind may be Godinton Park, Great Chart, of which a hall and wing of *c* 1400 survive. The property belonged to the Godintons until the time of Richard II, but by *c* 1373 it had been sold to the Goldwells who came from nearby.

*Figure 145 Lynsted Court, Lynsted. A two-storeyed 16th-century hall replaced, and partially reused, a 14th-century hall. Service wing of c 1500 (to right) and a wing of 1517\*, containing a parlour and kitchen, to the left (BB86/3969).*

According to Hasted, a younger branch of this family was established here, and it was probably they who had the earliest part of the present house built.[19] Old Chilmington, also in Great Chart, belonged to the Chilmingtons until the early 15th century when it passed via an heiress to the Twysdens, who retained it through the 15th and early 16th centuries. Some 14th-century work of an indeterminate nature remains, but the house was expanded and updated in the early 16th century when the surviving parlour wing was built (Figure 109). Although the Twysdens appear to have achieved no higher social status until later in the century, William, who died in 1539, left an extensive estate in Great Chart, Kingsnorth, Shadoxhurst and Romney Marsh totalling some 464 acres.[20]

Lynsted Court, formerly called Sewards, in Lynsted (Figure 145), has evidence of 14th-century work in the hall which probably dates from the time of the Sewards. But the original ancillary accommodation was rebuilt in the form of cross wings by the Finch family,[21] who added the service wing around 1500, and the larger upper-end wing, incorporating a great parlour and an integral kitchen, in 1517\*. Other examples of minor gentry houses are probably Bettenham Manor, Cranbrook, and Place Farmhouse and Great Engeham Manor, Woodchurch. All three are Wealdens of 15th-century date.[22]

A large number of lesser gentry seats were located in north-west Kent,[23] but surviving medieval gentry houses are rare. To some extent this may be explained by the fact that the part of medieval Kent nearest to the capital now lies beyond the border of the modern county and the area studied. But rebuilding must account for most of the scarcity. In the first place, the countryside round London continued to be attractive to wealthy city dwellers, and the high-quality properties of this area must have been exceptionally vulnerable to later updating and rebuilding. Secondly, much of north-west Kent has been heavily built up in recent times, and its early buildings have been swept away by the encroaching suburbs.

A tantalising example of what may once have been a fine gentry house remains at The Limes, Southfleet. Above substantial later remodelling, the roofs of a large three-bay hall and a four or five-bay cross wing of late 15th-century date survive. The house lies next to a great aisled barn and opposite an apparently later house known as Hook Green Farm. Hook Place, Southfleet, was a manor which was owned from the 14th century by a minor gentry family called Swan. Although there is no certainty, it is tempting to conclude that The Limes was the original manor house of the Swans.[24] No doubt a few large medieval gentry houses of this kind have left similar traces, but they are not common in this part of Kent.

*Figure 146 Riseden Hall, Goudhurst. Early 16th-century hall and cross-wing house (BB87/7).*

# The relationship between social status and type of house

All the houses mentioned so far were built by families among the 275 identified by P W Fleming as of gentry status between 1422 and 1509.[25] The extent to which the boundaries between gentry, yeomen and those engaged in trade or the professions was hard and fast in the 15th century is a matter of historical debate.[26] This book is not the place to engage directly in this discussion. But it can perhaps contribute to it by considering whether there is evidence to show that the status of the owners was a crucial factor in the design of houses: whether those built for knights and esquires can be distinguished from those of the lesser gentry, and whether their dwellings in turn were different from those erected by people who had no clear claims to gentility.

The first points to note are that stone buildings were exclusively built by knights and esquires and that, with the exception of Newlands Manor, Charing, all the houses mentioned above are either cross wings or Wealdens. Thus to this extent status and house seem to be related. However, this will hardly come as a surprise since stone houses are large and rare, and it has been established already that cross-wing and Wealden houses are as a rule larger than others.

The largest cross-wing houses were the largest of all timber-framed buildings, and in particular it was possible

for them to have more private accommodation in proportion to their halls, which must have suited the needs of prominent people with large households who required a number of different rooms for public and private use. As already shown, several men of high rank added high-quality, timber-framed wings to earlier houses in the years around 1500. In addition to these, some large, but not necessarily well-decorated, cross-wing houses belonged to the Church. They include The Deanery, Chartham, Court Lodge Farmhouse, Southfleet (Figure 70d), and Wingham Barton Manor, Ash next Sandwich.[27] Wings such as these, most of which lay at the upper end of the hall, quite certainly play a part in the increasing size of late 15th-century cross-wing houses illustrated in Figure 67.

Other, equally superior, cross wings were neither owned by the Church nor likely to have been the homes of knights or esquires. The most notable is Rectory Park, Horsmonden (Figures 88b, 108), one of the finest timber houses so far discovered in the county. Since the advowson was an appendage to the manor, it is conceivable that the property was owned by the knightly Poynings, but even so, it is unlikely to have been used by them, and may have been just the home of a succession of rectors.[28] Lynsted Court, particularly as remodelled in 1517*, and the early 16th-century wing at Old Chilmington, fall not far short of the same

*Figure 147 Boyke Manor, Elham. Early 16th-century Wealden (BB90/3006).*

architectural class, although they were only held by minor gentry families. That the wealthier gentry favoured the type is perhaps indicated by the noticeable decline in the size of cross-wing houses (Figure 67) during the first three-quarters of the 15th century, when few of the more prominent gentry families seem to have been building.

Several gentry families can be associated with Wealdens. The largest Wealden of all, the Manor House, Benenden, which has a hall of 65 sq m, was built by a knight, or by his wife's family.[29] Most other examples, however, were built for gentry families who were not in the top league, or who do not appear to have built for their personal occupation. Some, like cross wings, were constructed by the Church. West Court, Shepherdswell with Coldred, was built on a manor of St Martin's Priory, Dover, and Deanery Farm, Chartham, was erected by Christ Church Priory for the farmer of the manor at Chartham.[30] Several of these buildings were sizeable and well detailed, but Sutton Baron Hall, Borden, with a hall of only 33 sq m, lies well towards the smallest end of the scale for the type, and the majority can be matched by other Wealdens which have no known gentry connections.

A number of the houses recorded during the project can be associated with manors, estates or reputed manors, held by families identified by Hasted, but not included in Fleming's list of gentry.[31] Riseden Hall, Goudhurst (Figures 71c, 146), has

cross wings, and Brockton Manor, a sub-manor of Charing, Boyke Manor, Elham (Figure 147), and Posiers, Borden, are Wealdens;[32] in all of these, the size and quality of detailing match or exceed the work of some of the houses discussed above, such as Great Engeham Manor, Woodchurch, or Sutton Baron Hall, Borden. Meanwhile others, about whose origins nothing at all is at present known, are often of similar or even higher quality. Cross-wing houses, such as The Barracks, East Malling and Larkfield (Figures 70a, 121), and Campion House and Old Standen, Benenden (Figure 70e), are as large as some of the gentry houses discussed above; and Wealdens like Vane Court, Biddenden, of *c* 1419* (Figure 68i), The Old Palace, Brenchley, of 1485* (Figure 81b), Tong House, Eastling, of *c* 1500 (Figure 69e), and the group of Wealdens in Benenden,[33] are among the best late medieval houses in the county. It is unlikely that many, if any, of these were built by the gentry on Fleming's list.[34]

The geographical distribution of buildings of this sort reinforces the view that few of the better timber-framed houses can readily be distinguished by the status of their owners. As discussed above, high-ranking gentry in Kent have had at all times a predominantly easterly distribution, while lesser gentry were found in large numbers on the London fringes and in the Medway valley. However, as Figures 138 and 139 indicate, the greatest concentration of large timber-framed houses, both of cross-wing and Wealden form, lay in central and southern Kent where gentry estates were least common.

A few of these houses no doubt were built by gentry families, but many more must have been put up by wealthy yeomen or those in trade or the professions. The size and elaboration of some of these dwellings, as discussed in Chapter 8, suggests that their owners had plenty of money and thought of themselves as socially superior. Yet, if Fleming's analysis of the compositon of the gentry in Kent is correct – and some may argue that it is too restrictive[35] – then it would appear that, except at the very highest social levels, architecture was more a symbol of wealth and of social aspirations than of achieved status. This use of architecture is perhaps not dissimilar to that found elsewhere and at a later period.[36] From an architectural point of view, it seems artificial to differentiate these houses from many which were built by recognisable gentry families; whatever their status all these buildings were erected by people with considerable financial resources, and in the end it appears that this was what counted.[37]

If fine cross-wing and Wealden houses were erected by gentry and wealthy yeomen, merchants and professionals alike during the 15th century, it is legitimate to ask whether those in the latter groups were simply aping the well-established forms of their betters. It seems likely that houses of cross-wing form were built for the gentry before they were adopted by others. Stone cross wings can be found from the late 13th century, and despite the absence of early surviving examples in Kent, it is likely that two-storeyed timber-framed wings, possibly with low ground storeys, were also first erected by those of knightly rank. But the level at which the Wealden was first introduced is less easy to establish. The earliest known Wealden, Chart Hall (formerly Chart Bottom) Farmhouse of 1379/80*, is one of a group of late 14th-century houses in Chart Sutton which are very unlikely to have had gentry owners. On the other hand two at least of the Wealdens discussed above – the Manor House, Benenden, built sometime in the late 14th century, and West Court, Shepherdswell with Coldred, of *c* 1399* – are not much later in date. If, as has been suggested, the Wealden developed out of the cross-wing house in the later 14th century, then it is perhaps not impossible that it was the response of a newly developing class to a new situation. But, whoever invented the form, its advantages were speedily recognised by gentry and yeomen alike.

## Internal layout as a reflection of social distinctions

Throughout the 15th century everyone seems to have subscribed to the same view of the basic elements constituting an adequate house. All houses were centred on the open hall, with subsidiary rooms for private or service use at either end. Larger houses might have more elaborate subsidiary accommodation, and the external shape of the house fell into different categories which can be classified by type and size, but the central open hall and basic layout were remarkably standardised. In the early 16th century this began to change, and a divergence seems to have opened up between the way the recognised gentry and those on the fringes of gentry society perceived the function of their halls.

The architectural and documentary evidence discussed in Chapters 8 and 9 emphasised the growing importance of the ground-floor parlour from the late 15th century in all surviving houses of any quality. Late medieval society had become increasingly segregated, and the hall was ceasing to play such a dominant role at the centre of household life. The elaboration of the ground-floor parlour, and the introduction of enclosed fireplaces, reflected a growing desire for comfort, warmth and privacy. This trend can be documented clearly in royal and noble households,[38] but the physical evidence of timber-framed buildings in Kent shows that the change permeated much further down the social scale. However, it had different consequences at different social levels.

The gentry still required the impressive effect of an open hall for public occasions, and frequently retained such a room – which gradually took on more of the character of an entrance hall – for a long time to come. Houses like Penshurst Place and Ightham Mote never had upper storeys inserted into their open halls; and in smaller gentry houses, like Peirce House, Charing, and Hurst Farm, Chilham, part of the hall was left open for a very long time. In addition, a number of important early 16th-century houses were still erected with open halls, or at least with halls which rose through two storeys. In Kent it is likely that this was true of the now-demolished Shurland House, built by Sir Thomas Cheyney on the Isle of Sheppey in the 1520s.[39] Although the way it was used may have changed, the hall still had a role to play, and the demands for comfort and privacy were easily met by other rooms in the large houses of the wealthier gentry.

It appears that below this level there ceased to be a need for a public hall of the old sort. The earliest two-storey houses seem to have been built by wealthy yeomen, or by those involved in trade or minor administration. They are concentrated in that area of southern central Kent where the largest late medieval open-hall houses predominated and gentry were not thick on the ground. Although few of their builders are identifiable, such clues as there are point to them having been erected by those who were not of clearly defined gentry status. The agreement in 1500 to build a fully floored house in Cranbrook took place between Thomas a Crouch and Gyles Andrewe. Andrewe died in 1527, and the evidence of his will suggests that he was not only an affluent property owner but also a craftsman. Crouch has not been traced, but he was certainly not styled a gentleman in the document.[40] Smallhythe Place, Tenterden, erected in *c* 1514, is always claimed to have been built for an official of the port of Smallhythe, and the architectural evidence suggests that the building had more than the usual domestic accommodation.[41] Rocks, East Malling and Larkfield, built in 1507/8*, has details which imply that part of it may have been used for non-domestic purposes, perhaps as a workshop.

The fact that the hall did not diminish in size in the late Middle Ages suggests that the room itself remained important, but that the way it was used changed. The medieval arrangement, with its clear dais end, marked by a decorated beam and fixed bench, was abandoned immediately the open hall was floored over; and the way the room functioned must have altered as soon as a chimney was built between the hall and parlour, for there was no alternative wall free from windows or doorways against which to place the bench and table. Instead, all the inhabitants had to use the central space, so that the hierarchy which had been such a marked feature of the medieval hall must have disappeared altogether, implying that significant changes had taken place in household structure and relationships. In Kent this development was closely related to the emergence of those wealthy men who spanned the grey area dividing the gentry from the peasantry and were later to become the 'yeomanly gentry' so aptly described by Celia Fiennes.[42] Thus the similarities which make it sensible to study all late medieval houses together may have been starting to erode in the early part of the 16th century.

# 12 Late medieval houses in context

So far late medieval houses have been considered primarily in a formal manner. They have been sorted according to type and construction, numbers and dates have been discussed, and their geographical distribution has been plotted. The patterns which emerge are so pronounced that they are highly unlikely to have been the result of random survival. As demonstrated in Chapter 1, Kent is a county of contrasts, both geographical and historical, and this chapter sets out to explore the possible connections between these regional contrasts and the pattern of surviving buildings. This should provide a basis for putting the buildings into their historical context. Since this book is about buildings, no research into primary sources has been undertaken on the complex economic and social history of late medieval Kent. Much historical work remains to be done, and many problems remain unresolved. However, some observations can be made which seem to make sense in the light of current historical research, while others raise questions which point the way for future exploration.

## North Kent: the central and eastern areas

### The Stour valley and the north-eastern manors

North and north-east Kent together form the region where the majority of timber-framed houses of the late 13th and early 14th centuries were found. A few late 14th-century buildings are also scattered across this whole area. Later, the region seems to divide into two: in the central section, between Sittingbourne and Faversham, a considerable number of houses dating from the late 15th century occur, mostly of middling size and quality. Further east the numbers are fewer but the variety is far greater, ranging from large and fine to small and poor. This diversity might be thought to imply random survival, but in fact the evidence is not as contradictory as it at first appears.

The high levels of wealth and population recorded in north-east Kent in the 13th and 14th centuries were no longer so pronounced by the 16th century.[1] Detailed research on a number of ecclesiastical manors in the north east, such as Adisham, Chartham, Eastry, Ickham and Monkton, indicates that by the early 15th century there was severe depopulation accompanied by a reduction in tenants

and a redistribution of land resulting in an increasing disparity between a small number of tenants with large holdings, and a far greater number with small tenancies.[2] A picture of widening social and economic differentiation is common to all these studies, and it is more or less the same tale that the buildings tell. Although not lying in the most severely affected area, it is worth considering the case of Chartham in more detail. Here, a great deal of work has been done on the manorial history, and enough buildings survive to provide clues to what may have occurred there and elsewhere.[3]

The manor of Chartham, with about three-quarters of the land in the parish, was held by Christ Church Priory, and the manor house (now The Deanery) was located at a short distance from the church. There were three other small manors lying towards the parish boundaries,[4] of which Horton Manor has a large late 15th-century cross-wing house and earlier chapel remaining.[5] Apart from Deanery Farm, a Wealden erected by the Priory in 1495/6 for the farmer of the Priory lands,[6] there are seven other late medieval houses remaining in the parish, mostly lying along the river valley. They date from the late 15th or early 16th century and, with one exception, are relatively small in size, having hall areas of 40 sq m or less. One of them, Boxtree Cottage, has one of the smallest open halls recorded during the project, measuring only 15 sq m, and at Pilgrims' Cottage an equally small and smoke-blackened central area may also indicate an open hall, although too little survives below roof level for certain interpretation as a dwelling.

Through the 15th century significant changes were taking place in Chartham. Although the sharpest drop in both population and tenant numbers had occurred during the 14th century, the trend continued, and the land was redistributed with a polarisation between rich and poor. In 1450 only five of the sixty-five tenants rented land for more than 10 shillings per annum, and it was to some of these that the demesne was leased. By 1500 several of the tenants with the largest holdings were outsiders, including county gentry and citizens of Canterbury, so that by this date absentee tenants with resident sub-tenants had reached significant proportions, and many inhabitants of the parish may have been wage-earners with no land at all. The most dominant social group living within the parish by this time appears to have been the wealthier husbandmen, holding only medium-sized parcels of land. In these circumstances a lack of large numbers of sizeable houses is hardly surprising. Deanery Farm and the other two, somewhat smaller, Wealdens may reflect the better fortunes of those who farmed the largest acreages or had alternative sources of wealth, such as fulling. But it seems likely that few people could afford houses of this type. Most of the inhabitants probably had far smaller houses, like Boxtree Cottage or Pilgrims' Cottage. At later dates, houses of this size often came to be considered too small and inconvenient, and even if they survived for a long time, they were gradually engulfed by later additions, or demolished in rebuilding, so that few of them survive today.

Chartham may have more medieval houses remaining than most of the eastern parishes, but it is likely that the same pattern was repeated throughout the corn-growing manors of east Kent. Since the 16th-century population in this part of the county was possibly still decreasing, and certainly not increasing at the same rate as in the west, the number of surviving medieval houses set against the number of households recorded in 1557 and 1563 may give a relatively accurate guide to the proportion of houses which remain. In most parishes they form 10 per cent or less. The majority of the survivors are large and fine, and probably represent the homes of gentry, merchants or wealthy yeomen. But throughout the east of the county a few poorer houses, such as Ashby Cottage, Westbere (Figure 58), and Gander Court Farmhouse, Staple (Figure 112), are likely to be the rare survivors of the homes of the many tenants in the region who held only small parcels of land.[7]

However, the building evidence is by no means uniform. This can be demonstrated by considering the differences between Chartham and Chilham, which lie adjacent to one another in the Stour valley, for they have both similar and dissimilar features. The two parishes are much the same size, and they have an almost identical number of surviving medieval buildings, which formed an approximately similar proportion of the households recorded in 1557. But in Chilham the houses tend to be larger, several are of earlier date, and not one of them is as small as the smallest survivors in Chartham.

The manor of Chilham was held at Domesday by Odo of Bayeux. After his disgrace it was given to Fulbert of Dover who made it the main seat of his barony which was created for the defence of Dover Castle. By the late Middle Ages there were nine other small manors in the parish. Five of these were sub-manors of Chilham, and four of the five were specifically infeudated for the defence of Dover.[8] Of these, only the manor house of Hurst (today Hurst Farm) survives as a medieval building with an early 14th-century hall and mid 16th-century cross wing. All the other manor houses have been rebuilt. By 1281 a market had been granted in Chilham, and the town which grew up around it lay at the entrance to the castle. Apart from Hurst Farm eleven medieval houses were identified in the parish. Three of these, one large and two small, had cross wings and were situated in the built-up area. Five of them, located in both the town and the surrounding country, were certainly Wealdens, one of which, The Tudor Lodge Gift Shop and Peacock Antiques (situated in the Square), probably dates to the late 14th century. All the other houses are likely to be later than 1450, although four of them probably date to the third quarter of the century rather than later. Six of the nine houses for which measurements were obtained had halls of more than 40 sq m. Thus, although in terms of overall numbers Chilham hardly differs from Chartham, it definitely contains more sizeable 15th-century houses which are not manor houses.

Two potential reasons spring to mind. The first is that the market in Chilham might have advanced the prosperity of those in the vicinity who had the benefit of it. Other market centres, such as Elham and Charing, also have relatively high numbers of medieval houses surviving in the nucleated settlement. But this is not true of Wrotham or Appledore, so there is a question mark over the ability of markets by themselves to create wealth for those who lived nearby.

The second difference is that while Chartham was held largely by Christ Church Priory, Chilham was entirely in secular hands. One of the problems in estimating the effects of ecclesiastical versus secular control is that the availability of documents has concentrated attention on the ecclesiastical manors, and there have been no historical studies of the prosperity of tenants of lay manors. None the less, as noted throughout this chapter, the contrast between the size and quality of medieval houses in parishes which lay primarily under ecclesiastical jurisdiction and those, where the manors were held by secular lords, is consistent enough to be remarked upon and to require explanation. It is, for example, worth noting that both the levels of wealth and the number of surviving medieval houses built by yeomen or wealthy peasants are greater in the central section of north Kent where the Church owned little property.

## Parishes of the central northern plain

As discussed in Chapter 10 the 16th-century population in parishes such as Eastling and Sheldwich in the central region represents a significant decrease since the 14th century, but the levels of wealth, as indicated in the lay subsidies, remained remarkably and consistently high. Apart from one or two early and high-status houses, a number of small dwellings of end-jettied or unjettied form remain in both parishes. These are of reasonable quality, and form quite a contrast to the absence of small houses in parishes such as Eastry, Minster in Thanet or Shepherdswell with Coldred which lie to the north east.

However, even if this difference in survival rates suggests that ecclesiastical or secular overlordship made a difference to the prosperity of the tenants, it clearly had to be combined with other factors before it affected the quality of the houses that were built. This can be shown by comparing the buildings of Newington and Borden, which lie side by side just west of Sittingbourne, on the relatively flat land at the foot of the Downs where the soil is extremely fertile. The old London to Dover road (Watling Street) runs through the middle of Newington parish, and forms part of the northern boundary of Borden. The two parishes are similar in size, Newington having 2,115 acres and Borden 2,145, and in 1557 they contained sixty and fifty dwelling houses respectively. But in terms of their surviving medieval buildings they could hardly be more dissimilar, for only two were identified in Newington compared with sixteen in Borden (representing 3 per cent and 32 per cent of the number of households recorded in 1557). In Newington there are few instances of isolated farms or small hamlets of any period. Most of the houses lie along the London road and seem to date from the late 16th century and later, the only two surviving medieval buildings probably being manor houses. In Borden three or four medieval houses are situated not far from the church, but the rest are dotted throughout the parish as isolated farmsteads or in small hamlets such as Oad Street and Chestnut Street.

In his discussion of the evolution of the church of Milton, Everitt pointed out how Newington, which was once part of the Milton minsterland, early became a separate minster from which other parishes were founded.[9] In contrast Borden, which was largely woodland, remained ecclesiastically dependent on the parish of Milton until after the Conquest.[10] The land of both parishes was, and remained, subordinate to the royal manor of Milton. However, from an early date a number of manors or estates were established in Newington: in addition to the sub-manor of Newington, which later was divided into two, Hasted lists three manors, together with two 'formerly accounted' manors and two estates.[11] Borden on the other hand is likened by Everitt to the pastoral parishes of the Weald, inhabited by independent yeoman freeholders. No sub-manor of Borden was ever created, and there were only three small manors in the parish known to Hasted.[12]

In the absence of documentation, the circumstances of the 15th-century population in either parish are unknown; however, the presence in Borden of a sizeable group of relatively small medieval houses built between c 1440 and c 1510 possibly, as indicated by Figures 135 and 136, represents the houses of some 30 per cent of the population, which suggests that many of the inhabitants were reasonably well off. Although parts of several of these houses later were rebuilt or enlarged, there is little evidence of the wholesale clearance of earlier dwellings which appears to have been considered necessary in Newington in the later 16th and 17th centuries. This seems to imply that the medieval houses of the latter parish were too small, too low or too insubstantial to suit their later occupiers. The building evidence in these two adjacent parishes is so diverse that it is difficult not to accept Everitt's contention that the circumstances in which settlements originated may well have determined much of their subsequent history and character.[13]

### Parishes in the eastern Downs

Further to the east, Petham, Waltham, Upper Hardres and Elham form another group of contiguous parishes lying in the Downs south of the Stour valley. Surviving houses in all of them are generally late in date (except for two notable exceptions in Petham: Dormer Cottage and the Old Hall); they tend to be small (except in Elham), and several of those in Waltham and Petham, like others in neighbouring Crundale, are late aisled halls. A correlation between aisled halls and a downland environment has been noted elsewhere, and the condition of the tenantry adduced by way of explanation.[14] This may be so, but outmoded aisled construction is only one aspect of a larger issue. Late aisled halls can be found in many parts of Kent and are by no means confined to the Downs. No aisled halls were found in Upper Hardres but this parish, together with Waltham and Petham, contained some of the latest and smallest open-hall houses found during the survey (Figures 137, 139).

It is these qualities which must reflect the condition of men and make the region so distinctive. Yet interpreting this evidence is not straightforward. Landowners in these four parishes varied, ranging from the Archbishop and the

dean and canons of St Stephen's Chapel, Westminster, to the knightly Hautes and less wealthy secular families.[15] The area is isolated and difficult of access even today, with narrow valleys, and relatively poor quality farmland composed of clay-with-flints. The density of surviving houses is among the highest in north-east Kent, but the proportion of mid 16th-century households they represent is low. Lack of detailed figures for 1377 means that no comparison can be made between the population of the 14th and 16th centuries, although it is unlikely that it was increasing in the late Middle Ages. In terms of buildings there are differences between this region and the corn-growing areas further east, for there are hardly any early buildings and none of great size. Because the houses are small and late there is a tendency to think of the inhabitants as poor. But the mere fact that several people in these parishes were building open halls of survivable quality in the 16th century suggests that they had considerably more disposable wealth than their contemporaries on the great arable estates where so few small houses remain. The very isolation of the region may have worked in their favour and allowed small farmers to emerge who had a greater measure of independence than the peasants to the north east. Among the four parishes, Elham stands out as having houses of larger size and better quality. Hasted found it more congenial than other downland parishes,[16] and this may be because of its slightly more open situation and the presence of a market. As in the case of Chilham it may be wondered whether this had an effect on the prosperity of those who lived nearby.

The discussion in Chapter 10 suggested that houses can be categorised on a regional basis, but although in a general sense this is true, the three areas isolated above show that, within an overall framework, buildings can vary from one parish to the next. A book of this nature can only note these differences and speculate briefly about the local factors which may have played a part in determining the levels of prosperity reflected in the houses.

# Central Kent

It is clear that when numbers and quality are taken together, the medieval buildings of the centre far surpass those elsewhere in the county. In some respects the centre may be defined as running from the north coast to the Sussex border, and from Wrotham and Plaxtol in the west, to the River Stour in the east. But for present purposes the discussion is confined to the area south of the scarp of the Downs. Even then, there is no uniformity. Sub-regions exist, and the buildings of one parish can differ from those in the next.

In terms of wealth and population, some remarkable changes took place in central Kent south of the Downs between the 14th and 16th centuries. As discussed in Chapter 1, this region, apart from a small area round Maidstone, had one of the lowest assessments of wealth in England in 1334; yet by the time of the lay subsidy of 1524, assessments of 55–69 shillings per square mile placed it among the highest yielding parts of the country – even if the central section north of the Downs was assessed at an even higher rate. A similar growth is discernible in population between the Poll Tax figures of 1377 and the lists of communicants in the mid 16th century. In some cases these figures are available for individual parishes, and this suggests that the highest increases had taken place north east of Maidstone and in both low Weald and ragstone parishes, such as Headcorn, Egerton and Pluckley (no detailed figures are available for parishes further south).

## Christ Church Priory manors

Unpublished work by Butcher on the Christ Church Priory manors of East Peckham, East Farleigh and Loose – the parishes of the latter two incorporating parts of the modern parishes of Coxheath and Linton – has shown marked differences in the condition of the mid-Kent tenantry compared to the tenants on the manors of north-east Kent. There was a less marked decline in tenant numbers during the 15th century and less social stratification. Instead of a few large holdings at the top of the scale and a large number of small holdings at the bottom, there were many more tenants holding reasonable quantities of land in the middle range.[17] This impression of a sizeable proportion of the tenants enjoying a measure of prosperity not only complements the wealth and population evidence, but it is confirmed by the large numbers of late medieval houses in the centre of the county. As discussed in Chapter 10, the rapid increase of population in the second quarter of the 16th century almost certainly means that in many parishes a higher proportion of medieval houses survives than is apparent on Figure 141.

Figures 133–141, and in particular Figures 138 and 139, show considerable discrepancies between buildings in those parishes in which Christ Church Priory manors were centred and those round about. Figure 140 illustrates an unusually high density of surviving houses in East Peckham and Loose, with a reasonable number in East Farleigh (although rather less in modern Coxheath and in Linton). However, the quality of the houses hardly matches their quantity. Both East Peckham and East Farleigh have more end-jettied or unjettied houses than the surrounding parishes, and the median size of hall in all of them is the lowest on record in any part of central Kent. In addition, Loose was one of the few parishes in the area in which the population had declined, so the high survival rate of houses illustrated in Figure 141 is, in this case, misleading. Finally, although timber houses built before the mid 15th century can be found, they are by no means as numerous as in the Suttons and Staplehurst which lie just a little way to the south and east. Land in East Peckham and Loose was not exclusively held by Christ Church Priory, and it is not certain that all the recorded houses lay on the Priory's estates. But some of them must have done so, and probably enough for one to wonder whether the tenants of the Priory were in a less advantageous position than those of other manors. Otherwise the unusually small size of the surviving houses remains a mystery.

## Archbishop's manors

The principal landholder in several of the surveyed parishes in central Kent was the Archbishop. He held the manors of Wrotham, which included Plaxtol, and Charing, and the manor of the den of Smarden. The case of Wrotham and Plaxtol is particularly interesting, partly because the archi-tectural remains in the two modern parishes are so dissimilar, and partly because a considerable amount of research has been done on late medieval documents relating to the manor of Wrotham. In the late Middle Ages the manor stretched from Stansted above the scarp of the Downs, in the north, through Wrotham itself, across the Vale of Holmesdale and the Chart Hills to the edge of the Weald, taking in the modern parishes of Borough Green, Platt and Plaxtol.[18] The demesne of the manor lay in Wrotham itself, on the best agricultural land in the Vale of Holmesdale, to either side of the manor site next to the church.[19] The only nucleated settlement, incorporating a market, was here, and a rental of 1494 indicates that there were forty-two messuages located in Wrotham, including sixteen copyhold tenants. The other ninety-six free tenants were scattered through the rest of the manor, particularly to the south.[20]

Figure 140 shows that there is a considerable difference in the number of medieval houses surviving in Wrotham and Plaxtol, the latter being one of only five of the surveyed parishes in the county to have over five medieval buildings per 1,000 acres. Within the area of the manor, only three open-hall houses were identified in Wrotham as opposed to twelve in Plaxtol. Although two of the Plaxtol houses date from the late 14th century, Figures 135 and 136 show that the majority of cross-wing, Wealden and end-jetty buildings were probably built in the late 15th century. Semple's work on the manor of Wrotham in the late 15th and early 16th centuries has identified several of the Plaxtol builders or occupiers as butchers or graziers, and there are good reasons for seeing these houses as the dwellings of the wealthier farming community who had individual farms in the more pastoral area of the manor.[21] The Vale was partly occupied by 250 acres of demesne, which was predomi-nantly arable, and also contained two parks reserved for hunting. It contained a relatively large number of tenants who held at least part of their land in open fields, albeit cultivated in severalty. No outlying farmsteads survive in the Vale, and it seems likely that the majority of the forty-two messuages in Wrotham borough lay in the settlement around the church and the manor.[22] In contrast to the situation in the southern part of the manor, there are few remaining medieval buildings in Wrotham itself and, The Old Vicarage apart, the survivors are likely to be late in date. The only one of them to remain in the town centre, Workhouse Cottages, has a very low open hall, probably with an open end which was difficult to adapt to multi-storey living. Possibly this is a lone survivor of a once common type which has been swept away and replaced by houses of the mid–late 16th century and later. The combined documentary and building evidence indicates that even though some tenants in Wrotham had sizeable holdings, they were disadvantaged by farming scattered parcels, and possibly also by the fact that their land lay close to the manorial centre. Those whose land was further away, in the more pastoral parts of the parish, which is where the surviving houses are located, evidently managed to accumulate discrete and consolidated holdings from which they derived their greater prosperity.

This picture may be amplified by the somewhat different architectural evidence in Charing, another manor belonging to the Archbishop which lies towards the eastern end of the Vale of Holmesdale. The palace and the demesne which went with it were situated, as at Wrotham, in the Vale itself.[23] At the gates of the palace lay the church, the market and the nucleated settlement. At an early date several sub-manors had been created and they, together with a number of other isolated farmsteads, are mostly to be found in the southern part of the parish which extends into the sand and ragstone of the Chart Hills. Apart from one Wealden, which may have been erected for an official of the Archbishop,[24] only one of the surviving houses dates from before the mid 15th century, the majority having been built in the last quarter of the century.

In the rural areas there is little distinction between the size or quality of the houses of the sub-manors and other farmsteads, although Brockton Manor, the one probable manor house to remain almost in entirety, is the most finely detailed late medieval house in the parish. In the town, the survival of at least part of nine or more open-hall houses, most of which are of Wealden form, is testimony to the high quality of the medieval buildings there. This contrasts markedly with Wrotham, where the only partly surviving medieval house in the town centre is both small and low, and it is unlikely that so much would have been replaced if the houses there had been the equal of those in Charing town. However, despite the fact that the urban dwellings of Charing – which include clear evidence of a 15th-century shop – were never capable of later adaptation, they were never quite up to the standard of the rural houses in the parish, which are consistently larger and more pretentious. The halls of the town houses range between 31 and 34 sq m in area, while those in the rest of the parish are between 34 and 49 sq m. Thus it appears that, as in Wrotham, the holders of isolated farmsteads had certain advantages. That this is not just one of the standard differences between urban and rural buildings is suggested by the evidence of Chilham, where large and small houses were evenly distributed throughout the parish.

The final parish in which the Archbishop had property was Smarden, where he retained the manor of the den of Smarden until Archbishop Kempe settled it on his new college at Wye.[25] Most of the medieval houses are widely dispersed, although a small nucleus occurs round the church, where a market was established. Probably manorial control, in the proverbial manner of the Weald, was lightly exercised. The houses are predominantly late 15th or early 16th century in date, and are mostly of end-jetty form as in East Peckham, although on average they are not so small.

A number of interesting points emerge from the evidence of these parishes. In the first place, the number and location of houses on the large manors of Wrotham and Charing suggest that life may have been better for those who were primarily engaged in pastoral, as opposed to arable, farming, and for those whose homes were further from the manorial centre – although disentangling the relative benefits of these two aspects is not easy since the centre of the manor tended to lie on the best arable land.[26] Secondly, a majority among the parishes had, as Figure 140 indicates, a higher than average density of surviving medieval houses.[27] Charing is one of the parishes discussed in Chapter 10 in which surviving medieval buildings could have catered for over 30 per cent of the households recorded in 1557. Finally, as Figure 139 shows, in none of these parishes were medieval buildings as large as those further south, in the centre of the low and high Weald.

Put together these facts add up to the conclusion that there were considerable numbers of moderately wealthy people in the central parishes. Furthermore, the consistently smaller size of the houses in parishes dominated by Christ Church Priory estates may indicate that the Priory was a harsher landlord than the Archbishop. These inferences are by no means incompatible with the general picture that the documents present of medieval society in mid Kent; they augment it. The documentary evidence is plentiful only for ecclesiastical estates, whereas buildings remain on secular estates as well. It is therefore worth seeing what kind of houses were built on lay estates in central Kent.

## Secular estates

The parish of Pluckley lies between Charing and Smarden, and the land was divided between several manors. Although the main one belonged to the Archbishop at Domesday, it soon came to be held by knight service and passed through a succession of gentry families.[28] The parish is situated partly in the low Weald and partly on the ragstone, and the surviving medieval buildings are very similar in date, type and size to those of Smarden, though the density is greater. Like Charing, the houses probably catered for over 30 per cent of the households recorded in 1557. Thus Pluckley, where the manors were in lay hands, contains as many surviving medieval houses as parishes where the Archbishop held so much land; this suggests that the attitude of the landlord was not always the decisive factor in the prosperity of the tenants. Defining what the dominant influences were is less easy.

Among the many surviving Wealdens and end jetties in these central Kent parishes, one may catch rare glimpses of houses of smaller size and poorer quality. In Smarden the fragments of a single-aisled hall remain at Hadley House, and other aisled or quasi-aisled houses have been found in Boughton Malherbe (Figure 111) and East Farleigh. In Charing, Hunger Hatch Cottage is a small and probably late single-storey house; another example survives at Pimphurst Farmhouse, Bethersden (Figure 85b), and fragments of a third at The Dragon House, Smarden. Thus, despite the fact that by the early 16th century as much as 30 per cent of the population of this region may have been housed in the new types of medieval house, one may postulate that an even greater number lived in potentially durable, if somewhat smaller, dwellings which have mostly been swept away.

Not far to the west of Smarden and Pluckley lie Staplehurst and the Suttons, parishes in which the surviving timber-framed houses are of larger size, better quality and earlier date than anywhere else in the county. Chart Sutton and East Sutton are on the southern slopes of the greensand, running down to the River Beult in the low Weald below. The southern boundary of Chart Sutton forms the northern one of Staplehurst, which is located entirely in the Weald. Alluvium from the Beult, a tributary of the Medway, makes this part of the low Weald more fertile than regions further west or east (Figure 3), and possibly this was important. It is, for example, noticeable that the majority of the houses there date from the later years of the 14th century, when there was something of an economic and agricultural revival, and when this faded out in the first half of the 15th century,[29] the incidence of new houses dwindled. Nevertheless there must have been other causes at work, since the same prosperity is not apparent in Linton which lies almost immediately to the west and has similar topography and soil to Chart Sutton.

In terms of communications, the main road from London to Hastings via Maidstone lay just west of Chart Sutton and ran directly through Staplehurst where two of the late 14th-century houses, the King's Head Public House and Hill Crest and Kent Cottage, lie directly on its route. It has been claimed that the greatest peasant prosperity occurred in places which had easy access to two or more markets.[30] It is true that people in Staplehurst were within 3 and 4½ miles of Headcorn and Cranbrook markets respectively, and those in Chart Sutton within 3½ and 5 miles of Headcorn and Maidstone. But then, with nearby markets at Headcorn, Smarden and Charing, those who lived further east were hardly disadvantaged.[31]

Both Staplehurst and Chart Sutton shared the dispersed settlement pattern of a wide region of central Kent and the weak manorial structure common to the Weald. Staplehurst contained the detached lands of some ten manors whose centres lay at a considerable distance.[32] The largest part belonged to the manor of Sutton Valence, to which the manor of Chart Sutton was also an appendage, as was East Sutton before the early 15th century. Sutton Valence was held by the earls of Pembroke until the early 15th century when it was sold to the St Leger family, and shortly afterwards it passed to the Cliffords of Bobbing.[33] It seems unlikely that any of these overlords spent much time in Sutton Valence between the 13th and the early 16th centuries. All three parishes contained a number of small estates but, with the exception of Exhurst and Little Pagehurst in Staplehurst, none of them can be identified as the site of surviving medieval houses. In the absence of any likely candidates from the gentry, the alternative is that the houses were built for prosperous peasants or yeomen, many of whom, as elsewhere in the Weald, may have held land from more than one manor.

Yet none of this seems sufficient to explain why men in Staplehurst and Chart Sutton should have been able to build such fine houses some fifty years before their contemporaries elsewhere in the Weald or on the Chart Hills. As Figures 133–141 show, nearly all the surviving houses in these parishes date to the late 14th or early 15th century, with very few erected in the second half of the 15th century. From the 16th century, when the historical evidence is more plentiful, Staplehurst at least has been studied in some detail,[34] but nothing published on its history at this period helps to account for the earlier precocity of its buildings. For the moment the matter must be left as an unresolved puzzle. In the rest of the Weald the problem is less acute, for although the surviving houses may be larger, they are no earlier than the majority elsewhere.

## Disparities between Wealden parishes

Figures 135 and 136 suggest that many houses were built in the central section of both the low and high Weald in the late 15th century. Relevant surveyed parishes in the low Weald are Woodchurch, Pluckley and Smarden, and in the high Weald, Brenchley, Cranbrook and Benenden. All,

except Brenchley, have a considerable number of surviving medieval houses; but, as Figures 138–140 indicate, there are considerable differences in size, types and density.

The most obvious potential influence on late medieval prosperity in the central Weald was the broadcloth industry. Documents have linked wool and/or textiles with most Wealden parishes from Brenchley eastwards. The centre of production was Cranbrook, where the industry began in the 14th century. In the 15th century there is evidence for weavers and clothworkers at least as far afield as Pluckley and Smarden.[35] However, as noted in Chapter 1, documentation is neither detailed nor abundant until the mid 16th century. Since both wool production and the cloth trade faced problems in the 15th century, it is worth considering the extent to which textiles may have influenced house building in the Weald before the 16th century.[36]

Among those parishes where the majority of houses were erected in the second half of the 15th century, Brenchley, Benenden and Woodchurch have houses with halls as large as the earlier ones in Staplehurst and the Suttons. But surviving medieval houses in Cranbrook, as well as in Smarden and Pluckley, are noticeably smaller in size. It may be suggested that, because houses in the centre of Cranbrook town were not examined, larger and finer houses there were missed. This is not very likely, for, even if a number of medieval houses remain in the town, comparable evidence from other nucleated settlements, and from the 16th century in Cranbrook itself, indicates that the best dwellings are likely to have been situated on the outskirts or in the rural parts of the parish. A more valid objection to the method of extrapolating from surviving examples might be that the best of them were rebuilt by prosperous clothiers in the late 16th century or later. In part this is no doubt true, for a considerable number of fine houses of the late 16th and early 17th centuries in the parish are known to have been associated with wealthy clothiers. However, alongside these later houses are some medieval survivors of high quality. Old Wilsley is probably the largest complete medieval house remaining in the parish, and it is absolutely splendid (Figure 122). It is a Wealden, built in c 1500, with finely detailed timber work and an open hall which is likely to have been heated by an enclosed fireplace from the start. In the 16th and 17th centuries various modifications and extensions took place, but the basic structure was clearly considered perfectly adequate by the later owners, who are known to have belonged to the milieu of the more prosperous clothiers.[37]

Elsewhere, as at Freizley, The Freight and The Broadcloth, the original medieval house was partly rebuilt and enlarged, often in a magnificent way. In each of these cases the original house was considerably smaller than Old Wilsley, as can be gauged from the parts which remain. Although some of the owners of these properties cannot be identified, it is known that Freizley at least belonged to clothiers in the post-medieval period, and its later additions are among the finest in the parish.[38] It is not intended to argue that the medieval houses of Cranbrook were never rebuilt by the clothiers of the next century; in fact this is precisely what must have occurred at Goddards Green and Coursethorne.[39] What is very much in doubt is whether houses as large, as late and as splendid as Old Wilsley totally disappeared in the process; or whether the hypothetical rebuilding took place because what was there was too old, or even smaller than the Wealdens of which fragments do still remain.

Since Cranbrook was the centre of the textile industry, the fact that its surviving 15th-century houses are generally smaller than those of neighbouring parishes begs the question of whether, as has usually been assumed, wealth generated by textiles alone accounted for the finest medieval houses in the high Weald. Benenden certainly had its wealthy clothiers, such as the Gibbons, whose main seat was in Rolvenden and one of whose members built Pympne Manor, a fine close-studded Wealden, in Benenden.[40] But by the late 16th century if not before, there were not quite so many of them as in Cranbrook and Biddenden, and they never included the greatest names. Moreover, in addition to a number of large, late 15th-century houses, there are also Wealdens in Benenden of earlier date and similar size, such as the Manor House, The Moat and Dingleden, which were erected in or before the mid 15th century when the cloth trade was at a low ebb. The Manor House was probably built as a gentry residence, but no evidence has come to light to suggest this was true of the others. Thus even if their owners were involved in textiles, it is likely that at this date alternative or additional sources of wealth must be adduced.

The importance of farming as the backbone of Wealden prosperity in the late 16th century has been demonstrated by Zell. He has shown that farming was practised by a very large cross section of society, and that a sizeable number of medium and large farms of 100–150 acres were run by those below gentry status.[41] They tended, like the gentry, to have land in several locations, often held of more than one manor. In addition to farming, they might engage in subletting for rent and be involved in trade. By the late 16th century large farms in Benenden were perhaps the wealthiest in the Weald, with those of Cranbrook and Staplehurst not far behind. In general, the larger the farms, the higher the ratio of livestock to corn, thereby indicating a growing specialisation in stock rearing among the wealthy. On the smaller properties farming remained more truly mixed.[42]

How far back this state of affairs can be projected is not known, but the fact that the largest medieval houses in the Weald lie in Benenden, followed by Staplehurst and Woodchurch – parishes which lay at a little distance from the centre of cloth production – suggests that, despite a general slump in profits in the mid 15th century, farming was a source of wealth equal to, or even greater than, cloth. This seems to have been the clinching factor in Plaxtol, where several houses can be associated with butchers or graziers. The houses there were smaller than those in Benenden, but it is likely that the farms themselves were also of smaller size.[43] The acreage of farms may well have been a factor in determining the size of house. As Figures 136 and 140 show, this is implied by the distribution density of medieval houses. In the high Weald parishes, and in Staplehurst and Woodchurch, the houses are far more widely dispersed than in parishes where the houses were smaller. Although widespread distribution of houses does not necessarily mean that farms were larger, it is a potential indication of size. Only houses in the Suttons are seriously at odds with this inference. There large dwellings lie in close proximity to each other, implying that the farms to which they were attached were of no great extent, or had detached lands some distance away.

Whether the builders of houses in the high Weald were primarily farmers or clothiers, their houses suggest that they belonged to a different social group from those responsible for the surviving dwellings further north in mid Kent. Quite apart from their size, Figure 141 indicates that the medieval houses of Staplehurst, Cranbrook and Benenden represent the homes of under 10 per cent of the households recorded in 1557. There could be several reasons why this was so. In the first place, although the centre of Cranbrook was not surveyed, and the figure for medieval houses in that parish is probably too low, the eight buildings recorded would have to be increased to thirty for the proportion of houses to households to rise above 10 per cent, and it is unlikely that twenty-two medieval buildings remain undetected within the town. Second, the houses under discussion all have open halls, and this is a region where at least some two-storeyed dwellings were being built from the early 16th century onwards. Thirdly, Zell has shown that certainly from the 1560s and probably from the 1540s, the population of the high Weald parishes was increasing at a faster rate than the population further north. By the mid 16th century population density in the surveyed parishes of the high Weald ranged between 140 and 190 persons per 1,000 acres, while that in the surveyed parishes of the low Weald was between 80 and 150.[44]

All these reasons combine to make it unsurprising that the recorded houses cater for only a small proportion of the mid 16th-century population. Yet, when the relative scarcity of small open-hall houses of the type found further north in mid Kent, and the size and magnificence of the majority of surviving examples, are taken into account, these explanations do not seem to provide a totally satisfying answer to why the density of medieval houses in the high Weald is low. As Zell makes clear in his studies of Wealden society in the later 16th century, the prosperous farmers and wealthy clothiers who are likely to have built these houses formed only a small section of society. There were numerous small farmers, craftsmen, traders and others whose homes are largely unrepresented among the survivors, and from this one could conjecture that high Wealden society was more stratified than that in the low Weald and on the ragstone. The situation was obviously not the same as in north-east Kent, where a few held even larger amounts of land,[45] yet there are no signs of the numerous people of middling prosperity whose buildings remain in the centre of the county.

The houses suggest that this distinction between high and low Weald can be projected back into the previous century, and a measure of indirect support is provided by events in the mid 15th century when Kent, along with other parts of southern England, was shaken by considerable popular unrest. A connection between the men who took part in Cade's Rebellion of 1450 and the greater freedom and prosperity of mid-Kent tenants has been suggested by Butcher.[46] Many of those who took part are now known to have been wealthy peasants, including minor office-holders, protesting against corruption, greed and maladministration.[47] As Dyer remarked with reference to the earlier rising of 1381, any economic explanation of revolt is likely to be linked to rising but frustrated expectations.[48]

The evidence of the surviving houses could turn out to be one small piece in this jigsaw. The mid-Kent parishes from which the largest numbers of rebels came in 1450 were not Staplehurst and the Suttons, where surviving houses are large and early, nor Cranbrook, Benenden, Brenchley and Woodchurch where they were large and late. Instead they came from East Peckham, Smarden, Pluckley and Borden, all of which have a high incidence of middle-ranking medieval houses built in the second half of the 15th century. This could be no more than a coincidence, but it is tempting to speculate that those who were brave enough to show their discontent were those who were free and prosperous enough to have expectations which were not being fulfilled fast enough. Two decades later, a quite significant number of people from the very same parishes were in a position to build themselves substantial new homes. Exactly how this should be interpreted is by no means clear, but it is in marked contrast to the high Weald parishes where a handful of well-to-do entrepreneurs built some of the largest and finest medieval houses in England; and where less fortunate people had to make do with the sort of houses that fail to survive.

# North-west and west Kent

Understanding what occurred in west Kent is extremely difficult because of the paucity of documents and the lack of published work on those that have survived. As Figures 133–141 showed, the region is not uniform and the number and size of houses are generally less than in the centre of the county. To the north there are fewer houses altogether; in the Weald there are more, but they cannot compare with those in the centre, either in numbers, size or quality.

In some ways the north-western part of the county has similar characteristics to the central region further east: that is to say there are a number of high-status timber houses, ranging from the early or mid 14th-century Court Lodge, Fawkham, to the late 15th or early 16th-century houses at Court Lodge Farmhouse and The Limes, Southfleet. But these are not accompanied by the same scatter of late 14th-century buildings, or smaller late 15th-century houses, except perhaps in Southfleet, which stands out among the surveyed parishes. In part this was probably because the organisation of landholding was similar to that in north-east Kent, with tenant holdings increasingly divided between a few large parcels and many smaller ones, as has been revealed in Gillingham, on the eastern fringe of the north-west area.[49]

It is also probable that the poor quality of the land was partly responsible for reducing tenant prosperity. The soil is largely chalk mixed with sand, clay and gravel, which produces neither arable nor pasture land of high quality. The bishopric of Rochester, which held a large proportion of its estates in this region, was among the poorest in England and never achieved the sort of wealth enjoyed by the Canterbury ecclesiastical establishments;[50] and the Archbishop received less from his demesne farmers on the fringes of London than from those in the fertile lands of east Kent.[51] The extent to which good farmland may have played a significant role in creating wealth for the building of houses is suggested by Southfleet which, as remarked above, has more medieval houses than elsewhere in the region, and which Hasted describes as having more level and fertile soil than the surrounding parishes.[52] Even today a large part of Meopham, just to the south east of

Southfleet, is isolated and remote, with poor chalky soil set in wooded hills.

The subsidy assessment of 1334 indicates that there was considerable lay wealth in the corner of the historic county that now lies in London. But beyond that, in the area of modern Kent, assessments were low in both the 14th and the 16th centuries. When Londoners moved into Kent most of them did not go far beyond the county boundary. Some did acquire estates further into the county,[53] but those who stayed in the north west seem to have done nothing to improve the prosperity of the resident tenant population. Further south the subsidy figures paint an even bleaker picture, and the south-west corner emerges at all times as among the most sparsely populated and poorest parts of the county.[54] Yet despite this, the surviving building evidence becomes more abundant the further south one goes.

The parishes of Brasted and Sundridge are long and narrow, typical of this region in running from the Downs across the Vale of Holmesdale and the Chart Hills into the low Weald. In both parishes the manor and church lay in the Vale, as they did in Wrotham further east. Brasted was held by the Clares of Tonbridge until the late 15th century, and Sundridge by a wealthy local family, the Isleys; William Isley was among the entourage of the hated Lord Saye and Sele during the troubles of 1450.[55] Land in both parishes is of poor quality, even on the southern slopes of the greensand, and there is little evidence of the dispersed medieval farmhouses found in Plaxtol at the southern edge of the manor of Wrotham. In Brasted almost the only surviving medieval dwellings lie in the street settlement of the town founded by the Clares[56] – their presence forming a striking contrast to Wrotham where there is an absence of similarly dated buildings. In Sundridge a few medieval houses lie in the Vale, and a few more are dispersed through the rest of the parish. However, some of these, such as Dryhill Farmhouse and Yorkshill Farmhouse, are known to have been the centres of small manors or estates rather than the homes of prosperous tenant farmers. Whether lordship played any part in distinguishing these parishes from Wrotham and Plaxtol is difficult to say without further research.

Further south still the situation was again different. The elongated parish of Chiddingstone, which abuts the southern border of Sundridge, runs across the low and high Weald, and it is noticeable (Figure 136) that the majority of medieval houses lie within the high Weald region. Although houses in Edenbridge town, to the west, as well as isolated examples elsewhere, show that early 15th-century houses were not unknown in west Kent, the great majority date from the second half of the century. To this extent, the development in the western Weald was similar to that in the central high Weald. But in Speldhurst at least open-hall houses went on being built well into the 16th century.

This is not the only contrast with parishes further east. The houses are not the same, the majority being smaller with many of end-jetty or unjettied form, and they have a denser distribution as indicated on Figure 140 and confirmed by mid 16th-century population levels. Although there is no document covering the diocese of Rochester equivalent to Archdeacon Harpsfield's Visitation of 1557 for the diocese of Canterbury, Zell has worked on numerous parish registers of the 1560s, from which he has calculated the number of people per 1,000 acres throughout much of the Weald. These are unanimous in showing a very low density, of between 80 to 100 inhabitants per 1,000 acres, for Brasted, Sundridge, Chiddingstone and Speldhurst, in comparison with densities of 100 to 150 for the central low Weald and 140 to 190 for the central high Weald.[57] Thus the fact that the actual density of surviving houses in Chiddingstone is relatively high suggests that they may represent the homes of a high proportion of the population.

Neither the Wealden broadcloth industry, nor the iron industry which came to be important in the Brenchley and Goudhurst area in the 16th century, extended this far west. By the mid 16th century tanning and leatherwork were associated with western Kent, but it is unclear how widespread the prosperity generated from the industry might have been.[58] On the whole the major source of livelihood seems to have been the land. By the early 17th century it is clear that farms in Chiddingstone were, on average, no smaller than those in Headcorn, and somewhat larger than those in the mid-Kent parishes of Pluckley and Bethersden.[59] That small houses, representing the homes of a high proportion of the population, can be associated with medium-sized farms suggests that the social and economic fabric of the western high Weald had more in common with the central low Weald than with the greater extremes of wealth and poverty and high population of the central high Weald to which it is adjacent.

# Romney Marsh

One of the areas where very few medieval houses survive is Romney Marsh.[60] Four marshland parishes were investigated: Brookland, Brenzett, Newchurch and Lydd. To these may be added Appledore on the western edge and Aldington and Sellindge to the north. In Lydd about ten medieval dwellings remain in and on the outskirts of the town, but elsewhere on the Marsh proper none were found, and the question of the quantity and quality of the houses which undoubtedly existed on the Marsh in the 15th and early 16th centuries is something of a mystery. On the fringes, Appledore produced one medieval house apart from Hornes Place, but Aldington and Sellindge both have a fair number remaining.

Before the Black Death the Marsh was well populated, and the 1334 lay subsidy indicates areas of considerable wealth – particularly towards the east – as well as areas of great poverty. By the 16th century, the population density of the rural parishes was among the sparsest in the county, and the 1524 lay subsidy records some of the lowest yields in Kent, although the exclusion of the men of the Cinque Ports from the assessments almost certainly resulted in artificially low figures. Recent work by Butcher has helped to put this decline and the lack of building evidence into perspective.[61] A mid 15th-century survey reveals that some 40 per cent of the Marsh remained in ecclesiastical lordship throughout the Middle Ages. A substantial part was also held by the gentry – men like Robert Horne of Hornes Place, Appledore.

During the 15th century the towns of Hythe, New Romney and Lydd shrank considerably, but many of the townsmen who survived were taking up leases of property in the countryside, the wealthiest among them living off rents and

turning land to pasture for cattle and sheep in the same way as larger rural landowners elsewhere. The trend to large pastoral holdings held by those who lived off the Marsh had become so obvious by 1525 that it was reported to be in decay, with many great farms held by people who 'neither reside on them, nor till nor breed cattle, but use them for grazing'.[62] Although large numbers of those with smaller holdings were also engaged in mixed farming, a wide-ranging survey of 1457 shows that over half the holdings were of 10 acres or less, so they accounted for only a small proportion of the land. At the same time analysis of pottery finds from field walking shows a sharp decline in the number of houses in medieval occupation, particularly from the latter part of the 15th century onwards.[63] Despite this it is clear that there were still people living on the Marsh, but, as in all regions of Kent where the social and economic stratification was marked, the density of surviving buildings is slight.

On the outskirts of Lydd, one house survives which may represent the dwellings of the rural inhabitants of Romney Marsh. Rype Cottage (Figure 57) is a small, late, single-aisled hall, which had a loft at one end and may have been open at the other. After the Middle Ages it was substantially altered and enlarged to bring it up to date. Until recently another small, low medieval house remained not far away, but that has been demolished in recent years. Such houses have seldom lasted even when the site has been continuously inhabited, and since the Marsh suffered further depopulation after the Middle Ages, the wholesale destruction of such buildings is hardly surprising. In several of the later houses in Lydd, and one in Brookland, reused smoke-blackened rafters were found, indicating that many medieval houses were rebuilt after the Middle Ages. The fact that their timbers were fit for reuse suggests that the problem with them was not flimsy construction. In the towns they failed to measure up to the expectations of the late 16th century, and in the countryside they gradually fell into decay.

As remarked above, a number of late medieval houses remain in Lydd. They vary in size and quality, although even the largest among them are small in county-wide terms (Figure 139). Nonetheless the presence of high-walled Wealdens and end jetties in the town centre suggests that a degree of urban prosperity continued into the late 15th century. It may be wondered why no similar houses survive in Appledore which, although much smaller than Lydd, had a larger recorded population than the parishes of either Aldington or Sellindge in 1557. As recently pointed out by Gross, the earlier sea-based economy of Appledore changed to a land-based one during the Middle Ages, with pastoral farming in the rural area and a nucleated settlement and market serving a wide hinterland.[64] But Appledore was never as large as Lydd and, as a property of Christ Church Priory, it never enjoyed the same independence and privileges. By the late 18th century Hasted could describe it as having only forty-eight meanly built houses.[65]

However bustling Appledore may have been in the late Middle Ages, it is likely that the kind of houses which were built there were of the same poor quality as those in the rural parts of the Marsh. On the other hand, although the southern boundary of Aldington parish adjoins the Marsh, the surviving medieval houses lie considerably further north on the greensand of the Chart Hills where the mixed farming was totally untouched by the marshland tendency to pasture. The houses of Aldington and Sellindge share the same dispersed settlement pattern and the same characteristics as the houses of the low Weald and ragstone parishes of central Kent.

# The Isle of Sheppey

No mention has so far been made of medieval houses on Sheppey because the general scarcity of surviving dwellings observed over much of north-east Kent becomes a complete dearth there. The parishes of Eastchurch and Leysdown were surveyed, producing between them only one medieval building of uncertain form and date. The population on Sheppey was high in 1377, although the overall yield per square mile in the 1334 lay subsidy had been low, which suggests that the inhabitants may not have been wealthy. In 1557 the density of the population was among the lowest in the county, and by the 1570s bad management and over-rating on the part of the main landowners, the Cheneys of Shurland, is said to have led to depopulation on such a massive scale that the Crown had to step in with remedies.[66] If there is real substance in these claims, then the total lack of houses dating from before this time may be accounted for both by the poverty of the inhabitants and the effects of the 16th-century depopulation on such houses as there were.

# 13 Conclusion

It has often been said that Kent has more surviving medieval houses than any other county in England. Certainly, the largest and finest of them are extremely conspicuous, and it is easy to gain the impression that there are a great many of them. But as no attempt has yet been made to conduct a systematic census across the whole country, it would be premature to repeat any such claims here. Even in Kent previous estimates seem to have erred on the side of excess.

On the basis of the sample surveyed and discussed in this book, it is worth calculating just how many medieval buildings may remain over the county as a whole, and what proportion of the population may have lived in them. Appendix 2 shows that the total number of known open-hall houses in the sixty parishes is 395. If the parishes, which constitute 19 per cent of the parishes in the modern county, are a representative sample, then it might be expected that some 2,100 open halls would survive in the 319 administrative units of the modern county. This takes no account of concentrations of urban buildings, nor of the first fully floored houses which began to appear in the early 16th century, nor of the medieval buildings which have undoubtedly been missed during the survey. Thus the actual number of survivors built before *c* 1540 may be higher. Nevertheless, the grand total for the modern county is unlikely to be much above 2,500. This is a considerably lower figure than the 3,000–4,000 which was estimated at the start of the project,[1] but it seems to make sense in terms of the medieval population.

The population of the historic county in the early 16th century is unknown, but since it may have risen to only 80,000–85,000 by about 1560,[2] and had been growing rapidly in some areas during the second quarter of the century, the early 16th-century figure was almost certainly lower. However, on the basis of the mid 16th-century figures, which are the only guides we have, and allowing 4.75 people per household, there were something in the order of 17,500 households,[3] which means the surviving houses catered for approximately 14 per cent of the households. Given the growth of population between the erection of the houses and the moment of calculation, the inclusion of those who lived in the part of Kent now in Greater London, and the enormous variations between the regions, this overall figure seems remarkably high. Despite the margins of error it is useful for putting the scale of survival into perspective. In some parishes, mostly in the marshland and coastal regions, hardly any medieval houses were found, and the survival rate is well below the average. But in parts of central Kent over four houses remain per 1,000 acres, and this may represent as much as 40 per cent of the number required by the early 16th century. This density is not dissimilar to that proposed for parts of Essex and Oxfordshire,[4] and so far as is known, well above average for southern England as a whole.

Although Kent retains a large number of its medieval houses, this does not mean that the first survivors are of earlier date than those elsewhere in England. The earliest houses remaining are probably mid 13th-century, high-quality, two-storey stone ranges built by those of baronial class. It seems likely that they represent the subsidiary accommodation of large houses whose timber halls have vanished. In the years around 1300 these were followed by a number of complete stone houses in which both hall and ancillary ranges survive. The first timber buildings seem to date from the late 13th or early 14th century, and were not noticeably in advance of their time. They were built by those of knightly or gentry rank in the north of the county where the early manorial centres lay. Most of these buildings were aisled, and at this period the only surviving evidence for subsidiary accommodation is for single-storey end bays. This contrasts with the earliest timber structures known in East Anglia and the region south and east of Oxford, where 13th-century dates have been proposed for fully storeyed chamber ranges.[5] Although identification is uncertain, it is possible that the first 'peasant' dwellings also occur around 1300, but this is later than the dates proposed for some houses of comparable standing in Oxfordshire. It is this group of houses which first dispense with the open truss of aisled form and in which base-cruck construction appears for the first time in Kent.

Houses whose builders were quite certainly not of gentry status only start surviving in any number from the late 14th century, and then only in the same area of the central low Weald where the first putative peasant houses occurred. Although this was at a time when conditions improved after the prolonged social and economic depression of the 14th century, no satisfactory explanation has yet been found for the precocious houses of the Staplehurst and Chart Sutton region. They are as large and as fine as the best timber-framed houses erected fifty or a hundred years later, and they must have been built by those who, for want of a better word, were wealthy peasants or yeomen farmers. This is a phenomenon which appears to be of some significance for Kentish social history and needs drawing to the attention of social and economic historians. These houses also herald the introduction of new house types, in which aisles have been discarded and fully two-storeyed chamber accommodation introduced. It is by no means clear that the Wealden was invented at this level, but the earliest survivors are certainly among houses of this class.

Shortly thereafter the number of recognisable new houses tails off or even declines. The situation does not appear to improve until the mid 15th century, beginning perhaps in the 1450s and becoming more marked from the 1460s onwards. All writers on medieval England are agreed on the falling population and economic problems of the early to mid 15th century, so the correlation of documentary and building evidence may indicate that there was a real hiatus in the erection of new dwellings during this time. If the proposed dating of the buildings is correct, it is possible that the upsurge in building activity began before, or at exactly the same time as, the economic revival. This is an interesting point which deserves further exploration.

It has been argued here that a large number of well-built, but low and possibly aisled, open-hall houses are likely to have been swept away after the Middle Ages. While there is little evidence to associate the building of such houses with the first half of the 15th century in particular, the possibility that they were put up, and have since disappeared, should be borne in mind. Even if this was the case, it would still indicate a reduction in the prosperity of potential builders, for such houses would not have been the equivalent of the fine dwellings surviving from the late 14th century.

From the 1460s, and particularly towards the end of the century, the economic situation began to improve, and this is when the majority of surviving medieval houses were built. Leaving aside those which were quite certainly erected by gentlemen, they range from large to small. One of the important points which has emerged from this project is that density of survival and quality of building are two entirely separate issues. Those areas where the number of surviving houses is highest in relation to both acreage and population are not the same as those where houses are, on average, of the greatest size and highest quality. Among the buildings of this period are some of the finest timber houses of medieval England. They can be found dispersed throughout the county, but the marked concentration of large cross-wing and Wealden houses in the central high Weald calls for explanation. Neither the quality of Kentish cloth, nor the fertility of the land in the area, were outstanding in national terms; while the freedom of the men of the Weald was proverbial, the low density of the surviving distribution implies that the necessary levels of prosperity were reached by only a minority of the population.

In the centre of the county, in the low Weald and on the ragstone hills, smaller houses, many of which are of end-jetty form, were also built at this time. Although the houses are less pretentious, both absolute numbers and density of distribution are greater than further south. While it may be claimed that the wealthy parvenus who built the finest houses of the high Weald can hardly be called peasants in the accepted sense of the word, in parishes where 30–40 per cent of medieval houses survive, we must be looking at true peasant dwellings.

Although the smallest open-hall houses to remain are the least easy to date, the majority are likely to originate in this last period. They are not now as numerous as those of medium size, but it has here been suggested that well-built and potentially durable small houses were once far commoner. Low, small buildings were prone to adaptation and enlargement which was never necessary with the larger Kentish houses, and as a result most of them have been engulfed in later alterations or swept away. They are found throughout the county, and in the central areas their fragmentary remains may represent the homes of a poorer section of the community than that catered for by the numerous Wealden and end-jetty houses which survive. But in the east, where fewer large or medium-sized houses occur, few tenants on the large estates can have had surplus income to build better houses. It is highly unlikely that the homes of medieval wage-earners or the landless poor remain anywhere in the county.

By the mid 16th century the population in parts of Kent was increasing rapidly, but as far as can be seen there is little evidence of an immediate upsurge in new buildings. As the project was mainly concerned with open halls, purpose-built fully floored houses were not systematically surveyed, but the number of these encountered was not great – a conclusion already reached by Rigold.[6] In large part this is, no doubt, because the greatest increase was among just that poorer section of the population whose homes do not survive until long after the end of the Middle Ages.[7]

From the middle of the 16th century, and continuing well into the 17th century, new building increases.[8] This is most apparent in some of the nucleated settlements, such as Lydd, Newington next Sittingbourne and Wrotham, and in some of the low and high Weald cloth-producing parishes. It is beyond the scope of this project to assess these later developments or to relate them to medieval buildings. Sometimes the rebuilding of earlier structures can be detected, but many houses which were examined cursorily in the hope of finding medieval remains turned out to be new houses, presumably required by the expanding population, which had reached approximately 150,000 by the end of the 17th century.[9]

Much of the latter half of this book has been devoted to the late medieval houses of Kent. They have been classified by date, type and size, and their geographical distribution mapped. This approach, which perhaps represents a departure from the normal pattern of regional architectural studies, is a necessary precondition for any attempt to place the buildings in their proper historical context. Where buildings and documents can be studied together, it is usually found that they complement one another and form a single coherent picture of the past. Ultimately, given that they are all evidence, this must be so. But the building evidence does not depend upon the documents for its validity, and where there are no documents, the buildings, if correctly interpreted, can go some way towards filling the gaps. If the conclusions appear to be inconsistent with preconceived notions, there is a case for reopening the issues. This book is offered as an exploratory essay in the historical interpretation of Kentish houses, and if it contributes in a small way to a more balanced view of the social and economic history of medieval Kent, it will have achieved its purpose.

# Appendix 1
# Tree-ring dating

## The technique

From the outset of the project on medieval houses in Kent, it was clear that the accurate dating of buildings was a critical issue. One of the aims was to establish chronologies for different building types, and their relation to each other. Another was to see whether there were different rates of development in different regions of the county. A third was to assess whether there was a uniform increase over time in the number of medieval houses surviving, or whether the pattern of survival suggested bouts of activity and inactivity in the erection of new dwellings. Unless fairly specific dates could be obtained, there was little hope of these questions being answered, or of setting the buildings in a wider historical context.

The difficulties of dating domestic buildings, particularly if they are timber framed and of medieval date, and the need to establish as precise a chronology as possible have long been recognised.[1] A great deal of work has been done on this problem, notably on establishing the dates of various structural techniques.[2] But although this has gone a long way to clarify the general typological sequence, doubts still remain concerning the length of time particular techniques continued in use, and the extent to which there were regional differences in chronology.

In recent years, however, the possibility of a more objective method of dating timber structures has become available by means of dendrochronology or tree-ring analysis.[3] The annual growth of a tree is marked by the addition of a ring of new wood to the tree's circumference, the number of rings therefore indicating the age of the tree. Since the width of each ring varies according to climatic conditions, the sequence of ring-widths over the course of a tree's life forms a pattern which may be matched against the pattern from other trees within the same locality, and more generally matched against the pattern of ring-widths from trees over a wider region. By starting with a modern tree whose felling date is known, and overlapping the pattern of rings with successively older trees, a sequence of tree rings with firm dates may be established. This is known as a master chronology, and it is against this firmly dated sequence that timbers of unknown date may be matched. If bark is present on a tree dated in this way, then the felling date of the tree is clear. If only sapwood survives, the felling date may be estimated. Since it is known that most timber buildings were constructed with unseasoned timber,[4] the date of the buildings can, by these means, be gauged.

In this study a tree-ring dating project was set up in 1986, in collaboration with Nottingham University Tree-Ring Dating Laboratory, in order to establish a framework of accurate dates for a number of buildings. These were then used as controls for dating the rest of the medieval houses recorded. By the 1980s several laboratories engaged in tree-ring analysis were in existence, and master chronologies had been created for various parts of the British Isles. Nevertheless, in 1986 no one in England had conducted a systematic campaign of tree-ring dating on buildings of a defined period within a relatively confined area, and the chance to do so was particularly exciting. At that time no master chronology for oak timber in Kent was available against which to date the samples taken, and chronologies developed for other parts of England necessarily formed the basis for analysing the first material and obtaining the first tentative dates.[5] It was not possible, with the resources available, to establish a local master chronology tied to the present day. Instead a long and well-replicated floating chronology was built, produced by objective and independent means – in other words, taking no account of documented buildings or other external dates. This was then anchored to the period 1158 to 1540 by cross-matching with master chronologies from elsewhere. This long sequence had very high t-values[6] when compared with other British chronologies, especially those for the East Midlands and the south of England.

In all, seventy-four buildings, or phases of building, were sampled, and firm results were obtained for fifty-three of them. Three buildings had datable rings but no sapwood, which meant that the felling dates could not be estimated firmly, and two more were given dates which made little sense in architectural terms, probably because the timbers were reused. All these, together with the sixteen buildings, or phases of building, which remain undated, are listed below in Tables 5 and 6.

## The results

If bark, or traces of it, are present on a dated timber, the felling date is known. In Table 5 this is indicated by a date in brackets with no range to either side. Where two dates are shown in brackets (eg 1379/80), this indicates that the timber may have been felled in the second year, before March or April when the annual ring for that year began to grow. If no bark, but at least part of the sapwood is present, then an estimate of the felling date can be given. The number of sapwood rings may vary, but an average can be calculated. The original estimation of the number of sapwood rings likely to occur on timbers in Kent was based on the generally accepted number of about thirty for mature oak trees, with a range of fifteen to fifty estimated to include 95 per cent of all mature trees (30, -15 +20).[7] These estimations

| Name of parish and house, and brief description of dated structure | Date range | VA volume | No. of rings in site sequence | No. of samples in sequence |
|---|---|---|---|---|
| Meopham, Nurstead Court (aisled hall) | 1299–(1309)–1319 | 19 | 116 | 6 |
| East Farleigh, Gallants Manor (service wing) | 1312–(1322)–1332 | 23 | 149 | 2 |
| Ightham, Ightham Mote (solar wing) | 1321–(1331)–1341 | 19 | 155 | 11 |
| Ightham, Ightham Mote (roof of stone hall) | 1327–(1337)–1347 | 19 | 151 | 12 |
| Ightham, Ightham Mote (roof of stone chapel) | 1332–(1342)–1352 | 19 | 147 | 12 |
| Sutton Valence, Henikers (hall) | 1354–(1364)–1374 | 19 | 100 | 6 |
| Staplehurst, Coppwilliam (single aisled hall) | (1370/1) | 22 | 75 | 5 |
| Chart Sutton, Old Moat Farmhouse (service wing) | 1367–(1377)–1387 | 22 | 102 | 6 |
| Chart Sutton, Chart Hall Farmhouse (Wealden) | (1379/80) | 22 | 100 | 8 |
| Teynham, Lower Newlands (cross-wing house, hall dated) | 1370–(1380)–1390 | 19 | 89 | 5 |
| Plaxtol, Bartons Farmhouse (service wing) | 1373–(1383)–1393 | 21 | 81 | 5 |
| Staplehurst, Hill Crest and Kent Cottage (cross-wing house, wing dated) | 1379–(1389)–1399 | 22 | 84 | 5 |
| Shepherdswell with Coldred, West Court (Wealden) | 1397–(1399)–1409 | 23 | 74 | 2 |
| East Sutton, Walnut Tree Cottage (hall) | 1393–(1401)–1411 | 19 | 175 | 7 |
| Edenbridge, Country Fair and Light Horse (94, 96, High Street) (Wealden) | 1400–(1410)–1420 | 22 | 114 | 7 |
| Biddenden, Vane Court (Wealden) | 1417–(1419)–1429 | 21 | 104 | 7 |
| Plaxtol, Spoute House (end jetty, service end) | 1414–(1424)–1434 | 19 | 97 | 3 |
| Capel, Wenhams and Thistles (end jetty) | (1431)–1441 | 21 | 80 | 9 |
| Canterbury, 36–37 Burgate[a] (storeyed range) | 1425–(1435)–1445 | 19 | 85 | 4 |
| East Sutton, Parsonage Farmhouse (Wealden) | 1426–(1436)–1446 | 21 | 83 | 4 |
| Plaxtol, Spoute House (end jetty, hall) | 1435–(1445)–1455 | 21 | 57 | 3 |
| Plaxtol, Clakkers Hall (end jetty) | 1442–(1452)–1462 | 19 | 139 | 5 |
| East Sutton, Noah's Ark Farmhouse (end jetty) | 1446–(1456)–1466 | 19 | 110 | 9 |
| Aldington, Symnel Cottage (end jetty) | 1450–(1460)–1470 | 20 | 124 | 8 |
| Tenterden, The Man's Shop (18,20 High Street)[b] (Wealden) | 1450–(1460)–1470 | 19 | 149 | 5 |
| Sturry, Mead Manor (probably special-purpose range) | 1464–(1465)–1475 | 21 | 90 | 6 |
| Molash, Harts Farmhouse (cross-wing house) | (1466)–1469 | 21 | 132 | 1 |
| East Sutton, The Blue House (Wealden) | 1463–(1468)–1478 | 19 | 169 | 7 |
| Edenbridge, Farringtons, Edenbridge Bookshop (75, 77, 79 High Street) (Wealden) | (1476/7) | 23 | 124 | 10 |
| Brenchley, The Old Palace (Wealden) | (1485) | 22 | 181 | 6 |
| Gravesend, The Old Rectory House, Northfleet (unjettied) | (1488/9) | 20 | 113 | 7 |
| East Sutton, Luckhurst (Wealden) | (c 1490) | 20 | 93 | 10 |
| Chartham, Deanery Farm[c] (Wealden) | (1496/7) | 20 | 134 | 13 |
| Pluckley, Jennings Farmhouse (end jetty) | 1491–(1501)–1511 | 20 | 74 | 8 |
| Linton, Court Lodge (two-storey house) | 1496–(1506)–1516 | 21 | 79 | 6 |
| Staplehurst, Little Harts Heath (two-storey house) | (1507) | 24 | 120 | 6 |
| East Malling and Larkfield, Rocks (132 Rocks Road) (two-storey range) | (1507/8) | 21 | 97 | 8 |
| Sheldwich, Cobrahamsole Farmhouse (cross-wing house) | (1508) | 23 | 104 | 8 |
| Speldhurst, Manor Cottage (unjettied) | (1508/9) | 22 | 157 | 7 |
| Kenardington, Place Farmhouse (two-storey house) | (1512/13) | 20 | 80 | 6 |
| Lynsted, Tudor Cottage (two-storey hall) | (1514)–1520 | 20 | 111 | 8 |
| Petham, China Court (end jetty) | 1506–(1516)–1526 | 19 | 117 | 3 |
| Lynsted, Lynsted Court (parlour wing) | (1517) | 23 | 98 | 8 |
| Elmsted, Spong Farm House (partly floored hall) | (1520) | 22 | 162 | 5 |
| Lynsted, Tudor Cottage (parlour wing) | 1518–(1528)–1538 | 19 | 101 | 9 |
| Brenchley, Wat Tyler's Cottage (two-storey house) | (1529/30) | 22 | 229 | 8 |
| Hever, Hever Brocas (hall range) | 1524–(1532)–1542 | 21 | 117 | 7 |
| Speldhurst, Little Laverall (end jetty) | (c 1533) | 23 | 175 | 4 |
| Sittingbourne, Chilton Manor (reused rafters) | 1524–(1534)–1544 | 19 | 153 | 6 |
| Speldhurst, Linkhorns Farmhouse (end jetty) | (1540) | 22 | 198 | 7 |
| Plaxtol, Bartons Farmhouse (two-storey hall) | 1541–(1548)–1558 | 19 | 125 | 7 |
| Sittingbourne, Westfield (rear wing) | 1547–(1557)–1567 | 23 | 89 | 1 |
| Sevenoaks, 21–25 London Road (rear wing) | 1588–(1591)–1601 | 19 | 108 | 6 |

[a] Bowen 1986a.    [b] Recorded by Judith Roberts, see Roberts 1990.    [c] Tatton-Brown 1983a, 124–7.

*Table 5 Chronological sequence of tree-ring dated buildings. The firm or estimated felling date is in brackets.*
*No date range is given where the presence of bark leads to a precise date.*

were published in *Vernacular Architecture* **19–24** (1988–93).

However, at the end of the sampling in Kent, it was possible to reassess the sapwood estimates, using the evidence of the eighteen examples with bark, together with a small number of similarly firmly dated buildings elsewhere in south-east England and other samples which had substantial amounts of sapwood present. The results of the reassessment strongly suggest that most trees only had twenty-five sapwood rings, and that the 95 per cent confidence range should be fifteen to thirty-five such rings (25, +/-10).[8] Since the last measured ring-date for each building remains the same, the result has been to pull back all the estimated felling dates by five years.

In Table 5, the date range for the timbers of each building is given to either side of the estimated felling date. In some cases enough sapwood rings remain to make the start of the date range close to, or actually the same as, the estimated felling date. The estimated felling dates are the ones which have been used throughout this book, preceded by *circa* (*c*). All tree-ring dates quoted in the text have been identified by an asterisk. Since almost all buildings were dated on the evidence of several timbers, whose individual rings were combined to form a site sequence ranging from the earliest to the latest measured ring-date, the last two columns of Table 5 indicate the length of the site sequence, and how many timbers were used to construct it.

## Undated buildings

Not all timber buildings can be dated by dendrochronology. There are a number of known problems, several of which were encountered in Kent, where twenty-one buildings or phases of building sampled, remain undated. The overall effect of this, including evidence from buildings which were not considered suitable for sampling, has been illustrated in Figure 148.

In the first place, a number of buildings were not constructed of oak. So far, extensive tree-ring chronologies

*Figure 148 Tree-ring dating of medieval houses in Kent. The black symbols represent dated buildings, or phases of building. The white ones are those which were not dated; these include those which were sampled and proved impossible to date, those known not to be of oak, and those which were judged to have too few rings to sample for tree-ring dating.*

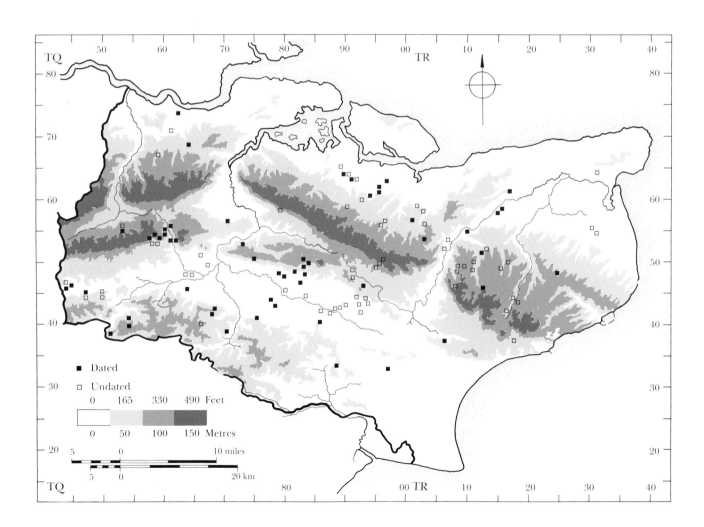

| Name of parish and building | Brief description of type | Suggested date range |
|---|---|---|
| Canterbury, Eastbridge Hospital[a] | Roof of stone chapel | Early 14th century |
| Chilham, Tudor Lodge Gift Shop and Peacock Antiques | Wealden with rear aisle | 1370–1410 |
| Eastry, Eastry Court | Aisled hall | 1294/5 (documented) |
| | | 1318/19 (alterations) |
| Elham, Boyke Manor | Wealden | 1490–1520 |
| Fawkham, Court Lodge | Aisled hall | 1310–50 |
| Hastingleigh, Coombe Manor | Base-cruck hall and cross wing | 1440–80 |
| Milstead and Kingsdown, Hoggeshaws | Wealden | 1420–60 |
| Petham, Dormer Cottage | Aisled hall | 1340–80 |
| Sevenoaks, 21–25 London Road | Wealden | 1500–20 |
| Sheldwich, Copton Manor | Roofs of stone hall and cross wing | 1310–40 |
| Sittingbourne, Chilton Manor | Aisled hall | 1270–1310 |
| Sittingbourne, Westfield | Wealden | 1410–50 |
| Upper Hardres, Cottage Farmhouse | End jetty | 1510–50 |
| Upper Hardres, Little Bursted Farmhouse | End jetty | 1500–30 |
| Waltham, Dennes House | Unjettied | 1510–40 |
| Waltham, Sarness Farm[b] | Barn | 18th century |

[a] Munby et al 1983, 128 and Tatton-Brown 1984, 155–7, where the roof is dated to the late 13th century. A tentative date of 1291–(1301)–1311 was obtained, but the site sequence of 69 rings from 5 timbers was too short for certain dating.

[b] This was sampled early in the project when the aim was to establish an absolute local master chronology, not a floating one. It was very soon clear that this would not be possible, but a few buildings of no direct relevance to the project were sampled in an initial foray (eg Canterbury Cathedral tower, 21–25 London Road, Sevenoaks, rear wing, and Westfield, Sittingbourne, rear wing).

*Table 6 Buildings where no tree-ring dating was possible.*

for the British Isles have only been established for oak among the hard woods, and cross matching with other species is not at present established practice. In parts of north and north-east Kent, where timber was always scarcer, considerable numbers of the medieval buildings – perhaps even as many as 20 per cent – are not built of oak. Where the timber has been identified it is elm, but since the buildings have not been examined by a timber expert it is not possible to state categorically that other timber was not used.[9]

A second problem concerns the large number of buildings which were built with timber from fast-grown trees and so have relatively few annual rings. These are listed in Table 6. In general, it is not possible confidently to cross match and date single timbers which have fewer than seventy annual rings remaining, and confidence is crucial in this study. In principle, it becomes progressively easier to obtain a date the more rings there are and the more samples that are involved. Where several samples are used, a site sequence, which is usually longer than any individual timber, can be obtained by cross matching all the timbers. In this project eight or more samples were normally taken, and dating was almost always based on site sequences.

In Kent it seems that many trees quickly grew to a large size and were felled when relatively young. The number of rings remaining, especially when sapwood has been lost, is frequently between thirty and fifty, even when the timber itself is of considerable scantling. This phenomenon occurred throughout the county, but was particularly noticeable in certain areas. For example, only one building with timber which looked suitable for sampling could be found at Elham, on the Downs, and when sampled the

sequence of rings in fact turned out to be too short. In Eastling, also on the Downs, no buildings appeared to have timbers with enough rings remaining, but two or three were found in the neighbouring parish of Sheldwich. Among parishes straddling the ragstone and low Weald, careful checking suggested that there was no point sampling buildings in Charing, Pluckley or Smarden, although only a few miles to the north west, in not dissimilar geographical conditions, the timbers of nearly every medieval house in Chart Sutton and East Sutton were slow grown and could be dated with ease. Some of these concentrations are plotted on Figure 148. Since, apart from these parishes, checking was done mostly in a random manner and was related largely to buildings which it was considered would be useful to have dated, it is not possible to assess how high a proportion of Kentish houses was built of fast-grown timber. A rough estimate, gauged from those houses inspected, suggests between 30–40 per cent may have had timbers with short ring-sequences. If this can be applied generally, it is a problem of some magnitude.

The reason why trees growing at the same time are of a different size may relate to variations in soil and situation. As local farmers pointed out, oaks planted on the well-drained ragstone grow far faster than their fellows on the Wealden clay. But the fact that the two groups of houses discussed above straddle both the greensand and the clay, with one cluster dating easily and the other not, indicates that the relationship between situation and growth is almost certainly a complex one which would have required research beyond the resources of this project to explore.

A third group of buildings where dendrochronology provided no easy answer consists of those with disputable dates: among the examples surveyed, two resulted in tree-ring dates for some timbers which caused problems from an archi-

Church House (72 High Street), Edenbridge. A cross-wing house

Comment
RCHME was puzzled by the fact that a crown post and saltire bracing of
c 1380–1410 were combined with evidence for shallow doorheads more appropriate to the late 15th century or after. The NUTRDL date of (1509)–1519 is based
on four timbers, including one which is certainly reused. But a last measured ring-
date of 1378 for one main post may indicate that the house was built around
c 1400 and was largely dismantled and rebuilt in the early 16th century.

The Old Farmhouse, Hadlow. An end-jetty house.

Comment
The RCHME date of c 1380–1420 indicates one of the earliest end-jetty houses
surveyed. The NUTRDL date is of 1316– (1326)–1336. This applies to two timbers
only; the rest have very few rings. Despite the early details of this end-jetty house,
it is difficult to accept that it is over eighty years earlier than any other examples.
Again reuse, although not obvious, may account for the tree-ring date.

*Table 7 Buildings with problematical dates.*

Canterbury Cathedral, timbers of the central tower.

Comment
It has been suggested that the tower was roofed as a simple lantern between
1486 and 1493. The four timbers sampled belong to this phase;[a] they were tree-
ring dated, but lack of sapwood means the felling date was only identified as
after the early 15th century.[b]

Rectory Park, Horsmonden. A cross-wing house.

Comment
The style and structure suggest a date range between 1480 and 1520. Lack of
sapwood means that the timbers could only be dated to the second half of the
15th century.[c]

Newbury Farmhouse, Tonge. An aisled hall.

Comment
The style and structure suggest a date range between 1280 and 1310. Only one
timber, an arcade post, could be tree-ring dated. It had 162 rings but no
sapwood, the length implying a large number of sapwood rings. Since the last
measured ring dates to 1099, the felling date could have been c 1150. If this is
accepted, the arcade post is likely to have been reused, although there is no
structural evidence for this.

[a] Hewett and Tatton-Brown 1976. [b] *VA* **19** 1988, 48. [c] *VA* **19** 1988, 48.

*Table 8 Sampled timbers with no sapwood remaining.*

tectural point of view. These are discussed in Table 7. Probably
these results indicate reused timbers, although it is not always
possible to prove this from examination of the structure.

In three more cases firm tree-ring dates were obtained
for timbers which had no sapwood remaining. It was
therefore impossible to estimate the actual felling dates of
the timbers or the construction dates of the buildings.
These are listed in Table 8. Newbury Farmhouse, Tonge,
has been included in this list, although it also falls into the
category of disputable dates discussed in Table 7.

# Discussion

It may be wondered whether these problems, and in particular
the absence of oak and the presence of fast-grown trees in
certain parts of Kent, have affected the conclusions of this
study. This does not appear to be very likely. As Figure 148
shows, the buildings which could not be dated are widely
distributed; they seem to occur in small pockets, interspersed
with areas where buildings could be tree-ring dated with ease.
In addition, as discussed below, the majority are likely to be

late, belonging to the period when most of the firmest results
were obtained, which means that in most cases another
building of the same type in more or less the same region
could be substituted. It is true that some building types are not
well dated, but this was not primarily a problem of distribution,
since it appeared to affect all such houses, wherever they lay.

It is considered good dendrochronological practice to
sample eight or more timbers in each structure in order to
produce reliable dates. But in some medieval buildings so few
timbers remain, at any rate so few that are potentially datable,
that tree-ring dating is not possible. Unfortunately, three
classes of building which frequently survive in fragmentary
condition in Kent – early buildings with aisles or base crucks,
late aisled halls, and the smallest medieval houses – also
tended to be those in which short sequences were common, so
the problem of dating was compounded.

The smallest houses and the late aisled halls were often
constructed with timbers of relatively slight scantling, and the
size of house, type of structure and relatively poor quality of
the materials led to them being enlarged and partly rebuilt.
Several of these lay on the Downs and in north-east Kent, but
they were not confined to those areas, for the problem was also
noticeable in East Peckham in the low Weald, where several
houses were identified from partial survivals which had too few
timbers remaining for sampling. Because of this, it was difficult
to establish whether small houses were contemporary with
large ones, or were generally later in date. Luckily some light
was thrown on the matter when four small open halls in
Speldhurst and Hever, in the western high Weald, were found
to be datable and proved to have been built well into the 16th
century. This evidence, together with the overall trends in size
indicated in Figure 67, suggests that the majority of small
houses are late in date.

Dating of structures in the first category of fragmentary
buildings – early aisled halls and base crucks – was likewise
hampered by the prevalence of fast-grown timber in some of
the better surviving examples.[10] But these seem to suffer from
a further problem of their own. At a national level it has long
been recognised that there are periods to which few buildings
can be dated, and this caused considerable difficulties in
constructing some of the earliest master chronologies. One of
these periods was the mid 14th century, which became known
as the '14th-century gap'. Over the British Isles as a whole the
hiatus centres on 1350, and the coincidence of this date with
the Black Death has given rise to speculation that the two
phenomena may be in some way related, possibly indicating a
depletion of tree stocks caused by earlier population pressure,
followed by a regeneration of oak on depopulated land.[11] This
is not quite the picture presented by the Kentish evidence.
Figure 149 shows that very few buildings in Kent have felling
dates before 1370, and that there were two completely blank
periods, one in the mid 14th century and the other around
1300.[12] However, although no dated timbers came from trees
felled during these periods, both are spanned by tree rings in
the unbroken sequence of the Kent master chronology, which
runs from 1158 to 1540, so that there is no 'gap' in the
chronology in the sense that dendrochronologists normally
use the term.[13] But the apparent absence of surviving buildings
around 1300 and in the mid 14th century still requires explanation. In fact the two gaps appear to represent lacunae of
different kinds.

During the project one or two buildings, which previously
had been thought to have mid 14th-century dates, such as

No. of rings in site sequence

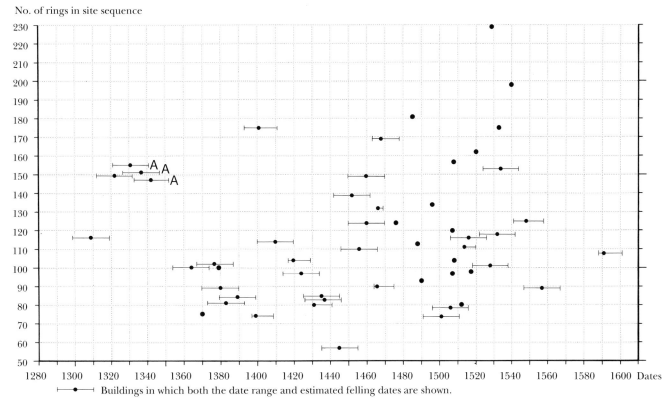

├──●──┤  Buildings in which both the date range and estimated felling dates are shown.

●  Buildings firmly dated by the presence of bark.

A  Three phases of Ightham Mote.

Walnut Tree Cottage, East Sutton, were shown to have been erected in the late 14th or early 15th century. This alteration affects not only tree-ring dated buildings, but depletes the list of all buildings likely to date from the mid 14th century. It is possible that the base crucks at Hamden, Smarden, and Nightingale Farmhouse and Burnt Oak, Yalding, were built at this time; it is equally possible that the tiny aisled hall at Dormer Cottage, Petham, should be assigned to this period. But the number of houses which belong neither with the group of proven early buildings, nor with the group for which there is abundant evidence of late 14th-century date, can be counted on the fingers of one hand. There does, therefore, seem to be a gap in buildings datable to the mid 14th century. It is, however, unlikely that this reflects a dearth of suitable timber, and more likely that adverse social and economic circumstances resulted in fewer people being able to build new houses at that time.

The earlier gap illustrated in Figure 149, around 1300, appears to have been caused by entirely different circumstances, for a number of structures were identified as likely to have been built during this period. Leaving aside those which were rejected as too fragmentary, or built of fast-grown timber, nine buildings were sampled and analysed. Three of the most sophisticated and typologically advanced among them – Nurstead Court, Gallants Manor and Ightham Mote – were dated to *c* 1309*, *c* 1322* and *c* 1331–*c* 1342* respectively, three ranges of the latter building accounting for the three dates marked A on Figure 149. No dates were obtained for the other six buildings, most of which were likely to have been built somewhat earlier. Five of them have several timbers with 60 to

*Figure 149 Chronological sequence of tree-ring dated buildings, or phases of building, illustrating firm dates, date ranges and numbers of rings in each site sequence.*

100 rings; yet they have not cross matched with each other or with the few buildings outside Kent which have been firmly dated to this time.[14] Initially it was thought this might be a regional problem, affecting buildings within a limited area. But in fact the examples lie strung out from Fawkham in the west to Eastry in the east, throughout the northern half of the county where the earliest timber houses occur.

Thus the most problematical period for tree-ring dating, from which we have plenty of buildings but very little material for cross matching, lies at the beginning of the 14th century and earlier. It was hoped that dated timbers from elsewhere in southern England, such as The Old Rectory, Warbleton, East Sussex (1292/3*),[15] the nave roof of Ely Cathedral (*c* 1295*),[16] the Pilgrims' Hall, Winchester (*c* 1308*),[17] and Upton Court, Slough (1319/20*),[18] would provide the key and help solve the problem. So far this has not proved possible.

It has been suggested that the trouble may have been caused by the medieval practices of pollarding and shredding, that is of cutting all the lower branches from a tree at regular intervals. This causes major disturbance to the tree and distorts its pattern of growth, producing sudden falls in ring widths followed by a gradual recovery over several years. In these circumstances the sequence will not match the master curve.[19] Tree management of this sort may have been associated with large estates, but more research is required to find out if this could have affected the earliest surviving buildings in Kent.

153

From a dendrochronological point of view, the inability to date the earliest surviving structures is extremely frustrating. But the newly found documentary date of 1294/5 for the timber aisled hall at Eastry Court, and the recent discovery that the single-aisled hall in West Street, New Romney, was built sometime after the great storm of 1287, together with the documented dates of 1303 and 1313 for the roofs over the stone halls at The Deanery, Chartham, and Court Lodge, Great Chart, mean that there are clues as to the dates of some of these early buildings.[20] Enough, at least, for us to be fairly certain that, in contrast to the situation in the mid 14th century, a considerable amount of building was being undertaken in the decades to either side of 1300.

Figure 149 illustrates the chronological distribution of the results from the fifty-three dated structures, and also indicates the number of annual rings in the site sequences from which the dates were obtained. In each case a circular symbol represents the felling date. Where the circle stands alone the building is firmly dated by the presence of bark. Horizontal lines to either side of the cirle mark the date ranges of those timbers whose felling dates can only be estimated. As discussed above, the majority of dated buildings were erected after 1370. It is apparent from Figure 149 that firmly dated timbers with traces of bark became more frequent as time went by, most of them occurring after 1470. However, bark was not confined to timbers of a certain age, but was fairly evenly distributed between sites with as few as 80 or as many as 229 rings in the sequence.

Perhaps the most important point to emerge from Figure 149 is the fact that the age of the timbers used varied over time. The few, high-status buildings dated in the first half of the 14th century were constructed with timbers from fairly long-lived trees, but from the 1370s to around 1450 few buildings used timbers which were more than 100 years old, and many were constructed with younger trees. This practice did not cease in the later period, for not only are sequences of 70 to 100 years common on Figure 149, but one must remember all those buildings whose timbers were too fast grown for tree-ring analysis to be possible. Yet timbers of more than 150 rings only come back into the picture after 1450. The meaning of this difference is not immediately apparent. The moment when the trees were felled must have depended upon their size, which in turn must have been closely related not only to soil and situation but also to overall climate, to the way they were managed and possibly to what the client was prepared to pay. Serious analysis of all these factors is not possible here. However, it is worth noting that the pattern is not simply regional, for sequences of over 150 rings, although primarily occurring in buildings in the high and low Weald where drainage was a problem, can also be found on the Downs and on the northern plain. Nor is it always a matter of social status, for the longest sequences are found both in grand houses, such as The Old Palace, Brenchley, and in tiny houses like Linkhorns Farmhouse and Little Laverall in Speldhurst. Thus, although patterns seem to be discernible in Figure 149, clear conclusions concerning their meaning cannot at present be postulated.

A final problem of tree-ring dating, which is not peculiar to Kent, concerns the reuse of timbers. It is self-evident that one should only sample timbers which are in their original positions and belong to the structure one is trying to date. Documents indicate that timbers were reused from other buildings. In 1352, for example, timber from the

Archbishop's derelict manor house at Wrotham was transported for reuse at his palace of Maidstone.[21] What occurred at this social level is presumably even more likely to have happened among people of lesser status, and in the 15th century a number of instances of tenants being allowed to reuse timber are recorded in the Sussex parish of Warminghurst.[22] Some buildings themselves have signs of reused materials, as at The Plestor, Borden, and 6 Adelaide Cottages, East Farleigh, where aisled halls, probably dating from the 14th or early 15th century, contain reused timbers with mortices for lap joints which are clearly of earlier date.

Nevertheless, in Kent the evidence for reuse in the Middle Ages is slight, and it seems likely that most of the surviving houses were built with new, unseasoned timber. In the 14th and 15th centuries there is considerable documentary evidence for tenants cutting high-quality timber in the Weald, and in the end the landlords were forced to give up their rights in favour of the tenants.[23] Moreover, few structures of the late 14th and 15th centuries show signs of reused material. However, a note of caution is advisable, for two such houses were sampled, unknowingly, for tree-ring dating. The Old Farmhouse, Hadlow, and Church House, Edenbridge, produced dates which were so far from what might reasonably be expected that reuse seems to be the only answer (Table 7). In the Edenbridge example further investigation suggested that a house of *c* 1400 had been largely rebuilt in the early 16th century. At The Old Farmhouse, where only two timbers had enough rings for dating, and the dates were 60 to 100 years earlier than expected, reuse is probable although there is no supporting evidence. This may also account for the exceptionally early date of one arcade post at Newbury Farmhouse, Tonge, although again this cannot be deduced from the structure itself.

# The uses of dendrochronology

Figure 149 shows that the majority of the fifty-three dated phases of building occurred after *c* 1370, and were fairly evenly spread over the next 180 years. It was in analysing buildings of this later period that tree-ring dating proved most effective. The firmly dated buildings, and the estimated felling dates for those in which no bark was present, were used to form a framework of dates against which other buildings could be assessed. This process helped to correct inaccurate dating tendencies. It indicated that some types of building or forms of construction had somewhat different date ranges from those previously proposed, and it confirmed the presumed development of others. Most importantly it provided a measure of objectivity and control which had previously been lacking in dating, and created greater confidence in dating the rest of the buildings investigated.

By the end of the project, significant mistakes in assigning dates to buildings which were subsequently tree-ring dated were no longer made, and it was sometimes possible to place them within a year or two of the estimated felling date. To a large extent this was no doubt due to increased experience of the region and its buildings, and there were indications that some of the same results might have been achieved without the aid of dendrochronology. But this does not detract from the importance of the exercise. Without the objectivity of tree-ring dating, our chronology would have remained open to debate. No doubt some conclusions will still be questioned, but this will have to be done from an informed viewpoint. It is this which makes tree-ring dating such a powerful tool for architectural historians.

It is difficult to be concise about the way the tree-ring dated buildings were used to date other structures. No formal diagram was ever devised, and attempts were made to take all aspects of each building into account.[24] Features such as location, overall size, general type of house, arrangement of accommodation and construction of frame and roof all played their part in the decision to assign houses to particular periods. But none of these can be used alone as abstract criteria. Neither can more detailed features such as the scantling of timbers, the type of mouldings or joints, the shape of openings and the form of framing, although they are likewise indicative of date spans of varying length. All these features are considered in more detail in *The House Within*. Because so many buildings have had their external walls rebuilt and their original openings renewed, it is not feasible to use tree-ring dated examples to demonstrate the extent to which shapes of openings and forms of framing can be precisely dated by these means. However, one structural feature – scarf joints – and two decorative ones – the caps and bases of crown posts and the mouldings of major members – are prolific enough in buildings dated by dendrochronology or documents to illus-trate the extent to which precise chronological dating of such features is and is not feasible.

## Scarf joints

Scarf joints have often been used to date timber structures, and tree-ring dated examples in Kent may be examined in order to see whether particular types have well-defined date ranges. Figure 150 illustrates those which occur in tree-ring dated buildings. They include all the basic types found in

*Figure 150 Dated scarf joints: a) Nurstead Court, Meopham, c 1309\*; b) Lower Newlands, Teynham, c 1380\*; c) Hill Crest and Kent Cottage, Staplehurst, c 1389\*; d) West Court, Shepherdswell with Coldred, c 1399\*; e) Country Fair, Edenbridge, c 1410\*; f) Parsonage Farmhouse, East Sutton, c 1436\*, and Harts Farmhouse, Molash, c 1466\*; g) Rocks, East Malling and Larkfield, 1507/8\*; h) Chart Hall Farmhouse, Chart Sutton, 1379/80\*, and Wenhams and Thistles, Capel, c 1431\*; i) Coppwilliam, Staplehurst, 1370/1\*, Clakkers Hall, Plaxtol, c 1452\*, Mead Manor, Sturry, c 1465\*, Luckhurst, East Sutton, c 1490\*, and Deanery Farm, Chartham, 1496/7\*; j) The Old Palace, Brenchley, 1485\*, The Old Rectory House, Northfleet, Gravesend, 1488/9\*, Court Lodge, Linton, c 1506\*, Place Farmhouse, Kenardington, 1512/13\*, and Spong Farm House, Elmsted, 1520\*; k) Lynsted Court, Lynsted, 1517\*.*

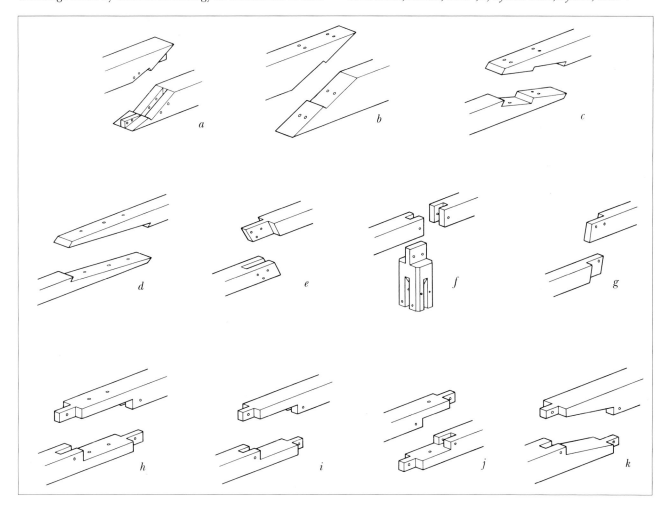

Kent but exclude a few variants which are not precisely dated. The latter are illustrated in *The House Within*.[25]

Splayed scarfs largely belong to the 14th century; among dated buildings tabled varieties, those in which the inclined surfaces are staggered, as in Figure 150 a–c, are more usually found towards the beginning of the 14th century, although they continue at least until 1400. Simple, untabled splays (d) are commoner in houses dated, or likely to date, from c 1400, but one undated example, at Hurst Farm, Chilham, almost certainly belongs in the early 14th century. From the late 14th century edge-halved and bridled joints became the commonest form (h–k). These might have edge pegs or face pegs, the former being by far the most frequently encountered. As the dated examples show, they continued in use throughout the 15th and the early part of the 16th centuries, the only development being a tendency for the length of the scarf to diminish. While this comes across quite clearly in dated examples, in other buildings scarfs of different length were often used within the same structure, and no absolute chronology is discernible. The splayed halving found at Lynsted Court in 1517* (k) is not very common and the type is not closely datable; other examples occur in houses which must date from the mid or even early 15th century.

The only houses with dated joints of simple bridled (e) form are found in Edenbridge in the early 15th century, but they are not confined to this period. Simple face or edge-halved scarfs without bridles (g) are rare, but also seem to have been used throughout the later Middle Ages, despite the fact that the only precisely dated example occurs in the early 16th century. Another undatable form is created by butting two timbers together to either side of the tenon of a supporting post (f); it is only by chance that the two dated examples fall in the mid 15th century.

The dated evidence is too incomplete to be very conclusive, but, such as it is, it suggests that although general trends can be identified, there was considerable overlap in the occurrence of different types of scarf joint, and that they can only be used as a dating feature if generous margins of error are allowed. In any given building this may be narrowed by considering other features as well, but on their own scarfs seldom provide evidence for dating within less than half a century and often far more.[26]

## Crown-post mouldings

The crown-post roof is the most common roof type found in medieval buildings in Kent, and some 370 such roofs were noted during the course of the project. Of these nearly 150 crown posts were measured and drawn.[27] Twenty-nine examples, dated by dendrochronology or documents, are illustrated in Figures 151 and 152. They span the years 1309 to 1532, and their number could be increased by including two absolutely plain open-truss posts dated 1512/13* and c 1548*.[28]

Examples in the first group, which date between c 1309 and 1331 (Figure 151 a–d), are mostly distinguished by the

*Figure 151 Dated crown posts of the 14th century: a) Nurstead Court, Meopham, c 1309*; b) Gallants Manor, East Farleigh, c 1322*; c) Salmestone Grange, Margate, chapel, 1326; d) Ightham Mote, Ightham, solar, c 1331*; e) Henikers, Sutton Valence, c 1364*; f) Old Moat Farmhouse, Chart Sutton, c 1377*; g) Chart Hall Farmhouse, Chart Sutton, 1379/80*; h) Lower Newlands, Teynham, c 1380*; i) Salmestone Grange, Margate, hall, before 1391; j) Hill Crest and Kent Cottage, Staplehurst, c 1389*.*

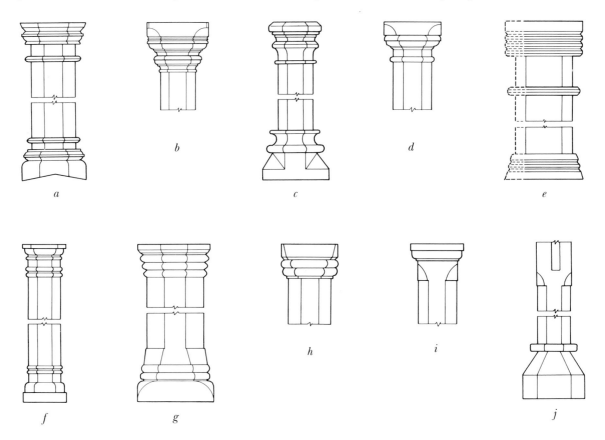

Figure 152 Dated crown posts of the **15th and 16th** centuries:
a) West Court, Shepherdswell with Coldred, c 1399*; b) Walnut Tree Cottage, East Sutton, c 1401*; c) Country Fair, Edenbridge, c 1410*; d) Vane Court, Biddenden, c 1419*; e) Wenhams and Thistles, Capel, c 1431*; f) Parsonage Farmhouse, East Sutton, hall, c 1436*; g) Spoute House, Plaxtol, c 1445*; h) Clakkers Hall, Plaxtol, c 1452*; i) Noah's Ark Farmhouse, East Sutton, c 1456*; j) Symnel Cottage, Aldington, c 1460*; k) **Harts Farmhouse, Molash,** c 1466*; l) The Blue House, East **Sutton,** c 1468*; m) The Old Palace, Brenchley, 1485*; n) Luckhurst, East Sutton, c 1490*; o) Jennings Farmhouse, Pluckley, c 1501*; p) Cobrahamsole Farmhouse, Sheldwich, wing, 1508*; q) Wat Tyler's Cottage, Brenchley, 1529/30*; r) Hever Brocas, Hever, hall, c 1532*.

use of quarter-round mouldings with a fillet or lip to the moulding. At Gallants Manor (b) the rolls are narrowly spaced, producing a complex outline. Since all these occur in high-status ranges, they have some pretensions towards artistic style which is noticeably lacking in the next group, from which they are easily distinguished. In part this may be a product of money and craftsmanship rather than a difference in date, but the simplicity of the late 14th-century crown post over the stone hall of Salmestone Grange (Figure 151i), built by St Augustine's Abbey sometime before 1391, suggests that there may have been a general move from complexity to simplicity towards the end of the century.

The crown posts in the second chronological group (Figure 151e–h) occur in much smaller, wholly timber-framed houses, and it is hardly surprising that they have none of the near elegance of their forebears. They are distinguished by an almost universal use of quarter-round mouldings and by tightly spaced rings with little or no splay between them, set more or less vertically one above the other. This group is, in fact, the most easily datable of all, particularly since the crown posts usually have heavy braces of square section, while other features, such as splayed scarf joints for which 14th-century dates are likely, are found in the same buildings. Nonetheless, while the dated examples are all in the late 14th century, it is perfectly possible that the forms continued into the early 15th century.

A third group, of more or less similar date, is very much simpler, with the capital often reduced to little more than a chamfer (Figure 151i–j). However, it is here that difficulties begin. Details not very different to those of the late 14th century occur in *c* 1419* at Vane Court, Biddenden (Figure 152d), and in 1529/30* at Wat Tyler's Cottage, Brenchley (Figure 152q). The latter would never be dated to the late 14th century, for every other feature places it firmly in the 16th. However, on the basis of the crown-post profile alone, precise dating would not be possible.

A curved splay between the top and the neck of most crown-post capitals became increasingly common from around 1400, and it is more and more difficult to distinguish examples by date. Rigold, writing over twenty years ago, noted the conservative nature of the decoration in Kentish timber-framed houses.[29] It has been argued in this book that some of his dating was over-cautious. But although it now seems likely that some features which he associated with the 16th century may be earlier, it is equally true that mouldings which first appeared in timber-framed buildings in the mid or even early 15th century continued until decorated crown posts disappeared. Cyma mouldings, for example, never very common for crown-post capitals, are usually dated late,[30] but they turn up in *c* 1456* at Noah's Ark Farmhouse, East Sutton (Figure 152i). In fact they were used long before, in the undated Manor House at Benenden which was probably built around 1400, and perhaps in 1393/4 in the wing of The Deanery, Chartham, which is discussed in more detail below. Few occur in later dated buildings, but they are found on the joists of Little Harts Heath, Staplehurst, in 1507* (Figure 155j) and on the beams at Court Lodge, Linton (Figures 155i, 156m), in *c* 1506*.

Bell-shaped crown-post bases are another feature which has usually been dated late, although the example at West Court, Shepherdswell with Coldred (Figure 152a), of 1399*, indicates that they could occur as early as 1400. Very much later dating has normally been applied when the base is raised

above a narrow pedestal. Among the dated crown posts is a group ranging from *c* 1466* to 1485* (Figure 152k–m), and the type persisted into the early 16th century, as indicated by Cobrahamsole Farmhouse (Figure 152p) of 1508*. But a narrow pedestal and bell-shaped base at Parsonage Farmhouse, East Sutton (Figure 152f), has been dated as early as *c* 1436*. This house not only has crown posts with raised bases but it has four-centred doorheads and evidence for close studding on both ground and first floors; all these details would suggest a date in the second half of the 15th century, although the presence of upwards and downwards braces to the crown posts of the closed trusses is more normally found in open halls of the earlier 15th century. External close studding for show has not previously been firmly identified in Kent before about 1460 except at Wye College, which was built by Cardinal Kempe, then Archbishop of York, shortly before 1448 when it opened its doors to the first students.[31] Its occurrence at Parsonage Farmhouse is therefore somewhat remarkable, but the tree-ring dating is difficult to dispute, since it includes main timbers from both the central and end trusses of the open hall. It is possible, given the concealed nature of much of the structure below roof level, that the four-centred doorheads and close studding are the result of later alterations, but the crown-post roof is almost certainly original, involving a considerable extension to the normal date range for bulbous bases on raised pedestals.

A peaked swelling in the centre of crown-post capitals is found in houses of *c* 1466* and 1508* (Figure 152k and p). A similar date range, spanning the mid 15th century to the early 16th century, is likely to apply to all other examples, with the possible exception of the cross wing at The Deanery, Chartham (Figure 153). This range has been dated to 1393/4, when Prior Chillenden of Christ Church Priory is known to have spent large sums on the buildings at Chartham.[32] The proportions of the wing are unusually tall for this date. The crown posts have caps with peaked swellings (albeit of slightly unusual form), bases which are tending towards the bulbous, and very thin and spindly braces; the tie

*Figure 153 The Deanery, Chartham, cross-wing details: a) Crown post and tie beam; b) Scarf joint in collar purlin; c) Scarf joint in wall plate.*

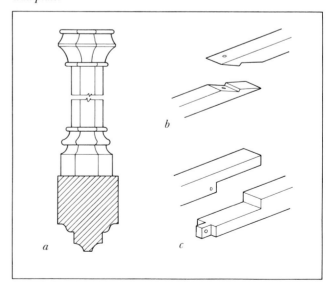

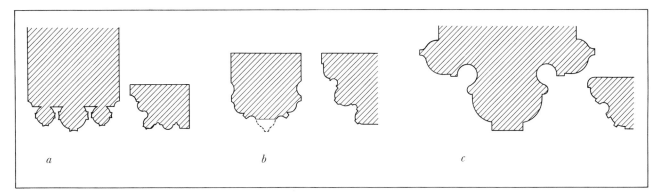

beams have cyma mouldings and the wall plate has an edge-halved and bridled scarf; in addition there is evidence that when this wing was built, the hall ceased to be heated by an open hearth. All these features, particularly when taken together, would fit more comfortably several decades later, in the mid 15th century.[33] Yet the collar purlin is scarfed with a splayed and tabled joint which would be entirely appropriate in the 1390s. If the range really was built in Chillenden's time, then most of the details are extremely precocious, perhaps because they were done by craftsmen from the ecclesiastical workshops. If the range is later – which is possible since the document which indicates that money was spent in Chillenden's time does not mention specific works – then the scarf in the collar purlin is exceptionally late for its type. This example neatly illustrates the problems which are frequently encountered when trying to date typologically, and when trying to marry buildings with documents. Unfortunately, in this case no tree-ring dating was done to settle the issue.

Many crown posts in small houses have block-like capitals perhaps accompanied by simple rolls and chamfered bases. There is little to distinguish the cap of Symnel Cottage, Aldington (c 1460*, Figure 152j), or the bases of Spoute House (1445*, Figure 152g) and Clakkers Hall (c 1452*, Figure 152h) in Plaxtol from the cap and base of Jennings Farmhouse, Pluckley, of c 1501* (Figure 152o). The reason is almost certainly because the smaller the house and the less money spent, the simpler the forms and the less datable they become.

*Figure 154 Dated mouldings in early buildings: a) Nurstead Court, Meopham, c 1309*. Tie beam and cornice; b) Salmestone Grange, Margate, chapel, 1326. Tie beam and cornice; c) Ightham Mote, Ightham, hall, c 1337*. Stone arch and timber cornice.*

## Mouldings on main timbers

Mouldings on main timbers are equally difficult to arrange typologically. Again, high-quality early 14th-century examples, whether in stone or timber (Figure 154), are instantly recognisable by their close approximation to contemporary detailing in major monuments of ecclesiastical origin.[34] The buildings dated by dendrochronology to the late 14th century and later were humbler structures altogether. The tie beams illustrated in Figure 155 show how very simple most of the mouldings were. In the late 14th century the quarter-round mouldings, noted on crown

*Figure 155 Dated mouldings on tie beams and ceiling beams. Tie beams: a) Coppwilliam, Staplehurst, 1370/1*; b) Old Moat Farmhouse, Chart Sutton, c 1377*; c) Vane Court, Biddenden, c 1419*; d) Wenhams and Thistles, Capel, c 1431*; e) Clakkers Hall, Plaxtol, c 1452*; f) Harts Farmhouse, Molash, c 1466*; g) The Old Palace, Brenchley, 1485*; h) Luckhurst, East Sutton, c 1490*. Ceiling beams: i) Court Lodge, Linton, c 1506*; j) Little Harts Heath, Staplehurst, 1507*; k) Tudor Cottage, Lynsted, c 1528*.*

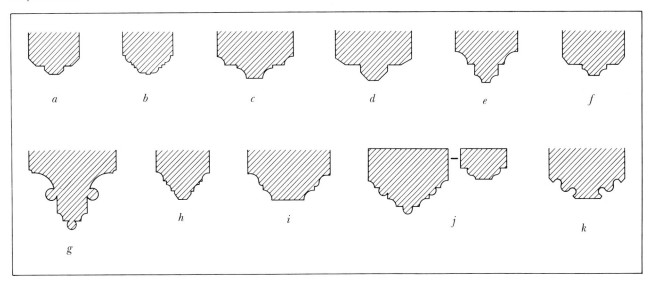

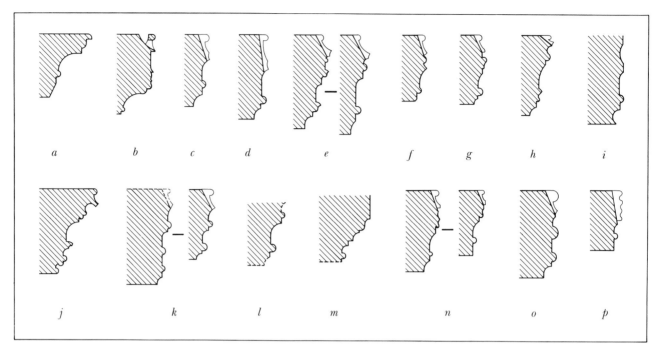

posts, might be found in other parts of the building, as at Old Moat Farmhouse, Chart Sutton (Figure 155b), in c 1377*. But this instance apart, it is difficult to classify mouldings by date since only in houses of high quality did they have any real character.

Decorative details at The Old Palace, Brenchley (Figures 155g, 156j), include rolls to the tie beams, double rolls to the dais beam, and engaged colonettes and capitals on the main posts of the open truss (Figure 81b). All these features occur on a group of high-quality open halls which used to be dated after 1510.[35] Tree-ring dating at The Old Palace establishes that such features were occurring already in 1485*, a date which is very much in line with the 1464–79 documented date range for Great Dixter which lies just over the Sussex border in Northiam.[36] However, with one or two exceptions of this kind, the dated dais beam profiles illustrated in Figure 156 indicate that any attempt at close dating through such features is likely to prove deceptive; although a large number of such beams were measured and drawn, very little chronological sense could be made of them.

Around 1500 a change does appear to have taken place which can, in a very general way, contribute to dating. It was from this time that other timbers, such as those used for doorways, windows, joists and fascia boards, started to be

Figure 156 (above) Dated dais and lower-end beam mouldings: a) Walnut Tree Cottage, East Sutton, c 1401*; b) Wenhams and Thistles, Capel, c 1431*; c) Spoute House, Plaxtol, c 1445*; d) Clakkers Hall, Plaxtol, c 1452*; e) Noah's Ark Farmhouse, East Sutton, c 1456*; f) Symnel Cottage, Aldington, c 1460*; g) Harts Farmhouse, Molash, c 1466*; h) The Blue House, East Sutton, c 1468*; i) Farringtons, Edenbridge Bookshop (75, 77, 79 High Street), Edenbridge, 1476/7*; j) The Old Palace, Brenchley, 1485*; k) Luckhurst, East Sutton, c 1490*; l) Jennings Farmhouse, Pluckley, c 1501*; m) Court Lodge, Linton, c 1506*; n) Cobrahamsole Farmhouse, Sheldwich, 1508*; o) Manor Cottage, Speldhurst, 1508/9*; p) Spong Farm House, Elmsted, 1520*.

Figure 157 (below) Miscellaneous dated mouldings: a) Luckhurst, East Sutton, c 1490*, door jamb of front doorway; b) Little Harts Heath, Staplehurst, 1507*, window sill in chamber over hall; c) Place Farmhouse, Kenardington, 1512/13*, door jamb of former service room doorway; d) Tudor Cottage, Lynsted, c 1514*, window sill in hall range; e) Lynsted Court, Lynsted, 1517*, door jamb and jetty fascia board in cross wing; f) Spong Farm House, Elmsted, 1520*, window sill in hall; g) Tudor Cottage, Lynsted, c 1528*, window sill in parlour; h) Wat Tyler's Cottage, Brenchley, 1529/30*, jetty fascia board.

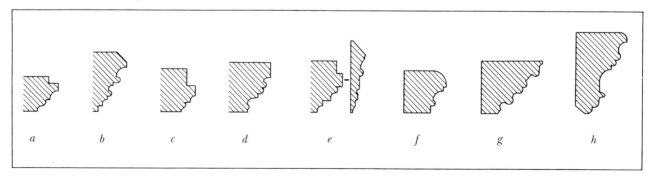

given more decoration than a simple chamfer (Figure 157). Since the appearance of these mouldings coincides with the demise of the medieval house, and the beginning of developments which were to flourish through the 16th century, the extent to which they can be used for dating cannot be fully explored in this book. But it seems likely that they ranged over as wide a period as their predecessors, and apart from being late, they introduce no greater precision.

From the 1490s cyma mouldings became common, and they continued to be used, often with simple hollow chamfers, for a long time. At about the same time, double rolls became popular. However, these cannot be used very precisely for, as the moulded window sills from the two phases of Tudor Cottage, Lynsted (Figure 157d and g), show, almost identical profiles could occur in c 1514* and c 1528*. The latter is slightly more elaborate, but then it is used on the windows of a new parlour and may simply reflect the grander nature of the structure it adorns.

## *Conclusions*

Discussed in isolation it seems that some details are of little value as dating evidence, and others can only be used in a general way for certain periods. However, by taking all the features of a building together, it frequently appears possible to date buildings with some degree of precision. Although in Kent no formal diagram of dated features was ever drawn up, the buildings were assessed and reassessed on more than one occasion, taking into account location in the county, presumed status, type, size, construction and decoration. In this way, dates have been increasingly refined and a high proportion of them are likely to be reasonably accurate.

Buildings which were not tree-ring dated were dated by comparing all their features with dated ones. Each building was assigned a date range which varied from twenty years, when there appeared good evidence for close dating, to a hundred years or even more, where no distinctive features could be identified. The majority of buildings were judged to be datable to within a range of forty years. Although this varies little from previous dating practices, the result of comparison with tree-ring dated buildings meant that the date ranges for particular houses sometimes changed. In some cases this was only by a decade or so, but in others the revision amounted to half a century or more. Looked at from one point of view, the period covered, from the mid or late 13th century to the second quarter of the 16th, remains the same as at the outset. Looked at from another, building activity now appears to be more concentrated at particular times.

# Appendix 2
# Numbers and types of open-hall houses found in
# each of the sixty fully surveyed parishes

In some cases medieval houses were located which were not recorded. Unless their type was readily identifiable from the exterior they have been included in the 'uncertain' category.

| | Houses pre-dating c 1370 | Late medieval timber-framed houses, c 1370 – c 1545 | | | | | Total |
|---|---|---|---|---|---|---|---|
| | | Cross wings | Wealdens | End jetties | Unjettied | Uncertain | |
| Aldington | 1 | 2 | 1 | 2 | | 2 | 8 |
| Alkham | | 1 | | | | 3 | 4 |
| Appledore | | 1 | | 1 | | | 2 |
| Ash next Sandwich | | 2 | 4 | | | | 6 |
| Benenden | | 2 | 8 | 3 | | 3 | 16 |
| Borden | | 4 | 7 | 3 | | 2 | 16 |
| Brasted | | 1 | 1 | 2 | | 4 | 8 |
| Brenchley | 1 | | 1 | 1 | | 3 | 6 |
| Brenzett | | | | | | | 0 |
| Brookland | | | | | | | 0 |
| Charing | 1 | 3 | 15 | 3 | 1 | 1 | 24 |
| Chartham | 1 | 3 | 3 | 2 | 1 | 1 | 11 |
| Chart Sutton | | 4 | 3 | 1 | | 2 | 10 |
| Chiddingstone | | | 3 | 3 | 3 | 8 | 17 |
| Chilham | 1 | 3 | 5 | 2 | | 1 | 12 |
| Chislet | | 4 | 1 | | | 1 | 6 |
| Cliffe-at-Hoo | 1 | | | 1 | | | 2 |
| Coxheath | | | 1 | | | | 1 |
| Cranbrook | | | 6 | 1 | | 1 | 8 |
| Detling | | 1 | 3 | 1 | | 2 | 7 |
| Eastchurch | | | | | | 1 | 1 |
| East Farleigh | 2 | | | 2 | 1 | | 5 |
| Eastling | 2 | 1 | 2 | 1 | | 3 | 9 |
| East Malling and Larkfield | | 4 | 2 | 2 | | 1 | 9 |
| East Peckham | 1 | 3 | 1 | 4 | | 9 | 18 |
| Eastry | 1 | 2 | | | | | 3 |
| East Sutton | | 1 | 6 | 2 | | | 9 |
| Elham | 1 | 2 | 4 | | | 1 | 8 |
| Eynsford | | | 1 | | 1 | | 2 |
| Fawkham | 1 | | | | | | 1 |
| Halling | | 1 | 2 | | | 2 | 5 |

| | Houses pre-dating *c* 1370 | Late medieval timber-framed houses, *c* 1370 – *c* 1545 | | | | | Total |
|---|---|---|---|---|---|---|---|
| | | Cross wings | Wealdens | End jetties | Unjettied | Uncertain | |
| Hawkinge | | | | 1 | | | 1 |
| Leysdown | | | | | | | 0 |
| Linton | | | | 2 | | | 2 |
| Loose | | 3 | | | | 3 | 6 |
| Luddenham | | | | | | 1 | 1 |
| Lydd | | 1 | 2 | 1 | | 4 | 8 |
| Meopham | 1 | 1 | | 3 | | 2 | 7 |
| Minster in Thanet | 1 | | 1 | | | 1 | 3 |
| Newchurch | | | | | | | 0 |
| Newington next Sittingbourne | | 1 | | | | 1 | 2 |
| Oare | | | | | | | 0 |
| Petham | 1 | 1 | 1 | 2 | | | 5 |
| Plaxtol | 1 | 4 | 2 | 2 | 1 | 3 | 13 |
| Pluckley | | 2 | 2 | 6 | 1 | 3 | 14 |
| Sellindge | | 1 | 3 | 1 | | 1 | 6 |
| Sheldwich | 1 | 2 | | 2 | | 2 | 7 |
| Shepherdswell with Coldred | | | 1 | | | | 1 |
| Smarden | 1 | 3 | 4 | 8 | | 5 | 21 |
| Southfleet | 1 | 3 | 4 | 1 | | | 9 |
| Speldhurst | | | | 3 | | 7 | 10 |
| Staple | | | | 1 | 1 | 1 | 3 |
| Staplehurst | | 6 | 1 | 1 | | 3 | 11 |
| Sundridge | | | 2 | | 1 | 2 | 5 |
| Thurnham | | 1 | 1 | 1 | | | 3 |
| Upper Hardres | | | | 4 | | | 4 |
| Waltham | | 1 | | 1 | | 1 | 3 |
| Westbere | | 1 | 1 | | 1 | | 3 |
| Woodchurch | | | 7 | 2 | 1 | | 10 |
| Wrotham | 2 | | | | | 2[a] | 4 |

[a] includes Yaldham Manor, the only post *c* 1370 stone building in the sixty surveyed parishes.

# Appendix 3
## List of medieval houses recorded during the
## course of the project and used in this book

The following is a list of those houses which were recorded in the course of the RCHME project and which are used in the three books arising from it. Except for those in italics, they are included in *A Gazetteer of Medieval Houses in Kent,* where further details may be obtained. *A Gazetteer of Medieval Houses in Kent* and the NMR files (NBR Index) also give details of those houses published elsewhere. Houses previously published in RCHME (1963) and Mercer (1975) are not included here.

| Parish | House name | NMR file number |
|---|---|---|
| Acrise | Hoad Farm | 40497 |
| Aldington | Church Farmhouse | 40138 |
| | Copperhurst | 40143 |
| | Court Lodge Farmhouse | 40148 |
| | Grove Cottage | 40144 |
| | Parsonage Farmhouse | 40150 |
| | Pattison's Farm | 40149 |
| | Poulton Manor Farmhouse | 40141 |
| | Symnel Cottage | 40142 |
| Alkham | Halton Court | 40184 |
| | Hogbrook | 40171 |
| Appledore | Hallhouse Farmhouse | 40357 |
| | Hornes Place | 39753 |
| Ashford | *Willesborough Labour Club* | *40047* |
| | *Worgers, High Street* | *40329* |
| Ash next Sandwich | The Chequer Inn | 40880 |
| | Lower Weddington Manor | 40476 |
| | The Ship Inn | 40112 |
| | 30, 32 The Street | 40172 |
| | Uphousden Farm | 40083 |
| | Wingham Barton Manor | 40111 |
| Aylesham | Ratling Court | 40019 |
| Benenden | Campion House | 40446 |
| | Coggers | 40449 |
| | Dingleden | 40447 |
| | Diprose Farmhouse | 40451 |
| | Little Standen | 40453 |
| | Manor House | 40173 |
| | The Moat | 40450 |
| | Old Eaton Farmhouse | 40448 |
| | Old Standen | 40452 |
| | The Paper Mill | 40337 |
| | Pympne Manor Farm | 40477 |
| | Watermill House | 40505 |
| Bethersden | Pimphurst Farmhouse | 40123 |
| Biddenden | Vane Court | 40166 |
| Bobbing | Church Farm | 40002 |
| Borden | Bannister Hall | 40282 |
| | Borden Hall | 40217 |
| | 245, 247 Borden Lane | 40266 |
| | Chestnut Street Farmhouse | 40269 |
| | Filmer House | 40273 |
| | Heart's Delight House | 40272 |
| | Hoad House | 40265 |
| | The Homestead | 40275 |
| | *The Plestor* | *40478* |
| | Posiers | 40268 |
| | Sharp's House | 40280 |
| | *Street Farm House* | *40500* |
| | Sutton Baron Hall | 40267 |
| | Thatch Cottage | 40270 |
| | Wren's Farmhouse | 40276 |
| | Yew Tree Cottage | 40274 |
| Boughton Aluph | Boughton Court | 40504 |
| Boughton Malherbe | Hazel Hill Cottage | 40182 |
| Brasted | 2, 3, 4, 5 Alms Row Cottages | 40007 |
| | Corner Cottage | 40008 |
| | 17 High Street | 40479 |
| | *Tilings Antiques, High Street* | *40481* |
| Brenchley | Cherry Trees | 40385 |
| | Old Cryals | 40433 |
| | The Old Palace | 40406 |
| | Studmore | 40383 |
| | Town Farm Cottage and Town Farmhouse | 40386 |
| | Wat Tyler's Cottage | 40387 |
| Brenzett | Godhall | 40340 |
| Brookland | *The Woolpack Inn* | *40343* |

| | | | | | |
|---|---|---|---|---|---|
| Capel | Wenhams and Thistles | 40190 | | Tudor Lodge Gift Shop | |
| Charing | Armada House, 9 High Street | 40087 | | and Peacock Antiques | 8845 |
| | Barnfield | 40084 | | Vergers Lodge and Thompsons House | 8864 |
| | Brockton Manor | 40085 | Chislet | Highstead Farmhouse | 40419 |
| | Burleigh Manor | 31667 | | Port Farmhouse | 40438 |
| | Elizabethan Court, High Street | 40089 | | Tudor House | 40263 |
| | Hope Haven and Ridgemount, | | | The Vision House | 40417 |
| | 26, 28 High Street | 40088 | Cliffe-at-Hoo | Allens Hill Farmhouse | 40457 |
| | Hunger Hatch Cottage | 40091 | | The Rectory House | 40434 |
| | Newlands Manor | 40515 | | | |
| | *Old Vicarage* | *40099* | | | |
| | *Payne Street Farmhouse* | *40485* | Coxheath | Westerhill | 40321 |
| | Peirce House, 33 High Street | 40503 | Cranbrook | Ashleigh, Hundred House | |
| | Pett Place | 40094 | | and Corner House | 40117 |
| | Sand Pett | 40093 | | The Broadcloth and The Old Studio | 40116 |
| | Swan Street Farm | 40094 | | *Chimney Sweeps Cottage,* | |
| | Vicarage Cottage | 40098 | | *Prunus Cottage* | *31671* |
| | Wady and Brett, 47 High Street | 40090 | | Collier's Green Farmhouse | 40107 |
| | Wellies, 19 High Street | 40155 | | The Freight | 40104 |
| Chartham | The Artichoke Inn | 40283 | | Freizley | 40176 |
| | The Bedford House | 40341 | | Old Wilsley | 40105 |
| | Boxtree Cottage | 40278 | | Whistlers | 40108 |
| | The Deanery | 40146 | Crundale | Crundale House | 8868 |
| | *Deanery Farm* | *40135* | | *Hunt Street Farmhouse* | *40192* |
| | The George Inn | 40285 | | *Little Winchcombe Farmhouse* | *40194* |
| | *The Old King's Head and* | | | | |
| | *King's Head Cottage* | *78469* | Detling | Harpole Farm | 8558 |
| | Underdown Cottages | 40284 | | The Homestead, 36 The Street | 8570 |
| Chart Sutton | Ashurst Lodge Farmhouse | 83709 | | Park Valley House | 8560 |
| | Chart Hall Farmhouse | 40445 | | Polle Hill Farmhouse | 8566 |
| | Dunbury Farmhouse | 40020 | | Pollyfields Farmhouse | 8568 |
| | Elderden Farmhouse | 40439 | | Well Cottage | 8579 |
| | Heronden | 40016 | | | |
| | Little Ashurst | 40442 | Eastchurch | Warden Manor | 40324 |
| | Old Moat Farmhouse | 40441 | East Farleigh | 6 Adelaide Cottages | 40058 |
| | White House Farmhouse | 40432 | | Gallants Manor | 40009 |
| Chiddingstone | The Castle Inn | 40175 | | Gate House Farm House | 40334 |
| | Hoath House | 39648 | | Malt House Cottages | 40333 |
| | Lockskinners | 40377 | | Thatchers | 40332 |
| | Oakenden | 40011 | | | |
| | Old Gilwyns and Gilwyns | 40012 | Eastling | Carpenters Arms Inn | 40394 |
| | Old Manor House and Post Office | 40372 | | Divan Court | 40411 |
| | Sharp's Place | 40366 | | Eastling Manor | 40044 |
| | Skipreed | 40376 | | North Court Farmhouse | 40416 |
| | Walnut Tree Cross Farmhouse | 40487 | | North Eastling Farmhouse | 40391 |
| | Withers | 39651 | | Plantation House, The Street | 40039 |
| | Woodgates | 40365 | | 2, 3, 4 The Street | 40392 |
| Chilham | Bagham Farmhouse | 8792 | | Tong Cottage | 40040 |
| | Burgoyne's | 8815 | | Tong House | 40410 |
| | Clifton Cottage | 8806 | East Malling and | The Barracks | 40160 |
| | Cumberland House | 8807 | Larkfield | 4, 6 Church Walk | 40154 |
| | Hurst Farm | 8832 | | Derbies | 40158 |
| | Monckton Cottage and Heron Manor | 8829 | | Ivy House Farmhouse | 39696 |
| | Monckton Manor | 8830 | | 1, 3, 5 Mill Street | 40157 |
| | Orions Cottage | 8858 | | 148, 150, 152 Mill Street | 40165 |
| | Phyllis Farmhouse | 8842 | | Rocks, 132 Rocks Road | 40461 |
| | Tavern Cottage | 8798 | | | |

| East Peckham | Bells Farmhouse | 83738 |
| | Beltring Green Farmhouse | 40298 |
| | Brookers Cottage | 40300 |
| | Bullen Cottage | 40306 |
| | Bullen Farmhouse | 40290 |
| | Bush Farm Cottage | 40304 |
| | Court Lodge Farmhouse | 40302 |
| | Forge Gate Farmhouse | 40305 |
| | Goose Green Cottages | 40299 |
| | Goose Green Farmhouse | 40388 |
| | Hale Street Farmhouse | 40390 |
| | Kent House Farmhouse | 40291 |
| | Little Mill | 40309 |
| | Little Moat Cottage | 40041 |
| | The Long Arm | 40288 |
| | The Old Post Office | 40301 |
| | 79 Old Road | 40293 |
| | Old Well House | 40311 |
| | Pinkham Cottages | 39702 |
| | Pond Farm | 40289 |
| | 23 Smithers Lane | 40303 |
| | Strettit Farm | 40310 |
| Eastry | Eastry Court | 40106 |
| | Old Selson House | 40179 |
| East Sutton | Barling Farmhouse | 40167 |
| | The Blue House | 40004 |
| | Divers Farmhouse | 40113 |
| | Hecton Farmhouse | 40163 |
| | Luckhurst | 40109 |
| | Noah's Ark Farmhouse | 40017 |
| | Parsonage Farmhouse | 40003 |
| | Street Farmhouse | 40168 |
| | Walnut Tree Cottage | 40015 |
| Edenbridge | Church House, 72 High Street | 39657 |
| | Farringtons, Edenbridge Bookshop, 75, 77, 79 High Street | 40357 |
| | Country Fair and Light Horse, 94, 96 High Street | 39662 |
| | Old Eden Inn, High Street | 39667 |
| | Old Stanfords End | 40031 |
| | Tanyard House, 92 High Street | 39669 |
| Egerton | The Bedewell | 40177 |
| | Hollis Farmhouse | 40198 |
| Elham | Boyke Manor | 40467 |
| | *Church Cottage* | *40435* |
| | Elham Manor | 40437 |
| | Exted Farm | 40436 |
| | King Post | 40428 |
| | Parsonage Farmhouse | 39671 |
| | The Rose and Crown Hotel | 40454 |
| | Stonebridge Farm | 40455 |
| Elmsted | Dean Farm | 40072 |
| | Spong Farm House | 40470 |
| Eynsford | Moat Farmhouse | 40050 |
| Fawkham | Court Lodge | 40431 |

| Frittenden | Balcombe Farmhouse | 40124 |
| Gillingham | Bloors Place | 40264 |
| | *94, 96 High Street* | *39676* |
| | *112, 114 High Street* | *40202* |
| Goodnestone | Griffins Head Inn | 40180 |
| Goudhurst | Lollards | 40443 |
| | The Old Eight Bells | 40463 |
| | Riseden Hall | 40051 |
| | Star and Eagle Inn | 40491 |
| Gravesend | The Old Rectory House, Northfleet | 40018 |
| Great Chart | Court Lodge | 31685 |
| | Godinton Park | 40164 |
| | Old Chilmington and Twysden | 40005 |
| Hadlow | Barnes Place | 40281 |
| | The Old Farmhouse | 40189 |
| Halling | *Clement's Farmhouse* | *83025* |
| | Court Farm | 40395 |
| | 94, 96 High Street | 40399 |
| | 122, 124 High Street | 40393 |
| | Prings | 40400 |
| Hartlip | *Ivy Cottage* | *40151* |
| Hastingleigh | Coombe Manor | 40188 |
| Hawkinge | Dane Farm | 40186 |
| Headcorn | Wick Farmhouse | 40210 |
| Hever | Hever Brocas | 40070 |
| Horsmonden | Rectory Park | 40006 |
| Ightham | Ightham Mote | 53012 |
| Kenardington | Place Farmhouse | 40153 |
| Langley | Shieling Hall | 40162 |
| Leeds | Battel Hall | 40490 |
| Leigh | *Ramhurst Manor House* | *40216* |
| Linton | Court Lodge | 40326 |
| Little Chart | *Rooting Manor* | *40218* |
| Loose | Brook House | 40323 |
| | Church House | 39733 |
| | Florence Cottage | 40338 |
| | Old Mill House | 40335 |
| | Peartree Cottages | 40325 |
| | *Pimp's Court* | *40336* |
| | *Tylers* | *40342* |
| Lower Hardres | *Young's Farmhouse* | *40384* |

| | | | | | |
|---|---|---|---|---|---|
| Luddesdown | Luddesdown Court | 40498 | | Little Damas | 40075 |
| | | | | Nut Tree Hall | 40057 |
| Lydd | 16 High Street, Elderwoods | 40191 | | Old Graingers | 40077 |
| | 5 New Street | 40154 | | Old Soar | 40237 |
| | 13, 15, 17 New Street | 40129 | | Rats Castle | 40076 |
| | 4, 5 Park Street | 40220 | | Spoute House | 40061 |
| | *Poplar House* | *40221* | | Tree House | 40074 |
| | Rype Cottage | 40222 | Pluckley | Bakers Mead | 40136 |
| Lynsted | Lynsted Court | 40224 | | Chambers Green Farm | 40134 |
| | Tudor Cottage | 55035 | | Cooper Farmhouse | 40121 |
| | | | | Dowle Street Cottages | 40120 |
| Margate | Salmestone Grange | 40178 | | Gore Court | 40119 |
| | | | | Jennings Farmhouse | 40118 |
| Meopham | Barncote Cottage | 40297 | | Lambden Cottage | 40122 |
| | Crickfield Farmhouse | 40295 | | *Ragstone* | *40147* |
| | Dene Manor | 40319 | | Rose Farmhouse | 40128 |
| | Forge Cottage | 40219 | | Stanford Bridge House | 40130 |
| | Nurstead Court | 40021 | | | |
| | Old Forge Cottage | 40294 | Rodmersham | Bakers Cottages | 40152 |
| | Owls Castle | 40318 | | | |
| | Somers | 40296 | Sellindge | 4, 5, 6, 7 Belle Vue | 40133 |
| | | | | 1, 2 Lees Cottages | 40140 |
| Mereworth | Laurel Cottage | 40183 | | Southenay Cottage | 40242 |
| | | | | Stone Hill and Old Forge Cottages | 40139 |
| Mersham | Mersham Manor | 40010 | | Talbot House | 40132 |
| Milstead and Kingsdown | Hoggeshaws | 40131 | Selling | Well House | 40320 |
| | | | Sevenoaks | *21-25 London Road* | *83105* |
| Minster in Thanet | *Eden Hall* | *40407* | | | |
| | Minster Abbey | 40474 | Sevington | *Bridge Cottage* | *40308* |
| | Wayborough Manor | 40408 | | | |
| | | | Sheldwich | Akhurst Cottage | 40381 |
| Molash | Harts Farmhouse | 8943 | | Cobrahamsole Farmhouse | 40101 |
| | | | | Copton Manor | 40100 |
| Nettlestead | Nettlestead Place | 40494 | | Halke Cottages | 40277 |
| | | | | Oast Cottage | 40389 |
| Newington next Hythe | *Old Kent Cottage* | *31811* | | Strawberry Fields | 40379 |
| | | | | The White House | 40380 |
| | | | | Yew Tree Cottage | 40382 |
| Newington next Sittingbourne | Church Farmhouse | 40127 | | | |
| | *Manor House* | *40049* | Shepherdswell with Coldred | West Court | 40185 |
| Newnham | Calico House | 40210 | | | |
| | | | Shoreham | *1-5 Chapel Alley Cottages* | *39715* |
| Otham | Belks | 40096 | | Reed Beds | 40243 |
| | The Rectory | 40084 | | | |
| | Stoneacre | 61511 | Sittingbourne | Chilton Manor | 40043 |
| | | | | Westfield | 40045 |
| Petham | China Court | 40069 | | | |
| | Cotterell Court | 40066 | Smarden | Ash Farmhouse | 40464 |
| | Dormer Cottage | 40060 | | Biddenden Green Cottage | 40465 |
| | *The Old Farmhouse* | *40488* | | Biddenden Green Farmhouse | 40492 |
| | Old Hall | 39706 | | The Brothers House | 40471 |
| | Yew Tree Farmhouse | 40068 | | Chessenden | 40250 |
| | | | | The Cloth Hall | 40466 |
| Plaxtol | Ashenden | 40103 | | The Dragon House | 40472 |
| | Bartons Farmhouse | 40056 | | Dreenagh House and Cottage | 40486 |
| | Clakkers Hall | 31818 | | The Fleete House | 40459 |
| | Claygate House | 40103 | | Hadley House | 40489 |
| | Crouchers Cottage | 40235 | | Little Ash | 40461 |
| | Ducks Farm | 40236 | | Mainey Wood | 40462 |

|  |  |  |  |  |  |
|---|---|---|---|---|---|
|  | Parsonage House | 40468 | Tenterden | *The Man's Shop, 18, 20 High Street* | *40252* |
|  | The Pent House | 40473 |  |  |  |
|  | The Thatched House | 83720 | Teynham | *Banks Farmhouse and Cottage* | *40253* |
|  | Tolhurst Farmhouse | 33625 |  | Lower Newlands | 40014 |
|  | Vesperhawk House | 40480 |  |  |  |
|  | West Hoy Farmhouse | 40458 | Thurnham | Howe Court | 8675 |
|  |  |  |  | Nether Milgate | 8669 |
| Smeeth | Evegate Manor | 40156 |  | Roundwell | 8680 |
|  |  |  |  | Stocks House, 70 Ware Street | 8700 |
| Southfleet | The Black Lion Public House | 40402 |  |  |  |
|  | Chapter Farmhouse | 40398 | Tonge | Newbury Farmhouse | 40238 |
|  | Church Cottages | 40403 |  |  |  |
|  | Church House | 40397 | Upper Hardres | Cottage Farmhouse | 39683 |
|  | Court Lodge Farmhouse | 40396 |  | Little Bursted Farmhouse | 40063 |
|  | Old Rectory (or Southfleet Rectory, |  |  | May Tree Farmhouse | 40073 |
|  | known now as Friary Court |  |  | Walnut Tree Farmhouse | 40062 |
|  | and Old Friary) | 40469 |  |  |  |
|  | The Limes | 40405 | Waltham | The Cottage, Anvil Green | 40067 |
|  | The Wheatsheaf Public House | 40404 |  | Dennes House | 40065 |
|  |  |  |  | Handville Green | 40071 |
| Speldhurst | The George and Dragon Public House | 40356 |  |  |  |
|  | Holly Cottage | 40345 | Westbere | Ashby Cottage | 40424 |
|  | Linkhorns Farmhouse | 40374 |  | Ye Olde Yew Tree Inn | 40418 |
|  | Little Laverall | 40350 |  | Yew Tree Cottage and White Cottage | 53066 |
|  | Manor Cottage | 40355 |  |  |  |
|  | The Old Farmhouse | 40360 | Westerham | *Apple Tree and Grape Vine Cottages* | *39728* |
|  | Old Place | 40364 |  | The Old Vicarage | 40501 |
|  | Searles | 40353 |  | Squerryes Lodge | 40499 |
|  | Stone Cross | 40352 |  |  |  |
|  | Stone Cross Farmhouse | 40351 | West Kingsdown | Crowhurst Farm Cottages | 40257 |
|  |  |  |  |  |  |
| Staple | The Black Pig Inn | 40079 | West Peckham | Dukes Place | 39703 |
|  | Gander Court Farmhouse | 83748 |  |  |  |
|  | *Summerfield Farmhouse* | *40078* | Westwell | Lacton Manor | 40261 |
|  |  |  |  |  |  |
| Staplehurst | Brigadoon | 40426 | Woodchurch | Great Engeham Manor | 40023 |
|  | Clapper Farmhouse | 40414 |  | Henden Place | 40022 |
|  | Coppwilliam | 40412 |  | New Diamond | 40025 |
|  | Cottons Farmhouse | 40430 |  | Oakmead | 40026 |
|  | Exhurst | 40429 |  | Place Farmhouse | 40027 |
|  | Hill Crest and Kent Cottage | 40421 |  | Redbrook Cottage | 40028 |
|  | King's Head Hotel | 40422 |  | Robhurst | 40024 |
|  | Lindridge | 40427 |  | Shirley Farmhouse | 40029 |
|  | Little Harts Heath | 40444 |  | Townland | 40030 |
|  | Little Pagehurst | 40415 |  |  |  |
|  | Old Newstead | 40420 | Woodnesborough | Summerfield Cottage | 40082 |
|  | *Tanyard and George Feltham,* |  |  |  |  |
|  | *Butchers* | *40413* | Wouldham | *Starkey Castle* | *39731* |
|  |  |  |  |  |  |
| Stelling Minnis | *High Chimney Farmhouse* | *39716* | Wrotham | The Old Farmhouse | 40258 |
|  |  |  |  | The Old Vicarage | 40259 |
| Sturry | Mead Manor | 40169 |  | Workhouse Cottages | 40260 |
|  |  |  |  | Yaldham Manor | 40170 |
| Sundridge | Dryhill Farmhouse | 40032 |  |  |  |
|  | Great Norman Street Farmhouse | 40034 | Yalding | Burnt Oak | 40046 |
|  | The Old Hall | 40035 |  | Crowplain Farmhouse | 40110 |
|  | Yorkshill Farmhouse | 40033 |  | Nightingale Farmhouse | 76924 |
|  |  |  |  | Rose Cottages | 40114 |
| Sutton Valence | Bardingley Farmhouse | 40001 |  | Rugmer Hill Farmhouse | 40115 |
|  | *Farthing Green Farmhouse* | *40036* |  |  |  |
|  | Henikers | 40038 |  |  |  |

# Notes

## Introduction

1 Turner and Parker 1851, 1853; Faulkner 1958; Wood 1950, 1965, 1974. For more recent work see Blair forthcoming; Howard 1987; and Thompson, M W 1991.

2 Barley 1961; Mercer 1975; Smith, J T 1970a.

3 Smith, J T 1992; Currie, 1992: this substantial article, published in 1993, appeared too late to be used in writing this book; however, references to it have been added to the notes as appropriate. Harding 1993 is another article which was not seen until after this book was finished.

4 Hewett 1969, 1980, 1985; Smith, J T 1955, 1958.

5 Dyer 1989; Mertes 1988.

6 Hallam 1988; Miller 1991b; Thirsk 1967.

7 This is, for example, noticeable in the study of late medieval Essex by Poos (1991). Given the general tenor of this book, it seems likely that statistical information on buildings would have been eagerly used had it been available. The one historian who has used building evidence constructively is Dyer (1986, 1989).

8 For England generally see, for example, Carpenter 1992, chapter 4, and Dyer 1989, 22–3. For Kent, see Du Boulay 1966, 162–3, and Harvey, I M W 1991, 9–10.

9 Du Boulay 1966, 162–3; for Celia Fiennes, see Morris, C 1982, 128.

10 These issues have been discussed in RCHME 1985, 56, 79, and Hall, L 1991; and by Robert Machin in a lecture to VAG, December 1990.

11 Currie 1988; Dyer 1986; Wrathmell 1984.

12 For joints, see works by Hewett. Moulding details have been studied in particular by Richard K Morris of Warwick University (1978; 1979). Most of his work is concerned with stone buildings, and the extent to which stone mouldings can be 'read' straight across into timber is uncertain.

13 Mercer 1975, 6.

14 For example, Barley 1986, 152; Mason 1969, 3; Mercer 1975, 11–12; and Smith J T, 1970a, 123.

15 Works by these authors are listed in the Bibliography and Further Reading. See also Roberts 1990 and several of the studies in Warren 1990. Quiney 1993 was published too late to be consulted in writing this book.

16 The area of the modern county has been taken from the OPCS Monitor for the 1981 Census. The civil parishes are those shown on the OS Administrative Areas Diagram for 1986. However, some large modern administrative units which incorporate several former civil parishes have been divided up for the purposes of this study. For example, Whitstable and Herne Bay have been separated, as have Rochester, Chatham and Gillingham. This should become clear from Figure 158.

17 For Canterbury, see the annual reports of the Canterbury Archaeological Trust, published in *AC*. For Sandwich, see Parkin 1984.

18 Everitt 1986, 40–2.

19 In the present project this led to 1 anomaly: in Cranbrook, where by 1557 1,500 communicants resided in 300 house-holds, the centre of the town was not investigated, although the rural part of the parish was surveyed. This means that figures for the number of surviving medieval houses in Cranbrook parish are almost certainly incomplete, and also means that no overall view of medieval housing in the parish as a whole was obtained.

20 Roberts 1990.

21 Rural ecclesiastical manor houses have been included, both because they seem to be relatively similar to secular manor houses, and because there is considerable documentary information concerning their building and the way they functioned.

22 In studies of vernacular architecture (as opposed to archae-ology), results obtained by random sampling have only been published by Meirion-Jones (1982), but its use, on a rigorous basis, has been advocated by Johnson (1988, 116). The full publication of his work is awaited with interest.

23 Notable areas of change affecting surveyed parishes are: the subsuming of Lullingstone into Eynsford, and Harty into Leysdown; alterations to the boundaries of Brenzett and Brookland (both surveyed), and of East Farleigh, Loose and Linton with the creation of Coxheath (all surveyed); and the splitting up of Wrotham into several parishes, of which Wrotham and Plaxtol have been surveyed.

24 The higher percentage of land area is almost certainly accounted for by the over-representation of large parishes in regions such as the Isles of Sheppey and Thanet, and Romney Marsh.

25 During the course of the project approximately 700 buildings were inspected internally; of these some 450 proved to have surviving medieval remains. DoE lists were used, where possible, as a guide. These were of varied assistance. In some cases relisting was not completed until after the fieldwork was finished. Of those that were available, the quality ranged from the excellent, to those of limited use, where blanket terms such as '17th century or earlier' had been applied. This simply highlights the virtual impossibility of accurately assessing Kentish buildings from the exterior: even after considerable experience, we could not always deduce which buildings might have medieval remains from exterior inspection alone. Although some buildings listed as 18th century proved to be medieval, and some buildings listed as medieval were not, only some half dozen unlisted houses were found which had substantial medieval remains.

26 For example, since this book was written, Margaret Lawrence, who provided valuable assistance through her knowledge of East Peckham, found 2 more medieval houses in the parish. Since East Peckham already has an unusually high number of medieval survivals, the recent discoveries have not resulted in changing East Peckham's position *vis-à-vis* other parishes, but

in strengthening it. So that although the absolute number of known survivals may increase, the general proportions suggested by the RCHME fieldwork are likely to remain valid.

27　Parkin 1970, 1973, 1976, 1981, 1989; Rigold 1967a; Sandall 1986.

28　Among others are Jones and Smith, J T 1961; Rigold 1963; and Coutin 1990.

29　Smith, J T 1970a, 123.

30　Rigold 1963, 353.

31　Rigold 1969a, 200; Gravett 1971, 4.

32　Rigold 1969a, 198; Everitt 1976, 12–13.

# 1　Historical background

1　The following account is based largely on Garrard 1954, 18–30, McRae and Burnham 1973, 52–6, 113–20, and Everitt 1976, 6–9.

2　McRae and Burnham 1973, pl 4.

3　Everitt 1976, 12, where he also notes the marked differences in the distribution of historic buildings throughout the county.

4　Comparative data for 1086, 1334 and 1524/5 are discussed in Darby *et al* 1979.

5　For a general discussion of the 1334 lay subsidy in Kent (PRO E179/123/12), see Glasscock 1975, xiv–xxix and map I, p xxvii. For comparison of the subsidy with the 1291 taxation of Pope Nicholas IV, which levied tax on annual clerical incomes, see Schofield, R 1965, including his table p 504.

6　This figure is not given by Schofield, R 1965 but can be deduced from his table, p 504.

7　Du Boulay 1966, 244–5. The problems of defining the geographical extent of manors, as well as the question of the reduction in revenues in the later Middle Ages, are discussed below.

8　Knowles 1959, 414. In 1086 Christ Church Priory was the second wealthiest, and St Augustine's the fourth wealthiest, religious house in England. By 1535 they had slipped to third and eleventh place respectively.

9　Smith, A 1963, 150.

10　*VCH* III, 186–93 and map opp p 177.

11　Du Boulay 1966, map 1; Everitt 1986, 172–80.

12　A transcription of the 1334 lay subsidy for Kent has been published by Hanley and Chalklin 1964, 71–170, where it is discussed in detail pp 58–70. For further discussion and maps, see Glasscock 1965 and 1975, xiv–xxix, 140–8. The following account is largely based on these works.

13　Schofield, R 1965, table p 504, provides the evidence for the ranking. Because he excluded the men of the Cinque Ports, Kent emerges as the fourteenth wealthiest county; but if their assessments are included it moves up to eighth place. Since their urban wealth is unknown, this may still be an underestimate.

14　Glasscock's maps vary between assessed wealth per square mile (1975, map 1) and yield per square mile (1965, 64).

15　Mate 1987, 523; 1991, 120. The evidence for a mid 14th-century swing away from arable to grass is briefly discussed in Campbell *et al* 1992, 21.

16　Bolton 1980, 290–4; Mate 1987, 525–32.

17　Witney 1976, 182.

18　Schofield, R 1965, 491–2.

19　Schofield, R 1965, table p 504.

20　Sheail 1968 and 1972.

21　Sheail (1968, 223) underlines the dangers of comparing the subsidies of 1334 and the 1520s, although he has contributed to the comparisons in Darby *et al* 1979.

22　Sheail 1972, map p 117.

23　The details for Kent are given as yields of shillings per square mile (Sheail 1968, map p 224).

24　This assessment, arrived at independently by the author, coincides with that undertaken by Darby *et al* 1979, 258 and fig 4.

25　Furley 1874, 201–4; Mate 1985, 63–5; Witney 1976, 177–86, and 1990.

26　Mate 1991, 134.

27　*VCH* III, 403.

28　Mate 1987, 526–7, 532. For Essex trade, see Britnell 1985, 248.

29　Mate 1987, 526–7, 532; Farmer 1991, 461–3.

30　*VCH* III, 406; Chalklin 1990, 79–80.

31　For cattle farming in the 16th-century Weald, see Zell 1985, 82–3.

32　Semple 1982, 27–9.

33　Semple 1982, 29; Mate 1991, 134.

34　Glasscock 1965, 64.

35　Hanley and Chalklin 1964, 67–70.

36　Sheail 1972, 116.

37　Mate 1991, 130–6.

38　Brown 1976, 145.

39　Du Boulay 1966, 227.

40　See Hatcher 1977 and Miller 1991a, 6 for general accounts of the problems.

41　PRO E 179/123/44.

42　Hanley and Chalklin 1964, 66. Alternative calculations, depending upon different assessments of the number of people under 14 or evading the tax (see Smith, R M 1988, 120), produce different figures, ranging between 78,000 and 99,000.

43　As discussed above, the 1524 lay subsidy returns for Kent are too incomplete to be used as evidence of population (Sheail 1972, 116–20). In addition, the validity of this source for this purpose has been questioned elsewhere (Poos 1985, 528–9).

44　Zell 1984a, 233.

45　Hatcher 1977, 68–9; Smith, R M 1988, 191–6; Dyer 1989, 4; Miller 1991, 6.

46　Hoskins 1959, 145.

47　The 1557 figures are based on Archdeacon Harpsfield's Visitation of 1557 (Sharp and Whatmore 1950, 1951).

48　*VCH* II, 89; Chalklin 1965, 27. Jordan (1961, 3) accepts a rather higher figure of 145,000 in 1600.

49　Smith, R M (1988, fig 9.4) indicates a slightly different pattern to the one the RCHME analysis shows. Nonetheless, the overall conclusions remain much the same.

50　1563 household survey: BL Harley MS 594, fols 63r – 84r. Of the 90 parishes for which 2 sets of household numbers exist, only 47 tally. In some of the rest, the discrepancies are small and probably insignificant, but 11 of the 14 increases, and 24 of the 29 decreases, differed by more than 10 per cent. In Sheldwich, for example, 16 households were listed in 1557 and 41 in 1563, an increase of 156 per cent. In Marden a decrease of 300 to 100 is equally suspicious. Zell (1983, 204), correlating these figures and information from other sources, suggests that the 1557 figures are the more accurate. This is supported by the fact that, when compared with the 1377 poll tax figures, the 1563 total shows a greater overall decrease in population than the 1557 figures, which suggests the latter are more reliable.

51　Zell 1984a, 235, 257.

52　Chalklin 1965, 218, map opp p 29. Also Everitt 1967, 410.

53　Everitt 1986, chapters 4 and 5; Witney 1976, 161–3, 176–83.

54 Du Boulay 1966, 48.

55 Du Boulay 1966, 57–8; *VCH* III, 190.

56 For discussion of the difficult questions of landholding and tenure in Kent, see Du Boulay 1966, chapters 3 and 4 and Mate 1991, 681–90.

57 Homans 1941, 112. His views are discussed briefly in Smith, R M 1984, 135–7.

58 For example, Du Boulay 1966, 147–8.

59 Baker 1965, 152–74; Du Boulay 1966, 146–50; Dyer 1989, 124.

60 For a general study of the peasant land market, see Harvey, P D A 1984. For Kent, see Du Boulay 1966, 135–7, Zell 1985, 73, and Mate 1991, 689–90.

61 Work done by David and Barbara Martin, quoted in Brandon and Short 1990, 110.

62 See, for example, work on Adisham: Campbell, S A 1981; Chartham: Langridge 1982 and 1984; Eastry: Mate 1991, 688; Gillingham: Baker 1964, 19; Ickham: Baker 1973, 410; Otford: Du Boulay 1959; Wrotham: Baker 1966 and Semple 1982.

63 I owe this comment to Andrew Butcher in connection with unpublished work on the Christ Church Priory manors of East Peckham, East Farleigh and Loose. It is also apparent at Wrotham: see Baker 1966, 10–11 and Semple 1982, 4–13.

64 Dyer 1989, 136. On the question of possible differences in labour dues on ecclesiastical and lay manors of earlier date, see *VCH* III, 338–44.

65 Dyer 1989, 8.

66 Dyer 1989, 120–3.

67 Clark 1977, 7; Everitt 1966, 35; Fleming 1985, 62, 96.

68 Everitt 1986, 172–80.

69 Witney 1976, 164–7.

70 Du Boulay 1966, 67–75.

71 Fleming 1985, 131–2.

72 Du Boulay 1966, 159–61; Fleming 1984, 36–7.

73 Fleming 1985, 150–1.

74 Brown 1976; Fleming 1985, 153–4; Webster 1984.

75 Fleming 1985, 153.

76 Witney 1976, 160–72.

77 The example of Barnes Place, Hadlow, is discussed in Chapter 3.


# 2 Houses of the early and mid 13th century

1 Turner and Parker 1851.

2 See in particular Wood 1950, 1965 and 1974; Faulkner 1958, and more recently Thompson, M W 1991 and Blair forthcoming.

3 All 3 houses have been published as first-floor halls in Newman 1980, 59, 385, 597. For Luddesdown Court, see also Peake 1920, *passim* and Wood 1950, 35.

4 None of the earlier authorities believed the surviving undercroft at Nettlestead Place lay beneath a hall; see Turner and Parker 1859, 307, and Oswald 1958 pt 2, 886. This view was also taken by Anthony Emery, unpublished notes, 1988. I am grateful to Mr Emery for corresponding with me about the house.

5 Thompson, M W 1991, 90–1.

6 Blair forthcoming.

7 Rigold 1969b and 1971a.

8 Biddle 1986, 6; Blair 1987, 77 note 35, and forthcoming.

9 Tatton-Brown 1991, 5; but the fenestration of the hall as illustrated in 17th-century drawings (ibid pls IA and B),

appears to be raised over an undercroft.

10 Blair 1987, 63; Thompson, M W 1991, 179.

11 Lethaby 1907, 142–5.

12 Description by de Joinville in 1241, *The History of St Louis*, as quoted in Thompson, M W 1991, 44–5.

13 Necham's description of the components of a house are published in Turner and Parker 1851, 3–6. Blair (forthcoming) discusses the introduction and early development of the aisled hall.

14 The excavated evidence of Sulgrave, Northamptonshire, suggests the standard arrangement might have been developed considerably earlier (Davison 1977, 109–11).

15 Wood 1965, 29.

16 The hall in the bailey at Rochester was in need of repair in 1230–1 (*King's Works* II, 808).

17 Thompson, M W 1991, 160.

18 Biddle 1986, 4–5.

19 Wood 1950, 17–19; 1974, 21–2. These examples are also mentioned by Blair forthcoming.

20 I am grateful to Eric Mercer and Madge Moran for bringing the Shropshire buildings to my attention.

21 Wood 1974, 19–22, 59. The interpretation of Little Chesterford Manor is discussed in Smith, J T 1992, 4–5. Swalcliffe Manor was published by Wood-Jones 1963, 25–8, but the plan is inaccurate and the development much more complex than presented there.

22 This feature was recorded by Cecil Hewett who made a model of the arrangement. He has kindly supplied me with a photograph of this, now in the NMR file. The evidence is no longer visible, but the site of the doorway is still recognisable on the first floor.

23 Eames 1965, *passim*; James and Robinson 1988, 9–10, 160–5.

24 *King's Works* II, 903, 919, 931, 943, 975.

25 Kipps 1934, 78–9; Rigold 1969f. It is also likely that there was a detached ground-floor hall at the Archbishop's palace in Maidstone.

26 C R J Currie, in a lecture to VAG, April 1987, and 1992, 88, 139.

27 Timber-framed examples in Oxfordshire are discussed in Currie 1992, 88.

28 Beresford, G 1974, 99–109.

29 Hurst 1984, 94, and Beresford, M and Hurst 1990, 45, where a timber attached hall is postulated; more recently doubts have been expressed as to the location of the hall.

30 Ketteringham 1976, 6–12.

31 Although the plan published in Dornier (1971–2, 25) indicates that there were 2 first-floor doorways in the front wall of the main range, no comment was passed on the fact that the rear face of these doorways lies on the inside, indicating that they were both intended to allow access into the range, and did not lead from this range to subsidiary structures. The timber doorways leading to the rear wings have now been dated by NUTRDL to *c* 1287*, while the roof has been shown to have been replaced in 1618/19* (*VA* **20**, 40).

32 Wood 1950, 76–81; 1965, 22.

33 Rigold 1965, 93–7, 118–21.

34 Oswald 1958, pt 2, 887; unpublished notes by A Emery in NMR file.

35 Rigold (1965, 118) argues that the undercroft of a first-floor hall was normally subdivided, and that there was usually communication between the 2 floors. There is evidence for neither at Luddesdown Court and Nettlestead Place. The ground floor of Squerryes Lodge was divided, but there is no evidence of an internal stair to the upper chamber.

36 Wood 1950, 96; RCHME 1993, 201–12. It has been suggested

that the immensely thick walls of the Bedford Range at Penshurst Place, normally dated to the 15th century, indicate an earlier origin, perhaps in the time of Stephen de Penchester in the late 13th century. The internal area, of approximately 190 sq m, is large, and whether the range could have functioned as a chamber block can only be speculated. I am grateful to Dr Jill Allibone for discussing her work on Penshurst Place with me.

37  Rigold 1965, 118.

38  Such a study is currently being undertaken by Eric Mercer in Shropshire, and I have benefited from numerous discussions with him on the problems which these early buildings pose.

39  Thompson, M W 1991, 114.

40  Hasted II, 453; III, 337, 395; V, 338; Round 1902, 158; Farrer 1925, 103–7; Sanders 1960, 144–5.

41  For Matthew Paris, see Luard 1880, 504.

42  Lecture by Joan Thirsk to the Hadlow Historical Society, September 1991. I am grateful to Dr Thirsk for this suggestion and for discussing her work with me.

43  *King's Works* II, 1017–18.

44  Farrer 1923, 61–102; Sanders 1960, 68–9.

45  PRO C.133/161 (24).

46  *Cal Fine Rolls* 1216–66, 296; *Cal Feudal Aids III*, 1284–1431, 8.

47  *Cal Close Rolls* 1234–7, 47; *DNB* Thomas de Camvill; typescript by H W Knocker, The Manor of the Rectory of Westerham (undated), in possession of Mr W S Churchill.

# 3  Ground-floor halls: late 13th and early 14th centuries

1  Tatton-Brown 1991.

2  Wood 1950, 33–5.

3  This by no means includes all the surviving houses of this period, although it is hoped that it forms a representative sample.

4  Canterbury Cathedral Archives, DCc Eastry 21, 22, 41, 47, 57, 58. Another timber aisled hall which was clad in stone in the late 13th or early 14th century has been excavated at Salehurst, East Sussex (Gardiner *et al* 1991, 84–5).

5  Leigh: Rigold in Parfitt 1976; Pivington: Rigold 1962; Joydens Wood: Tester 1979; Tester and Caiger 1958.

6  BL MS Cotton Galba EIV, fol 102v.

7  Andrew Butcher, in a seminar at the University of Kent, February 1989, drew attention to the omission of work from the *Memorandum Book*, indicating that the Eastry Court case is not an isolated example.

8  Mate (1984b, 12) discusses the effect that the Statute of Mortmain had on the building policy of Christ Church Priory.

9  Canterbury Cathedral Archives, DCc Eastry 58; DCc Mersham 11. The long distance transport of timber for building in the Middle Ages is well attested and has been discussed by a number of researchers (Rackham 1986, 263–4; C R J Currie, lecture to VAG, April 1987; W G Simpson, lecture at Rewley House, Oxford, May 1992).

10  Witney 1990, 29.

11  The 7 are Eastry Court, Newbury Farmhouse, Old Soar (where the width can be deduced although the hall has gone), Chilton Manor, Nurstead Court (stone), Hurst Farm (unaisled) and Ratling Court. In several cases the aisle widths are conjectural on the basis of circumstantial evidence. The widths range between 8.5 and 9.5 m.

12  The status of stone for building and its use for ecclesiastical manor houses is discussed in Smith, J T 1992, 17–18.

13  The unaisled stone halls range in width from 8.4 m at The Deanery, Chartham, down to 5.8 m at Hoad Farm, Acrise.

14  Ketteringham 1976, 9–17; Martin 1990, 99.

15  Reported at a meeting of the Royal Archaeological Institute by Major Luard Selby in 1863 (*Archaeol J* **20** 1863, 387).

16  For Court Lodge, Godmersham, see Wood 1965, pl LV; a reconstruction of the Archbishop's Hall, drawn by John Bowen, is reproduced in Tatton-Brown 1991, fig 2. Other examples are cited in Smith, J T 1992, 16.

17  Cherry, M 1989, 453–4; Cave-Browne 1895, 204.

18  Arnold, A A 1900, 161.

19  Robertson 1883, 223–8.

20  Binney 1972, 556–8.

21  The earliest reference to Cawne in Kent occurs in 1363 (24 Sept 1363, Roger Assbournham to Thomas Caven Kt, moiety of a tenement called Nelcombe in Zele and Ightham, BL Charter 16, 473). There is no definite reference to connect him to the Mote before his death in *c* 1372 (deed drawn up at Ightham, the Saturday after St Lawrence 1372, conveying land to trustees, BL Harl. Roll V.9; and will of Sir Thomas Couen, Kt, undated, CKS U601 T134–137; see also *AC* 4, 1861–2, 221–5).

22  Jayne Semple, pers comm; Hasted V, 23 gives the *Inquisitions Post Mortem* of Walter Culpeper, 1326/7 as a source. But this does not, in fact, refer to Old Soar or any property in the correct area (*Cal Inq P M* VII, p 39, no. 74).

23  In 1319 the Culpepers acquired land in East Farleigh between the wood of the prior of Christ Church, called le Frith, the heath of Est Farleghe, a lane called Gonnyldde Lane and a highway called Denestrete (*Cat Anct Deeds* I, p 466, C. 808). This almost certainly describes the site of Gallants Manor.

24  Several transactions of land in East Farleigh are recorded by the Culpepers during the 14th century, and since various of them are called 'of East Farleigh', it is likely that the house was used as a family residence (*Cat Anct Deeds* I, p 395, C.94; p 396, C.105; p 420, C.352; II, p 469, C.1983; p 557, C.2787).

25  Several of the fragments plotted are too ruinous for serious analysis. This includes Pimp's Court, Loose, the chapel at Pett Place, Charing, and the stonework at Rooting Manor, Little Chart, Coombe Manor, Hastingleigh, and Evegate Manor, Smeeth. At Boughton Court, Boughton Aluph, Parsonage Farmhouse, Elham, and Dean Farm, Elmsted, vaulted undercrofts survive.

26  As already stated, the RCHME's coverage of early houses is by no means exhaustive, but it is likely that further additions will not greatly alter the distribution pattern. It is far easier to extend the list of substantially surviving early stone houses in central and west Kent (eg Little Buckland near Maidstone, and Court Lodge, Horton Kirby [Tester 1981]) than in the east of the county.

27  List of sheriffs in Hasted I, 182–7; list of knights of the shire in Cave-Browne 1895, 200–10.

28  See Chapter 2, p23 and note 40.

29  DoE, *Lists of Buildings of Special Architectural or Historic Interest*; Newman 1980, 1983.

30  The medieval remains in west Kent are Hever Castle, Nurstead Court, Nettlestead Place and Morants Court, Chevening. In east Kent the medieval buildings are Walmer Castle, North Court Farmhouse, Eastling, and Sharsted Manor, Doddington, which is said to have medieval remains within a rebuild of 1711.

31  Analysis of the 15th-century gentry by P W Fleming (1985, 150–1) revealed that the north and east of Kent had a higher proportion of knights and esquires than elsewhere in the county. In contrast, the western part of the county had many

32 more families of parish gentry status. For later work on the Kentish gentry, see Clark 1977 and Everitt 1966.

32 Hasted VI, 140, 158; VII, 278–9; IX, 252.

33 Hasted VII, 278–9; *Cal Feudal Aids* III, 1284–1431, 6, 25, 34; *Cal Inq P M* VII, p 93, no. 104; *Cal Inq P M* VIII p 51, no. 82; IX p 42, no. 52.

34 Hasted, IX, 252; Colvin 1964, 5, 25; Du Boulay 1966, 387; Parkin 1976, 53–6; Fleming 1985, 169–70.

35 Colvin 1964, 4–6.

36 Burnt Oak and Nightingale Farmhouse, Yalding; The Old Farmhouse, Speldhurst. Because of the difficulty of dating, these houses have been discussed with those of the late 14th century in Chapter 6.

37 Hasted V, 283–4; VIII, 69–70.

38 Joan Thirsk, lecture to the Hadlow Historical Society, September 1991 and pers comm.

39 Hasted VII, 482; Rigold 1967a, 248.

40 In Oxfordshire, in the Vale of White Horse, the first surviving peasant dwellings appear to date from the late 13th century (Currie 1992, 103–7, 152–3, 174–5). In Shropshire there seems to have been a difference in social status between the buildings of base crucks and full crucks (Eric Mercer, pers comm), which in some ways may match the Kentish distinction between aisled halls and base crucks at this time.

# 4 Subsidiary accommodation: late 13th and early 14th centuries

1 Faulkner 1958, 178–80.

2 The 10 with upper ends remaining are Hoad Farm, Acrise; The Rectory House, Cliffe-at-Hoo; Copton Manor, Sheldwich; Ightham Mote; Battel Hall, Leeds; Nurstead Court; Old Soar, Plaxtol; Penshurst Place; Southfleet Rectory; and Newbury Farmhouse, Tonge. Evidence for upper ends is visible at The Deanery, Chartham; Court Lodge, Great Chart; and Mersham Manor. Only at Gallants Manor, East Farleigh, has the hall gone taking with it all trace of upper-end accommodation.

3 Service ends remain at Hoad Farm; Copton Manor; Gallants Manor; Court Lodge, Great Chart; Mersham Manor; and Penshurst Place. One was drawn before demolition at Nurstead Court. Evidence for such ends is visible at The Deanery, Chartham; The Rectory House, Cliffe-at-Hoo; and Ightham Mote. There is no evidence surviving at Southfleet Rectory, Battel Hall, Old Soar and Newbury Farmhouse.

4 BL MS Cotton Galba EIV, fol 102v.

5 See Chapter 3, p26 and note 7, for the fact that the *Memorandum Book* does not cover all building work undertaken by the Priory during this time.

6 Sparks and Parkin 1974, 170–1.

7 Turner and Parker 1853, 88.

8 Blair 1978, 353–4.

9 Once the solar was combined with a cellar only, once with a cellar and pantry, and once with a pantry and buttery.

10 Cotton 1925, 158. These were built with the new hall in the time of Thomas Ikham, sacrist of St Augustine's, sometime before 1391.

11 For a discussion of the roles of monks and serjeants on the manors in the late 13th and early 14th centuries when these houses were built, see Mate 1983, 335–6.

12 References to garderobes are numerous in royal documents. See *King's Works* II, *passim*; Wood 1950, 135; 1965, 177–8.

13 Wood 1950, 113–14.

14 For example, Rigold 1969a, 200.

15 Other houses where the ceilings have clear evidence of raising are Ightham Mote and Hoad Farm, Acrise.

16 Wood 1965, 74.

17 Barley 1986, 121.

18 Hussey, A 1911, 217; Eastry *Memorandum Book*; and architectural remains. The total from these sources is a little under 100, but Everitt (1986, 205–6), using the place-name evidence as well, calculates that there were a great many more than this.

19 Bensted and Hussey 1911; Tatton-Brown 1982, 88–101.

20 Wood 1950, 8–10.

21 *King's Works* II, 809.

22 Wood 1950, 76–81.

23 Mertes 1988, 148, 159.

24 *Dictionary of the Christian Church* 1988, 319. Wood (1965, 231–2, 235–6) cites several 13th and 14th-century houses where squints or galleries look into chapels.

25 The RCHME's work on Nurstead Court has already been published in Cherry, M 1989.

26 Gravett and Renn 1981; Rigold 1969d.

27 Since writing this chapter, the publication of a new VAG bibliography (Pattison 1992) brought to light an article on Southfleet Rectory, published by the late Stuart Rigold in 1967 (1967b). As always it contains a number of illuminating insights, including an outline of the same sequence of the high and low end development in the 13th and early 14th centuries.

28 Rigold 1967a.

29 Stylistically the wing is of 14th-century date and it may have been part of the campaign documented in 1330–1, even though no work on the chamber was recorded at that time (Canterbury Cathedral Archives, DCc Eastry 58).

30 Rigold in Parfitt 1976, 177, 180.

31 Gardiner *et al* 1991, 84–5.

32 C R J Currie, lecture to VAG, April 1987.

33 A similar lack of evidence for accommodation at either end of the hall has been noted in Hertfordshire by J T Smith (1992, 14).

34 This occurs at the lower ends of Chilton Manor, Sittingbourne; Ratling Court, Aylesham; Newbury Farmhouse, Tonge; and Hurst Farm, Chilham; at the upper end of Old Cryals, Brenchley; and at 1 end, possibly the upper end, at Little Moat Cottages, East Peckham. The evidence of the arcade post at Barnes Place is illustrated in *The House Within*, fig 95a and b.

35 The Plestor, Borden; Eastling Manor; Bardingley Farmhouse, Sutton Valence; Crundale House, Crundale.

36 Tester and Caiger 1958, 21; Tester 1979, 290; Rigold 1962, 36; Rigold in Parfitt 1976, 180; Martin 1990, 99.

37 A timber-framed range with a semi-basement of just the type proposed was discovered by C R J Currie at The Cottage, Aston Tirrold, Oxfordshire, and has been tree-ring dated to *c* 1282/4* (Currie 1992, 103–7).

# 5 Construction and roofs: late 13th and early 14th centuries

1 Rigold in West 1970, 101; Smith, J T 1992, 12.

2 Hewett 1989, 189; Smith, J T 1992, 12.

3 Rigold in Parfitt 1976, 179. The relevant phase of Park Farm, Salehurst, has been dated to before 1250 on the basis of this

construction (Gardiner *et al* 1991, 88).

4 Interrupted sills were used with the main corner posts in Copton Manor barn, Sheldwich (Wade 1988, 42–3). Door jambs sometimes pass across high sill beams until a late date, as occurs at The Tudor Lodge Gift Shop and Peacock Antiques, Chilham, in the late 14th century, and at Hoggeshaws, Milstead and Kingsdown, probably built in the second quarter of the 15th century.

5 Smith, J T 1965, 153–6.

6 Parkin 1970, 123–38; Bowen 1986b, 224–5. This house has timber arcade posts and external stone walls. Rigold (1973, 184) thought it had stone walls from the start, but the roof is cut back and does not reach the walls at either side.

7 Smith, J T 1992, 12, 175.

8 Smith, J T 1992, 12–14.

9 For The Old Rectory, Warbleton, see Martin and Martin 1981, 37–40 and *VA* 22, 1991, 40.

10 Mason 1966, 130–7; Smith, J T 1974, 250.

11 Unfortunately the matrices face the gable wall and had to be explored by feel, so there is a little uncertainty over their precise form. Notched laps were also used in the earliest phase of the Copton Manor barn, Sheldwich (Wade 1988, 42–3).

12 Tatton-Brown 1983b, 256.

13 Samson posts have been found in a number of 13th or early 14th-century stone buildings. One of the closest analogies is at St Etheldreda's, Ely Place, London (Hewett 1980, 123–4).

14 Scissors with collars span the roof of the *Necessarium* of Christ Church Priory itself (Tatton-Brown 1983b, 256; Sparks and Tatton-Brown 1989, 24–5).

15 Sparks and Tatton-Brown 1984, 2–6.

16 This crown strut is studded with a series of unexplained peg holes similar to those reported in other examples by Warren and Hallam 1990, 116, and Warren 1992, 8.

17 Among other publications which discuss these issues, see Smith, J T 1970b; Mercer 1975; Hewett 1980; Munby *et al* 1983; Warren and Hallam 1990; Warren 1992.

18 Munby *et al* 1983.

19 *c* 1290 – *c* 1340, Richard K Morris of Warwick University, pers comm. A very similar moulding to that at the Table Hall was used for the dais beam in 3–4 West Street, New Romney, built some time after 1287. The beam was measured and drawn by E W Parkin (notebook EWP 107, 53 in NMR) and reproduced at small scale in Parkin 1973, 125.

20 The tree-ring date, of 1291–(1301)–1311, for the chapel of the Eastbridge Hospital is based on a site sequence of 69 rings taken from 5 timbers. It is considered too tentative to publish in *VA*. Tatton-Brown in Munby *et al* 1983, 130 suggests that the nave roof of Chartham Church, which has a king strut, may be earlier than the chancel which was being rebuilt in 1294. However, Rigold (1969e, 266) thought all the roofs could be as late as *c* 1315. Warren (1992, 6) believes the roof of the hall at Robertsbridge Abbey may date to the early 13th century. Tatton-Brown (p 128) thought it was of the third quarter of the century; but quotes (p 134, n 22) Rigold's opinion that it was built nearer 1280. Judging by the published illustrations, the latter date seems more likely. Possibly this would be a prime subject for tree-ring dating.

21 Drinkwater 1964; RCHME 1968, 24–5; Mercer 1975, 82; Munby *et al* 1983, 132. Warren (1992, 5) quotes a date of *c* 1230 for the crown-post roof over the Dominican Friary in Bristol, but the form of this roof looks later, and it is not clear what evidence there is to support such an early date.

22 Martin and Martin 1981, 37–40, and *VA* 22, 1991, 40.

23 Munby *et al* 1983, 130; Parkin 1976, 57.

24 This roof type also occurs at Manor Farm, Frittenden

(information from Kenneth Gravett). Most examples lie over timber-framed ranges, but they are combined with stone walls at Bilsington Priory, Kent, and at The Pilgrim's Hall, Winchester, possibly of *c* 1308 (Crook 1991).

25 Fletcher and Spokes 1964, 169–73.

26 I am grateful to Kenneth Gravett for pointing out that both Christ Church Priory and St Augustine's Abbey used crown posts over their barns. However, the earliest surviving barns (Copton Manor for Christ Church and Littlebourne for St Augustine's) are of several phases, and the dates of the crown posts may be somewhat later. See Rigold 1966 and Wade 1985, 27–35; 1988, 38–44.

27 In Canterbury itself Christ Church Priory erected at least 2 crown-post roofs in the years around 1400 (Tatton-Brown 1983b, 256), and St Augustine's used crown posts over the halls of Minster Abbey, Minster in Thanet, and Salmestone Grange, Margate.

28 Hewett 1980, 322.

29 Munby *et al* 1983, 131–2; Warren 1992, 5–9.

30 See in particular Currie and Fletcher 1972, and the articles by N W Alcock, G I Meirion-Jones and J T Smith in Alcock 1981, 5, 16–20, 55, 56–7.

31 The main reason for suggesting that the crown-post roof is added concerns the fact that the collar purlin has an edge-halved scarf which otherwise does not occur in the county before the late 14th century. In addition the capital of the crown post of the open truss has simple, tightly spaced roll mouldings, without the lip which occurs on the surviving fragment of an arcade-post capital below.

32 Jones 1975–6; tree-ring date in *VA* **20** 1989, 41. For the general characteristics of early base-cruck construction, see Alcock and Barley 1972.

33 Parkin 1981.

34 Alcock and Barley 1972, 134–9.

35 The problem of origins is discussed in most detail by J T Smith in Alcock 1981, 16–20.

# 6 The evolution of the late medieval house

1 Rigold 1963, 351; 1969a, 200; Rigold in Parfitt 1976, 180.

2 Among the most important contributions to the debate are Brunskill 1970, 26–8; Mercer 1975, 3–4 and 1990; Alcock 1981, 58; Wrathmell 1984, 1989a, 248 and 1989b, 3–8; Dyer 1986, 36; Currie 1988 and 1990; Smith, J T 1992, 31–4.

3 Wrathmell 1984 and 1989b.

4 As will be discussed later, some buildings, such as Ashby Cottage, Westbere, were never given upper storeys, but few of these survive.

5 Walker 1987.

6 Currie (1988, 5) discusses the heightening of low-eaved houses and the fact that they had a higher attrition rate than their high-eaved successors.

7 C R J Currie, lecture to VAG, December 1991, and 1992, 91–3, 103–7.

8 Another example is The Old Vicarage, Linton, published by Mercer 1975, 13, 175–6.

9 Eg, in end-jetty houses at Tolhurst Farmhouse, Smarden, The Black Pig Inn, Staple, and Farthing Green Farmhouse, Sutton Valance.

10 East Sutton: The Blue House, *c* 1420 and 1468*; Parsonage Farmhouse, *c* 1436*; Walnut Tree Cottage, *c* 1401*.

Staplehurst: Clapper Farmhouse, *c* 1420; Coppwilliam 1370/1*; Exhurst, *c* 1385; Hill Crest and Kent Cottage, *c* 1389*; King's Head Hotel, *c* 1385. Sutton Valence (parish not fully surveyed): Bardingley Farmhouse, 1270–1300; Farthing Green Farmhouse, *c* 1435 and *c* 1455; Greenways Farmhouse, *c* 1450; Henikers, *c* 1364*.

11 This point has also been made with reference to Hertfordshire by J T Smith (1992, 34).

12 Rates of replacement due to a variety of causes are discussed by Currie 1988, especially pp 3, 5.

13 Rigold 1963, 354; 1969a, 199; Gravett 1971, 7.

14 Rigold (1969a, 198) noted the rarity of continuous jetty houses in Kent in comparison with the number found in Essex and Suffolk.

15 Gravett 1971 4; Parkin 1986, 184–5.

16 Martin and Martin 1989, 6–7.

17 Dyer 1986, 33, 42.

18 For Sussex, see Martin and Martin 1989, 6–9. I am grateful to Joan Harding for supplying the Surrey figures.

19 Mercer 1975, 13; Lewis *et al* 1988, 18 and Machin 1989.

20 Smith, J T 1992, 39.

# 7  The construction of late medieval houses

1 Before the tree-ring date was obtained, Walnut Tree Cottage was ascribed to the mid 14th century (see Mason 1973, 93–8, DoE list, District of Maidstone, 1985, 57).

2 Another aisled Wealden has been reported in Wingham (information from David Cox). A single-aisled Wealden at Barham has been interpreted as an earlier aisled hall remodelled as a Wealden in the 15th century (Parkin 1989, 225–33). In Sussex several aisled Wealdens have been discovered (Martin and Martin 1979, 53–5; 1986, 64), and another is known in Hampshire (Lewis 1990, 121).

3 For Skinners House Cottages, see Gray 1975.

4 Dunsters Mill, Ticehurst, dated to *c* 1450 in Martin and Martin 1989, 133; earlier dating had been proposed in Mason 1969, 22.

5 Reports by R W McDowall (1959) and E W Parkin (1970 and 1978), deposited in NMR, file no. 31676.

6 The other examples are Hogbrook in Alkham, and Little Winchcombe Farmhouse in Crundale, the latter recorded by students from the Canterbury School of Art in 1986.

7 Arcade posts supported on cross beams also occur in Hampshire (Lewis 1990, 120).

8 Sandall 1986; for the Sussex evidence, see Mason 1978, 155.

9 Colman 1974.

10 Evidence from the London *eyre* of 1244 (Chew and Weinbaum 1970, nos 396, 481) discussed in Schofield, J 1984, 76.

11 48–9 Churchgate Street and 1 College Street, Bury St Edmunds, discussed by Philip Aitkens in a lecture to VAG, December 1992. RCHME report in NMR, file no. 86421.

12 Currie 1992, 129, 132. I am grateful to Chris Currie for sending me a list of early jetties in the Vale of White Horse in advance of publication.

13 Hewett 1976, 56, 58–9; 1980, 110–11, 126–8; Smith, J T 1965, 152; Walker 1987, 33.

14 Leach 1992, 3.3. Tree-ring dating of this range was carried out by NUTRDL.

15 The various forms of jetty construction are discussed in *The House Within*, Chapter 2, p39–43.

16 The dating and distribution of Wealden houses are discussed in Rigold 1963.

17 The second earliest tree-ring dated Wealden, of 1392/3*, is Scolfes, Boreham Street, Wartling in East Sussex (*VA* **22** 1991, 40). It is one of a group of early examples identified in the Rape of Hastings by David and Barbara Martin.

18 The Tudor Lodge Gift Shop and Peacock Antiques, Chilham.

19 See *The House Within*, Chapter 3, p52–7; Chapter 4, p64–75. Details of Sussex Wealden construction are discussed in Martin and Martin 1979, 69–70; 1981, 54–6; 1989, 21–3, 123–34.

20 Gravett 1971, 4; Rigold 1969a, 200.

21 Gravett 1971, 6.

22 Gravett 1971, 6; Smith, J T 1970a, 125 and Mercer 1975, 176–7, where late 15th or early 16th-century dates were proposed.

23 As a post-medieval house, Summerfield Farmhouse has not been included in *A Gazetteer of Medieval Houses in Kent*; RCHME report in NMR, file no. 40078. For cruck-like forms in external walls in Suffolk, see Colman 1990.

24 Mercer 1975, 82–95.

25 Rigold 1969a, 198–9.

26 Eg at Mead Manor, Sturry, of *c* 1465*, Old Newstead, Staplehurst, and at two sites in Chiddingstone: the Old Manor House and Post Office, and Old Gilwyns and Gilwyns.

27 Warren and Hallam 1990, 116–23.

28 Rigold 1965, 117; 1969a, 199.

29 Gray 1990, 55, fig 2.

30 Tatton-Brown 1983a, 125.

31 Bowen 1990, 63.

32 Bowen 1990, 67–78; Hewett 1980, 197.

33 Rigold 1969a, 199; Gravett 1971, 11–12.

# 8  Form and function: the internal organisation of houses in the late Middle Ages

1 Furnivall 1877, 239–40.

2 Results of a preliminary study of the inventories were presented in lectures by Richard Harris to the Wealden Buildings Study Group in May 1989, and the Regional Furniture Society/Vernacular Architecture Group conference in Oxford in May 1991. I am extremely grateful to him for providing me with copies of the transcripts (CKS PRC 10/1) and for allowing me to read the lectures in advance of publication. Where his transcript has been quoted, the CKS reference is followed by the initials RH and the number he has given to each inventory. 10 of the inventories which refer to properties in Canterbury and Sandwich have been excluded from this study as relating to urban dwellings (a few others in which no location is noted may also refer to urban dwellings but have, in the absence of further information, been included). Out of the 94 potential rural examples, 44 itemise contents by room, although it is clear that not all of them describe complete houses.

3 Notably in Barley 1961, 41–6; Cowper 1914; Melling 1965, 16–30; de Launay 1984.

4 Field 1965; Martin and Martin 1977, 6–12; Dyer 1986.

5 Hanawalt 1986, 31–43 and *passim*.

6 Rigold 1963, 354; 1969a, 199.

7 For the Luttrell Psalter, BL Add. MS 42130, fol 208, see Millar 1932, 168.

8 Inventory of Christopher Badcocke CKS PRC 10/1 fol 83– 83v (RH 76).

9 Harding 1976, 16; Alcock and Laithwaite 1973, 103, 111– 18; Lewis *et al* 1988, 18.

10 Sections of the panelling at Shieling Hall and The Old Palace are illustrated in *The House Within*, fig 97.

11 Martin and Martin 1989, 83–4 where the point is made that some of the finest houses in Sussex, such as Great Dixter, Northiam, never had panelling, and may have been designed for hangings at the dais end.

12 This was also noted by J T Smith 1970a, 125.

13 Alcock and Currie 1989.

14 This point was made by Barley 1961, 29. An unusual exception is the Manor House, Benenden, a grand Wealden which was built *c* 1400. The ground-floor room at the upper end has quarter-round mouldings to the ceiling beam and its supporting braces.

15 The latrine at Bayleaf has been reconstructed with a free overhang. Most examples found during the project have evidence for an attached chute. For a reconstruction, see *The House Within*, fig 22b.

16 The point was discussed by members of the VAG at the meeting in Kent, April 1992. For a similar lack of original parlour or chamber heating in medieval Hertfordshire houses, see J T Smith 1992, 42.

17 2 relevant wills, both from Tenterden, are published in Cowper 1914, nos 3 and 4; 14 relevant wills from Cranbrook are published in de Launay 1984, nos 3, 5, 13, 15, 27, 33, 39, 42, 60, 65, 77, 78, 85 and 101; and 6 more from Charing were kindly supplied by Patricia Winzar, CKS PRC 32/2/209, 565; 4/105; 5/21; 7/46; 8/76. Extracts from 10 other wills (CKS PRC 17/4–17/7), are published in Melling 1965, 7–9. The inventories cited are those of Henry Bodiham of Goudhurst, 30 Sept 1490 (PRO Prob. 2/35), John Caysar of East Peckham, 1491 (Prob. 2/47), Agnes Robert of West Peckham, 11 April 1496 (Prob. 2/113), John Pympye of Nettlestead, 14 Sept 1496 (Prob. 2/115), William Wodcock of Mill hall, 18 Aug 1507 (Prob. 2/184); and William Brent of Charing, 2 Feb 1495/6, transcribed by Leland Duncan, notebook in KAS Library, Maidstone. I am grateful to Mrs P M Winzar for providing me with a copy of the latter.

18 For William Brent and his association with Peirce House, Charing, see Winzar 1993.

19 The extent to which probate inventories in Kent reflect the households of the more prosperous members of the community is discussed in Zell 1984b.

20 The presence of 2 doorways and no sign of subdivision has also been found in some Hampshire houses (Lewis 1990, 121).

21 This excludes late 15th-century houses, such as The Old Rectory House, Northfleet, Gravesend, in which the end bay formed a large heated kitchen.

22 Harding 1976, 9; Martin and Martin 1977, 18–20; Lewis *et al* 1988, 12 and *passim*.

23 The problem was noted by Richard Harris who considers the use of the lower end of the house and the kitchen in some detail (see note 2).

24 For example, the presence of buttery and pantry in late 13th and early 14th-century Christ Church Priory manor houses is recorded in the Eastry *Memorandum Book* (BL MS Cotton Galba EIV, fol 102v), in the Archbishop's manor house at Wrotham in 1330/1 (Lambeth Pal Lib MS ED 1139 *Compotus Wrotham 4 Ed II Jan* 1330–31), and in the manor of Westehalle, owned by Cobham College, in the late 14th century (BL Harley Roll C.18).

25 CKS PRC 17/4 fol 130v. Will of John Overer, the younger, of Throwley, 7 Nov 1487, quoted in Melling 1965, 7.

26 See note 2.

27 CKS PRC 10/1, inventories of John Tooke Esq of [Godinton Park] Great Chart, fol 56v–59v (RH 45); Harry Elner of Ripple, fol 60v–61v (RH 48); Thomas Abarrowe of Tenterden, fol 67(a)–68v (RH 58).

28 Attention was first drawn to provision for widows in Kentish wills by H S Cowper (1914). The complexity and variety of the arrangements which might be made for members of an older generation have been discussed by Richard Smith (1982, 34–5).

29 Many 17th and early 18th-century documents make clear that kitchens were frequently still detached, even if they were sometimes used for other purposes. See, for example, the terriers in CKS DR6/At 24, 34, 64, 76, and various surveys of 1608 in PRO L R 2/345.

30 These are not to be confused with a group of very late open-hall houses, such as Headcorn vicarage (now Headcorn Manor), and The Paper Mill, Benenden, where the central doorway opens on to stairs rising to a divided chamber end above.

31 Fairfield House, Eastry: unpublished notes by E W Parkin, 1970, NMR file no. 31676; Filborough Farmhouse, Gravesend (Arnold, G M 1895, 161); Gore Court, Otham (DoE list, District of Maidstone, 1987, 114–15).

32 Cowper 1914, no. 9; de Launay 1984, no. 65; Martin and Martin 1981, 47–9.

33 For 13, 15, 17 New Street, Lydd, see Pearson forthcoming. For The Castle Inn, see Gray 1988. Both examples lie next to churches in the centre of nucleated settlements, raising the possibility of a specialised ecclesiastical or communal function for the buildings.

34 Two other wings of early date and similar form occur at Iden House, Goudhurst (unpublished report by Wealden Buildings Study Group, NMR file no. 31679) and at Selbys Farm, Hildenborough, where the wing lies at the upper end of the hall (Mercer 1975, 174).

35 Mason and Wood 1968; Mercer 1975, 173; re-interpreted by Richard Harris in 1986, unpublished notes in NMR, file no. 31827.

36 Martin and Martin 1977, 18–20.

37 Lewis *et al* 1988, 27.


# 9 The demise of the open hall

1 Harding 1976, 19.

2 The date of the cross wing at The Deanery is discussed in Appendix 1.

3 The first lateral stacks heating Hertfordshire open halls seem to date to shortly before 1450 (Smith, J T 1992, 27).

4 Gray 1978, 11.

5 Mercer 1975, 20–1.

6 Martin and Martin 1978, 44–5.

7 Lewis 1980 and Lewis *et al* 1988, 18. It is possible that another example in Kent occurred at Longport House, Newington near Folkestone, recently dismantled for re-erection at The Weald and Downland Open Air Museum.

8 Martin and Martin 1978, 46–7; Swain 1968, 127–45; Harding 1976, 14–15, 26.

9 Parkin 1981, 225–330. The timber chimney is illustrated in

*The House Within,* fig 155.

10 Melling 1965, 9–10.

11 Martin and Martin 1977, 22–3; the same point is discussed by J T Smith (1992, 95).

12 Roberts 1990, 135–6.

13 Another fully floored Wealden occurs at Strawberry Hole Farmhouse, Northiam, East Sussex (Martin and Martin 1977, 5–6).

14 For The Priest's House, see Gravett 1971, 13 and Roberts 1990, 71. Outside Kent other surviving examples of early brick stacks in the south east are Whitehall, Cheam, Surrey (Gravett 1966; Quiney 1983) and Paycockes, Coggeshall, Essex (Hewett 1980, 211).

15 '...Also all the seid house to be tyled of Nockoll tyle and a chymney with 2 fyres. Also to be a oven in the kechyn with a reredoyse in the same kechyn...' (Melling 1965, 9).

16 Lambeth Pal Lib MS ED 1206: vouchers for Aldington Bailiwick *c* 1513–14.

17 Parkin 1971; Quiney 1984, 460–2; 1990, 108. The suggestion that the house was formerly larger is based on the existence of a full-size doorway leading from the chamber over the hall westwards into thin air; the doorway is too large to have led to a latrine, and since the present hall and parlour lack any clear sign of an original stair position or service rooms, it seems likely that the house was originally larger or, as at Little Harts Heath, a new two-storey range was added to earlier service accommodation which was subsequently demolished, taking with it the evidence for the original entrance.

18 CKS PRC 10/1; inventories of Elizabeth Sheaffe, fol 29v–31v (RH 26) and Stephen Forde, fol 48v–51v (RH 38).

19 Roberts 1990, 133.

# 10 The regional distribution of late medieval houses

1 Lecture by Andrew Butcher to the VAG Spring Conference in Kent, April 1992.

2 Mercer 1975, 1.

3 Rigold 1963, 352–3.

4 Rigold 1969a, 199–200; 1973, 187.

5 Rigold 1969a, 200.

6 The Wealden houses in Charing High Street tend to be smaller than those in the rural part of the parish, but none of the Charing houses were particularly large. It may be suggested that houses in nucleated settlements will always be smaller, but in Chilham several of the largest medieval houses in the parish lie in the village, with smaller ones in the surrounding countryside.

7 Work done by John McCann, 1987, and used in a lecture by C R J Currie 'Surviving Medieval Peasant Buildings in Southern England', Leeds, September 1988.

8 For a discussion of the 1557 and 1563 surveys, see Chapter 1, p14 and notes 47 and 50. In some cases the 1557 survey lists both households and communicants, in others only the number of communicants is recorded. Where both are known, the average number of communicants per household was 3.4, and this figure has been used to calculate household numbers in parishes where only communicants were listed. It is almost identical to the 3.5 and 3.4 figures used by Zell in Staplehurst and Cranbrook (1984a, 250–1).

9 See Chapter 1, p14.

# 11 Late medieval gentry houses

1 Mate 1984a; Prestwich 1980, 260–4.

2 *Cal Pat Rolls* 1392, 326.

3 Faulkner 1970, 140–6.

4 *Cal Charter Rolls* 1448, 102.

5 Bennett *et al* 1990, 247. See also Swain 1966 and report and drawings in the NMR, file no. 39731.

6 Du Boulay 1966, 154–6.

7 Flaherty 1860, 70, 79; Cave-Browne 1895, 219, 224; Hull and Keen 1957, 208.

8 Hasted VII, 176.

9 Conway 1930.

10 Tatton-Brown 1982, 102–3.

11 For Peirce House, owned by the Brent family, see Winzar 1993.

12 As seen in a perusal of *The Buildings of England* (Newman 1980, 1983). The distribution of the gentry in Kent is discussed in Chapter 1, p16–17.

13 A similar dearth of 15th-century gentry houses has been noted in Shropshire (E Mercer, pers comm) and in Oxfordshire (Currie 1992, 89–90).

14 Hasted VI, 69–70.

15 Parkin 1976, 53–6; Fleming 1985, 169–70.

16 Hasted V, 283–4; VIII, 69–70.

17 Hasted VII, 278–9.

18 Hasted VII, 440.

19 Hasted VII, 506.

20 Twisden 1939, *passim.*

21 Hasted VI, 301–4.

22 Hasted VII, 104–5, 229–30, 233–4, 587–8.

23 Fleming 1985, 150–1. The acquisition of property in northwest Kent by Londoners, including the gentry, is discussed in Brown 1976, Du Boulay 1966, 148–9 and Webster 1984.

24 Hasted II, 435; Fleming 1985, 171 and ch 5, n 17.

25 Fleming 1985, 95–9, 444–6.

26 For Kent, in addition to Fleming 1985, see Du Boulay 1966, 162–3; Harvey, I M W 1991, 9–10. The matter has been addressed by many writers in relation to other parts of England; for a recent discussion and bibliography see Carpenter 1992, 73–9, 96–7, 134–8.

27 Hasted II, 425–30; VII, 304–5; IX, 207–8.

28 Hasted V, 313–14, 320; list of rectors in the church.

29 Hasted VII, 176.

30 Hasted IX, 379–81; Sparks and Parkin 1974, 179–81.

31 Fleming 1985, 444–6.

32 In the 17th century, Riseden Hall belonged to a clothier family called Sabbe (Hasted VII, 73) whose association with the property can be traced back into the 16th century. In the mid 15th century Risedens of Riseden were recorded, and their tenure may go back to the 13th century (Oswald 1937, 43–4). Hasted VI, 73; VII, 440; VIII, 100–1.

33 For example, Dingleden, Pympne Manor, The Moat, The Paper Mill and Watermill House.

34 See note 30.

35 Fleming himself (1985, 153) acknowledges that in the Weald the distinction between gentry and others was less clear cut than elsewhere.

36 See Introduction note 10.

37 The wealth of yeomen in Kent is suggested, among other things, by the fact that by the early 16th century it was yeomen, not gentry, who were taking on the largest and dearest leases on the Archbishop's estates (Du Boulay 1965, 450).

38 Girouard 1978, 58–9.

39 Howard 1987, 82.

40   Melling 1965, 9–10.
41   Roberts 1990, 477–83.
42   Morris, C 1982, 128.

## 12 Late medieval houses in context

1   1334 lay subsidy: PRO E179/123/12; 1524 lay subsidy: Sheail 1968 and 1972; 1377 poll tax: PRO E179/123/44; 1557 survey: Sharp and Whatmore 1950, 1951; 1563 survey: BL Harley MS 594, fols 63r–84r; for a discussion of these documents and of the literature relating to them, see Chapter 1.
2   See Chapter 1, note 62. I am also grateful to Andrew Butcher for discussing these issues on more than one occasion.
3   The following account is based on Langridge 1982, 124–69; and 1984, 229–39.
4   Langridge 1982, 9–11; Hasted VII, 297–315.
5   Tatton-Brown 1982.
6   Sparks and Parkin 1974, 179–81.
7   Similarly poor, small and probably late, medieval houses have been identified outside the surveyed parishes, such as Southdown Cottage, Nonington (recorded by E W Parkin in 1968, report in NMR, file no. 39700), Old Kent Cottage, Newington near Folkestone, and St Mary's Grove Cottage, Tilmanstone (Mercer 1975, 177–9).
8   Hasted VII, 269–86.
9   Everitt 1986, 312.
10   Everitt 1986, 323.
11   Hasted VI, 50–64. Everitt (1986, 322) suggests that many of the 'reputed' manors in Kent were never true manors, but were woodland farms or small gentry estates.
12   Hasted VI, 69–74. Everitt 1986, 323–5.
13   Everitt 1986, 332.
14   Mason 1978, 155. Further aisled halls are currently being found on the Sussex Downs by David and Barbara Martin.
15   Hasted VIII, 95–110; IX, 304–28; Du Boulay 1966, 362–4.
16   Hasted VIII, 95–6.
17   Andrew Butcher, seminar at the University of Kent, February 1989.
18   Baker 1966, 5–7; Semple 1982, 1–2 and map.
19   Baker 1966, 7.
20   Baker 1966, 12–14.
21   Semple 1982, 33–8.
22   Baker 1966; Du Boulay 1966, 147; Baker 1973, 386–7.
23   In the late 13th century there were 67½ acres of arable demesne in Eastfield and 155 acres in Westfield, identifiable as lying a short distance to east and west of the palace: 'A survey of the archbishop's estates, 1283–5', Lambeth Pal Lib MS 2068. Some of this land can be traced as belonging to Charing manor in the 16th and 17th centuries. I am grateful to Patricia Winzar for this information.
24   The Old Vicarage; Patricia Winzar, pers comm.
25   Hasted VII, 480, where the date is given as 10 Henry VI (1431/2), when Kempe was still Archbishop of York.
26   For the view that lords had more control over close-knit arable communities, see Dyer 1989, 136.
27   The density of houses in Charing parish would have been greater before the parish was enlarged to the north by the addition of chalkland where no medieval houses have been found.
28   Hasted VII, 464–7.
29   Hatcher 1977, 31–6.
30   Biddick 1985, 826–7; Roberts 1990, 67, fig 7.
31   For information on Wealden markets, see Roberts 1990, 67

and fig 7; Gulley 1960, 518–20; and Streeten 1982, 92.
32   Thompson, A 1982, 2, map 2.
33   Hasted V, 352–85.
34   Zell 1984a, 240–1.
35   A number of weavers and clothworkers from Pluckley and Smarden are listed among those who were pardoned after Cade's Rebellion of 1450 (Cooper 1868, 262–5).
36   Few records of the Wealden broadcloth industry in the 14th and 15th centuries are known, and no detailed work has taken place on its extent or organisation at this time. See VCH III, 403, 406; Mate 1987, 526–7, 532; 1991, 135; Chalklin 1990, 79–80.
37   Hasted VII, 93–4; Hussey, C 1948.
38   Hasted VII, 97.
39   Hasted VII, 93, 105–6; Zell 1983, 210.
40   Hasted VII, 175, 187.
41   Zell 1983, 212–15, table 4; 1985, 85–8.
42   Zell 1983, 214–15; 1985, 83.
43   By the late 15th century the situation was improving for pastoral farmers, and anyway those who specialised in beef, as Benenden and Cranbrook men came to do in the 16th century, were less affected by the mid-century problems (Mate 1987, 527–8; 1991, 135–6). For Plaxtol, see Semple 1982, 33–8.
44   For Zell's calculations concerning population figures in the 1560s, see Zell 1984a, 236–7, 257.
45   Zell 1983, 216.
46   Andrew Butcher, seminar at the University of Kent, February 1989.
47   Harvey, I M W 1991, 105–6.
48   Dyer 1984, 9–10.
49   Baker 1964, 18–19.
50   Brown 1976, 145–6.
51   Du Boulay 1965, 446.
52   Hasted II, 422.
53   For the distribution of Londoners' purchases in Kent, see Brown 1976; Webster 1984.
54   The poverty is suggested by the 1524 lay subsidy, and the low population density is indicated by Zell 1984a, 257.
55   Hasted III, 128–30, 147–9; Harvey, I M W 1991, 40, 178–9.
56   Beresford, M W 1967, 67.
57   Zell 1984a, 257. Woodchurch, towards the east end of the low Weald, had a very low population density of 80 inhabitants per 1,000 acres; it has not been included in the low Weald figures cited here as its medieval buildings are rather different to those in the more central part of Kent.
58   Zell 1983, 211.
59   Zell 1985, 78.
60   This is discussed further in Pearson forthcoming.
61   Butcher 1974; and 'Citizens and Farmers in the Romney Marshes, 1350–1540', lecture to The Second Romney Marsh Conference, September 1992.
62   Furley 1874, 450.
63   Reeves forthcoming.
64   Anthony Gross 'Medieval Appledore and its Hinterland', lecture to the Second Romney Marsh Conference, September 1992.
65   Hasted VII, 253.
66   Cave-Browne 1898, 90–2.

## 13 Conclusion

1   In 1977 Everitt suggested there might be up to 8,000 medieval and sub-medieval buildings in Kent (1977, 12).

2  Zell 1984a, 233 and dicussion in Chapter 1.

3  The 4.75 figure for family size in the early 16th century is based on various studies in Kent and elsewhere. See Langridge 1984, 239–41; Zell 1984a, 233; and Smith, R M 1988, 190.

4  C R J Currie in lectures to VAG Spring Conference 1987, and in Leeds, 1989; the Essex figures are taken from work by J McCann and quoted by Currie in his 1989 lecture.

5  Early dates for Essex buildings have been advanced in Hewett 1980 and 1985. More recently very early dates have been suggested for Fyfield Hall, Essex (reported in Smith, J T 1992, 12). Early tree-ring dates have been recorded in Oxfordshire and Buckinghamshire (N W Alcock 'Dating the Medieval Peasant House in the Midlands', lecture to Royal Archaeological Institute, November 1992), and Currie 1992.

6  Rigold 1969a, 198; 1973, 188.

7  Taylor (1992) explores the possibility that the first response to housing an increasing population was the subdivision of existing dwellings, not new building.

8  Many of the finest examples are illustrated in Gravett 1971.

9  Chalkin 1965, 27.

# Appendix 1 Tree-ring dating

1  Articles in the early issues of *VA* by Stuart Rigold and J T Smith were concerned with these problems (Rigold 1971b; Smith, J T 1972). See also Smith, J T 1970a, 126–7 and the discussion in Mercer 1975, 6.

2  The seminal work on structural techniques, such as methods of jointing, was undertaken in Essex by Cecil Hewett who has expanded his field of study, notably into ecclesiastical carpentry of the 14th century and earlier (Hewett 1980, 1985).

3  For a general introduction to tree-ring dating, see Baillie 1982; Laxton and Litton 1988.

4  Salzman 1952, 237–9.

5  The method of constructing the Kent master chronology is discussed in Laxton and Litton 1989, 90–8.

6  A t-value is a statistical measure of probability.

7  Hughes *et al* 1981.

8  This reassessment of the results is discussed by Dr Laxton of NUTRDL in *VA* **24** 1993, 46.

9  Rackham (1980, 145) suggests that 97 per cent of ancient building timber was oak; we believe this would be far too high a proportion in Kent. Ibid, 267, 329–31 for the use of other species of timber for building.

10  In addition to buildings sampled by the RCHME, 3–4 West Street, New Romney, an early aisled hall (published by Parkin 1973) was sampled for tree-ring dating by Roland Harris for the Romney Marsh Research Trust. He found the rings to be few in number and undatable, and I am grateful to him for discussing this, and for forwarding the cores for examination and confirmation by NUTRDL.

11  Baillie 1982, 211–15.

12  I am grateful to Dr Laxton of NUTRDL for suggesting the final form of Figure 149.

13  For the buildings whose timbers were used to span the mid 14th century in constructing the Kent master chronology, see Laxton and Litton 1989, fig 2.

14  The 5 buildings are Eastry Court, Eastry (timbers with 82, 84 and 106 rings); Chilton Manor, Sittingbourne (63, 66, 70, 73, 80); Court Lodge, Fawkham (60, 61, 65, 71); Copton Manor, Sheldwich (62, 64, 67, 71, 76, 80, 84, 86); and Newbury Farmhouse, Tonge (68, 87, 106, 162). The sixth building is the Eastbridge Hospital, Canterbury.

15  *VA* **22** 1991, 40.

16  *VA* **21** 1990, 37.

17  Crook 1991, 146.

18  *VA* **19** 1988, 46.

19  Rackham 1980, 5, 158–9, 186–7. Dr Rackham (pers comm) would expect both pollarding and shredding to have been common in non-woodland trees in medieval Kent.

20  For Eastry Court, see Canterbury Cathedral Archives, DCc Eastry 22. The house in New Romney has recently been excavated by Roland Harris (*The Romney Marsh Irregular*, 7 January, 1992, and lecture to The Second Romney Marsh Conference, September, 1992). An early 14th-century date had previously been suggested by Rigold (1973, 184). The dates of the halls at The Deanery, Chartham, and Court Lodge, Great Chart, are provided by the *Memorandum Book* of Prior Eastry, BL MS Cotton Galba EIV, fol 102v.

21  Sheppard 1888, 79.

22  Currie 1983, 53.

23  Furley 1874, 201–4, 331–3; Mate 1985, 63–4; Roberts 1990, 18–20.

24  In East Sussex, David and Barbara Martin underwent a similar, if slightly more formal, process, using features from dated buildings to create a chart against which to check all their buildings in the period 1300–1750. In the Middle Ages, dated buildings are few in number and accumulated experience almost certainly played a large part in assigning date ranges to particular features. The Sussex buildings are each given an optimum date with a range of 25 years to either side. The success of the method was demonstrated when the Martins proved able to date a number of Kent tree-ring dated buildings with a fair degree of accuracy. This suggests that experience of an area combined with periodical self-scrutiny and reassessment can lead to accurate dating by conventional means. Nonetheless, tree-ring dating plays an essential part in proving that this is the case. For the Martins' dating methods, see Martin and Martin 1987 and 1989, 5–6.

25  *The House Within*, figs 75, 77, 79.

26  Very similar conclusions emerged from a study of scarf joints in Oxfordshire: see Currie 1972.

27  Many examples were inaccessible for measuring and others were only known from the presence of pegs and mortices for posts and braces.

28  These occur at Place Farmhouse, Kenardington, and in the hall range of Bartons Farmhouse, Plaxtol.

29  Rigold 1963, 354; 1969a, 198.

30  Rigold 1963, 354.

31  Parkin 1985, 213 suggests 1447 for the start of building; Rigold 1973, 186 dated the close studding at Wye to *c* 1445. Internal close studding, for security purposes, was used at the Court Hall in Milton Regis, probably in the second quarter of the 15th century (Rigold 1968, 16–17).

32  Sparks and Parkin 1974, 171, 179.

33  Although there is no record of later building work, some might have taken place just prior to 1446/7 when an altar in the chapel was consecrated; Sparks and Parkin 1974, 171.

34  Morris, R K 1978; 1979.

35  Rigold 1963, 354.

36  Martin and Martin 1987, 18–22.

# Bibliography and Further Reading

Alcock, N W 1981a. *Cruck Construction: an Introduction and Catalogue* (Counc Brit Archaeol Res Rep 42)
1981b. The origin and spread of cruck construction in Britain. In Alcock 1981a, 56–60

Alcock, N W and Barley, M W 1972. Medieval roofs with base-crucks and short principals. *Antiq J* **52**, 132–68
1981. Medieval roofs with base-crucks and short principals: additional evidence. *Antiq J* **61**, 322–8

Alcock, N W and Currie, C R J 1989. Upstairs or downstairs? *VA* **20**, 21–3

Alcock, N W and Laithwaite, M 1973. Medieval houses in Devon and their modernisation. *Medieval Archaeol* **17**, 100–25.

Arnold, A A 1900. Chancellors of the Diocese of Rochester. *AC* **24**, 160–74

Arnold, G M 1893. On the Old Rectory at Northfleet. *AC* **20**, 70–5
1895. Filborough Farmhouse, East Chalk, Gravesend. *AC* **21**, 161–71

Astill, G and Grant, A (eds) 1988. *The Countryside of Medieval England*

Aston, M, Austin, D and Dyer, C (eds) 1989. *Rural Settlement of Medieval England: Studies Dedicated to Maurice Beresford and John Hurst*

Baillie, M G L 1982. *Tree-Ring Dating and Archaeology*

Baker, A R H 1964. Open fields and partible inheritance on a Kent manor. *Econ Hist Rev 2 ser* **17**, 3–23.
1965. Some fields and farms in medieval Kent. *AC* **80**, 152–74
1966. Field systems in the Vale of Holmesdale. *Agr Hist Rev* **14**, 1–24
1973. Field systems of south east England. In Baker and Butlin 1973, 377–411

Baker, A R H and Butlin, R A (eds) 1973. *Studies of Field Systems in the British Isles*

Barley, M W 1961. *The English Farmhouse and Cottage*
1986. *Houses and History*

Bennett, P, Cross, R and Ward, A 1990. Starkey Castle. *AC* **108**, 244–52

Bensted, H and Hussey, A 1911. Newlands Chapel. *AC* **29**, 85–6

Beresford, G 1974. The medieval manor of Penhallam, Cornwall. *Medieval Archaeol* **18**, 90–145

Beresford, M W 1967. *New Towns of the Middle Ages*

Beresford, M W and Hurst, J 1990. *Wharram Percy, Deserted Medieval Village*

Berger, R (ed) 1970. *Scientific Methods in Medieval Archaeology*

Biddick, K 1985. Medieval English peasants and market involvement. *J Econ Hist* **45**, 823–31

Biddle, M 1986. *Wolvesey, The Old Bishop's Palace, Winchester*

Binney, M 1972. Penshurst Place, Kent – I. *Country Life* March **9**, 554–8

Blair, J 1978. A late thirteenth-century survey of buildings on estates of Southwark Priory. *Antiq J* **58**, 353–4
1987. The twelfth-century bishop's palace at Hereford. *Medieval Archaeol* **31**, 59–72
forthcoming. Hall and chamber: English domestic planning 1000–1250'. In Meirion-Jones and Jones forthcoming

Blair, J and Ramsay, N (eds) 1991. *English Medieval Industries*

Bolton, J L 1980. *The Medieval English Economy 1150–1500*

Bowen, J 1986a. Nos. 36–37 Burgate (formerly part of The Sun). *AC* **103**, 224
1986b. 'Cogan House', no. 53 St Peter's Street. *AC* **103**, 224–5
1990. The architectural history of 'Meister Omers' and the buildings to the north. In Driver, Rady and Sparks 1990, 67–78

Brandon, P and Short, B 1990. *The South East from AD 1000*

Britnell, R H 1985. *Growth and Decline in Colchester 1300–1525*

Brown, A 1976. London and north-west Kent in the later Middle Ages: the development of a land market. *AC* **92**, 145–56

Brunskill, R W 1970. *Illustrated Handbook of Vernacular Architecture*

Butcher, A F 1974. The origins of Romney freemen, 1433–1523. *Econ Hist Rev 2 ser* **27**, 16–27

Campbell, B M S 1981. The population of early Tudor England: a re-examination of the 1522 muster returns and 1524 and 1525 lay subsidies. *J Hist Geogr* **7**, 145–54

Campbell, B M S, Galloway, J A and Murphy, M 1992. Rural land-use in the metropolitan hinterland, 1270–1339: the evidence of *Inquisitiones post mortem*. *Agr Hist Rev* **40** I, 1–22

Campbell, S A 1981. *Some Aspects of the Social and Economic History of the Manor of Adisham*. Unpub M Phil thesis, University of Kent

Carpenter, C 1992. *Locality and Polity, a study of Warwickshire landed society 1401–1499*

Cave-Browne, J 1895. Knights of the Shire for Kent from A.D. 1275 to A.D. 1831. *AC* **21**, 198–243
1898. Shurland House. *AC* **23**, 86–93

Chalklin, C W 1965. *Seventeenth Century Kent*
1990. Sources for Kentish history: trade and industry. *AC* **108**, 73–89

Cherry, M 1989. Nurstead Court, Kent: a re-appraisal. *Archaeol J* **146**, 451–64

Chew, H M and Weinbaum, M (eds) 1970. *The London Eyre of 1244*. London Rec Soc, **6**

Clapham, A W 1928. An early hall at Chilham Castle, Kent. *Antiq J* **8**, 350–3

Clark, P 1977. *English Provincial Society from the Reformation to the Revolution: Religion, Politics and Society in Kent, 1500–1640*

Cleere, H and Crossley, D 1985. *The Iron Industry of the Weald*

Colman, S 1974. A late aisled house in Suffolk. *VA* **5**, 14–17
1990 Base-cruck usages in Suffolk. *VA* **21**, 10–15

Colvin, H M 1964. A list of the archbishop of Canterbury's tenants by knight service in the reign of Henry II. In *Kent Records, Documents Illustrative of Medieval Kentish Society* (KAS) **18**, 1–40

Conway, M 1930. Stoneacre, near Otham. *Country Life* **65** no 2, 420–68

Cooper, W D 1868. Jack Cade's followers in Kent. *AC* **7**, 233–71

Cotton, C 1925. A contemporary list of the benefactions of Thomas Ikham, sacrist of St Austin's Abbey, Canterbury. *AC* **37**, 152–9

Coutin, K 1990. The wealden house. In Warren 1990, 73–87

Cowper, H S 1911. Some timber-framed houses in the Kentish Weald. *AC* **29**, 169–205
1914. A note on some fifteenth and sixteenth century Kentish wills. *AC* **30**, 127–31

Crook, J 1991. The Pilgrim's Hall, Winchester. Hammerbeams, base crucks and aisle-derivative roof structures. *Archaeologia* **109**, 129–59

Currie, C R J 1972. Scarf-joints in the North Berkshire and Oxford area. *Oxoniensia* **37**, 177–86

1983. Timber supply and timber building in a Sussex parish. *VA* **14**, 52–4

1987. Harwell houses to 1700: an interim gazetteer. Vernacular Architecture Group, unpublished Spring Conference Programme

1988. Time and chance: modelling the attrition of old houses. *VA* **19**, 1–9

1990. Time and chance: a reply to comments. *VA* 21, 5–9

1992. Larger medieval houses in the Vale of White Horse. *Oxoniensia* **57**, 81–244

Currie, C R J and Fletcher, J M 1972. Two early cruck houses in north Berkshire identified by radiocarbon. *Medieval Archaeol* **16**, 136–42

Darby, H C, Glasscock, R E, Sheail, J and Versey, G R 1979. The changing geographical distribution of wealth in England: 1086–1334–1525. *J Hist Geogr* **5**, 3, 247–62

Davison, B K 1977. Excavations at Sulgrave, Northamptonshire, 1960–76. *Archaeol J* **134**, 105–14

de Launay, J 1984. *Cranbrook, Kent. Wills 1396–1640* (Kent Record Collections and Kent Archaeological Trust)

Detsicas, A (ed) 1981. *Collectanea Historica: Essays in Memory of Stuart Rigold*

Detsicas, A and Yates, N 1983. *Studies in Modern Kentish History, presented to Felix Hull and Elizabeth Melling* (KAS)

Dornier, A 1971–2. Donington le Heath. *Leicestershire Archaeol Hist Soc Trans* **47**, 22–42

Drinkwater, N 1964. The Old Deanery, Salisbury. *Antiq J* **44**, 41–59

Driver, J C, Rady, J and Sparks, M 1990. *The Archaeology of Canterbury, Excavations in the Cathedral Precincts, 2 Linacre Garden, "Meister Omers" and St Gabriel's Chapel* (Kent Archaeol Soc for Canterbury Archaeol Trust)

Du Boulay, F R H 1959. Late-continued demesne farming at Otford. *AC* **73**, 116–24

1961. Denns, droving and danger. *AC* **86**, 75–87

1962. Gavelkind and knight's fee in medieval Kent. *Engl Hist Rev* **77**, 504–11

1963–4. A rentier economy in the later Middle Ages. The archbishopric of Canterbury. *Econ Hist Rev 2 ser* **16**, 427–38

1965. Who were farming the English demesnes at the end of the Middle Ages? *Econ Hist Rev 2 ser* **17**, 443–55

1966. *The Lordship of Canterbury: an Essay on Medieval Society*

Dyer, C 1984. The social and economic background to the rural revolt of 1381. In Hilton and Aston 1984, 9–42

1986. English peasant buildings in the later Middle Ages. *Medieval Archaeol* 30, 19–45

1989. *Standards of Living in the Later Middle Ages*

Eames, E 1965. The royal apartments at Clarendon Palace in the reign of Henry III. *J Brit Archaeol Ass 3 ser* **27**, 57–85

Eddison, J (ed) forthcoming. *Romney Marsh: The Debatable Ground* (Oxford University Committee for Archaeology Monograph)

Everitt, A M 1966. *The Community of Kent and the Great Rebellion 1640–60*

1967. The marketing of agricultural produce. In Thirsk 1967, 466–592

1975. The primary towns of England. *Local Historian* **11**, no. 5, 263–77

1976. The making of the agrarian landscape of Kent. *AC* **92**, 1–31

1986. *Continuity and Colonization: the Evolution of Kentish Settlement*

Farmer, D L 1991. Prices and wages, 1350–1500. In Miller 1991b, 431–525

Farrer, W 1923, 1924, 1925. *Honors and Knights' Fees 1, 2 and 3*

Faulkner, P A 1958. Domestic planning from the twelfth to the fourteenth centuries. *Archaeol J* **115**, 150–83

1970. Some medieval archiepiscopal palaces. *Archaeol J* **127**, 130–46

Field, R K 1965. Worcestershire peasant buildings, household goods and farming equipment in the later Middle Ages. *Medieval Archaeol* **9**, 105–49

Flaherty, W E 1860. The great rebellion in Kent of 1381 illustrated from the Public Records. *AC* **3**, 65–96

Fleming, P W 1984. Charity, faith and the gentry of Kent, 1422–1529. In Pollard 1984, 36–58

1985. *The Character and Private Concerns of the Gentry of Kent, 1422–1509*. Unpub PhD thesis, University of Swansea

1990. The Lovelace dispute: concepts of property and inheritance in fifteenth-century Kent. *Southern Hist* **12**, 1–18

Fletcher, J M and Spokes, P S 1964. The origin and development of crown-post roofs. *Medieval Archaeol* **8**, 152–83

Fordham, S J and Green, R D 1980. *Soils of Kent* (Soil Survey Bulletin **9**)

Foster, I LL and Alcock, L (eds) 1963. *Culture and Environment: Essays in Honour of Sir Cyril Fox*

Furley, R 1871, 1874. *A History of the Weald of Kent with an Outline of the Early History of the County* (parts 1 and 2)

Furnivall, F J (ed) 1877. *Harrison's Description of England in Shakespeare's Youth*, pt I, book 2

Gardiner, M, Jones, G and Martin, D 1991. The excavation of a medieval aisled hall at Park Farm, Salehurst, East Sussex. *Sussex Archaeol Collect* **129**, 81–97

Garrard, G H 1954. *A Survey of the Agriculture of Kent*

Girouard, M 1978. *Life in the English Country House, a Social and Architectural History*

Given-Wilson, C 1987. *The English Nobility in the Late Middle Ages*

Glasscock, R E 1965. The distribution of lay wealth in Kent, Surrey and Sussex, in the early fourteenth century. *AC* **80**, 61–8

1975. *The Lay Subsidy of 1334*. The British Academy, Records of Social and Economic History, n ser **2**

Goose, N R 1976. Wage labour on a Kentish manor, Meopham 1307–75. *AC* **92**, 203–23

Gravett, K 1966. Whitehall, Cheam. *Surrey Archaeol Collect* **63**, 138–50

1971. *Timber and Brick Building in Kent*

1972. Timber building in Sturry. In McIntosh 1972, 24–8

1981. The Rectory House at Cliffe-at-Hoo. In Detsicas 1981, 187–91

Gravett, K W E and Renn, D F 1981. The tower of Stone Castle, Greenhithe. *AC* **97**, 312–18

Gray, P J 1975. Skinners House, Chiddingstone. *AC* **91**, 179–82

1978. *Charlwood Houses: A Comparative Analysis of the Early Buildings in a Wealden Surrey Parish*. Unpub typescript, privately circulated

1988. The Castle Inn, Chiddingstone, Kent. *VA* **19**, 42

1990. Dating buildings in the Weald. In Warren 1990, 47–60

Greenstreet, J 1876. Assessment in Kent for the aid to knight the Black Prince, anno 20 Edward III, ed J Greenstreet. *AC* **10**, 99–162

Gulley, J L M 1960. *The Wealden Landscape in the early Seventeenth Century and its Antecedents*. Unpub PhD thesis, London University

Hall, A D and Russell, E J 1911. *A Report on the Agriculture and Soils of Kent, Surrey and Sussex* (Board of Agriculture and Fisheries)

Hall, L 1991. Yeoman or Gentleman? Problems in defining social status in seventeenth and eighteenth century Gloucestershire. *VA* **22**, 2–19

Hall, R de Z 1972. *A Bibliography of Vernacular Architecture*

Hallam, H E (ed) 1988. *The Agrarian History of England and Wales 1042–1350*

Hanawalt, B 1986. *The Ties that Bound: Peasant Families in Medieval England*

Hanley, H A and Chalklin, C W 1964. The Kent lay subsidy roll of 1334/5. In *Kent Records, Documents Illustrative of Medieval Kentish Society* (KAS) **18**, 58–172

Harding, J M 1976. *Four Centuries of Charlwood Houses, Medieval to 1840*

— 1993. Timber-framed early buildings in Surrey. A pattern for development, c 1300–1650. *Trans Ancient Monuments Soc* **37**, 117–45

Harvey, I M W 1991. *Jack Cade's Rebellion of 1450*

Harvey, P D A (ed) 1984. *The Peasant Land Market in Medieval England*

Hasted, E 1797–1801. *The History and Topographical Survey of the County of Kent*. 12 volumes, 2nd edn, reprinted 1972 with introduction by A M Everitt

Hatcher, J 1977. *Plague, Population and the English Economy, 1348–1500*

Hewett, C A 1969. *The Development of Carpentry, 1200–1700: an Essex Study*

— 1976. Aisled timber halls and related buildings, mostly in Essex. *Trans Ancient Monuments Soc* **21**, 45–99.

— 1980. *English Historic Carpentry*

— 1985. *English Cathedral and Monastic Carpentry*

— 1989. Evidence for an intermediate stage between earth-fast and sill-mounted posts. *Trans Ancient Monuments Soc* **33**, 181–92

Hewett, C A and Tatton-Brown, T 1976. New structural evidence regarding Bell Harry Tower and the south-east spire at Canterbury. *AC* **92**, 129–36

Hilton, R H 1975. *The English Peasantry in the Later Middle Ages*

Hilton, R H and Aston, T H (eds) 1984. *The English Rising of 1381*

Homans, G C 1941. *English Villagers of the Thirteenth Century*

Hoskins, W G 1953. The rebuilding of rural England 1570–1640. *Past and Present* **4**, 44–59

— 1959. *Local History in England*

Howard, M 1987. *The Early Tudor Country House, Architecture and Politics 1490–1550*

Hughes, M K, Milson, S J and Legett, P A 1981. Sapwood estimates in the interpretation of Tree-Ring Dates. *J Archaeol Sci* **8**, 381–90

Hull, F and Keen, R A 1957. English politics and the sheriff of Kent, 1378. *AC* **71**, 206–13

Hurst, J G 1984. The Wharram Research Project: Results to 1983. *Medieval Archaeol* **28**, 77–111

Hussey, A 1911. Chapels in Kent. *AC* **29**, 217–58

Hussey, C 1948. Old Wilsley, Cranbrook, Kent. *Country Life* **104**, 26–30, 78–82

James, T B and Robinson, A M 1988. *Clarendon Palace, the History and Archaeology of a Medieval Palace and Hunting Lodge near Salisbury, Wiltshire*

Johnson, M 1988. Late medieval houses in western Suffolk: new directions in the study of vernacular architecture. *Scot Archaeol Rev* **5**, 1–2, 114–20

Jones, M (ed) 1986. *Gentry and Lesser Nobility in Late Medieval Europe*

Jones, S R 1975–6. West Bromwich (Staffs) manor-house. *Trans South Staffordshire Archaeol Hist Soc* **17**, 1–63

Jones, S R and Smith, J T 1961. The Wealden houses of Warwickshire and their significance. *Trans Birmingham Warwickshire Archaeol Soc* **79**, 24–35

Jope, E M 1963. The regional cultures of medieval Britain. In Foster and Alcock 1963, 327–50.

Jordan, W K 1961. Social Institutions in Kent 1480–1660. *AC* **75**

Ketteringham, L L 1976. *Alsted: Excavation of a Thirteenth–Fourteenth Century Sub-Manor House with its Ironworks in Netherne Wood, Merstham, Surrey*

*King's Works. The History of the King's Works* (gen ed H M Colvin),

vol II (1963), III (1975), IV (1982)

Kipps, P K 1934. The palace of the Archbishops of Canterbury at Charing, Kent, now called Palace Farm. *Archaeol J* **90**, 78–97

Knocker, H W 1915. 'The valley of Holmesdale', its evolution and development. *AC* **31**, 155–77

— 1932. The evolution of the Holmesdale. No 3, the manor of Sundrish. *AC* **44**, 189–210

Knowles, D 1959. *The Religious Orders in England*

Langridge, A M 1982. *The Tenantry of Chartham from c1200 to c1550*. Unpub M A thesis, University of Kent

— 1984. The population of Chartham from 1086 to 1600. *AC* **101**, 217–44

Laxton, R R and Litton, C D 1988. *An East Midlands Master Tree-Ring Chronology, and its Use for Dating Vernacular Buildings*

— 1989. Construction of a Kent master dendrochronological sequence for oak, AD 1158 to 1540. *Medieval Archaeol* **33**, 90–8

Leach, P (ed) 1982. *Archaeology in Kent to AD 1500* (Counc Brit Archaeol Res Rep 48)

— 1992. *Archaeological Studies Undertaken During Building Restoration Work of Ightham Mote. I, North East Quarter 1989–1992*. Report for The National Trust

Lethaby, W 1907. The Palace of Westminster in the eleventh and twelfth centuries. *Archaeologia* **60**, 131–48

Lewis, E 1980. A jettied house at Wickham, Hampshire. *Proc Hampshire Fld Club Archaeol Soc* **36**, 203–17

— 1990. Three Hampshire Wealden houses. *Proc Hampshire Fld Club Archaeol Soc* **46**, 113–30

Lewis, E, Roberts, E and Roberts, K 1988. *Medieval Hall Houses of the Winchester Area*

Luard, H R (ed) 1880. Matthew Paris. *Chronica Maiora* **5** (Rolls Series 57)

Machin, R 1977. The great rebuilding: a reassessment. *Past and Present* **77**, 33–56

— 1989. Review of Lewis *et al* 1988. *Medieval Archaeol* **33**, 268

McIntosh, K H (ed) 1972. *Sturry, the Changing Scene*

McRae, S G and Burnham, C P 1973. *The Rural Landscape of Kent*

Martin, D 1990. Three moated sites in north-east Sussex. Part 2: Hawksden and Bodiam. *Sussex Archaeol Collect* **128**, 89–116

Martin, D and Martin, B 1977. *Historic Buildings in Eastern Sussex* (Rape of Hastings Architectural Survey) **1**, no. 1

— 1978. *Historic Buildings in Eastern Sussex* (Rape of Hastings Architectural Survey) **1**, no. 2

— 1979. *Historic Buildings in Eastern Sussex* (Rape of Hastings Architectural Survey) **1**, no. 3

— 1981. *Historic Buildings in Eastern Sussex* (Rape of Hastings Architectural Survey) **2**, no. 2

— 1986. *Historic Buildings in Eastern Sussex* (Rape of Hastings Architectural Survey) **2**, no. 3

— 1987. *Dated Houses in Eastern Sussex 1400–1750*. Historic Buildings in Eastern Sussex (Rape of Hastings Architectural Survey) **4**

— 1989. *Domestic Building in the Eastern High Weald 1300–1750, pt I, Wall Construction*. Historic Buildings in Eastern Sussex (Rape of Hastings Architectural Survey) **5**

— 1991. *Domestic Buildings in the Eastern High Weald 1300– 1750, pt 2, Windows and Doorways*. Historic Buildings in Eastern Sussex (Rape of Hastings Architectural Survey) **6**

Mason, R T 1966. Old Court Cottage, Limpsfield. *Surrey Archaeol Collect* **63**, 130–7

— 1969. *Framed Buildings of the Weald*

— 1973. *Framed Buildings of England*

— 1978. Single-aisled halls in Sussex. *Sussex Archaeol Collect* **116**, 155–8

Mason, R T and Wood, R H 1968. Winkhurst Farm, Bough Beech. *AC* **83**, 33–7

Mate, M 1983. The farming out of manors: a new look at the evidence from Canterbury Cathedral Priory. *J Medieval History* **9**, 331–43

1984a. Agrarian economy after the Black Death: the manors of Canterbury Cathedral Priory, 1348–91. *Econ Hist Rev 2 ser* **37**, 341–54

1984b. Property investment by Canterbury Cathedral Priory, 1250–1400. *J British Studies* **23**, 1–21

1985. Labour and labour services on the estates of Canterbury Cathedral Priory. *Southern Hist* **7**, 55–67

1987. Pastoral farming in south-east England in the fifteenth century. *Econ Hist Rev 2 ser* **40**, 523–36

1991. Kent and Sussex. In Miller 1991b, 119–36, 268–85, 680 –703

Meirion-Jones, G I 1981. Cruck construction: the European evidence. In Alcock 1981a, 39–56

1982. *The Vernacular Architecture of Brittany*

Meirion-Jones, G and Jones, M (eds) forthcoming. *Manorial Domestic Buildings in England and Northern France* (Soc of Antiq London Occas Pap n ser **15**)

Melling, E 1965. *Some Kentish Houses* (Kentish Sources 5)

Mercer, E 1975. *English Vernacular Houses: a Study of Traditional Farmhouses and Cottages*

1990. Time and chance: a timely rejoinder. *VA* **21**, 1–3

Mertes, K 1988. *The English Noble Household 1250–1600*

Michelmore, D J H 1979. *A Current Bibliography of Vernacular Architecture 1970–1976*

Millar, E G 1932. *The Luttrell Psalter*

Miller, E 1991a. Introduction: land and people. In Miller 1991b, 1–33

Miller, E (ed) 1991b. *The Agrarian History of England and Wales 1348–1500.*

Moreton, C E 1991. A social gulf? The upper and lesser gentry of later medieval England. *J Medieval Hist* **17**, 255–62

Morgan, D A L 1986. The individual style of the English gentleman. In Jones, M (ed) 1986, 15–35

Morris, C (ed) 1982. *The Illustrated Journeys of Celia Fiennes, c 1682–c 1712*

Morris, R K 1978. The development of later gothic mouldings in England, *c* 1250–1400 – part I. *Architect Hist* **21**, 18–57

1979. The development of later gothic mouldings in England, *c* 1250–1400 – part II. *Architect Hist* **22**, 1–48

Munby, J, Sparks, M and Tatton-Brown, T 1983. Crown-post and king-strut roofs in south-east England. *Medieval Archaeol* **27**, 123–34

Newman, J 1980. *West Kent and the Weald* (The Buildings of England series) 2nd edn

1983. *North East and East Kent* (The Buildings of England series) 3rd edn

Oswald, A 1933. *Country Houses of Kent*

1937. Gatehouse, near Goudhurst, Kent. *Country Life* 9 Jan, 42–7

1958. Nettlestead Place, Kent. *Country Life* **124** pt 1, 16 October, 832–5; pt 2, 23 October, 886–9

Parfitt, J H 1976 (with contribution by S E Rigold). A moated site at Moat Farm, Leigh, Kent. *AC* **92**, 173–201

Parkin, E W 1962. The vanishing houses of Kent. 1. Durlock Grange, Minster-in-Thanet. *AC* **77**, 82–91

1968. Lake House, Eastwell. *AC* **83**, 151–61

1970. Cogan House, St Peter's, Canterbury. *AC* **85**, 123–38

1971. Cobbs's Hall, Aldington, and the Holy Maid of Kent. *AC* **86**, 15–24

1973. The ancient buildings of New Romney. *AC* **88**, 117–28

1976. Ratling Court, Aylesham. *AC* **92**, 53–64

1981. A unique aisled cottage at Petham. In Detsicas 1981, 225–30

1984. The ancient Cinque Port of Sandwich. *AC* **100**, 189–216

1985. The medieval origins of Wye College. *AC* **102**, 209–31

1986. Newington, near Hythe: the threatened village. *AC* **103**, 167–89

1989. Barham: the old aisled house. *AC* **107**, 225–37

Pattison, I R, Pattison D S, Alcock, N W 1992. *A Bibliography of Vernacular Architecture III, 1977–89*

Peake, W B 1920. *Luddesdown, The Story of a Kentish Manor*

Pearson, S forthcoming. The medieval houses of the Marsh: the missing evidence. In Eddison forthcoming

Pile, C C R 1955. *Cranbrook. A Wealden Town*

Pollard, A (ed) 1984. *Property and Politics: Essays in Later Medieval English History*

Poos, L R 1985. The rural population of Essex in the later Middle Ages. *Econ Hist Rev 2 ser* **38**, 515–30

1991. *A Rural Society after the Black Death: Essex, 1350–1525*

Prestwich, M 1980. *The Three Edwards, War and State in England 1272–1377*

Quiney, A 1983. Whitehall, Cheam: an early jettied house reconsidered. *Surrey Archaeol Collect* **74**, 135–40

1984. The lobby-entry house: its origins and distribution. *Architect Hist* **27**, 456–66

1990. *The Traditional Buildings of England*

1993. *Kent Houses*

Rackham, O 1980. *Ancient Woodland, its History, Vegetation and Uses in England*

1986. *The History of the Countryside*

Rawcliffe, C 1978. *The Staffords, Earls of Stafford and Dukes of Buckingham, 1394–1521*

Reeves, A forthcoming. Romney Marsh: the fieldwalking evidence. In Eddison forthcoming

Rigold, S E 1962. Excavation of a moated site at Pivington. *AC* **77**, 27–47

1963. The distribution of the Wealden house. Appendix to Jope 1963, 351–4

1965. Two camerae of the military orders. *Archaeol J* **122**, 86–132

1966. Some major Kentish timber barns. *AC* **81**, 1–30

1967a. Fourteenth-century halls in the east Weald. *AC* **82**, 246–56

1967b. Southfleet Old Rectory. *Dartford District Antiquarian Soc Newsletter* **4**, 18–21

1968. Two types of Court Hall. *AC* **83**, 1–22

1969a. Timber-framed buildings in Kent. *Archaeol J* **126**, 198–200

1969b. Walmer Old Manor House. *Archaeol J* **126**, 215–17

1969c. Battel Hall, Leeds. *Archaeol J* **126**, 255–9

1969d. Lympne Castle. *Archaeol J* **126**, 260–2

1969e. Chartham Church. *Archaeol J* **126**, 265–6

1969f. Charing Palace. *Archaeol J* **126**, 267

1969g. Yardhurst, Daniel's Water. *Archaeol J* 126, 267–9

1971a. Eynsford Castle and its excavation. *AC* **76**, 109–71

1971b. Dated buildings relevant to vernacular practice before 1550. *VA* **2**, 10–12

1973. Domestic buildings. In McRae and Burnham 1973, 184–90

Roberts, J 1990. *Tenterden Houses: A Study of the Domestic Buildings of a Kent Parish in their Social and Economic Environment.* Unpub PhD thesis, University of Nottingham

Robertson, Canon W A Scott 1883. The rectors of Cliffe at Hoo. *AC* **15**, 217–54

Round, J H 1902. Castle Guard. *Archaeol J* **59**, 144–59

RCHME 1968. *Cambridgeshire. Volume I West Cambridgeshire*

1963. *Monuments Threatened or Destroyed. A Select List: 1956 –1962*

1985. *Rural Houses of the Lancashire Pennines 1560–1760*

1993. *Salisbury, The Houses of the Close*

Salzman, L F 1952. *Building in England down to 1540*

Sandall, K 1986. Aisled halls in England and Wales. *VA* **17**, 21– 35

Sanders, I J 1960. *English Baronies: A Study of their Origins and Descent, 1086–1327*

Schofield, J 1984. *The Building of London from the Conquest to the Great Fire*

Schofield, R 1965. The geographical distribution of wealth in

England, 1334–1649. *Econ Hist Rev 2 ser* **18**, 483–510

Semple, J L 1982. *The Manor of Wrotham in the Early Sixteenth Century: Some Aspects of Land Holding and Population*. Unpub thesis for Diploma in Local History, University of Kent

Sharp, W and Whatmore, L E 1950 (ed L E Whatmore). Archdeacon Harpsfield's Visitation Returns. *Catholic Record Society* **45**

—— 1951 (ed L E Whatmore). Archdeacon Harpsfield's Visitation Returns. *Catholic Record Society* **46**

Sheail, J 1968. *The Regional Distribution of Wealth in England as indicated in the 1524/5 Lay Subsidy Returns*. Unpub PhD thesis, London University

—— 1972. The distribution of taxable population and wealth in England during the early sixteenth century. *Trans Inst Brit Geogr n ser* **55**, 111–26

Sheppard, J Brigstocke (ed) 1887–9. *Literae Cantuarienses* 3 vols (Rolls Series **85**)

Smith, A 1963. Regional differences in crop production in medieval Kent. *AC* **78**, 147–60

Smith, J T 1955. Medieval aisled halls and their derivatives. *Archaeol J* **112**, 76–94

—— 1958. Medieval roofs: a classification. *Archaeol J* **115**, 111–49

—— 1965. Timber-framed building in England. *Archaeol J* **122**, 133–58

—— 1970a. The evolution of the English peasant house to the late seventeenth century: the evidence of the buildings. *J Brit Archaeol Ass 3 ser* **33**, 122–47

—— 1970b. The reliability of typological dating of medieval English roofs. In Berger 1970, 239–69

—— 1972. The dating of buildings: problems and fallacies. *VA* **3**, 16–20

—— 1974. The early development of timber buildings: the passing-brace and reversed assembly. *Archaeol J* **131**, 238–63

—— 1981. The problems of cruck construction and the evidence of distribution maps. In Alcock 1981a, 5–24

—— 1992. *English Houses 1200–1800, The Hertfordshire Evidence*

Smith, R A L 1943. *Canterbury Cathedral Priory*

Smith, R M 1982. Rooms, relatives and residential arrangements: some evidence in manor court rolls 1250–1500. *Medieval Village Research Group Annual Report* **30**, 34–5

—— 1984a. Families and their land in an area of partible inheritance: Redgrave, Suffolk, 1260–1320. In Smith, R M 1984b, 135–95

—— 1988. Human resources. In Astill and Grant 1988, 188–212

Smith, R M (ed) 1984b. *Land, Kinship and Life-cycle*

Sparks, M J and Parkin, E W 1974. 'The Deanery', Chartham. *AC* **89**, 169–82

Sparks, M J and Tatton-Brown, T 1984. *The Blackfriars in Canterbury*

—— 1989. 19, The Precincts. *Canterbury Chronicle*, 23–8

Straker, E 1931. *Wealden Iron*

Streeten, A D F 1982. Potters, kilns and markets in medieval Kent: a preliminary study. In Leach 1982, 87–95

Swain, E R 1964. A hall-house at Upper Bush. *AC* **79**, 149–57

—— 1966. Starkey Castle, Wouldham. *AC* **81**, 118–25

—— 1968. Divided and galleried hall-houses. *Medieval Archaeol* **12**, 127–45

Tatton-Brown, T 1982. The topography and buildings of Horton Manor, near Canterbury. *AC* **98**, 77–105

—— 1983a. Deanery Farm, Chartham. *AC* **99**, 124–5

—— 1983b. The Precincts Survey *AC* **99**, 255–6

—— 1984. The 13th century roof of the chapel of the hospital of St Thomas-upon-the-Eastbridge, Canterbury. *Medieval Archaeol* **28**, 155–7

—— 1991. The Archbishop's Palace, Canterbury. *J Brit Archaeol Ass* **144**, 1–60

Taylor, R 1992. Population explosions and housing, 1550–1850. *VA* **23**, 24–9

Tester, P J 1979. A re-assessment of some features of the medieval house in the Joyden's Wood square earthwork. *AC* **95**, 289–90

—— 1981. The Court Lodge, Horton Kirby. In Detsicas 1981, 163–72

Tester, P J and Caiger, J E L 1958. Medieval buildings in the Joyden's Wood square earthwork. *AC* **72**, 18–40

Thirsk, J (ed) 1967. *The Agrarian History of England and Wales 1500–1640*

Thompson, A 1982. *Family and Society in Staplehurst 1450–1600*. Unpub thesis for Diploma in Local History, University of Kent

Thompson, M W 1991. *The Rise of the Castle*

Turner, T H and Parker, J H 1851, 1853, 1859. *Domestic Architecture in England*, pt I 1851, pt II 1853, pt III 1859

Twisden, J R 1939. *The Family of Twysden and Twisden*.

VCH. *The Victoria History of the Counties of England, Kent* **II** 1926, **III** 1932

Wade, J (ed) 1980–88. *Traditional Kent Buildings*, **1–6**. (Studies by students at the School of Architecture, Canterbury College of Art and Design)

Walker, J 1987. Wynter's Armourie: a base-cruck hall in Essex and its significance. *VA* **18**, 25–33

Wallenberg, J K 1931. *Kentish Place-Names*

—— 1934. *The Place-Names of Kent*

Warren, J 1992. Great and lesser gothic roofs: a study of the crown-post roof and its antecedents. *VA* **23**, 1–9

Warren, J and Hallam, M 1990. Anglo-Norman: crown strut and crown post roofs. In Warren 1990, 101–25

Warren, J (ed) 1990. *Wealden Buildings: Studies in the Timber-framed Tradition of Building in Kent, Sussex and Surrey* (Wealden Buildings Study Group)

Webster, B 1984. The community of Kent in the reign of Richard II. *AC* **100** 217–29

West, S E 1970 (with contribution by S E Rigold). Brome, Suffolk. The excavation of a moated site, 1967. *J Brit Archaeol Ass 3 ser* **33**, 89–121

Winzar, P 1993. Peirce House, Charing: the house and its owners. *AC* **111**, 131–200

Witney, K P 1976. *The Jutish Forest: a Study of the Weald of Kent from 450 to 1380AD*

—— 1990. The woodland economy of Kent, 1066–1348. *Agr Hist Rev* **38**, 20–39

Wood, M E 1950. Thirteenth-century domestic architecture in England. *Archaeol J* **105** (supplement), 1–150

—— 1965. *The English Medieval House*

—— 1974. *Norman Domestic Architecture*

Wood-Jones, R B 1963. *Traditional Domestic Architecture of the Banbury Region*

Wrathmell, S 1984. The vernacular threshold of northern peasant houses. *VA* **15**, 29–33

—— 1989a. Peasant houses, farmsteads and villages in north-east England. In Aston *et al* 1989, 247–67

—— 1989b *Domestic Settlement 2: Medieval Peasant Farmsteads* (Wharram: a study of settlement on the Yorkshire wolds, 6)

Zell, M 1983. Wealth, trades and agriculture in the Elizabethan Weald. In Detsicas and Yates 1983, 203–18

—— 1984a. Population and family structure in the sixteenth-century weald. *AC* **100**, 231–57

—— 1984b. The social parameters of probate records in the sixteenth-century. *Bull Inst Hist Res* **57**, 107–13

—— 1985. A wood-pasture agrarian regime: the Kentish Weald in the sixteenth century. *Southern Hist* **7**, 69–93

# Index

Figures in **bold** refer to illustrations. Houses in Kent are listed under the parish name, while other houses referred to in the text are under the name of the house or parish and county. Endnotes are indicated by n and nn after page references.

# D

# T

status of 95, 128, 130, 131, 132–4, 141–2
subsidiary accommodation 95–6, 98
two-storeyed 82, 112–13
wealth
taxable 12, 13
geographical distribution of 12–14, 31, 136, 146–7
ecclesiastical 12–14, 143
lay 12–13, 140–1, 142, 143
*see also* ecclesiastical estates; land and landholding; taxation
Wells, Somerset, Bishop's Palace 19
Westbere 163
Ashby Cottage **63,** 64, 67, 123, 137, 168, 174n
Ye Olde Yew Tree Inn 168
Yew Tree Cottage and White Cottage 168
West Bromwich Manor House, Staffordshire 56
Westerham
Apple Tree and Grape Vine Cottages 168
The Old Vicarage 93, 168
Squerryes Lodge 18, 19, **20,** 21, 22, 23, 29, 31, 42, 51, 168, 171n
West Hagbourne, Oxfordshire, York Farm 79
West Kingsdown
Crowhurst Farm Cottages 168
West Peckham
Dukes Place 168
Westwell
Lacton Manor **60, 78,** 102, 111, 168
Wharram Percy, North Yorkshire 21, 171n
White Horse, Vale of, Oxfordshire 45, 79, 173n, 175n
Wimbish, Essex, Tiptofts 79
Winchester, Hampshire
Bishop's Palace 19
Pilgrims' Hall 153, 174n
windows
in chambers 40, 43–4, 63, 97, 99, 114
in halls 31, 80, 90, 94
mullioned 96, 114, and transomed 94
in parlours 96, 114, 161
projecting (including oriels) 94, 96, 99, 114
provision for 40, 47, 61, 80, 82
traceried 18, 20, 29, 31, 94, 96, 99
Wingham, bailiwick of 12
house in 175n

wings
rear 73, 106–7
*see also* cross wings
Woodchurch 121, 123, 124, 126, 141, 142, 143, 163, 178n
Great Engeham Manor 131, 133, 168
Henden Place 168
New Diamond 168
Oakmead 168
Place Farmhouse 131, 168
Redbrook Cottage 168
Robhurst 168
Shirley Farmhouse 168
Townland 168
Woodnesborough
Summerfield Cottage 168, 175n
Woolmer, Hampshire, Hunting Lodge 23
Wouldham
Starkey Castle 87, 88, 128, 168
Wrotham 5, 123, 125, 137, 138, 139, 147, 163
Archbishop's manor house 154, 176n
manor of 13, 139, 140, 143, 171n
The Old Farmhouse 168
The Old Vicarage 139, 168
Workhouse Cottages 139, 168
Yaldham Manor 87, **104,** 105, 128, 163, 168
Wye
The Old Flying Horse **92,** 93
Wye College 93, 140, 158, 179n

# Y

Yalding 33, 56, 117
Burnt Oak, Benover 56, **77,** 82, 153, 168, 173n
Crowplain Farmhouse 168
Nightingale Farmhouse 56, 61, 62, 63, **64,** 77, 112, 153, 168, 173n
Rose Cottages **98,** 168
Rugmer Hill Farmhouse **93,** 103, 168
yeomen 2, 8, 16, 17, 33, 67, 95, 100, 115, 132, 134, 138, 141, 146, 177n
*see also* peasants